# BECOME THE MUSIC

## AUTHORS

ELAINE MEI AOKI
VIRGINIA A. ARNOLD
JAMES FLOOD
JAMES V. HOFFMAN
DIANE LAPP
MIRIAM MARTINEZ

ANNEMARIE SULLIVAN
 PALINCSAR
MICHAEL PRIESTLEY
NANCY ROSER
CARL B. SMITH

WILLIAM H. TEALE
JOSEFINA VILLAMIL
 TINAJERO
ARNOLD W. WEBB
PEGGY E. WILLIAMS
KAREN D. WOOD

**MACMILLAN/McGRAW-HILL SCHOOL PUBLISHING COMPANY**

**NEW YORK      CHICAGO      COLUMBUS**

# AUTHORS, CONSULTANTS, AND REVIEWERS

## WRITE IDEA! Authors

Elaine Mei Aoki, James Flood, James V. Hoffman, Diane Lapp, Ana Huerta Macias, Miriam Martinez, Ann McCallum, Michael Priestley, Nancy Roser, Carl B. Smith, William Strong, William H. Teale, Charles Temple, Josefina Villamil Tinajero, Arnold W. Webb, Peggy E. Williams

The approach to writing in Macmillan/McGraw-Hill Reading/Language Arts is based on the strategies and approaches to composition and conventions of language in Macmillan/McGraw-Hill's writing-centered language arts program, WRITE IDEA!

## Multicultural and Educational Consultants

Alma Flor Ada, Yvonne Beamer, Joyce Buckner, Helen Gillotte, Cheryl Hudson, Narcita Medina, Lorraine Monroe, James R. Murphy, Sylvia Peña, Joseph B. Rubin, Ramon Santiago, Cliff Trafzer, Hai Tran, Esther Lee Yao

## Literature Consultants

Ashley Bryan, Joan I. Glazer, Paul Janeczko, Margaret H. Lippert

## International Consultants

Edward B. Adams, Barbara Johnson, Raymond L. Marshall

## Music and Audio Consultants

John Farrell, Marilyn C. Davidson, Vincent Lawrence, Sarah Pirtle, Susan R. Snyder, Rick and Deborah Witkowski

## Teacher Reviewers

Terry Baker, Jane Bauer, James Bedi, Nora Bickel, Vernell Bowen, Donald Cason, Jean Chaney, Carolyn Clark, Alan Cox, Kathryn DesCarpentrie, Carol L. Ellis, Roberta Gale, Brenda Huffman, Erma Inscore, Sharon Kidwell, Elizabeth Love, Isabel Marcus, Elaine McCraney, Michelle Moraros, Earlene Parr, Dr. Richard Potts, Jeanette Pulliam, Michael Rubin, Henrietta Sakamaki, Kathleen Cultron Sanders, Belinda Snow, Dr. Jayne Steubing, Margaret Mary Sulentic, Barbara Tate, Seretta Vincent, Willard Waite, Barbara Wilson, Veronica York

# ACKNOWLEDGMENTS

*The publisher gratefully acknowledges permission to reprint the following copyrighted material:*

"Aïda" from AÏDA by Leontyne Price with illustrations by Leo and Diane Dillon. Text copyright © 1990 by Leontyne Price. Illustrations copyright © 1990 by Leo and Diane Dillon. Reprinted by permission of Harcourt Brace Jovanovich, Inc.

"All of You Was Singing" from ALL OF YOU WAS SINGING by Richard Lewis and illustrations by Ed Young. Copyright © 1991 by Richard Lewis. Illustrations copyright © 1991 by Ed Young. Reprinted with permission from Atheneum Publishers, an imprint of Macmillan Publishing Company.

"American Women: Their Lives in Their Words" from AMERICAN WOMEN: THEIR LIVES IN THEIR WORDS by Doreen Rappaport. Copyright © 1990 by Doreen Rappaport. Reprinted by permission of HarperCollins Publishers.

"Anne Frank Remembered" from ANNE FRANK REMEMBERED by Miep Gies with Alison Leslie Gold. Copyright © 1987 by Miep Gies and Alison Leslie Gold. By permission of Simon & Schuster, Inc.

"Anne Frank: The Diary of a Young Girl" from ANNE FRANK: THE DIARY OF A YOUNG GIRL by Anne Frank. Copyright © 1952 by Otto H. Frank. Used by permission of Dell Books, a division of Bantam Doubleday Dell Publishing Group, Inc. By permission also of Valentine, Mitchell Co. Ltd., London.

"Backroads" from THE GOOD RED ROAD by Kenneth Lincoln with Al Logan Slagle. Copyright © 1987 by Kenneth Lincoln and Al Logan Slagle. Reprinted by permission of HarperCollins Publishers.

"Beyond the Divide" from BEYOND THE DIVIDE by Kathryn Lasky. Copyright © 1983 by Kathryn Laskey. Reprinted with permission of Macmillan Publishing Company.

"Blue Highway" from BLUE HIGHWAY: A JOURNEY INTO AMERICA by William Least Heat-Moon. Copyright © 1982 by William Least Heat-Moon. By permission of Little, Brown and Company.

Cover illustration from THE BONE WARS by Kathryn Lasky, jacket illustration by Stephen Marchesi. Copyright © 1989 by Stephen Marchesi. Used by permission of Puffin Books, a division of Penguin Books USA Inc.

Jacket cover from CAN YOU SUE YOUR PARENTS FOR MALPRACTICE? by Paula Danzinger. Copyright © 1979 by Paula Danzinger. Used by permission of Dell Books, a division of Bantam Doubleday Dell Publishing Group, Inc.

Jacket cover from THE CAT ATE MY GYMSUIT by Paula Danzinger. Copyright © 1974 by Paula Danzinger. Used by permission of Dell Books, a division of Bantam Doubleday Dell Publishing Group, Inc.

"Checkouts" from A COUPLE OF KOOKS: AND OTHER STORIES ABOUT LOVE by Cynthia Rylant. Copyright © 1990 by Cynthia Rylant. All rights reserved. Used by permission of Orchard Books, New York.

"The Circuit" by Francisco Jiménez from THE ARIZONA QUARTERLY, Autumn 1973. Copyright © 1973 by Francisco Jiménez. Used by permission of the author.

"A Crown of Wild Olive" from HEATHER, OAK, AND OLIVE by Rosemary Sutcliff. Originally published in the U.S. by E. P. Dutton (Penguin USA Inc.) and in the United Kingdom by Hamish Hamilton Ltd. where it was titled TRUCE OF THE GAMES. Used by permission of Murray Pollinger Literary Agent.

Excerpt "Dogsong" by Gary Paulsen. Copyright © 1985 by Gary Paulsen. Reprinted with permission of Bradbury Press, an Affiliate of Macmillan, Inc.

Jacket cover from DRAGONDRUMS by Anne McCaffrey with cover art by Rowena Morrill. Copyright © 1979 by Anne McCaffrey. Cover art © 1986 by Rowena Morrill. Used by permission of Bantam Books, a division of Bantam Doubleday Dell Publishing Group, Inc.

Jacket cover from DRAGONSINGER by Anne McCaffrey with cover art by Rowena Morrill. Copyright © 1977 by Anne McCaffrey. Cover art © 1986 by Rowena Morrill. Used by permission of Bantam Books, a division of Bantam Doubleday Dell Publishing Group, Inc.

"Dragonsong" from DRAGONSONG by Anne McCaffrey. Copyright © 1976 by Anne McCaffrey. Reprinted with permission by Atheneum Publishers, an imprint of Macmillan Publishing Company.

Jacket cover from DRAGONSONG by Anne McCaffrey with cover art by Rowena Morrill. Copyright © 1976 by Anne McCaffrey. Cover art © 1986 by Rowena Morrill. Used by permission of Bantam Books, a division of Bantam

*(Continued on page 591)*

**1995 Printing**

DEDICATION FROM THE DEVELOPMENT TEAM. . .

To our
children:

*Allison McNeal-Halliburton,
Matthew, Daniel, and
Erika Goodman,*

and all the
others who
hear a different
drum and
walk to
their own
beat.

*Joellyn Goodman · Renée Beach*

# SAY IT WITH MUSIC

# Dare TO Dream

#   JUST US!

# Getting the Message

# 340
## Seeing Earth from Space

An excerpt from the nonfiction science book
*by Patricia Lauber*
**Newbery Honor and Washington Post–Children's
Book Guild Nonfiction Award–winning author**

There's more to be seen than meets the eye. An
entirely new world is being explored through the
aid of technology.

# REACH OUT

Pablo Casals

# FINDING YOUR WAY

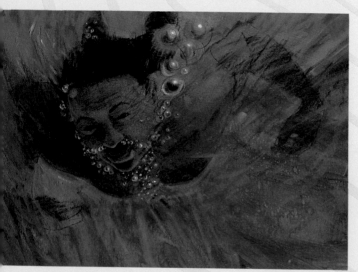
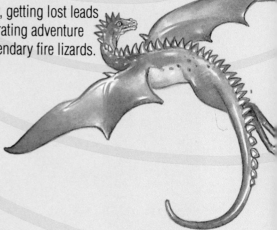

# 490
## The Gorgon's Head

A Greek myth
*Retold by Nathaniel Hawthorne, illustrated by Robert Roth*

In a distant kingdom, Perseus is ordered by the evil King Polydectes to carry out an impossible mission.

# CONTENTS

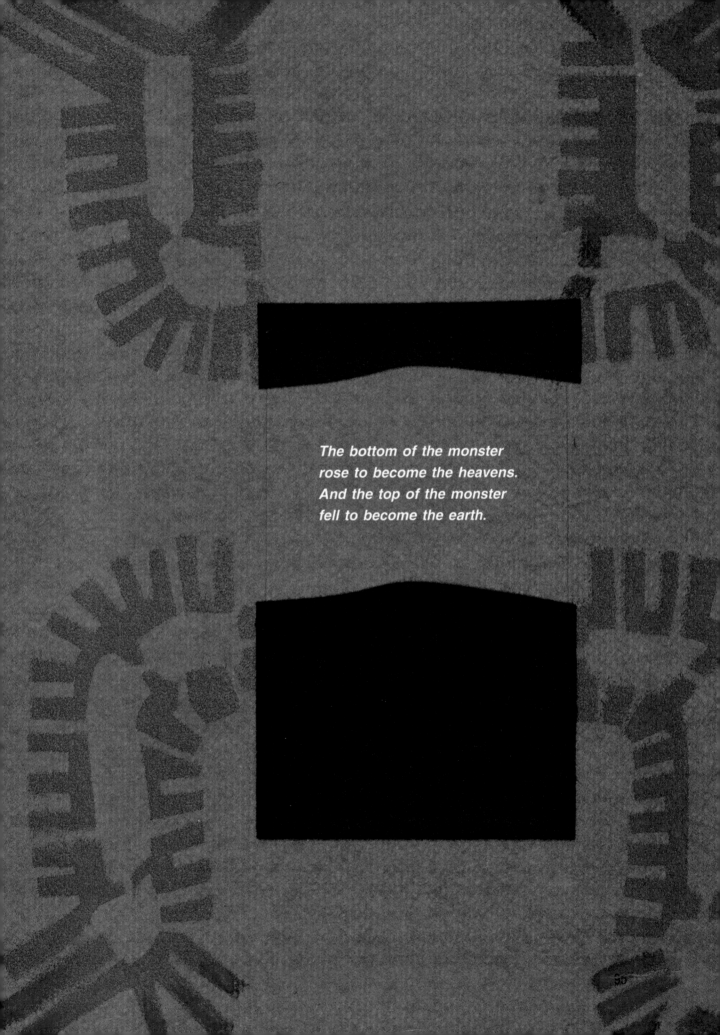

The bottom of the monster
rose to become the heavens.
And the top of the monster
fell to become the earth.

And before there was night or day
on the earth and in the sky,
there was a terrible darkness . . . .

# SAY IT WITH

# MUSIC

We sing to each other
or listen to music together
or make music together
in the knowledge that
the sharing of sound
makes us all belong
to each other.

—MARY TRAVERS
lead singer of the
Peter, Paul, and Mary trio

# Aïda

TOLD BY

*Leontyne Price*

ILLUSTRATED BY

**LEO & DIANE DILLON**

*L*ong ago, in the faraway land of Ethiopia, there lived a Princess named Aïda. She was fair as the sunrise and gentle as starlight touching a flower. Her father, the great King Amonasro, loved her dearly.

It was a time of terrible fear and danger in Ethiopia, for the kingdom was at war with its neighbor, Egypt. Both countries raided each other's lands, killing or enslaving their enemies.

For the safety of his people, King Amonasro set strict boundaries at the borders of his country, and no Ethiopian was allowed beyond them.

The Princess Aïda was young and, locked within the palace, she grew restless. So, one morning, Aïda and her trusted friends disobeyed the King's command. They disguised themselves and slipped away from the palace guards.

It was a glorious day of freedom, out in the gentle breezes and lush green fields of their beautiful country. But Aïda wandered farther than she should have. Off on her own, enjoying the warm sun and fresh country air, she did not hear her friends in the distance when they shouted, "Aïda! Beware! Come back!"

Once again, Egyptian soldiers had invaded Ethiopia, crossing the south edge of the River Nile. Now they marched toward Aïda.

When she finally did hear her friends' warning, it was too late. Soldiers seized her. Bound with ropes and chains, Aïda, the royal Princess of Ethiopia, was carried off to Egypt as a slave.

Aïda had learned her royal lessons well. She revealed to no one that she was the daughter of King Amonasro of Ethiopia. But her beauty and noble bearing attracted great attention. So sparkling and unusual was she that the all-powerful Pharaoh, the ruler of Egypt, chose her from among thousands of captured slaves to be his gift—a personal handmaiden—to his only daughter, the Princess Amneris.

It was easy for Aïda to perform the duties of a servant, for she remembered what her own handmaidens had done. The Egyptian Princess Amneris was fascinated, for Aïda was different from any slave she had ever seen. She wanted her new handmaiden to be her closest companion.

Even with the special privileges granted to one so close to the Royal Princess, Aïda felt nothing but despair. All her life she had been the beloved daughter of Ethiopia's King, and now she was a slave to her father's enemy. She knew there was no hope of seeing Ethiopia again.

There was one source of light in her life, however. For Radames, the handsome young captain of the Egyptian Army, had fallen in love with the gentle, beautiful slave the moment he saw her. She, too, had fallen for Radames, despite his position as an enemy of her homeland.

They met often, in secret, by the Temple of Isis, and in the joy of their moments together, Radames confided his dreams to Aïda.

"I will lead the Egyptian Army to victory," he told her, "and when I return, our countries will be united, and you will become my bride and reign as the Queen of your people. It will not be long, I promise."

The day finally came when the Pharaoh was to hold court and announce the new leader of the war against Ethiopia.

Amid the majestic columns of a great hall in the palace, Egypt's High Priest, Ramfis, confided to Radames: "There are rumors that the Ethiopians plan to attack. Prepare yourself, for the Goddess Isis has chosen, and the great honor of leadership may be bestowed upon you."

All his life, Radames had dreamed of this day. If he became the new leader, he could return triumphant to free Aïda and marry her. "Ah, heavenly Aïda," he thought. "I could finally enthrone you in your native land."

Radames was deep in thought when Princess Amneris stepped from the shadows. She, too, was in love with the handsome leader, but she suspected he loved another.

Aïda suddenly appeared.

Oh, how Radames's eyes filled with passion! And when Amneris

saw the look that passed between them, she was seized with suspicion and jealousy. Could Radames prefer a *slave* to the Princess of Egypt? It was intolerable! But her fury was interrupted by trumpets heralding the arrival of the Pharaoh.

A messenger came forward to give his report.

"Mighty Pharaoh, the Ethiopians have attacked. They are led by the fierce warrior King Amonasro, who has invaded Egypt!"

A thunder of anger broke out in court, and upon hearing her father's name, Aïda quietly cried out in fear.

The Pharaoh rose, and the crowd grew still.

"Radames will lead our army," he cried. "It is the decree of the Goddess Isis. Death to the Ethiopians! Victory to Egypt!" he shouted. "Return victorious, Radames!" he commanded.

"Return victorious! Return victorious!" the throng shouted, and Aïda, too, was stirred by the cry. In spite of herself, she also began to shout, "Return victorious! Return victorious!" as the court led the soldiers off to battle. Aïda was now left alone.

"Return victorious!" she called after Radames, but as her own voice echoed in the great hall, she suddenly realized she was asking for the death of her father, her mother, her friends, and all those she cherished. Yet how could she pray for the death of the man she loved?

Aïda was shocked. Her heart was torn between Radames and her loyalty to her father and Ethiopia. She fell to her knees and prayed.

"Oh, great gods of my youth!" she cried. "Pity me!"

That night, the halls of the temple rang as the priestesses chanted the sacred consecration song. The High Priest, Ramfis, led prayers to Phtha, the creator of life and mightiest Egyptian god, as he gave the great hero the sacred sword of Egypt.

"Let the sword of Radames be the strength of our nation! Let his bravery in battle crush the Ethiopians! Protect our land," they prayed, "and make Radames the most magnificent warrior of all."

"Praise to Phtha! Praise to Phtha!" the Egyptians chanted, and the priestesses danced a sacred dance to please the great god and ensure death to their enemies.

With Radames gone, time passed slowly for Aïda. But soon the prayers of the priests were granted. A special day dawned for Egypt—a day of ceremony and grandeur, of pomp and pageantry. The Ethiopians had been defeated at last.

Amneris sat before her mirror. Surrounded by slaves and adorned in her most beautiful gown and jewels, she was pleased with her reflection. Surely today when Radames returned, he would be struck by her radiance. Yet despite her vanity, she secretly burned with jealousy to think that Aïda, a mere handmaiden, might truly be loved by Radames.

So Amneris decided to test her privileged slave. And when gentle Aïda entered the royal chambers, Amneris sobbed, pretending great grief.

"Oh, Aïda, Aïda!" she cried in a shaking voice. "Egypt has lost its finest warrior. Radames has been killed in battle!"

Immediately Aïda wept with the pain of one whose heart has been broken forever. There was no longer any doubt in Amneris's mind.

"It is all a lie!" she shouted. "Radames was not killed. He lives!"

Aïda's tears of sorrow turned to tears of joy.

Overcome with fury, Amneris hurled Aïda to the floor. "How dare you, a lowly slave, love the same man loved by the Princess of Egypt?"

But Aïda, too, was a Princess. She rose proudly. She was about to tell Amneris the truth, but she stopped herself. Instead, with great difficulty, she asked to be forgiven.

"Have mercy on me," she begged. "Your power is unquestioned—you have all that a person could want. But what do I have to live for? My love of Radames, and that alone."

Aïda's plea only fueled Amneris's rage. She stormed out of the chamber, leaving Aïda to fear the worst.

Flags flew, and the entire city gathered to see the grand spectacle of the victory parade led by the Pharaoh, the Princess, and the High

Priest. Trumpets blared, and dancing girls threw rose petals to form a welcoming carpet before the magnificent chariot of Radames.

The handsome warrior dismounted and knelt before the royal throne. When Amneris placed a laurel wreath on his head, the crowd was wild with joy.

"Hail to the conqueror!" they roared. "Hail to Radames!"

The Pharaoh proclaimed, "Radames, you are my greatest soldier. As a reward, whatever you wish shall be yours."

When Radames rose, he saw Aïda. Amneris saw the look of love on his face, and she was consumed with jealousy. Yet he dared not ask for Aïda's hand, not at that moment in public court.

"Mighty Pharaoh," he said instead, "I ask that you allow me to call forth our prisoners of war."

The Pharaoh granted Radames's request, and the Ethiopians were led into the square in chains. One tall, proud man stood out above the rest. Aïda gasped. It was her father!

The crowd was shocked to see her run and embrace him, but he whispered to her, "Do not betray that I am King."

Amonasro addressed the Pharaoh. "I am Aïda's father, and I have faithfully fought for my sovereign, who died in battle. I am prepared to die for him and my country, but I beseech you to have mercy on those who have been defeated."

With outstretched arms, Aïda joined the Ethiopians. "Let the prisoners go free," she begged Radames and the Pharaoh.

So moved by her appeal, the Egyptian people joined in, and their cries urged the Pharaoh to allow the captured soldiers to be released.

"No!" the High Priest, Ramfis, cried. "The Ethiopians are still a threat and should be put to death."

"Their freedom is my wish," Radames told the Pharaoh.

"Unchain the Ethiopians!" the Pharaoh ordered. "But you, Aïda's father, must remain my prisoner as a pledge of your people's good faith."

An even greater reward was now to be bestowed upon Egypt's greatest warrior. The Pharaoh led Amneris to Radames.

"My daughter will be your bride," he proclaimed, joining their hands. "One day, you shall be Pharaoh, and together you will rule."

Radames was horrified. He dared not refuse the Pharaoh. He bowed and pretended gratitude, but his heart was filled with sorrow. Amneris looked scornfully at her handmaiden.

Aïda wept in her father's arms as the triumphant Egyptian Princess held Radames's hand and led him to the palace.

"Do not lose faith," Amonasro whispered to his daughter. "Ethiopia will soon avenge our conquerors."

It was the eve of the great wedding, and a full moon shone on the dark waters of the River Nile beside the Temple of Isis. By boat, the High Priest, Ramfis, brought Amneris to the Temple. There she was to pray that her marriage be blessed. Little did she know that Radames had sent a message to Aïda, who was waiting to meet him nearby.

Aïda sadly watched the moonlit river and longed with all her heart and soul to return to her beloved homeland. Suddenly she heard Radames approach. But when the man came closer, she was stunned to see that it was her father, King Amonasro.

"Listen carefully, Aïda," he said sternly. "My plan will bring both you and Radames back to Ethiopia. Our soldiers stand ready to attack when I signal. There is a secret, unguarded road, but only Radames knows it. It is your duty as the Princess of Ethiopia to make him reveal this path."

"Father!" she cried, "I *cannot* betray Radames!"

With anger and disdain, King Amonasro forced her to her knees. "You are no longer my daughter! You are nothing more than a lowly slave of the Egyptians and a betrayer of your country! Have you forgotten your loved ones who were slaughtered without mercy by these, your enemies?"

"You are wrong! I am *not* and will *never* be a slave to anyone. I am the Princess of Ethiopia, and I have never forgotten my royal blood. My duty to you and to my country will always be first in my heart!"

Even as she swore to obey his command, she cried inside for what her father and her dear country would cost her. Amonasro embraced her to give her courage, and he hid in the bushes to listen.

When Radames finally came, he was breathless with love. But Aïda turned on him scornfully.

"How could you betray me and marry Amneris as your reward?"

"Aïda, you have always been my love. My passion for you is deeper than the Nile, deeper than life itself," Radames told her.

"Then show me," Aïda demanded. "You have betrayed me. And if you truly love me, you will leave Egypt tonight and flee with me to Ethiopia. Only there will we find happiness and peace."

Radames was torn. The thought of leaving Egypt was unbearable, but the thought of living without Aïda was even more painful. At last, after much persuasion, he agreed to flee.

"The roads are heavily guarded by your soldiers. How will we escape?" she asked.

"All the roads are guarded except one," he told her. "The Gorges of Napata."

"The Gorges of Napata!" a voice rang out. Amonasro sprang from his hiding place. He was ready to attack with his army.

Radames could not believe it. "You, Aïda's father, are King of Ethiopia?" He was overcome. "I have sacrificed my country for my love of you!" he cried to Aïda.

"Come with us now," Amonasro told Radames. "You and Aïda will reign happily in Ethiopia."

But as the King took Radames's hand to lead him away, a shout rang out in the darkness. "Traitor!"

It was Amneris. She and the High Priest had come from the temple and had overheard the plot.

"Traitor!" she screamed again.

Amonasro leapt to kill Amneris with his dagger, but Radames ran between them to shield her.

"Go quickly!" he warned Aïda and Amonasro, and the King ran, dragging Aïda with him.

Radames stood before Amneris and the High Priest. He did not try to escape. Instead, he threw down his sword.

"I surrender!" he cried. "I am your prisoner!"

The treason of Radames shocked and infuriated all of Egypt. Guards locked him in the deepest dungeon in the palace. Soon his trial would begin, and he would be sentenced to a horrible death.

Amneris was in a state of grief. Her love for Radames had not diminished. Deep in her heart, she knew he had not meant to betray his country. Her own jealousy had made the mighty warrior a prisoner. She longed to beg her father, the Pharaoh, to release him, but she knew Radames still loved Aïda. She also knew soldiers had killed Amonasro, but Aïda had escaped and was still alive—somewhere.

In desperation, Amneris commanded the guards to bring Radames to her. She humbled herself and pleaded with him to forget Aïda.

"I will find a way to set you free, free to marry me and share the throne of Egypt," she said. "But you must never see Aïda again."

Radames refused. "You are Princess of Egypt, my country; and you have all that anyone could ask for. Yet I will always love Aïda, and there will never be room in my heart for anyone else."

The more Amneris begged him, the more strongly he refused.

When the priests came to take Radames, Amneris was in a rage of anger and jealousy, and she made no attempt to stop them. But when he left, she fell to the ground in tears, cringing as she heard the priests loudly accuse Radames of betrayal.

"Traitor! Traitor!" the High Priest, Ramfis, shouted again and again, but Radames never uttered a word to defend himself. Louder and louder the cruel accusations were hurled at him.

Amneris prayed to Isis and the other gods of Egypt to show mercy and save the man she loved, but the gods were silent.

The tribunal of priests pronounced Radames guilty of treason and sentenced him to be buried alive.

As the priests passed from the trial, Amneris flung herself before the High Priest. She insulted him and threatened revenge, but her cries were in vain.

"Radames, the traitor, will die," he said coldly.

Only the priests and guards were allowed to watch Radames walk into the deepest vault below. They sealed the last opening, shutting out all light and the last

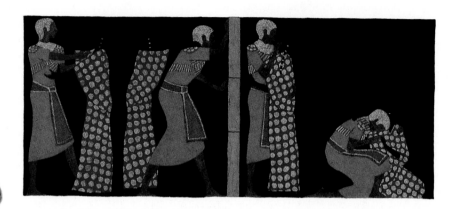

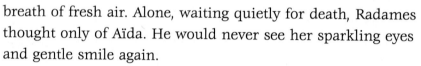

breath of fresh air. Alone, waiting quietly for death, Radames thought only of Aïda. He would never see her sparkling eyes and gentle smile again.

Suddenly, in the darkness, he heard Aïda's voice. At first, Radames thought it was a dream. But no—she had escaped and was hiding in the vault, waiting for him.

"Aïda, my love, you are too young and too beautiful to die."

Radames pushed in vain, trying to open the vault.

But Aïda gently placed her arms around him. With a tender kiss, she told him to stop.

"Remember, we will never be separated again. For eternity, we will be together."

And with all the love in the world, they held each other close—so close—as if they would never part.

Above their tomb, dressed in black, Princess Amneris prayed to the gods to forgive her and to grant heavenly rest to Radames, her love.

The gods granted her wish, but not as she hoped. For as she prayed to the gods and wept, a peaceful death had come to the Ethiopian Princess Aïda and Radames, the greatest warrior of Egypt. Finally they were together—forever in each other's arms.

# MEET *Leontyne Price*

## Storyteller's Note

Aïda as a heroine—and *Aïda* as an opera—has been meaningful, poignant, and personal for me. In many ways, I believe Aïda is a portrait of my inner self.

She was my best friend operatically and was a natural for me because my skin was my costume. This fact was a positive and strong feeling and allowed me a freedom of expression, of movement, and of interpretation that other operatic heroines I performed did not. I always felt, while performing Aïda, that I was expressing all of myself—as an American, as a woman, and as a human being.

Vocally, the role was perfectly suited to my voice in every respect—lyrically, dramatically, and in timbre. The role presented no difficulties, and because my voice was infused with the emotions I felt about Aïda, I sang with vocal ease and great enjoyment.

My first Grand Opera performance of this noble Ethiopian Princess's story was on the stage of the War Memorial Opera House in San Francisco in 1957. Totally prepared, eager, and excited, I performed my debut Aïda with great success. I went on to perform Aïda at the Chicago Lyric Opera House, the Arena di Verona and La Scala in Italy, the Vienna Staatsoper, the Paris Opera House, Covent Garden in London, the Hamburg Staatsoper in Germany, and my home opera house, the Metropolitan Opera House in New York City—where I performed the role more often than in any other opera house.

Aïda has given me great inspiration onstage and off. Her deep devotion and love for her country and for her people—her nobility, strength, and courage—are all qualities I aspire to as a human being. I will never forget her.

—**Leontyne Price**

# *Leo & Diane Dillon*

On her first day attending Parsons School of Design in New York City, Diane Dillon saw a painting done by another student. The painting, she thought, was extraordinary. "I was immediately overcome by two feelings: 'I'm in over my head' and 'Here is a challenge I *must* meet.' The painting was Leo's." A few years later, the two artists were married. Their marriage was the beginning of a life together creating bold, beautiful illustrations for books.

They describe the drawings they create together as being done by "an agent we call 'the third artist.' The third artist is a combination of the two of us and is different than either of us individually. . . . It comes up with things neither of us would have done."

For their illustration of *Aïda,* the Dillons received the Coretta Scott King Award, given annually to an author or illustrator whose work promotes a better understanding of the culture and contribution of all people to the American dream. They are also two-time winners of the Caldecott Medal, given to the illustrator of the most distinguished children's picture book published in the United States—in 1976 for the African folk tale *Why Mosquitoes Buzz in People's Ears* and in 1977 for *Ashanti to Zulu: African Traditions.*

# GIVE MY REGARDS TO

The theater lights dim, and a hush falls over the audience. The orchestra conductor raises a baton, and suddenly the air becomes alive with music. The curtain parts, and you're off on a wonderful musical adventure.

If you have seen an opera or a musical show, you know how enjoyable it can be. If you haven't, put it on your list of things to do! You might even get a chance to see some of the shows featured on these show bills.

# WEST SIDE STORY

Music by Leonard Bernstein
Lyrics by Stephen Sondheim
Book by Arthur Laurents

William Shakespeare's play *Romeo and Juliet*, a tragic story of young lovers, is retold in this modern musical version set in New York City in the 1950s.

Through music, song, and dance, the love story of Tony and Maria unfolds. He, a native-born New Yorker from a Polish family, and she, a recent arrival from Puerto Rico, fall in love. But prejudice, the tough street life on the city's West Side, and gang loyalties get in the way of their dreams. Tony and Maria's hope for finding a place for themselves is beautifully expressed in their duet "Somewhere."

## MY FAIR LADY

Music by Frederick Loewe
Lyrics and book by Alan Jay Lerner

The British author George Bernard Shaw wrote a play called *Pygmalion*. It describes how Eliza Doolittle changes into a self-assured, well-spoken Englishwoman under the guidance of the very stuffy Professor Henry Higgins.

In *My Fair Lady,* the musical adaptation of this play, Eliza's progress in speaking proper English results in the singing of the song "The Rain in Spain."

## THE WIZ

Music and Lyrics by Charlie Smalls
Book by William F. Brown

*The Wiz,* inspired by the children's story *The Wonderful Wizard of Oz* and by the 1939 movie version, features a rock score, an African-American cast, and modern dialog. Yet the story—a young girl's attempt to return to Kansas from the Land of Oz—remains unchanged. A special treat in the show is watching Dorothy, the Lion, the Tinman, and the Scarecrow sing and dance to the lively tune "Ease on Down the Road."

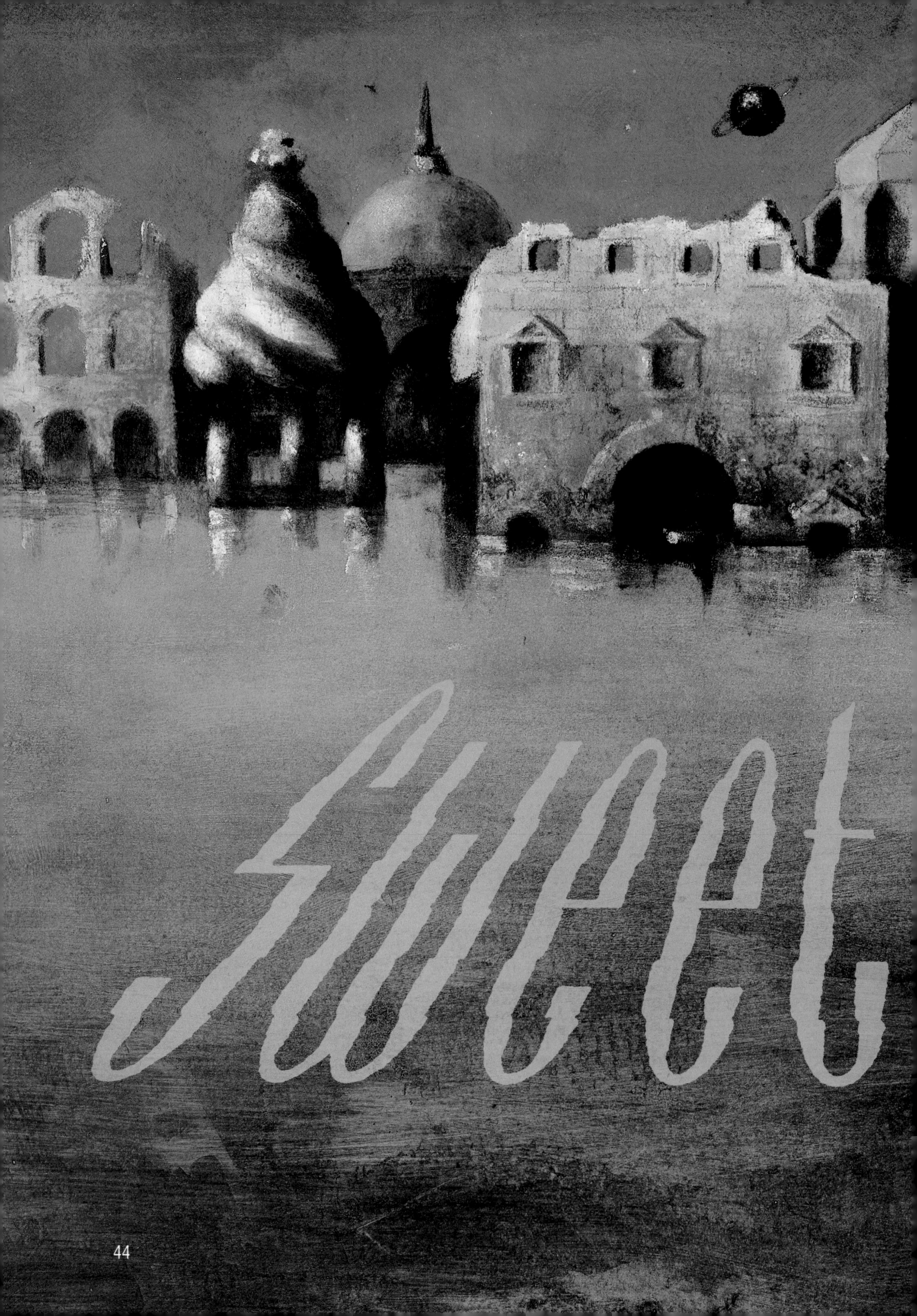
Sweet

# Water

BY LAURENCE YEP          ILLUSTRATED BY PAOLA PIGLIA

*Tyree and his family
live in the flooded city
of Old Sion on the
planet Harmony. The
residents of Old Sion,
called Silkies, are de-
scendants of long-ago
settlers from Earth.
When Tyree hears the
music created by a
master fiddler at a
winter festival, he be-
comes so entranced
with it that he whittles
a flute and tries to
teach himself to play.
Tyree's father, a stern
fishing captain, be-
lieves that music is
frivolous. He is
angered by Tyree's
attempts to play the
flute. He tells Tyree,
"I won't have the
Captain's son become
the laughingstock of
the Commune. I don't
want any Silkie to ever
hear you play again. Is
that understood?"*

I figured that Pa's order could be taken two ways, his way and my way. I could play the flute as long as no Silkie heard me, and I knew there was one place at night in Old Sion where no Silkie would hear me, because no Silkie would dare go there. I was willing to go there that very night to find a place where I could practice. I planned to go to Sheol. I was that desperate.

We still called the area by its old name, given when Sheol was the most elegant and expensive area in Old Sion, but now after the floods the mansions were occupied by the Argans, the only intelligent race native to Harmony. The Argans were a strange race, and they liked to keep their secrets. No human ever knew how they repro-duced, though their words for fam-ily relations translated loosely into "uncle" and "nephew."

There were some humans who had never forgiven the aliens be-cause they didn't warn the colo-nists about the tides, but then we weren't asked to come to their world. And anyway, the colonists weren't exactly kind to the aliens.

Later when the city, Old Sion, was abandoned, the Argans drifted back from the wastelands, claiming that the land was still theirs, and by that time it did not matter who Old Sion belonged to legally, be-cause the sea had already filled most of the city. There was a silent agreement between the humans and the Argans—though both would have been the first to deny it—not to go into certain sectors, or at least never to be seen there. No man ever saw an Argan in Old Sion unless that Argan wanted him to, not even if it was in that human's own home. So when I went into the Argan's area, I was the one in the wrong. I was the invader.

At night Sheol didn't look like it belonged to man anymore. The half-submerged elegant houses looked like ancient monsters surfacing. Their great stone faces were covered with delicate beards of green sea-weed or soft mustachios of barnacles. The seaworn doors opened like the mouths of Seadragons through which the water twisted and un-twisted, and the windows were like eyes, hollow and black and wait-ing—with ripples fanning outward as though from some creature sleeping inside.

It was really scary, but I thought like a human in those days and I figured that whether the Argans and the animals and the houses liked it or not, I was going to practice there. On purpose I picked out the finest and biggest mansion, which had been built on a hill. It had belonged to Nimrod Senaar, the Governor who had cheated my ances-tors. The statue of our old enemy rose from the water lonely and proud, frowning at the change in his old city. I thumbed my nose at him as I passed.

I moored my skiff to one of the pillars of the portico and splashed up the steps. My bare feet made wet slapping sounds as I walked across the portico and through the entrance hall with its huge rotunda. I checked the rooms on both floors for the acoustics until I found one that satisfied me. Then for about an hour I practiced my scales until I heard something strange.

At first I thought it was the wind but then I realized it was mu-sic, and the more I listened, the more I felt that I had never heard anything more lovely. The song was at once sad and yet beautiful, moving like the veiled ghosts of bold knights or unfulfilled maidens. The echoes floated up the street over the hissing water, past the empty, slime-covered apartment houses, bounced and danced past walls whose rotting mortar slowly spilled stone after stone into the sea. It was a song for Old Sion.

I had to find the musician and I searched the entire mansion un-til I found him sitting on the portico by my skiff. It was an Argan, an

old one, sitting there calmly. The
bristly fur on his back and arm-
legs was a peppery gray, the flesh
on his belly was all wrinkled, and
he stooped slightly from old age.
He looked very much like a four-
foot-high Earth spider, though you
would never suggest that to an
Argan. They hate to be reminded of
their resemblance to their Earth
cousins the way humans hate to be
reminded that they look like apes.

He put down his reed pipes
when he saw me and with six of
his arm-legs slowly pushed himself
off the portico. He seemed surprised and walked around me. He
walked delicately on two arm-legs
like a ballet dancer imitating an
old man, with his six other arm-
legs stretched out to balance his
overpuffed body. He stepped back
in front of me and examined me
boldly, even though Argans usually
kept their eyelids down low because they knew how their eyes
bothered humans. Argans have
myriads of tiny eyes on their orbs.
They shine like clouds of stars in
dim light and it takes some getting
used to—it's like being watched by
a one-man crowd.

"What can I do for you,
Manchild?" he asked in Intergal.

I shifted uncomfortably from
one foot to the other. I told myself
that it was silly to feel like I had
invaded this Argan's home. In

those days I believed I had as much right to this place as the Argans did. "I heard you playing," I said finally.

"And my nephews and my neighbors heard your free concert," the old Argan said. "They found me and told me so I could come home and hear my competition."

"There's no competition," I mumbled. It was easy enough to get embarrassed about my playing in those days. I could even be shamed by aliens. "Well," I added, "I guess I'll be moving on. I don't want to drive folk away from their homes."

The old Argan grabbed hold of me and I knew I couldn't get away. The Argans had small but very strong disc-shaped suction pads at the base of their finger-toes. They could retract the suction pads into their skin or extend them so that the bottoms of their hand-feet appeared to be rimmed with tiny white circles. When he used his suction pads, his grip was unbreakable.

"What do they know? It's the song that counts, not the singer." He pointed at the flute. "And that's a mighty nice flute. Did you carve it?"

I turned my ornate flute over in my hands self-consciously. "I'm afraid I spent more time carving pictures into it than I did playing it."

"Do you like music?"

"More than anything," I said. "But there's no one to teach me."

"Of course." The old Argan was thoughtful for a moment. "What did you think of my song? It was just a little night music."

"I thought it was beautiful," I said and added truthfully, "it was the most beautiful thing I've ever heard."

I don't know what he was looking for, but he studied me for a long time. His myriad eyes reflected my image so I saw a hundred Tyrees—each a perfect miniature.

"Would you like me to teach you?" the old Argan said.

"But what about your nephews and your neighbors?"

"I told you to forget them. Music's the only important thing."

I felt a warm rush of gratitude inside me. "I'd like it an awful lot if you would teach me, Mister..." I realized that I had almost made a bad mistake, because Argans, like some people on Earth, don't believe in giving their true names because that gives the listener power over the person named. Argans have what they call use-names, which they change every so often.

"My use-name is Amadeus." The old Argan let go of my wrist with a slight popping noise.

I rubbed the small circles on my wrist where the suction pads had gripped me. A new question had occurred to me but it took me a while before I worked up enough nerve to ask him. "Since you're an Argan, how can you teach me to play a human musical instrument?"

"It's enough that I know," Amadeus snapped. "Now no more questions if you want me to teach you."

It was a puzzle how an alien could teach me about human music, but I was willing to try anything. "All right," I said.

"Come back tomorrow night and I'll see if I can teach you that you have only two thumbs and not ten."

I knew that I had met one of the aliens' songsmiths, and all the way home I felt warm and good inside, knowing what a privilege I was being given. If there is one thing the Argans love, it's their music—you could hear one or more of them playing on their reed pipes whenever you passed near Sheol. The Argans think that the gods directly choose someone to be a songsmith. Important councils have been moved to decisions by an inspired songsmith suddenly getting up and playing a particular song in a particular way.

The Argans don't think of music as we humans do. An Argan song seems skimpy by human standards. It just has a basic story line—like how the three moons were created—and a theme of music which represents the song. It's up to the musician to improvise and create variations on the theme and to combine these with certain other established themes which the audience recognizes as representing a castle, or a feast, or a heroic battle, or anything like that.

In Argan music, songs keep on evolving and changing as they are played. The Argans think that the human style is the mark of a mediocre musician. Only mediocre musicians play a song in the same way all the time. In human music, since you usually have a song sheet, the musician is limited to an already-fixed pattern of themes and variations and his performance is judged by his skill in playing the song. But in Argan music, the best musicians have to be not only skilled craftsmen but also geniuses at finding new and original patterns.

Of course, Argan music isn't really that loose. When I first started to play it, I wondered how a musician knew what to play next, since you had to choose while performing at the same time; but there's a

kind of logic to it—like knowing the ending to a story halfway through the telling. For example, if two Argan heroes meet, you have to describe both of them, and their battle, and the funeral for the loser.

Amadeus was very patient about explaining things like that about music. He really earned his title, the Ultimate Uncle—which was his social position among the Argans, though Amadeus would never tell me any more. He hated to talk about himself and Argan affairs, but about music there was almost no stopping him. I took to visiting Sheol three times a week, and Amadeus would listen patiently as I butchered his people's music. Whenever I tried to apologize for a particularly clumsy performance, he would encourage me by telling me that my song and I had not found one another yet. According to Argan belief, it's the song that finds the singer and not the other way around.

After a while, though, not even that belief could satisfy me. I was tired from having to do my chores during the daytime, keep my secret from my parents, and still have nothing to show for all my sacrifices but some bad playing.

"It's no use, Amadeus, I'm never going to be a musician."

Amadeus sighed and shook his head. "Manchild, you have everything that a person needs to make music: you have the talent, you have the skills now, but you still hold your soul back from the music—like you can't forget you're a human playing Argan music. You just have to remember that it's the music that counts—not the one who plays it."

And with that he put the reed pipes to his mouth and began to play the human song, "Moonspring." I sat in astonishment as he slipped next into "Shall We Gather by the Stars" and "These Happy Golden Years."

"Amadeus, where did you ever learn to play human songs?" I asked in amazement.

He made a disappointed noise. "Manchild, didn't I just tell you that a real musician can play both 'human' and 'Argan' music? I'm not an Argan playing human songs. I'm a musician making music. The only thing that matters in this changing universe is the song, the eternal song that waits for you."

"Yes, but—"

"Play," Amadeus angrily ordered me, so I played. It was strange. Amadeus wouldn't talk about himself and he wouldn't let me talk about myself; and yet despite my ignorance, I felt closer to him than I had to anyone else. And in the moments when I doubted myself, Amadeus somehow always managed to keep me looking for my song.

Anybody who thinks Argan music is easy to learn has never really tried to. A lot of it was boring work when I had to master all the conventional themes so I would have a variety to choose from; but eventually after a year's work I got so that I could play two songs tolerably well. Even Amadeus had to admit I was a tolerable backup man— though I had yet to be found by my own song. But then one night he sat for a long time and smoothed the hair down on his arms thoughtfully before he finally looked up at me again. "I don't know what to do, Manchild. You're not going to develop any more unless you listen to others play—and you play for others."

Amadeus knew all about my first bad experiences with an audience, so he knew how shy I was of those situations. "Amadeus," I finally said, "have they been staying away because of me or have you been keeping them away so I wouldn't be nervous?"

"A little of both," Amadeus said reluctantly.

"The Argans don't like the idea of your giving me lessons, do they?"

"Who told you?" he asked angrily. "You pay those fools no mind. They've heard you play but they just won't believe."

"Believe what?" I asked.

"That an Argan song will ever find a human," Amadeus was forced to admit.

"Have they been giving you trouble?" I asked.

"It doesn't matter," Amadeus said.

I had noticed that the rooms were a lot dustier of late, as if most of the house was no longer occupied. A brilliant songsmith like Amadeus should have had quite a few Argans around him—not only to hear him play but also to serve him as befitted his status. Yet whenever I went over there, Amadeus was alone.

"Do your family come back after I leave, or do they stay away all the time now?"

"Mind your own business," Amadeus snapped.

"But, Amadeus—"

Amadeus held up one hand-foot as a warning. "Let's get something straight, Manchild. We're here to play music, not to talk."

I gave up asking any more questions and just thought for a while. After all he had done for my sake I could hardly do less. "If you can get some of them together, I'll play for them," I said. "We'll show them."

Amadeus made sure I wanted to go through with it before he named the next night for my test. I had to trade twenty feet of my best nylon fishing line to Red Genteel, but he agreed to do my chores in the garden for that day while I napped. I wanted to be at my best for the Argans.

That night there must have been some twenty Argans sitting on the porch; six of them were my "classmates" while the others were nephews, skeptics, critics, and creatures who liked to see minor disasters. The moment I sat down to warm up they began to crack jokes in the clicking language of the Argans. I did not know the words but their jokes were obviously about me. They might not be able to make fun of Amadeus, but I was fair game.

One of them, Sebastian, had painfully learned some Intergal, so I could understand. "My cousin, he say, are your fingers broke? But I say, no, you just sitting on your hands."

I started to blush but Amadeus, he gave me a wink—which for an Argan is a considerable maneuver. It was a mannerism that I thought he had picked up from me. "You just start whenever you like, Manchild. Don't you mind the noise. 'Pears to be an undue number of insects out tonight." Amadeus stopped their jokes for maybe a minute and then they started in again. If I had been Amadeus, I would have been jumping up and down with anxiety, but Amadeus had a quiet kind of strength. He was like a calm pool of water that you could have dropped anything into and it wouldn't have disturbed the pool besides a momentary ripple. Just having Amadeus there gave me confidence.

"I'd like to play now, Amadeus," I said.

"Well," and Amadeus nodded to me approvingly, "well, go on."

I shut my eyes against all the furry faces and the star-clustered eyes and I tilted my head up toward the night sky, toward the real stars. Suddenly my song had found me. It was "Sweetwater," the song Jubal had played at that winter fête—but now I made it my own. I took the melody and I played it like an Argan, modeling my song after an Argan song about a lost child looking for its mother. All the months of frustration and loneliness poured out of me and I played like *I* was the lost, lonely child calling across the empty light-years of space to Mother Earth.

The notes blended into a song that floated majestically over the rooftops, wheeling like a bird fighting through the wind and the rain, striving to break into the open, free sky, where the sun would dry his wings so he could turn toward home: to ride the winter winds to his home. I felt as lonely as when I used to lie on the roof watching the flocks of birds overhead and imagining what it was like to fly. Gliding with long, strong wings—floating along through the light, so far above the world that land and sea blurred into one. The wind raced through their pinions, bore them up on an invisible hand, and then, passing through their bodies, there came the smell of sweetwater.

When I felt the song was finished, I put the flute down to see Amadeus chuckling to himself. The other Argans looked a little stunned. Amadeus started to play a theme, this time an Argan song, "The Enchanted Reed Pipes." I played backup man but he was the master, sending his song ringing and echoing up the abandoned streets, the two of us gone mad with music.

# MEET Laurence Yep

Growing up in San Francisco in the fifties, Laurence Yep often felt like a "double" outsider. To the majority of people, he looked Chinese; to the Chinese, he was an "American," since he spoke only English. "It was as if all the features on my face had been erased," Yep remembers, "and I was simply a blank mirror. . . ." This theme of being an outsider runs through much of Yep's work. His characters are outsiders with big dreams.

Laurence Yep's first books were science fiction. They explored the lives of outsiders on distant planets. He recalls that when he was a child, science fiction and fantasy were "truer." "In those books," he explains, "children were taken to other lands and other worlds where they had to learn strange customs and languages—and that was something I did every time I got on and off the bus." Yep comments, "Even my contemporary books Kind Hearts and Gentle Monsters and Liar, Liar are about teenagers who place themselves outside of society."

Writing and researching Dragonwings, a book about a young Chinese boy and his father who, having arrived in the United States, dream of building a flying machine, rewarded Yep in two ways. It helped him anchor his identity as a Chinese American. It also earned him the prestigious Newbery Honor, given each year to authors of the most distinguished children's books published in the United States, as well as six other national literary awards.

SWEETWATER
by Laurence Yep
Pictures by Julia Noonan

DRAGONWINGS
by Laurence Yep

# IN THE MUSIC

Yarrow liked it
when his uncles came
the house a sounding board
around their instruments
He lay upon the chesterfield
let the hours go humming by
till someone thought of clocks
remembering him
and sent him off to bed

Beneath the frosted rafters
he pulled the quilt up to his chin
shivered with the welcome chill
let the music wash him
tumbling in the waves of song
floating easy on a sound
he rode his uncle's fiddle bow
into the warming dawn

**by
Robert
Currie**

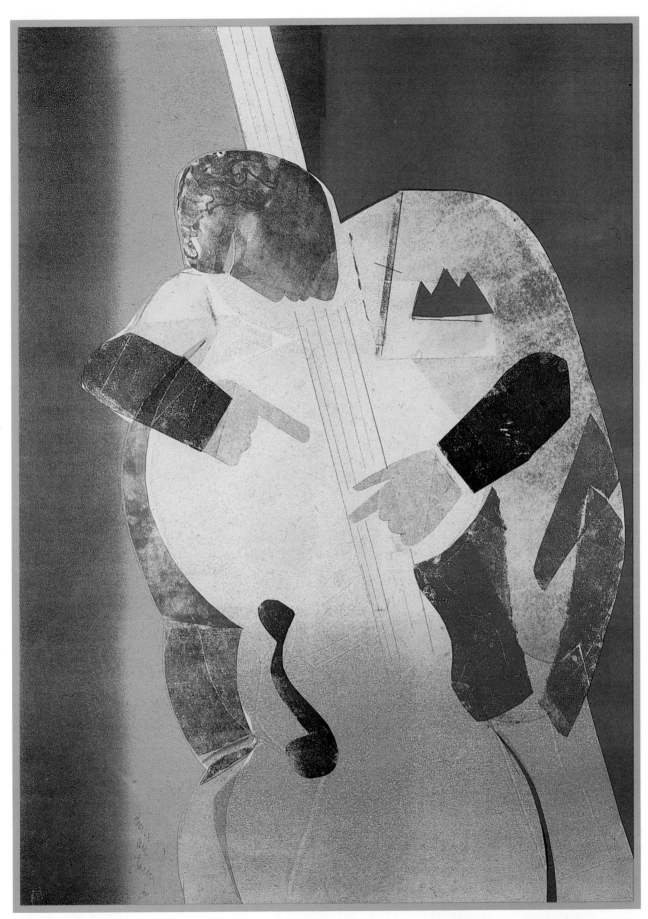

**Bass Concerto**, a collage by Romare Beardon

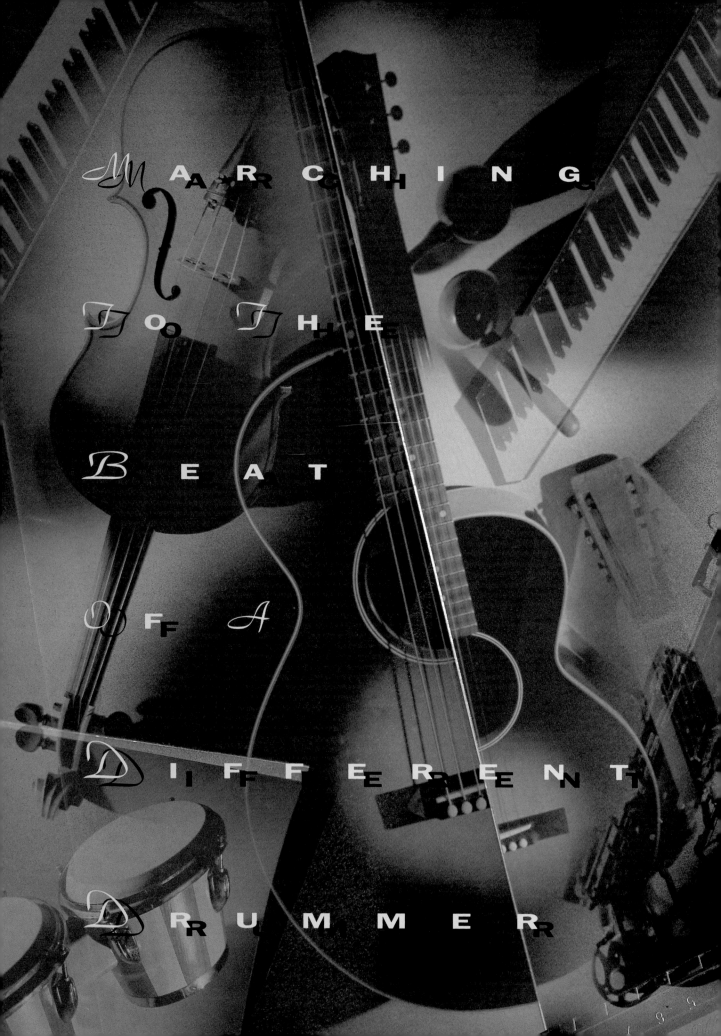

MARCHING TO THE BEAT OF A DIFFERENT DRUMMER

### Duke Ellington
by James Lincoln Collier
Macmillan, 1991

The legacy Duke Ellington left us is all those great records, hundreds of them, like "Black and Tan Fantasy," "Rockin' in Rhythm," "Mood Indigo," "Creole Love Call," "Ko-Ko," "Harlem Airshaft," "Cotton Tail," and so many others.

### Dogsong
by Gary Paulsen
Puffin, 1987

"People were afraid to sing and dance and we lost our songs."

Russel frowned. "Can we get them back? Could I get a song?"

Oogruk thought for a time. "It is not like that. You don't get songs, you *are* a song."

# ROCK'S
## Finest Hour

**Charity finds a singing voice at a historic recording session.**

A sign outside Studio A bore a single admonition: "Please check your egos at the door." Bold instructions, perhaps, since polished limousines were already nosing down La Brea Avenue toward these L.A. recording studios bearing 45 of the most luminous stars—and well-developed egos—in rock, pop and country music. Some, like Cyndi Lauper and Lionel Richie, were coming straight from the American Music Awards, an annual TV confection designed to pass out trophies and pull in Nielsens. Here at A&M's studios, however, something far more substantial was about to take place. Before this glorious hard day's night would end, the ego

Harry Belafonte

check-in counter would be the bus-
iest spot in town.

Singers whose life-styles sometimes seem to celebrate excess
were coming here to alleviate want.
Their project: recording a song that
could be used to raise funds for
African famine relief. Their work
would put a Yankee twist to a similar Band Aid project by British rock-
ers that has raised nearly $9 million
since December. But it would also
make for one of the most moving
nights in music history.

The progenitor of the project
was singer Harry Belafonte who,
impressed by the British famine effort and stunned by news accounts
of the Ethiopian tragedy, had first
conceived the American initiative
last December.

Several days before Christmas,
Belafonte called pal Ken Kragen, a
high-octane manager, with fund-
raising ideas. "He figured, after all,
the national song charts are domi-

nated by black artists," says
Kragen. "If Jews were starving in
Israel, American Jews would have
raised millions." Belafonte initially
suggested staging a megastar-
studded concert. Too difficult to
pull off, said Kragen, recalling the
money woes of the 1971 performance for Bangladesh. "Why not
a record?" asked Kragen, whose
interest in world hunger had first
been aroused by the late Harry
Chapin, an earlier singer client.
"After all, the Band Aid people
didn't copyright the idea." Kragen
then contacted Kenny Rogers and
Lionel Richie, both of whom he
also manages. Having taken over
Chapin's antihunger crusade in
1981 when the latter died, Rogers
readily agreed to participate. So did
Richie, who had spent the past several days talking about just such a
project with his wife, Brenda.

Kragen next tried to phone
Stevie Wonder, but without success. Then, shortly before Christmas,
Brenda Richie was shopping in
Beverly Hills when Wonder walked
into the store to buy some jewelry.
She helped him select several items
and asked him to return the favor
by telephoning her husband about
a special project. He did—and was
quickly enlisted.

Lionel, meanwhile, was busy
contacting Michael Jackson, whom
he had been seeing socially for

several weeks. Michael, too, agreed to join—provided he could help write the song that would be recorded. No problem, said Lionel happily. Needing a producer for the record, Kragen rang up Quincy Jones, who dropped his work on a new album to donate his services to the project.

At the Jackson home in Encino, Michael and Lionel set to work writing the anthemlike song *We Are the World*. Progress came in bits and pieces. "I'd go into the room while they were writing," remembers Michael's sister, LaToya, "and it would be very quiet, which is odd, since Michael's usually cheery when he works. It was very emotional for them. Some nights they'd just talk until 2 in the morning."

In the days between Christmas and New Year's, Kragen expanded his search for stars. "Basically, I started at the top of the record charts and began making phone calls," he says. Steve Perry, lead singer and creative heart of Journey, came home to a message on his telephone answering machine. Sign me up, he said. Then Bruce Springsteen, on tour, was called. "Do they really want me?" asked the Boss modestly. Assured that he was indeed wanted, Springsteen also came aboard. "That was something of

Quincy Jones

Lionel Richie
Daryl Hall
Paul Simon
Stevie Wonder

Billy Joel
Cyndi Lauper

a turning point," concedes Kragen. "It gave the project a great deal more stature in the eyes of others."

Kragen's final lineup—all of whom performed for free—reads like a Who's Who of gold record collectors. Among them: Tina Turner, Bette Midler, Willie Nelson, Billy Joel, Huey Lewis and Waylon Jennings. Jeffrey Osborne was approached by Richie just hours before the taping, while both were rehearsing for the American Music Awards. "Keep it silent," cautioned Lionel. Kragen, who had first envisioned only 10 or 15 performers, eventually had trouble stopping the project's momentum. "In the last week we went from 28 to more than 40 artists," he says. "I had to turn down something like 50 or 60 performers who wanted to participate."

Many of those who came did so with difficulty. Springsteen, because of his notoriously long concerts, never travels and seldom arises before 5 P.M. the day after a show. Yet the next afternoon, after finishing his American tour in Syracuse, N.Y., he boarded a plane and flew to L.A. Daryl Hall and John Oates were also in the East rehearsing for a tour that would start a week and a half after the taping. Stevie Wonder managed to get out of Philadelphia despite terrible weather. James Ingram flew in from London, and Paul Simon showed up despite having spent the entire previous night at work in a recording studio.

On the last Monday in January, as the American Music Awards were ending at the Shrine Auditorium across town, all was in readiness at A&M. Studio C had been set aside as a makeup room, Studio B stocked with fruit, cheese and juices for incoming singers. The building's large Charlie Chaplin soundstage creaked under a $15,000 spread of roast beef, tortellini, imported cheese and other goodies for the performers' guests— all provided gratis by Someone's in The Kitchen catering. The onlookers and guests (each performer was allowed five) included Ali MacGraw, Jane Fonda, Dick Clark and many family members, and all watched the night's proceedings through TV monitors and the lenses of five video cameras.

At 9 P.M. people began arriving in streams. "During the first hour it was impossible to get anything done," says Osborne. "Everyone was congratulating each other, meeting people they hadn't met before." "Saying 'hi'; exchanging lies," echoes Ray Charles. "It was just like Thanksgiving, all of us together." Ruth Pointer of the Pointer Sisters came with a camera and quickly shot some snaps of Michael Jackson ("I have two kids, and they would've killed me if I hadn't").

Then sister June Pointer entered the studio with Bruce Springsteen, and the pair plopped down together on the only chair then available.

**B**ob Dylan showed typical reserve at first, sitting off by himself. But even the legendary loner couldn't withstand the warmth. Hours later he could be found in a corner, rehearsing his solo lines as Stevie Wonder accompanied him on the piano, singing in Dylan's own nasal style. Fleetwood Mac's Lindsey Buckingham found himself chatting with Harry Belafonte. When Buckingham mentioned how much he loved Belafonte's Calypso classic, *The Banana Boat Song,* everyone nearby suddenly broke into a spontaneous chorus of day-o's. Ray Charles asked for a drink of water, and another singer volunteered to lead him to the fountain. Stevie Wonder. And so it went. "For me, the first couple hours were highly charged," says Kenny Loggins. "I've never before felt that strong a sense of community."

Around 10 P.M. the sheet music was passed out, and several people stepped forth to address the group. Kragen talked of plans for the funds they hoped to raise. Mindful of the decade-long "Bangladesh situation, I assured the artists that if it came down to seeing that the money got to the right places, I would go over with the supplies personally." Then Bob Geldof, leader of the Boomtown

Ray Charles

Bob Dylan

Bruce Springsteen

Rats and organizer of the British Band Aid sing-along, offered a moving speech about his own travels in Ethiopia, telling of a "good day" in one village he had visited when only five people had died. "Geldof's opening speech was pretty intense," noted Loggins later. "You could hear the truth in his voice."

After Michael Jackson shyly described the piece he and Richie had written—"a love song to inspire concern about a faraway place close to home"—the taping began. Quincy Jones sat on a stool directing his multimillion dollar chorus, Richie on a chair next to him, Michael with the others but off to one side. At one point during the long hours that followed, emotions swept up the 400 guests, who joined the singing from their soundproof stage. During a break, Brenda Richie took orders for Fat Burgers (from Springsteen, Dionne Warwick and others) and sent a chauffeur off to a nearby hamburger stand.

By 3 A.M. the choral section of the song was recorded, and only the solo sections remained. "Everybody was drained, but also hanging on to the thread of magic in the night," says Ingram. "You could see the fatigue on people's faces," remembers Osborne. The group took another break and, prompted by Diana Ross, began autographing each other's sheet music. Suddenly

Michael Jackson
Diana Ross

Wonder came into the room with two African women, representatives of the very people the performers were trying to help. The women, nervous and exhausted, spoke through trembling lips in their native Swahili, thanking the group for all they were doing. Says Ingram, "Everybody was humbled."

Then Jones positioned the 21 soloists in a semicircle around him. Starting with Richie, they all sang their parts, and the singing moved round and round the semicircle until it was completed. Loggins was stationed between Springsteen and Steve Perry during the solos; Springsteen sang his part in a huge, booming voice. "I wanted to do my very best," Loggins says, "and with Springsteen belting his line like a loud Joe Cocker, I wondered how I should do mine." Just be yourself, Perry advised. "I think that pretty much sums up how everybody was acting," says Loggins.

By dawn most of the performers had finished. Dylan and Springsteen, obviously drained by the marathon, remained until around 7:30. His own solo work long since completed, Perry also stuck around to witness the ending. Osborne, after trading a few ad lib vocal licks with Wonder, Richie and others, finally walked out the studio door with Michael Jackson sometime before 8. Off to one side an exhausted Diana Ross sat on the floor, tears filling her eyes. "I just don't want this to end," she said.

## Meet Todd Gold

When the reporter Todd Gold tried to get permission to attend the famous "We Are the World" recording session, he recalls, "I was told *no, no, no,* and for added measure, I was told *no* one more time." But Gold knew that the story of the music world's biggest stars getting together for a worthy cause was important. So he kept trying until, the next day, some of the stars agreed to talk to him. Gold's talent and persistence have made him a top reporter for *People* magazine. Based in Los Angeles, he has interviewed such music legends as Michael Jackson, Quincy Jones, Phil Collins, and Paula Abdul.

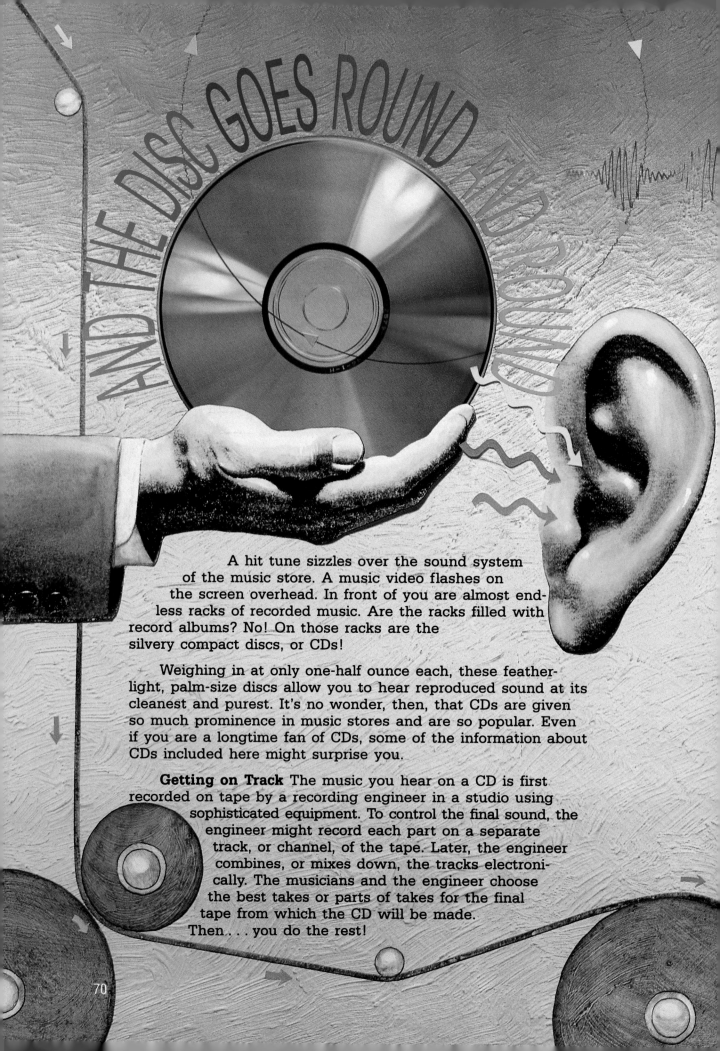

A hit tune sizzles over the sound system of the music store. A music video flashes on the screen overhead. In front of you are almost endless racks of recorded music. Are the racks filled with record albums? No! On those racks are the silvery compact discs, or CDs!

Weighing in at only one-half ounce each, these featherlight, palm-size discs allow you to hear reproduced sound at its cleanest and purest. It's no wonder, then, that CDs are given so much prominence in music stores and are so popular. Even if you are a longtime fan of CDs, some of the information about CDs included here might surprise you.

**Getting on Track** The music you hear on a CD is first recorded on tape by a recording engineer in a studio using sophisticated equipment. To control the final sound, the engineer might record each part on a separate track, or channel, of the tape. Later, the engineer combines, or mixes down, the tracks electronically. The musicians and the engineer choose the best takes or parts of takes for the final tape from which the CD will be made. Then. . . you do the rest!

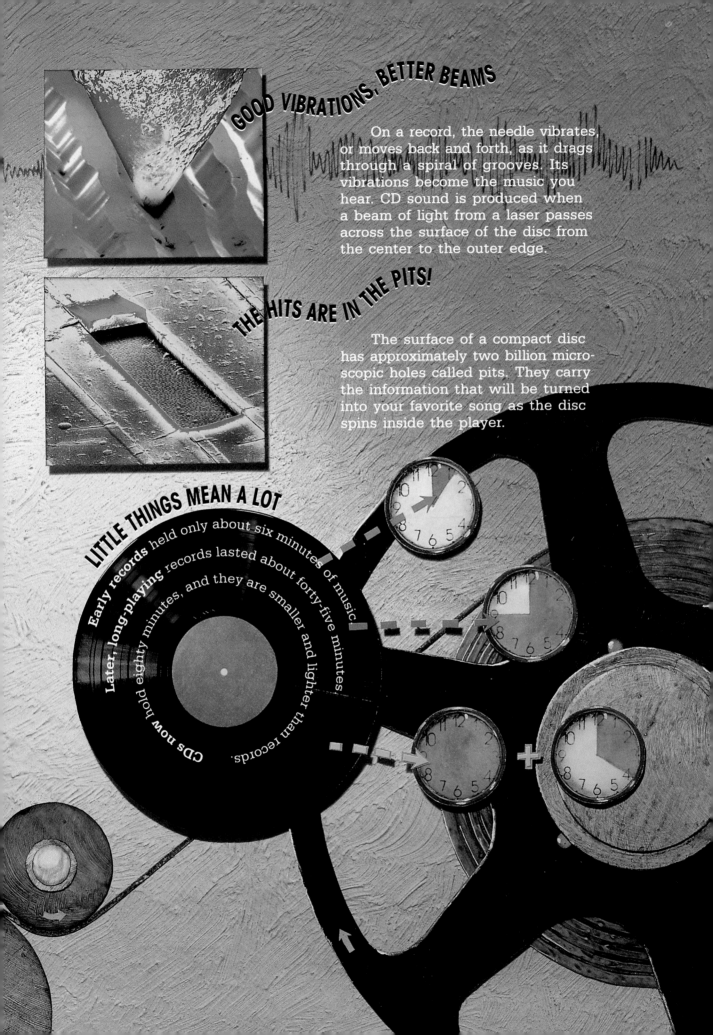

## GOOD VIBRATIONS, BETTER BEAMS

On a record, the needle vibrates, or moves back and forth, as it drags through a spiral of grooves. Its vibrations become the music you hear. CD sound is produced when a beam of light from a laser passes across the surface of the disc from the center to the outer edge.

## THE HITS ARE IN THE PITS!

The surface of a compact disc has approximately two billion microscopic holes called pits. They carry the information that will be turned into your favorite song as the disc spins inside the player.

## LITTLE THINGS MEAN A LOT

Early records held only about six minutes of music. Later, long-playing records lasted about forty-five minutes, and they are smaller and lighter than records. CDs now hold eighty minutes.

# I·HEAR·AMERICA·

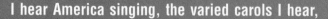

I hear America singing, the varied carols I hear,
Those of mechanics, each one singing his as it should
    be blithe and strong,
The carpenter singing his as he measures his plank
    or beam,
The mason singing his as he makes ready for work, or
    leaves off work,
The boatman singing what belongs to him in his boat,
    the deckhand singing on the steamboat deck,
The shoemaker singing as he sits on his bench, the
    hatter singing as he stands,
The wood-cutter's song, the ploughboy's on his way in
    the morning, or at noon intermission or at sundown,
The delicious singing of the mother, or of the young
    wife at work, or of the girl sewing or washing,
Each singing what belongs to him or her and to none
    else,
The day what belongs to the day—at night the party
    of young fellows, robust, friendly,
Singing with open mouths their strong melodious songs.

—WALT WHITMAN

# TWO TALES

## MEET JANE ANNE VOLKMER

WHILE Jane Anne Volkmer was a student in graduate school, her professor suggested she try to write and illustrate a book. Since she already knew something about Guatemalan folklore and had a foster child in that country, Volkmer seized this opportunity. In Guatemala, she researched the background material for *Song of the Chirimia* and took the photographs on which she based her illustrations.

## MEET RICHARD LEWIS

UNTIL Richard Lewis was about thirteen years old, books held little attraction for him. "At that time," he says, "the reading bug caught up with me, and . . . I, with a strong inclination towards daydreaming, began to find in books a private corner for my thoughts. The specific titles escape me now but the glow of that discovery is still with me."

This glow obviously has remained with Lewis. His career has centered on teaching writing and literature to children and on the writing and editing of books for young people. His goal is to make the poetry and song of various cultures known to his readers.

Among Lewis's books are *Out of the Earth I Sing* and *The Moment of Wonder*, both American Library Association Notable Books.

# ABOUT MUSIC

## MEET ED YOUNG

EVEN as a young child, Ed Young showed a talent for drawing. When he was nineteen, he moved from his home in China to the United States, where he studied art.

Young received an award from the American Institute of Graphic Artists in 1962 for *The Mean House and Other Mean Stories,* the first book he illustrated. Among his other award-winning books are *The Emperor and the Kite* and *Lon Po Po,* both of which were awarded Caldecott Medals.

*Music is one of the oldest forms of self-expression. It delights, soothes, comforts, and touches us deeply. The joy of music is universal, and the richness of its tradition is presented here in the retelling of the Mayan folk tale* Song of the Chirimia *and the Aztec myth* All of You Was Singing. *Both celebrate the emotion and dramatic power of song and remind us that music begins within us.*

# SONG OF THE CHIRIMIA

## A GUATEMALAN FOLK TALE

retold and illustrated by
*narrada e ilustrada por*
JANE ANNE VOLKMER

AUTHOR'S NOTE

Dear Reader,

When I first heard the legend of the chirimia, I wanted to share it with as many people as possible. It is a story that has been told for generations in the country of Guatemala.

Each year hundreds of people from around the world travel to Guatemala to visit the ruins of ancient Mayan cities. I often go there myself, and every time I try to imagine what it was like over 2,000 years ago when Mayan kings and queens ruled. It's not hard to picture what they looked like because the Maya left behind stone carvings of themselves. Many of this book's characters were drawn from these carvings.

I hope you enjoy this story and will want to learn more about Guatemala— the people, the music, and the history. I believe that through books we can all become world travelers.

Sincerely,
Jane Anne Volkmer

## NOTA DE LA AUTORA

Estimado Lector,

La primera vez que oí la leyenda de la chirimía quería compartirla con todo el mundo. Es un cuento que ha sido contado a través de las generaciones en el país de Guatemala.

Cada año viajan las personas, a centenares, desde todos sitios, a visitar las ruínas de las ciudades Mayas. Voy allá a menudo, y cada vez intento imaginar como eran las cosas hace 2,000 años cuando los reyes Mayas gobernaban. No es difícil imaginar como eran los Mayas, porque dejaron figuras esculpidas de piedra. Muchos de los personajes en este libro vienen de estas figuras esculpidas.

Espero que disfrutes de este cuento y que quieras aprender más sobre Guatemala—la gente, la música, y la historia. Creo que a través de los libros podemos todos ser viajeros del mundo.

Sinceramente,
Jane Anne Volkmer

# LA MÚSICA DE LA CHIRIMÍA

## FOLKLORE GUATEMALTECO

traducida por
LORI ANN SCHATSCHNEIDER

On the night of the 20th full moon of Clear Sky's kingly reign, a child was born to him. Under the moon's bright light, he stood motionless, gazing at the baby girl in his servant's arms.

"I shall name my daughter Moonlight," Clear Sky declared, "to honor the light in which I first saw her." The child was all the king had now. His beloved queen had died at Moonlight's birth.

As Moonlight grew, Clear Sky's love for her deepened. Some days he would take her out in a boat on a nearby lake. They would watch the fishermen throw their nets into the clear blue waters. Patiently the two would wait until the men lifted the nets wriggling with fish.

Other days the two would walk through the marketplace to see the merchants' displays. Moonlight's eyes reflected the sun's sparkle on gold necklaces. Her voice had the softness and warmth of woven cloth.

As she talked gaily to Clear Sky, she danced past the displays, breathing the fragrance of cacao beans.

But one day, the happiness ended. Moonlight sat on the palace steps, staring at the

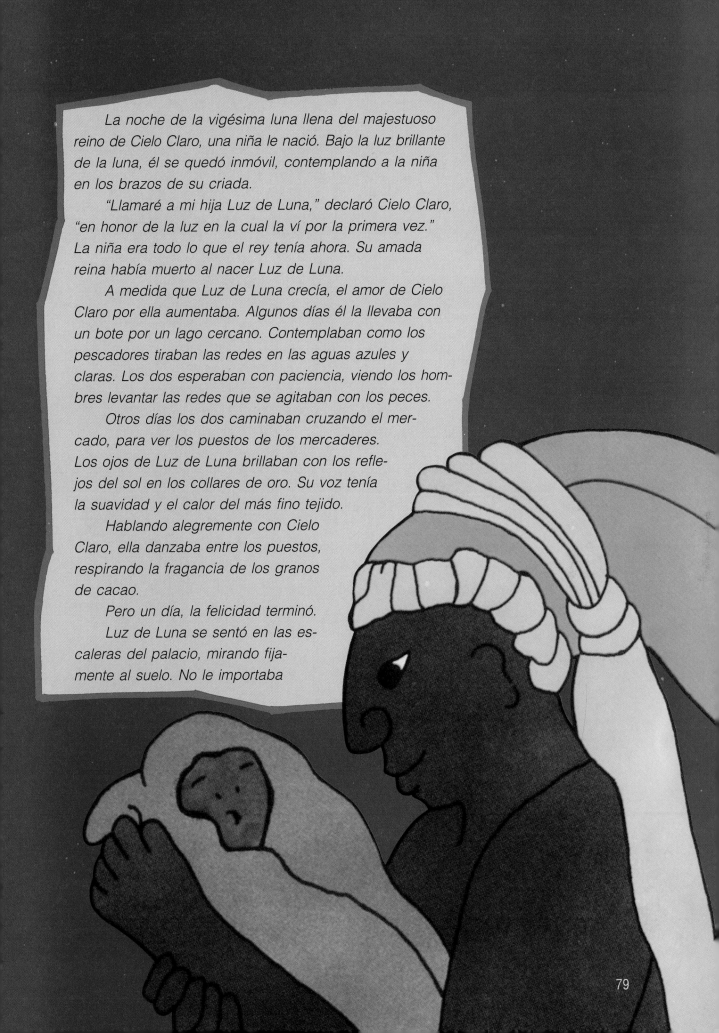

La noche de la vigésima luna llena del majestuoso reino de Cielo Claro, una niña le nació. Bajo la luz brillante de la luna, él se quedó inmóvil, contemplando a la niña en los brazos de su criada.

"Llamaré a mi hija Luz de Luna," declaró Cielo Claro, "en honor de la luz en la cual la ví por la primera vez." La niña era todo lo que el rey tenía ahora. Su amada reina había muerto al nacer Luz de Luna.

A medida que Luz de Luna crecía, el amor de Cielo Claro por ella aumentaba. Algunos días él la llevaba con un bote por un lago cercano. Contemplaban como los pescadores tiraban las redes en las aguas azules y claras. Los dos esperaban con paciencia, viendo los hombres levantar las redes que se agitaban con los peces.

Otros días los dos caminaban cruzando el mercado, para ver los puestos de los mercaderes. Los ojos de Luz de Luna brillaban con los reflejos del sol en los collares de oro. Su voz tenía la suavidad y el calor del más fino tejido.

Hablando alegremente con Cielo Claro, ella danzaba entre los puestos, respirando la fragancia de los granos de cacao.

Pero un día, la felicidad terminó.

Luz de Luna se sentó en las escaleras del palacio, mirando fijamente al suelo. No le importaba

ground, not caring what could be seen at the market or how many fish were netted. She would not talk to anyone, not even her father.

She wanted to be alone.

Her father tried to bring back her laughter and chatter.

He gave her glistening jade beads from the highlands. He had his hunters bring exotic birds to her from the jungle. He called the best ballplayers in the kingdom to play in the ballcourt before her.

But Moonlight remained silent.

Clear Sky could not sleep.

He told his counselors, "My grieving will not end until I see a smile on Moonlight's face."

Clear Sky summoned governors, priests, and scribes to his chambers to ponder this problem of gloom. The learned men sat quietly for many hours, trying to think of a solution.

Finally, a scribe who recorded marriages in his village broke the silence. "Moonlight has become a young woman. It is the time of her life to marry. When she marries, her sorrow will leave."

**"She shall be married!"** proclaimed the king.

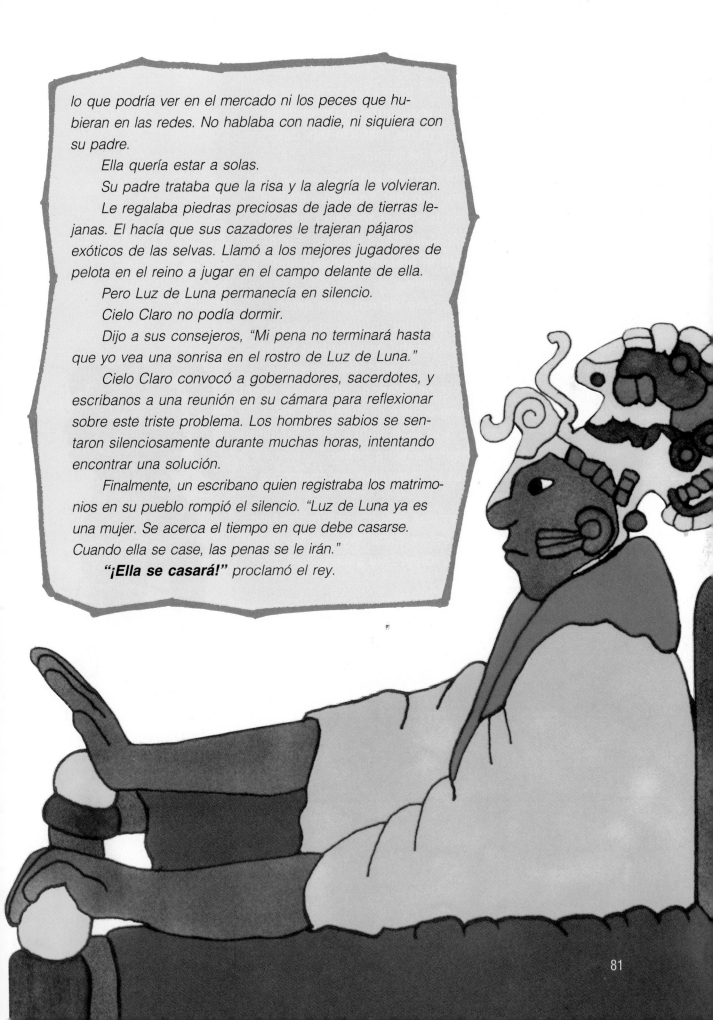

lo que podría ver en el mercado ni los peces que hubieran en las redes. No hablaba con nadie, ni siquiera con su padre.

Ella quería estar a solas.

Su padre trataba que la risa y la alegría le volvieran. Le regalaba piedras preciosas de jade de tierras lejanas. El hacía que sus cazadores le trajeran pájaros exóticos de las selvas. Llamó a los mejores jugadores de pelota en el reino a jugar en el campo delante de ella.

Pero Luz de Luna permanecía en silencio.

Cielo Claro no podía dormir.

Dijo a sus consejeros, "Mi pena no terminará hasta que yo vea una sonrisa en el rostro de Luz de Luna."

Cielo Claro convocó a gobernadores, sacerdotes, y escribanos a una reunión en su cámara para reflexionar sobre este triste problema. Los hombres sabios se sentaron silenciosamente durante muchas horas, intentando encontrar una solución.

Finalmente, un escribano quien registraba los matrimonios en su pueblo rompió el silencio. "Luz de Luna ya es una mujer. Se acerca el tiempo en que debe casarse. Cuando ella se case, las penas se le irán."

**"¡Ella se casará!"** proclamó el rey.

Clear Sky ordered all the young, unmarried men in the kingdom to come to the central plaza on the day of the 224th full moon of his rule. On this day, Moonlight could choose her husband.

As ordered, the suitors arrived at the palace on the day of the full moon. Many brought expensive gifts of jade, pottery, gold, and birds. Handsome men, strong men, knowledgeable men—all stood waiting. Each paraded before Moonlight in elegant clothing and spoke to her of his best qualities.

But she did not smile. She did not even listen.

As the sun lowered, the faint sounds of a song drifted through the crowd. On the path leading to the plaza, a man walked. He had no gifts. He carried no weapons. His clothes were not elegant. He was singing a joyful song. The evening breeze captured his low, sweet voice and carried it to Moonlight's ears. Smiling, she lifted her head to hear the song better.

"Tell that young man to come into my chambers," the king commanded.

The dark-haired singer was brought before the king. He stood tall and slender before Clear Sky and Moonlight.

"What is your name?" Clear Sky asked.

Cielo Claro ordenó venir a todos los jóvenes solteros del reino a la plaza central, el día de la luna llena 224 de su ley. En este día Luz de Luna podría escoger a su esposo.

Tal como les había ordenado el rey, los pretendientes llegaron al palacio el día de la luna llena. Muchos trajeron regalos caros de jade, cerámica, oro, y pájaros. Hombres atractivos, hombres fuertes, hombres inteligentes—todos esperaban. Cada uno desfilaba ante Luz de Luna vestido con ropas elegantes, y le hablaba de sus mejores cualidades.

Pero ella no sonreía. Ni siquiera escuchaba.

Al ocultarse el sol, el sonido tierno de una canción le llegó a través de la multitud. En el sendero que conducía a la plaza, un hombre caminaba. No tenía regalos. No llevaba armas. Sus ropas no eran elegantes. El estaba cantando una canción alegre. La brisa nocturna capturó su voz dulce y baja, y la llevó a los oídos de Luz de Luna. Sonriendo, ella levantó la cabeza para oír mejor la canción.

"Digan a ese joven que venga a mi cámara," ordenó el rey.

El cantante del pelo oscuro fue traído ante el rey. Se mantuvo erguido ante Cielo Claro y Luz de Luna.

"¿Cómo te llamas?" Cielo Claro preguntó.

"I am called Black Feather," he replied.

"Black Feather, you have brought pleasure to my daughter. If she wishes, you may marry her."

Moonlight smiled at Black Feather. "Your voice is clear and your song more pure than any I have ever heard," she said. "But I still prefer to listen to the harmony of singing birds. If you can make your song and your voice become one as the birds do, I shall marry you."

"I will learn to sing like the birds," he said, "but it will take me some time. Will you grant me time to learn?"

"How much time will you need?" she asked.

"Three full moons," he answered.

"I shall listen for your return."

With love in his heart, Black Feather left the king's chambers. He hurried down the palace steps. A large cluster of ceiba trees at the plaza's edge rustled for him to come to them. A small opening between the trees led to a path. This path would take him far into the woods, where it was said that the birds never stop singing.

Black Feather disappeared down the steep and narrow path. He walked through the darkness till he could go no farther. Black Feather lay on the ground and fell asleep.

At dawn, Black Feather woke to the sound of singing birds. He listened intently. Morning, noon, and evening, Black Feather tried his best to sing as sweetly as they did.

But he could not.

Two full moons passed, and Black Feather grew weary from trying.

Alone in the woods, Black Feather thought he would never be able to return to Moonlight. Suddenly, leaves started falling around him, and the wind blew cold and moist.

"Me llaman Pluma Negra," el respondió.

"Pluma Negra, has traído placer a mi hija. Si ella desea, podrán casarse."

Luz de Luna sonrió a Pluma Negra. "Tu voz es clara y tu canción la más pura que haya escuchado," dijo ella. "Pero todavía prefiero escuchar la melodía del canto de los pájaros. Si tú puedes hacer que tu canción y tu voz se unan como hacen los pájaros, me casaré contigo."

"Yo aprenderé a cantar como los pájaros," dijo él, "pero me tomará algún tiempo. ¿Me concederá usted tiempo para aprender?"

"¿Cuánto tiempo necesitarás?" ella preguntó.

"Tres lunas llenas," él respondió.

"Esperaré tu regreso."

Con amor en su corazón, Pluma Negra salió de la cámara del rey. Con prisa bajó las escaleras del palacio. Un grupo grande de árboles de ceiba en el borde de la plaza susurraban para que se acercara hacia ellos. Una pequeña abertura entre los árboles seguía hacia un sendero. Este sendero le llevaría lejos al interior del bosque donde se decía que los pájaros nunca cesaban de cantar.

Pluma Negra desapareció por el sendero empinado y estrecho. Caminaba en la oscuridad hasta que no pudo más. Pluma Negra se acostó en el suelo y se durmió.

Al amanecer, Pluma Negra se despertó con el canto de los pájaros. Escuchó atentamente. Por la mañana, al medio día, y por la noche, Pluma Negra intentaba cantar tan dulcemente como ellos.

Pero no podía hacerlo.

Pasaron dos lunas llenas, y Pluma Negra se fatigaba de tanto intentarlo.

A solas en el bosque, Pluma Negra pensó que nunca podría volver a ver a Luz de Luna. De repente, las hojas empezaron a caer a su alrededor y el viento sopló frío y húmedo.

Startled, Black Feather looked up. Like a large tree bent in the wind, the Great Spirit of the Woods floated above him.

"Why do you look so sad?" whispered the Great Spirit.

With much dismay, Black Feather told the spirit his story.

"I know a way for your voice and your song to join in harmony so you can sing like a bird," crackled the Great Spirit. "But you must do as I tell you. First, cut a branch from that tree."

Black Feather took his knife and cut the branch. He handed it to the Great Spirit. Howling, the spirit flew into a treetop, setting it ablaze. The spirit roared and hissed as he transformed the branch into a long, hollow pipe with holes in one side.

The flames vanished, and the spirit drifted slowly back to Black Feather.

The Great Spirit gave the pipe to the young man saying, "What you hold in your hands is called a chirimia, and its song is more pleasing to the ear than that of the birds. Learn to play it well, and when the princess hears the chirimia's song, she will marry you."

Black Feather stared at the pipe.

"Take it to your lips and blow through it," the spirit commanded. "Move your fingers along the holes and listen."

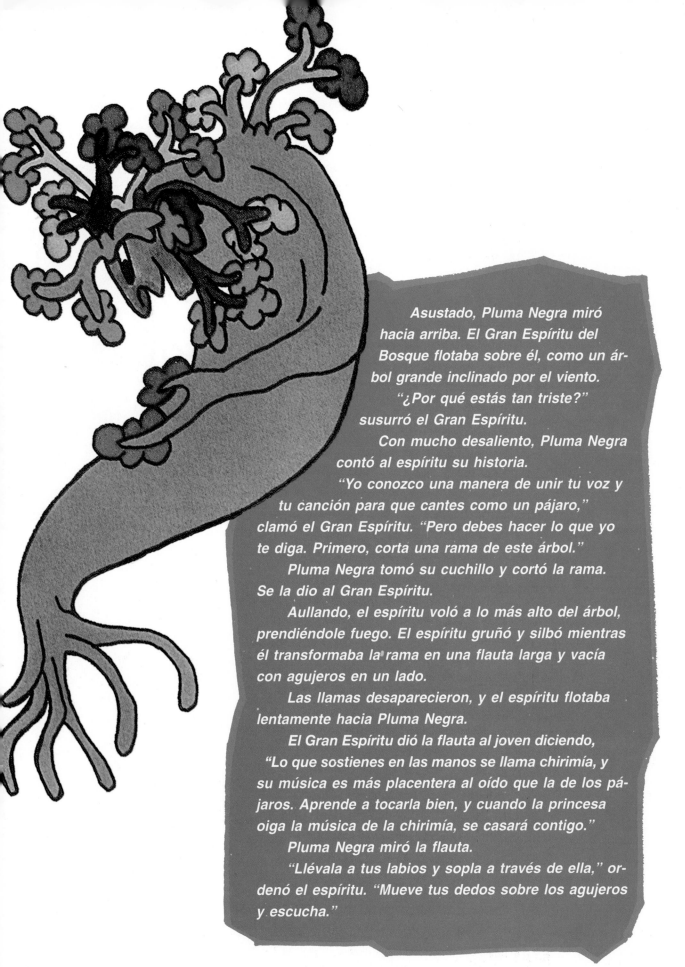

Asustado, Pluma Negra miró hacia arriba. El Gran Espíritu del Bosque flotaba sobre él, como un árbol grande inclinado por el viento.

"¿Por qué estás tan triste?" susurró el Gran Espíritu.

Con mucho desaliento, Pluma Negra contó al espíritu su historia.

"Yo conozco una manera de unir tu voz y tu canción para que cantes como un pájaro," clamó el Gran Espíritu. "Pero debes hacer lo que yo te diga. Primero, corta una rama de este árbol."

Pluma Negra tomó su cuchillo y cortó la rama. Se la dio al Gran Espíritu.

Aullando, el espíritu voló a lo más alto del árbol, prendiéndole fuego. El espíritu gruñó y silbó mientras él transformaba la rama en una flauta larga y vacía con agujeros en un lado.

Las llamas desaparecieron, y el espíritu flotaba lentamente hacia Pluma Negra.

El Gran Espíritu dió la flauta al joven diciendo, "Lo que sostienes en las manos se llama chirimía, y su música es más placentera al oído que la de los pájaros. Aprende a tocarla bien, y cuando la princesa oiga la música de la chirimía, se casará contigo."

Pluma Negra miró la flauta.

"Llévala a tus labios y sopla a través de ella," ordenó el espíritu. "Mueve tus dedos sobre los agujeros y escucha."

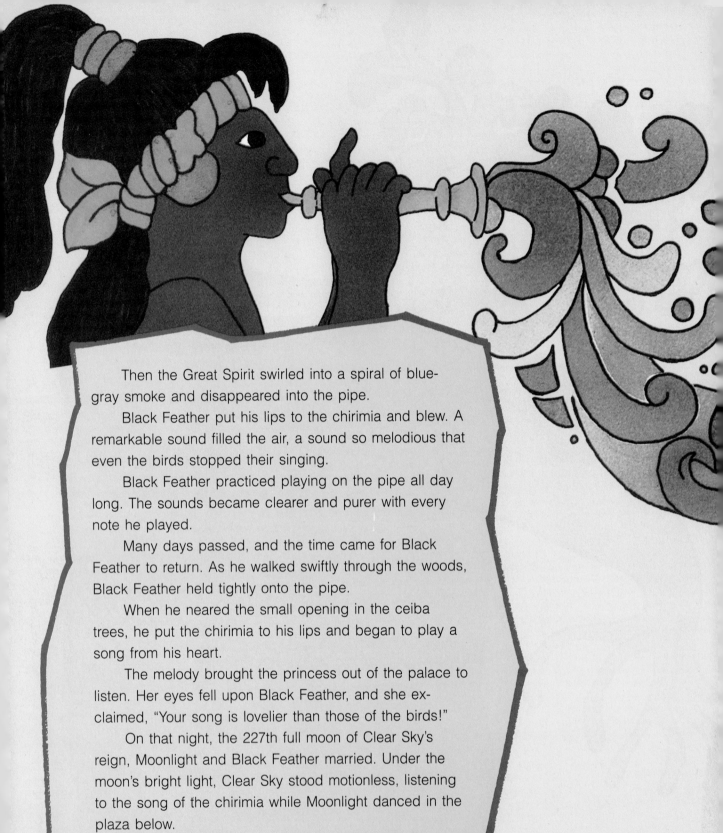

Then the Great Spirit swirled into a spiral of blue-gray smoke and disappeared into the pipe.

Black Feather put his lips to the chirimia and blew. A remarkable sound filled the air, a sound so melodious that even the birds stopped their singing.

Black Feather practiced playing on the pipe all day long. The sounds became clearer and purer with every note he played.

Many days passed, and the time came for Black Feather to return. As he walked swiftly through the woods, Black Feather held tightly onto the pipe.

When he neared the small opening in the ceiba trees, he put the chirimia to his lips and began to play a song from his heart.

The melody brought the princess out of the palace to listen. Her eyes fell upon Black Feather, and she exclaimed, "Your song is lovelier than those of the birds!"

On that night, the 227th full moon of Clear Sky's reign, Moonlight and Black Feather married. Under the moon's bright light, Clear Sky stood motionless, listening to the song of the chirimia while Moonlight danced in the plaza below.

Today, if you travel to Guatemala, you may hear music sweeter than that of any bird, lilting in the wind. If you ask what it is you hear, the reply will be, "It is the song of the chirimia, the most harmonious song in the woods."

Entonces el Gran Espíritu giró en un remolino de humo azul y gris, y desapareció en el interior de la flauta.

Pluma Negra puso los labios en la chirimía y sopló. Un sonido extraordinario llenó el aire, tan melodioso que los pájaros detuvieron su canto.

Pluma Negra practicó tocando la flauta todo el día. Los sonidos se volvían más claros y puros con cada nota que tocaba.

Pasaron muchos días, y llegó el momento para que regresara Pluma Negra. Caminando rapidamente a través del bosque, Pluma Negra cogía la flauta fuertemente.

Al acercarse a la pequeña abertura entre los árboles de ceiba, él puso la chirimía en sus labios y comenzó a tocar una canción, que salía de lo más profundo de su corazón.

La melodía atrajo a la princesa fuera del palacio. Sus ojos cayeron sobre Pluma Negra y ella exclamó, "¡Tu canción es más hermosa que la de los pájaros!"

Esa noche, la luna llena 227 del reino de Cielo Claro, Luz de Luna y Pluma Negra se casaron. Bajo la luz brillante de la luna, Cielo Claro se quedó inmóvil, escuchando la música de la chirimía mientras Luz de Luna danzaba abajo en la plaza.

Hoy en dia, si tú viajas a Guatemala, podrás oír música más dulce que cualquier otro canto alegre de pájaro en el viento. Si tú preguntas que es lo que se escucha, la respuesta será, "Es el sonido de la chirimía, la música más armoniosa en el bosque."

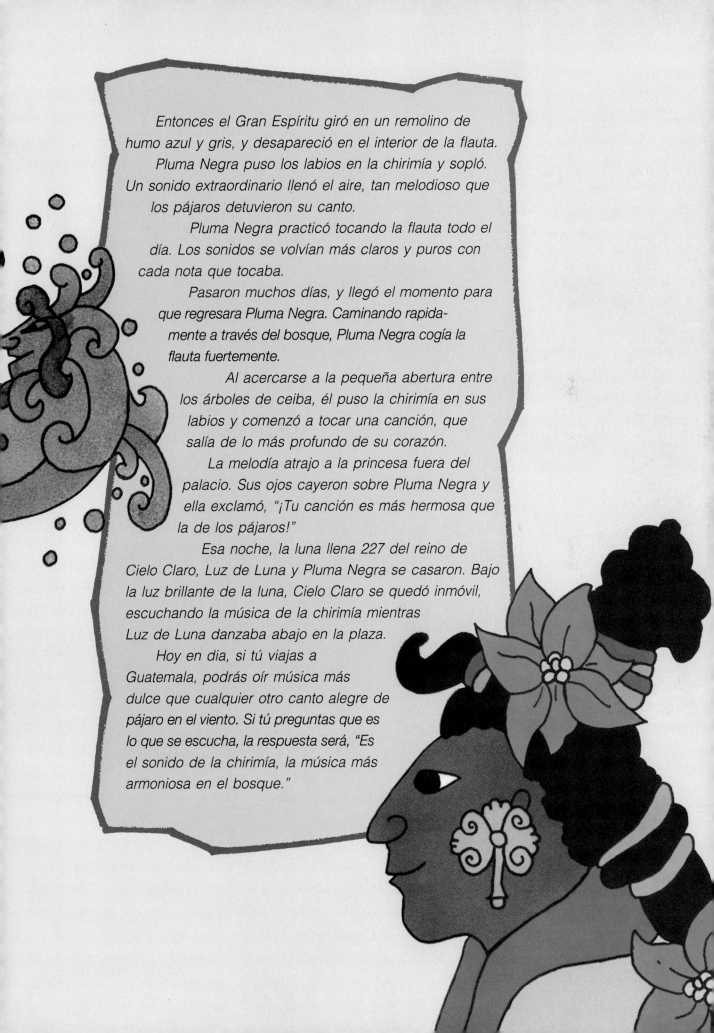

To the Aztecs in Mexico and their neighbors to the South, the Mayans, the world is suffused with an almost supernatural quality of aliveness. Colors, flowers, wind, water—even the silence between the stars—are seen as symbols of the workings of the universe and of our place within it. The Aztecs believed in a complex system of gods, who personified many of the forces of nature. The sun itself was a god who lived in a house in the sky where there was much singing and dancing. Another god, Tezcatlipoca, like many Aztec gods, took on different forms, but most often represented night. It was Tezcatlipoca who asked Quetzalcoatl—an important Aztec god who represented the spirit and the wind—to journey to the sun and bring the musicians there back to Earth.

ALL OF YOU WAS SINGING is a retelling of this myth about how music came to Earth. As with all myths, many meanings can be read into it. My own sense of this myth is the profound importance of music to the well-being of life. To sing is an affirmation of the melody and rhythm of life. And such singing continues, as in the Aztec song, even after us:

*My flowers shall not perish*
*Nor shall my chants cease*
*They spread, they scatter.*

—R.L.

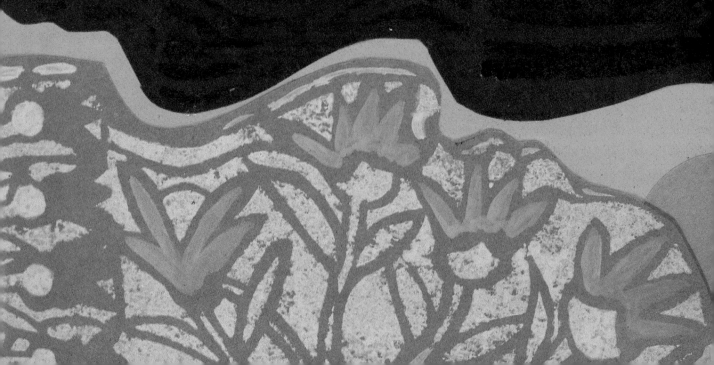

# ALL OF YOU WAS SINGING

RICHARD LEWIS

Art by ED YOUNG

When things were beginning,
there was water
everywhere.

And the earth-monster
swam everywhere,

eating everything
it saw.

93

*From out of everywhere,*
*there came two serpents*
*who tore*
*the earth-monster*
*in half.*

And the sky, speaking to the earth, said:
I am your sky.
You are my earth.

From your eyes, the gods made springs
of cold water.
From your mouth, they made the deep caves
and echoing caverns.

From your skin, they brought the lawns
of jeweled flowers.
From your hair, they fashioned the long grass
and the noble trees.

And the first sound I heard in my heavens
was the sound
of moving air
becoming
the wind.

The sound of the wind grew
and became the glowing of stars.

The sound of the wind grew
and became the music of the sun.

But whenever I, the sky, reached toward you,
the earth,
the music of the sun stood still,
and you, the earth, which had light to see
the colors of your flowers and birds . . .
you had no music;
you wore upon your body only
a mist of silence.

My sadness shook, pleading with the wind:

"Wind, we must bring music to the earth.
We must bring music to the waking dawn.
We must bring music to the dreaming man.
We must bring music to the moving waters and
the flying birds.
Wind, life upon the earth must be music.

"Wind, go to the house of the sun, where you shall
find a music whose burning sounds bring me
my light.

"Wind, bring back to the silent earth these
flowers of sounds;
bring back clusters of the most
beautiful music."

And the wind, hearing my plea,
gathered into itself
all of your earth's silence
and, in a great rush of air,
swept past the roofs of my sky,
where it found the sun
and the melodies of its music,
playing in a nest of light.

In the east, the singer in white sang
the songs of the newborn.

In the west, the singer in red played
the songs of love and war.

In the north, the singer in blue sang
the songs of wandering clouds.

In the south, the singer in yellow sang
the songs of gold.

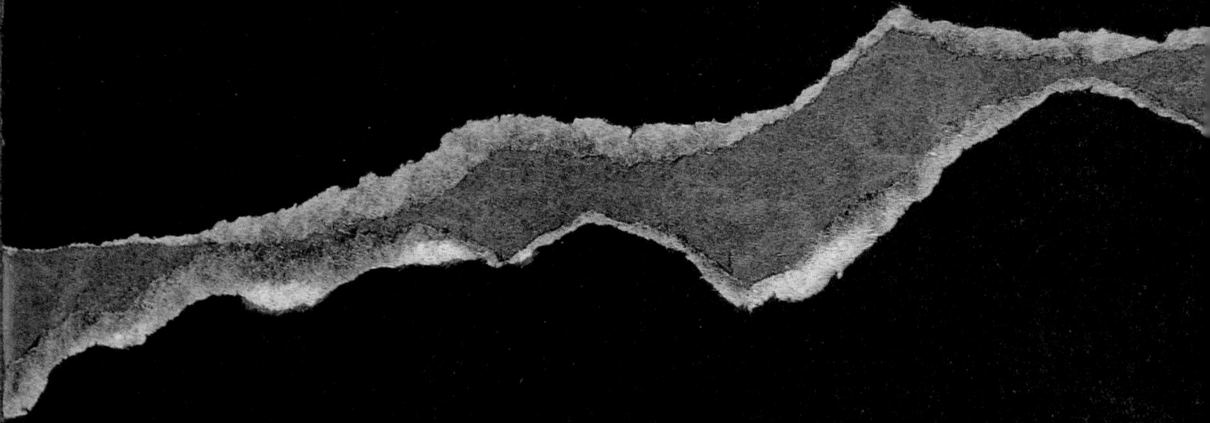

All of my sky was filled with the surging
of wind,
And the sun cried to the musicians:

"The earth's wind comes closer.
Do not answer the wind."

And the wind cried:

"Come, come, musicians of the sun.
The earth is calling you."

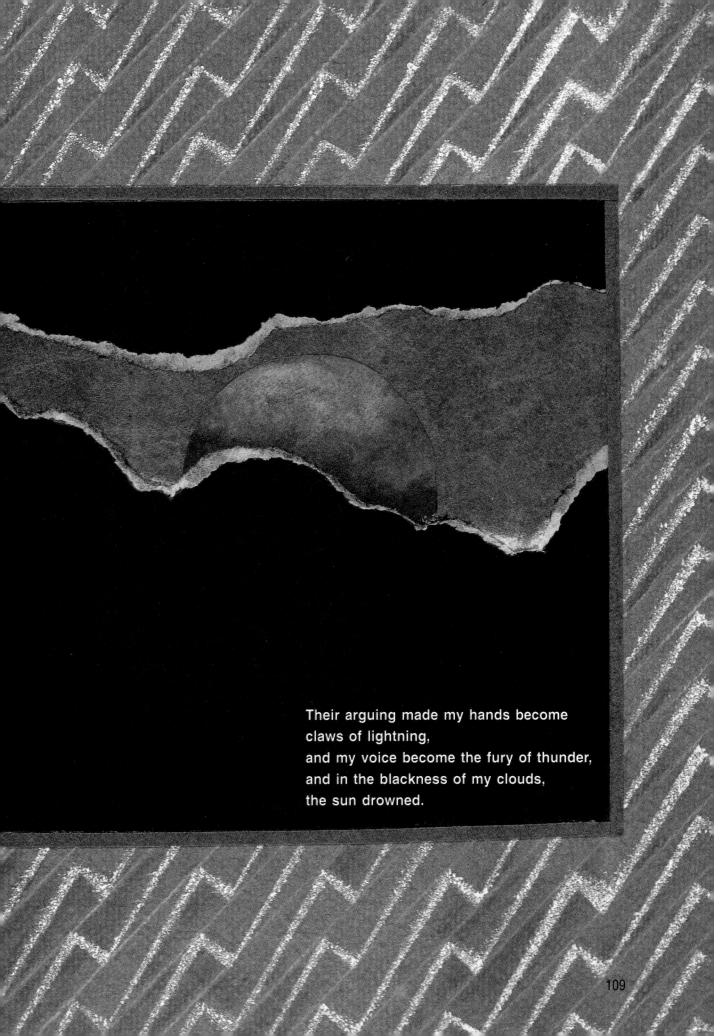

Their arguing made my hands become
claws of lightning,
and my voice become the fury of thunder,
and in the blackness of my clouds,
the sun drowned.

Afraid, the musicians of the sun
ran into the arms of the wind,
which gently carried their melodies
into the arms
of you,
the earth.

Your silence opened.

Your waking dawn sang.

Your dreaming man sang.

Your moving waters and your flying birds sang.

Your waiting mother sang.

All of you was singing.
Music had come to the earth.

# Listening to the nightingale singing

Listening to the nightingale singing
among the flowers
or to the cry of the frog
which dwells in the water,
we recognize the truth
that of all living things
there is not one
which does not utter song.

 KI TSURAYUKI

PLATE: OLD KUTANI WARE
EDO PERIOD, 17th CENTURY
TOKYO NATIONAL MUSEUM

116

# CONTENTS

# DARE
## to
## DREAM
## DREAM

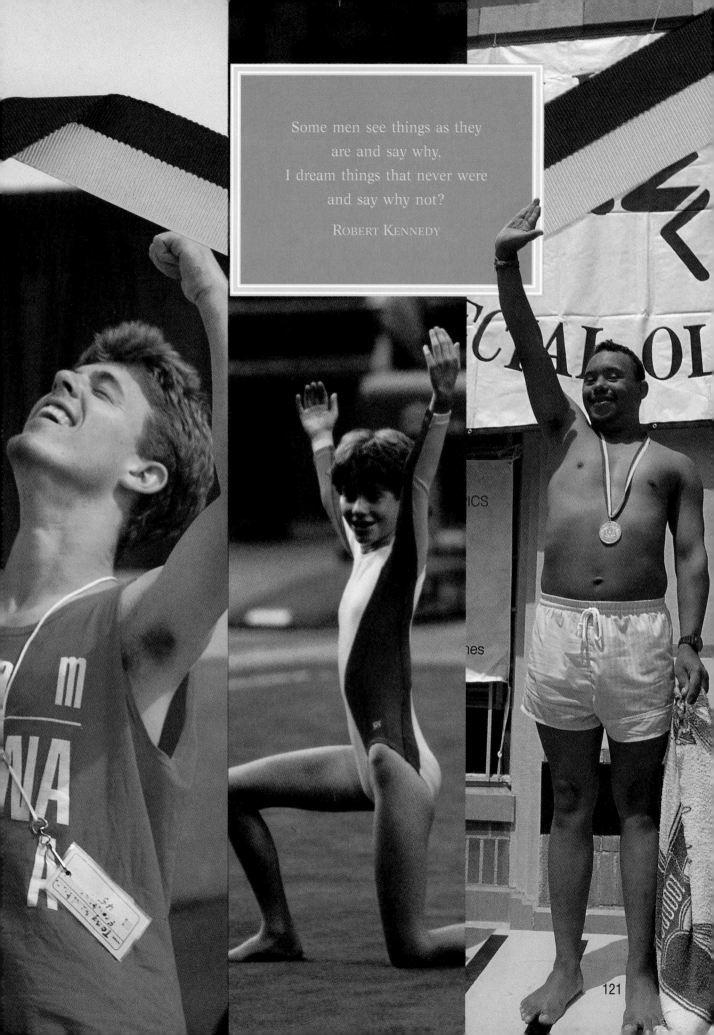

Some men see things as they
are and say why,
I dream things that never were
and say why not?

ROBERT KENNEDY

121

# Meet Ryan White and Ann Marie Cunningham

**M**ost thirteen-year-olds have their entire lives in front of them. Ryan White did not. He knew he had AIDS. But he dared to dream that he would beat it. He fought the disease with the help of doctors and medication. He fought people's fear of the disease with his own courageous words. "The press had started to say that I was dying," he said. "My personal philosophy on that subject was no complaints, baby, no surrender. I wasn't quitting."

**T**here have been outstanding shows on public television—from dance and drama to programs about the Civil War and drug wars. But perhaps none shook the nation more than *I Have AIDS—A Teenager's Story*. Ann Marie Cunningham was the associate producer of this show, which won an award for Children's Television Workshop. The teenager, Ryan White, won Cunningham's admiration.

Cunningham has written speeches, newspaper stories, and magazine articles. She has coauthored books on science and technology. But coauthoring with Ryan White was special. They worked together for a year—the last year of Ryan's life.

# RYAN WHITE:

## MY OWN STORY

### BY RYAN WHITE

### AND ANN MARIE CUNNINGHAM

*Ryan White was born in Kokomo, Indiana, in 1971.*
*Soon after his birth, his doctors discovered that he had severe hemophilia, a hereditary disease in which the blood clots very slowly, so that a small injury can result in excessive bleeding. To help Ryan lead as normal a life as possible, he was given injections of Factor VIII, a blood product that helps blood to clot. Factor VIII is made from donated blood. Unknowingly, Ryan received an injection of Factor VIII that was infected by Human Immunodeficiency Virus, the virus believed to cause AIDS. When he turned thirteen, Ryan began to display symptoms of the disease. A group of parents, believing incorrectly that he would infect others, petitioned the Board of Education to keep Ryan at home. Ryan, however, was determined to attend classes with his friends. After a series of legal battles, the courts agreed that he was entitled to return to school. Angered by this decision, many students and parents made it clear that Ryan was unwelcome both at school and in the town of Kokomo. After several unpleasant incidents, Ryan, his mother, and his sister, Andrea, reluctantly moved to the neighboring town of Cicero.*

Jeanne and Ryan, eighteen months old

Cicero was something different—just a little lake community, maybe 4500 people. More come on vacation in the summer. There's one central street, and not a lot to do except drive around, visit your friends, and hang out at the Dairy Queen. That was fine with me. All I wanted, I thought, was peace and quiet.

As you come into Cicero, you drive past farmers' fields and the town cemetery, and then cross a lake with several docks to get to the main street, which has old-fashioned gas lanterns all along it. Our house was a brand-new Cape Codder, right on the lake. The first time we saw our future home, it was only half-built. Andrea and I could pick which of the three bedrooms we wanted. The ones we ended up

with were joined by a door, but each room had a separate staircase. So we could walk back and forth and visit each other easily, but feel like we had our own apartments. There was a deck that looked out over the boats on the lake, and from the kitchen window you could see birds and chipmunks and squirrels in the woods out back. When we moved to Cicero in May, I finally had all the shelf space I needed for Herbie's cage and my G.I. Joe figures and my comics—just as I was beginning to get hooked on other things. Like skateboarding.

> "I discovered Maui Surf and Sport, a skateboard shop that carried surfer T-shirts."

I had another year to go before I could get a learner's permit, so skateboarding was the next best thing to driving. Whenever Mom and I drove into Indianapolis to see Dr. Kleiman—just about once a week right then—we passed through Castleton, a part of the city where all the malls are. It's the best place around to see movies and shop. One day in Castleton I discovered Maui Surf and Sport, a skateboard shop that carried surfer T-shirts and shorts—the kind I liked from California that you couldn't find anywhere else around us. John Riser, the owner, was a young, athletic guy who let me grill

him about the best wheels and boards. Since I was just starting to skate, he gave me some videotapes to inspire me.

Ryan is pulled along by his dog Wally outside his new home in Cicero (top). Ryan with his brand-new Mustang, a present from Michael Jackson (right).

I bought plenty of clothes. When I finally got to California, I wanted to look like I belonged. I also picked up a board, several pairs of Oakleys—mirrored sunglasses in wild colors like orange—and copies of the skateboarding magazines John carried. I read every page of *Skateboarding, Poweredge,* and my favorite, *Thrasher,* which is the best for skateboarders. At least I could study tricks, even if a wall ride was way beyond me. I began to think all I wanted in life was to work for John when I turned sixteen, so I could learn how to be in business for myself. A long time ago in Kokomo I'd started a little company called Odd Jobs, Inc. I was president, and a girl who lived down the street was vice-president. We mowed lawns and cleaned out garages. Now I wanted to see how to really work on my own—and skate around in the mall parking lot during my lunch hour.

> "Some letters I got made the hair on the back of my neck stand up on end."

I didn't ride a skateboard much at first. Not because Dr. Kleiman wasn't happy about a hemophiliac doing that. Not because my best move wasn't a curb grind or an ollie. The fact is, I was having a bad summer. My lungs put me back in the hospital for a short while, though I turned out not to have pneumonia. That was a big relief. Mom knew the drill by now: She brought me my Alyssa Milano poster for my room, and my own surf shirts and shorts so I wouldn't have to wear hospital gowns. She sent me a card that said, "Ryan, get well so the mail will slow down."

Moving hadn't cut back my cards and letters. Some reached me even though they were addressed just "To the Boy With AIDS, Indiana."

But it's creepy to be famous because you're sick. Now and again my mail reminded me about that. Some letters I got made the hair on the back of my neck stand up on end. Like the lists of strange questions I'd get from a man in Oregon. Mostly he wanted to know, "When will my friend Ryan write to me?" Never, buddy! Then there was the man who had seen my picture in *People* and had decided he was my father. This man even hitchhiked to Cicero and called us. He said he was on his way over to live with me and look after me. We let the police station handle that one. I didn't want to mess with it!

Besides, all the fame in the world wasn't making me well. I seemed to be tired all the time, even if I slept twenty hours a day. I'm not exaggerating. Laura would come down from intensive care and leave me notes like, "I stopped by twice and you were asleep both times. Don't you ever do anything else?"

I certainly was cold—constantly. If I was outside, I buttoned my jacket up to my chin no matter how warm it was. Once I got home, I always wore jeans and sweaters and furry Big Foot slippers with claws. If I was sitting still, I wrapped myself up in a blanket as well and got Wally and Gizzy to nap on my feet. A friend of Mom's bought me a portable hand-heater that I carried around with me. Now and then I had to turn Mom's electric stove all the way up and hold my blue fingers over the hot coil to warm them. Sometimes I burnt them first, and collected a scar or two.

We went to Daytona with my grandparents at spring break, but I had to take my heater along. We stayed in a condo with a balcony looking out over the beach. The weather wasn't great, so Andrea and I spent hours on the balcony feeding the sea gulls. Someone had written "INDIANA" in huge letters along the sand, like they knew we were coming. Actually, they were celebrating because I.U. had won the National Collegiate Basketball Championship again.

When I breathed, I rattled. Sometimes I ran out of breath completely. In the middle of a conversation, I'd have to stop talking, rest my head on my hands, and take some short pants. My voice sounded thin and squeaky, like I had permanent bronchitis. My nose ran, and my chest felt tight. My hearing had gotten peculiar. Sometimes it was so sensitive that when Mom cooked bacon, the hissing sound hurt my ears. Other times, I could barely hear what someone was saying to me.

Ryan White with Wally, 1989

I hardly ever went out. Now and again we had to go see Dr. Kleiman, or I went along on Mom's errands, or we'd go for Mexican food in Noblesville, the next town. Sometimes people stared, but only because they recognized us—not because they didn't want us around. At least we were just another family here. But I couldn't be far from a bathroom because I was throwing up a lot, or I might need to warm my hands under the hot-air dryer.

Even though I was having trouble keeping food down, you could still tell I was a teenager—I always wanted to eat. Whenever we ordered dinner, I'd ask for nachos to start, and then French fries, steak, and cheesecake. After a few bites, though, I was usually too worn out to finish. Long before dessert, I'd start bugging Mom and Andrea to take me home again. Once we got there, the first thing

I'd do was turn off the air conditioning. They probably weren't pleased—Indiana summers can be up in the nineties and sticky—but they never complained. My whole family was very worried about me, except for Andrea, who always told everyone, "Nothing is ever going to happen to Ryan. He'll pull through." The press had started to say that I was dying.

My personal philosophy on that subject was no complaints, baby, no surrender. I wasn't quitting. I could get better, so I would. I liked the Cicero cemetery fine. It looked green and peaceful. But I wasn't about to be carried out there yet.

I watched TV 'til I thought I was going to disappear inside the set. Nothing had changed—the Cubs were underdogs again. Every week I saw some outfielder trying to dig a ball out of the ivy on the wall of Wrigley Field. You'd have thought the Cubs would be world champs now that they had a player named Ryne—Sandberg that is, the star second baseman. I was glad I was called "Ry-man" instead of "Ryno," the fans' name for Sandberg. I decided I liked Vanna White on *Wheel of Fortune,* though not as much as Alyssa Milano.

When *Playboy* published some photographs of Vanna, I kept after Mom to buy the issue for me. Mom said she was embarrassed, but one day she came home with the magazine inside a grocery bag. "From now on, you're not getting *everything* you want," she scolded me.

Ryan and Greg Louganis with Greg's gold medals from the 1987 Pan-American games

I tried to keep my mind on stuff I wanted, good stuff. In spite of all the grief we got in Kokomo, we'd been able to see and do a lot. Like the times Greg Louganis, the diving champion who won four gold medals at the Olympics, had visited with us in Indianapolis. He turned out to be not all that tall, but *there* was someone with muscles! Dr. Kleiman wouldn't give me steroids, but maybe there was another way I could look more like Greg. The first time he called us up, we were still living in Kokomo. He'd heard about us on CNN, and he was coming to Indianapolis for the U.S. Diving Championships. Lots of famous athletes show up sooner or later in Indianapolis because of all the great sports facilities that have been built there for events.

Greg invited all three of us to come watch him compete a couple of times. The first time, he gave me the medal he won, the 38th National Title Medal. While he was talking to some reporters, he let me climb up to the ten-meter platform. The platform was tiny, and it was a *long* way down to that pool. I held on tight to the railing the whole time.

Once both my feet were flat on the ground again, I told Greg, "Man, you gotta be nuts to *dive* off that thing!"

Greg laughed. I guess he's heard that from lots of people besides me. He told me he knew how it felt to have other kids in school give you a hard time. All the way through school, he had a lot of trouble doing his work. His classmates called him "stupid" and most of his teachers decided he was retarded. He didn't find out what was really wrong until he was eighteen. It turned out that he has dyslexia, which means you see letters in the wrong order when you read. It must be really tough to have everyone tell you you're stupid, know you're really not, but not be able to get them to believe you.

> "Greg was really excited when he found out that my sister was a champion too."

Later on, Greg invited the three of us plus my grandparents to come see him again at a theater in Indianapolis. He was making his debut as a professional dancer. I liked that—he was already a big deal diver, but he wanted to plunge into something new. Greg was really excited when he found out that my sister was a champion too. Andrea had been invited to roller skate in the opening ceremonies for the 1987 Pan-American Games which were going to be held in Indianapolis. It was a giant step forward for her—and for roller skating. Greg was competing in the Games, and gave Andrea some exercises and tips so she wouldn't get leg cramps. And he gave me one of the two gold medals he won at the Pan-American Games. He said, "I'd give you both, but I'm afraid my mother will kill me. She'll want one of them."

Next time we were in L.A., Greg said we could come visit him

Ryan in his room decorated with his *Max Headroom* poster, 1988

(Counterclockwise, starting from the top): Ryan and Lukas Haas sitting on their director's chairs during filming of *The Ryan White Story,* 1988; Ryan and his prom date Dee Laux, spring 1989; the family relaxes at home with cat Chi Chi and dog Wally, 1986

at his house in Malibu. He thought I would love his new pool and his view of the Pacific surf. I couldn't wait to try surfing. I remembered the party Elton had thrown for me at Disneyland the fall before. Ever since then I'd wanted to go back to California really, really badly. When I had finally gotten out of the hospital, Elton had flown all three of us out to L.A. I couldn't believe we were actually there until we walked out of the airport. There in front of us was a row of palm trees. And I was finally warm enough!

Before we had left Indiana, Mom reminded me that when I was first trying to go back to school, we'd heard that Rock Hudson had AIDS. "Everyone is running scared now," Mom said. "So please don't do anything like sharing sodas or lollipops—that might upset people."

But we didn't have to worry. Elton passed cans of Coke back and forth with me, and hugged and kissed and joked around with all of us. Elton's always like that, the whole time you're with him.

From L.A., Elton flew us in his private jet to two of his concerts, one in Oakland and one in San Diego. Andrea and I got special sweatshirts and scarves and sunglasses to wear at the concerts. Elton even gave me the beanie he wore on stage.

When we got back to L.A., Elton had arranged a tour of Universal Studios and a party at Disneyland for us. To get us there,

Andrea and Ryan backstage at an Elton John concert in San Francisco, November 1986

he had two limos, and a bus for his band and their families. Elton rode in one limo, which had a sunroof, and we followed in the other. Every now and again, Elton's limo would pull over and he'd stand up and wave at us and anyone else around! It was pretty funny.

At Universal, we got to see Marty McFly's high school and the soda shop from *Back to the Future!* I was still pretty weak from being in the hospital for so long, but there was no way I wanted to miss a minute of this. So at Disneyland, Elton got me a wheelchair and pushed me around himself.

Elton didn't forget about us afterward. When Andrea's birthday rolled around in October, he sent her red roses. He called us now and again from wherever he was touring, to see how we were getting along. We got handwritten letters from him, postmarked all over the world.

I looked over our Disneyland photos, of Elton and me in wild sunglasses. At least I wasn't quite as skinny now as I had been last fall. I could use a few extra pounds though. Maybe I could talk Mom into taking up Mexican cooking.

> "I was pleased, but I've never liked starting a new school."

Something else I thought about was where I'd go from here. After all, the fighting was over, and we'd won. I *was* back in school, though I wasn't sure what my new one, Hamilton Heights, was going to be like—assuming I could keep awake long enough to go. Mom and I had gone to see Mr. Cook and Mr. Dillon, the principal and the assistant principal, about my registering. It turned out that they were expecting us. One parent who was a real estate agent had

Elton John and Ryan at Disneyland, 1987

already called to tell them that we had bought a house in the school district. Hamilton Heights was happy to have me, Mr. Cook said, if I was really serious about school.

I said what I always said. "I like school. I want to be with other kids."

Mr. Cook smiled. "Let's go register," he said, and he led us to the cafeteria to line up at the registration tables with everybody else.

I was pleased, but I've never liked starting a new school. Especially not this time—I had no idea what to expect. I'd managed to open a few doors for myself, but that could mean that I'd find more of them slammed shut in my face than ever. For starters, I wasn't sure I'd feel well enough to start school at all. If I did, things were going to be a little awkward because I was going to be a freshman when I should be a sophomore. And there was something else I wasn't sure of: I'd meet plenty of kids who had only seen me on television. They didn't know the first thing about the real me, and they might not bother to find out.

Ryan answers questions at Boys Town, 1988.

Around this time a reporter asked me, "Who's your best friend?"

I had to tell the truth. "I don't have one," I replied.

Now that we were in Cicero, I wanted more than a quiet life. I wanted friends my age. We'd left everyone we knew behind in Kokomo. In one way, that was good. I really wanted to put the past behind me so I wouldn't be bitter. But now there was no one except my relatives who would know what I meant when I said, "Remember back *before* I was in the news so much?"

> "Dr. Woodrow Myers, the state health commissioner, invited Mom and me to speak at a state conference on AIDS."

Maybe everyone I met at Hamilton Heights would think, He's friends with Elton John—he

doesn't need us. That was one thing I'd noticed: Fame can isolate you just as much as AIDS. Or maybe kids would try to get close to me only because I was famous, not because they liked me.

Well, I wasn't going to find out by sitting home in front of the TV. I had to move ahead, or else things would start gaining on me. I had to believe that I had a purpose. I must be good for something. The winter before, when I was still feeling pretty well, Dr. Woodrow Myers, the state health commissioner, invited Mom and me to speak at a state conference on AIDS. Dr. Myers asked me to give the crowd some advice.

"Whatever you do, please don't isolate us," I said.

Guess I had to take my own advice right now. I certainly knew I had to keep on getting myself out of the house, just to educate people. They kept imagining that AIDS was a dirty word, a slimy disease. If they saw me walking around, shopping, looking normal, I figured they might have more compassion for people like me.

In Kokomo, fear had gotten the better of everybody. I understood that. No one was really

against me; they were against my disease. Parents were worried about their own kids. When I first heard I had AIDS, I was just like everybody else in Kokomo: I was scared, and so was my family.

But the more I thought about what had happened, the more it seemed to me that fear had taken control of adults in Kokomo. Once that happened, they believed whatever they wanted to believe about me and AIDS. Many kids who called me names were only repeating what they'd heard grown-ups say. Kids in Kokomo were doing just what kids do—listening to their parents.

So when I thought about what I'd do next, I decided that if adults ignored the medical facts, I ought to concentrate on talking to kids. Most adults are pretty set in their ways, but kids are still learning. If I hung out with kids, talked to them, maybe they'd go home and change their parents' minds.

I wasn't the only one who had this idea. I mentioned that we were able to move because we got some money from a movie company, plus Elton lent us enough extra to make a down payment on our house in Cicero. Actually, we had had several movie offers, but we picked the Landsburg Company. I had seen a couple of TV movies they'd already made about real people, and I really liked them. One called *Adam* was about a kid, younger than I

was, who was kidnapped from a parking lot. Another movie, named *Bill,* was about a retarded man, and a filmmaker who starts to make a documentary about him. The filmmaker winds up making friends with Bill, helping him find a job and learn to look after himself. The real Bill even ended up visiting the White House (the *real* White House). These movies were grim in places, but they kind of gave you hope at the same time. I liked that.

Andrea, Ryan, Judith Light, and Heather meet at Linda Otto's house in Malibu, 1988.

Something else I liked was that Linda Otto, the producer from Landsburg, came out to Indiana from Los Angeles to meet us. No one else did. We sat with Linda around our kitchen table, talking about what our movie might be like. I liked knowing that Mom and Andrea would get some money because of me—I'm a practical person. But I was fairly amazed

Ryan and Jill Stewart sightsee at the Capitol in Washington, D.C., March 1988. (Right) Ryan plays pool at a neighbor's in Cicero with, from left to right, Andrea, Wendy Baker, and Jill Stewart.

that a movie producer was sitting right there in front of me, much less interested in me.

"We want to show what you *really* went through in Kokomo, not just the court hearings," Linda explained. "We'll tell the story from your point of view."

That sounded like a neat idea, but I had to ask, "Why would anyone want to make a movie about *me,* anyway? You really think people will watch it?"

Linda told me she thought it was very important to stand up for children's rights. She said she'd picked filmmaking as the way to do it, because you could reach so many people. She tried to make movies that would help kids. When

*Adam* was shown on TV, there was a roll call of missing kids at the end, and an 800 number you could call if you had seen any of them. Linda said that over a hundred missing children were found after that—even though poor Adam had ended up dead.

Lots of times, though, producers in Hollywood want to make a certain movie, but it never works out. They just can't find a script that's good enough, or hire the actors they want. Or they do make the film, but they can't make a deal with a network to show it on television. Linda said to me, "I promise you, Ryan. I'll get this movie done."

I hoped it would happen, but I tried not to get too excited. Meanwhile, I had another visitor—totally unexpected this time. One afternoon Mom called down to me. I was in our basement family room, watching

TV, as usual. I saw *Who's the Boss?* as often as it was on. It was a chance to catch Alyssa Milano, and besides, Linda Otto was hoping that Judith Light would play Mom in our movie. "Ryan," she said, "there's a girl here to see you."

A girl? I thought Mom must mean a reporter. I climbed the stairs halfheartedly. I wasn't thrilled about talking to some other magazine or newspaper who'd probably end up claiming I was dying. Whoever they were, I planned on giving them five minutes—no more. Instead, there was a girl with long blonde hair standing in our living room with Mom, smiling at me. She was about my height and my age—too young to be a reporter.

"Hi, Ryan," she said. She had a nice smile and a small, sweet voice. "I'm Jill Stewart. I live two doors down from you."

Ryan and Jill Stewart during a hearing at the President's Commission on AIDS, March 1988

> "I had another visitor—totally unexpected this time."

A new neighbor dropping in! It seemed like years and years since *that* had happened. I'd spent so much time by myself, watching other people talk on TV, I was rusty when it came to conversations with anyone who wasn't family. My mouth almost creaked when I spoke, and I squeaked, as usual.

"Hi," I managed to say.

"I'm president of the student body at Hamilton Heights High," Jill added. That meant she must be one of the most popular kids there. Jill was a senior, but she was only a year older than I was. She explained, "I wanted to invite you to our school. Now you'll know someone when you come your first day."

Jill said that Hamilton Heights had already stepped up their AIDS education program in case I enrolled. "No one is planning on treating you badly," she told me. "We just want to be normal."

"I'll second that," I said.

Jill came back again with her father and mother, a nurse. A few days later, Wendy Baker, a friend of Jill's from Hamilton Heights, knocked on our door too. They made a good pair—Jill had fair hair and Wendy's was dark. Wendy was a junior and my age. She lived over on the other side of the lake. Later, after we got to be close friends and visited each other a lot, Wendy told me that she had been really nervous when we first met.

"Why?" I asked her.

> "Mr. Cook and Mr. Dillon asked me to come two weeks late. 'We want to make sure everyone at school is educated and prepared.'"

Sometimes I make people nervous because I look so young. I stopped growing when I was twelve, thanks to AIDS. Luckily the hoarse rasp in my voice makes me *sound* my age, at least. When I see that someone who's just been introduced is jumpy around me, I stay calm and wait for them to settle down too.

"Well," Wendy said, "I thought you might want to be left alone. And besides," she added, "you were better looking than on TV."

I laughed. That second part was certainly good to hear.

"The last thing I need is people running away from me," I said. "I was really glad you stopped by."

Wendy and Jill brought me photos of all the teachers at Hamilton Heights, so I'd recognize them when I got to classes. The girls called me every week just to

Ryan White and Anthony Cook, principal of Hamilton Heights High School, August 1987

say hi, and brought some of their other friends over to meet me and tell me about what would go on at school. By the time school started, I would know about fifteen of the six hundred and fifty kids there.

"What those girls have done!" Mom exclaimed. She was getting to be very good friends with the Stewarts and the Bakers. "These kids are *glad* they'll be going to school with you. They think you're a hero!"

With all this encouragement, I wasn't surprised that I did begin to get better, just as I thought I would, plus I finally started on AZT. I was definitely looking forward to school. Mr. Cook and Mr. Dillon asked me to come two weeks late. "We want to make sure everyone at school is educated and prepared," Jill explained to me. "So we're dropping everything for a crash course on AIDS."

**R**yan continued to speak out on behalf of people with AIDS. He died at age 18 at James Whitcomb Riley Hospital in Indianapolis on April 8, 1990.

Ryan and Jeanne at home, 1990

# The Quilt of Remembrance

The placards taped to San Francisco's Old Federal Building, hand-lettered with the names of people who had died of AIDS, were tattered and windblown. Nonetheless, thousands walked by on November 27, 1985, deeply affected by the tributes to hundreds of those who had died of this terrible disease.

Cleve Jones was one of those who passed by, and the images of those names haunted him. "I knew then that we needed a monument, a memorial," he said. In October 1987, Jones's dream was displayed in Washington, D.C.— nearly 200 three-by-six-foot panels commemorating mothers and fathers, sons and daughters, and loved ones and strangers who died of AIDS.

The NAMES Project, as it is called, has had a profound effect both on those who have viewed the huge quilt and on those who have labored over it. And as the panels continue to arrive, the quilt grows even more massive.

The NAMES Project has been showing the quilt since 1987 to raise money for services to people with AIDS, although the quilt is now so large that each region of the country tours its own quilt. Flashy and forthright, sad and joyous, the panels of the quilt represent not only the suffering of thousands but also the belief that love can triumph.

The Quilt, displayed on the Great Mall Lawn in front of the United States Capitol.

140

**DAVID R. THOMPSON**
1949-1986
COLUMBIA · STANFORD

A week after the death of a Stanford librarian, David Thompson, about three hundred of his coworkers at the library received a single yellow rose from him, along with a note. David's coworkers later quilted their panel for him in a noontime sewing circle, making sure to include a yellow rose.

Each letter in Tom Biscotto's panel was designed and put together by a different group of Tom's friends. The *S* represents his lifelong involvement with the theater and his affection for his pet boa constrictors.

Baby Jessica

After reading *Newsweek*'s story about two-year-old Jessica Hazard, who died of AIDS, Kim Kubik and his girlfriend made this panel to remember a child they hadn't known.

QUEEN CHRISTINE

Craig Pierce, a hospice nurse in San Francisco, made this panel for his patient Christine Williams. "To be able to express my feelings in memory of a beautiful black woman who touched my heart with laughter is very special," he wrote.

141

# "HOPE"
## *is the thing with feathers*

BY EMILY DICKINSON

"Hope" is the thing with feathers—

That perches in the soul—

And sings the tune without the words—

And never stops—at all—


And sweetest—in the Gale—is heard—

And sore must be the storm—

That could abash the little Bird

That kept so many warm—


I've heard it in the chillest land—

And on the strangest Sea—

Yet, never, in Extremity,

It asked a crumb—of Me.

*The Large Family* by René Magritte

# Always to Remember

## THE VISION OF MAYA YING LIN

*In the 1960s and 1970s, the United States was involved in a war in Vietnam. Because many people opposed the war, Vietnam veterans were not honored as veterans of other wars had been. Jan Scruggs, a Vietnam veteran, thought that the 58,000 U.S. servicemen and women killed or reported missing in Vietnam should be honored with a memorial. With the help of lawyers Robert Doubek and John Wheeler, Scruggs worked to gain support for his idea. In 1980, Congress authorized the building of the Vietnam Veterans Memorial in Washington, D.C., between the Washington Monument and the Lincoln Memorial.*

## by Brent Ashabranner
### photographs by Jennifer Ashabranner

The memorial had been authorized by Congress "in honor and recognition of the men and women of the Armed Forces of the United States who served in the Vietnam War." The law, however, said not a word about what the memorial should be or what it should look like. That was left up to the Vietnam Veterans Memorial Fund, but the law did state that the memorial design and plans would have to be approved by the Secretary of the Interior, the Commission of Fine Arts, and the National Capital Planning Commission.

What would the memorial be? What should it look like? Who would design it? Scruggs, Doubek, and

The western side of the wall as it aligns with the Lincoln Memorial, seen in the background.

Wheeler didn't know, but they were determined that the memorial should help bring closer together a nation still bitterly divided by the Vietnam War. It couldn't be something like the Marine Corps Memorial showing American troops planting a flag on enemy soil at Iwo Jima. It couldn't be a giant dove with an olive branch of peace in its beak. It had to soothe passions, not stir them up. But there was one thing Jan Scruggs insisted on: the memorial, whatever it turned out to be, would have to show the name of every man and woman killed or missing in the war.

The answer, they decided, was to hold a national design competition open to all Americans. The winning design would receive a prize of $20,000, but the real prize would be the winner's knowledge that the memorial would become a part of American history on the Mall in Washington, D.C. Although fund raising was only well started at this point, the choosing of a memorial design could not be delayed if the memorial was to be built by Veterans Day, 1982. H. Ross Perot contributed the $160,000 necessary to hold the competition, and a panel of distinguished architects, landscape architects, sculptors, and design specialists was chosen to decide the winner.

Announcement of the competition in October, 1980, brought an astonishing response. The Vietnam Veterans Memorial Fund received over five thousand inquiries. They came from every state in the nation and from every field of design; as expected, architects and sculptors were particularly interested. Everyone who inquired received a booklet explaining the criteria. Among the most important: the memorial could not make a political statement about the war; it must contain the names of all persons killed or missing in action in the war; it must be in harmony with its location on the Mall.

A total of 2,573 individuals and teams registered for the competition. They were sent photographs of the memorial site, maps of the area around the site and of the entire Mall, and other technical design information. The competitors had three months to prepare their designs, which had to be received by March 31, 1981.

Of the 2,573 registrants, 1,421 submitted designs, a record number for such a design competition. When the designs were spread out for jury selection, they filled a large airplane hangar. The jury's task was to select the design which, in their judgment, was the best in meeting these criteria:

★ a design that honored the memory of those Americans who served and died in the Vietnam War.

★ a design of high artistic merit.

★ a design which would be harmonious with its site, including visual harmony with the Lincoln Memorial and the Washington Monument.

★ a design that could take its place in the "historic continuity" of America's national art.

★ a design that would be buildable, durable, and not too hard to maintain.

The designs were displayed without any indication of the designer's name so that they could be judged anonymously, on their design merits alone. The jury spent one week reviewing all the designs in the airplane

**The eastern side of the memorial points to the Washington Monument, which it resembles in the clarity and abstract simplicity of its design.**

ONLY
ONE
SON

hangar. On May 1 it made its report to the Vietnam Veterans Memorial Fund; the experts declared Entry Number 1,026 the winner. The report called it "the finest and most appropriate" of all submitted and said it was "superbly harmonious" with the site on the Mall. Remarking upon the "simple and forthright" materials needed to build the winning entry, the report concludes:

This memorial with its wall of names, becomes a place of quiet reflection, and a tribute to those who served their nation in difficult times. All who come here can find it a place of healing. This will be a quiet memorial, one that achieves an excellent relationship with both the Lincoln Memorial or Washington Monument, and relates the visitor to them. It is uniquely horizontal, entering the earth rather than piercing the sky.

This is very much a memorial of our own times, one that could not have been achieved in another time and place. The designer has created an eloquent place where the simple meeting of earth, sky and remembered names contain messages for all who will know this place.

The eight jurors signed their names to the report, a unanimous decision.

When the name of the winner was revealed, the art and architecture worlds were stunned. It was not the name of a nationally famous architect or sculptor, as most people had been sure it would be. The creator of Entry Number 1,026 was a twenty-one-year-old student at Yale University. Her name—unknown as yet in any field of art or architecture—was Maya Ying Lin.

How could this be? How could an undergraduate student win one of the most important design competitions ever held? How could she beat out some of the top names in American art and architecture? Who was Maya Ying Lin?

The answer to that question provided some of the other answers, at least in part. Maya Lin, reporters soon discovered, was a Chinese-American girl who had been born and raised in the small midwestern city of Athens, Ohio. Her father, Henry Huan Lin, was a ceramicist of considerable reputation and dean of fine arts at Ohio University in Athens. Her mother, Julia C. Lin, was a poet and professor of Oriental and English literature. Maya Lin's parents were born to culturally prominent families in China. When the Communists came to power in China in the 1940s, Henry and Julia Lin left the country and in time made their way to the United States.

Maya Lin grew up in an environment of art and literature. She was interested in sculpture and made both small and large sculptural figures, one cast in bronze. She learned silversmithing and made jewelry. She was surrounded by books and read a great deal, especially fantasies such as *The Hobbit* and *Lord of the Rings*.

But she also found time to work at McDonald's. "It was about the only way to make money in the summer," she said.

A covaledictorian at high school

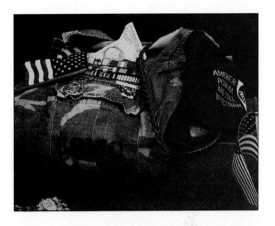

An elaborate remembrance to a son (facing page), a Marine Corps uniform, and combat boots (above), are some of the tokens left by visitors.

**Maya Ying Lin at work.**

graduation, Maya Lin went to Yale without a clear notion of what she wanted to study and eventually decided to major in Yale's undergraduate program in architecture. During her junior year she studied in Europe and found herself increasingly interested in cemetery architecture. "In Europe there's very little space, so graveyards are used as parks," she said. "Cemeteries are cities of the dead in European countries, but they are also living gardens."

In France, Maya Lin was deeply moved by the war memorial to those who died in the Somme offensive in 1916 during World War I. The great arch by architect Sir Edwin Lutyens is considered one of the world's most outstanding war memorials.

Back at Yale for her senior year, Maya Lin enrolled in Professor Andrus Burr's course in funerary (burial) architecture. The Vietnam Veterans Memorial competition had

recently been announced, and although the memorial would be a cenotaph—a monument in honor of persons buried someplace else—Professor Burr thought that having his students prepare a design of the memorial would be a worthwhile course assignment.

Surely, no classroom exercise ever had such spectacular results.

After receiving the assignment, Maya Lin and two of her classmates decided to make the day's journey from New Haven, Connecticut, to Washington to look at the site where the memorial would be built. On the day of their visit, Maya Lin remembers, Constitution

Gardens was awash with a late November sun; the park was full of light, alive with joggers and people walking beside the lake.

"It was while I was at the site that I designed it," Maya Lin said later in an interview about the memorial with *Washington Post* writer Phil McCombs. "I just sort of visualized it. It just popped into my head. Some people were playing Frisbee. It was a beautiful park. I didn't want to destroy a living park. You use the landscape. You don't fight with it. You absorb the landscape . . . When I looked at the site I just knew I wanted something horizontal that took you in, that made you feel safe within the park, yet at the same time reminding you of the dead. So I just imagined opening up the earth. . . . "

The statue of the three servicemen, near the western side of the wall, is remarkable for its realistic detail.

When Maya Lin returned to Yale, she made a clay model of the vision that had come to her in Constitution Gardens. She showed it to Professor Burr; he liked her conception and encouraged her to enter the memorial competition. She put her design on paper, a task that took six weeks, and mailed it to Washington barely in time to meet the March 31 deadline.

A month and a day later, Maya Lin was attending class. Her roommate slipped into the classroom and handed her a note. Washington was calling and would call back in fifteen minutes. Maya Lin hurried to her room. The call came. She had won the memorial competition.

# Meet Brent Ashabranner

"My books frequently examine complex social issues," Brent Ashabranner comments, "but I think these issues can be made of interest to readers of all ages." Ashabranner creates interest by focusing on the people connected with an issue. In his award-winning book *Morning Star, Black Sun: The Northern Cheyenne Indians and America's Energy Crisis,* for example, readers view the problems of Native Americans through the eyes of a Cheyenne Indian. In recounting the story of the controversial Vietnam Veterans Memorial, Ashabranner personalizes the struggle by including a warm biographical sketch of its young designer. "Recognizing good story material, giving it shape and life, is a creative act that constantly renews the writer," he says.

Brent Ashabranner's award-winning books include *To Live in Two Worlds, The New Americans,* and *Into a Strange Land.* All three books were named American Library Association Best Books for Young Adults.

HITCH YOUR WAGON

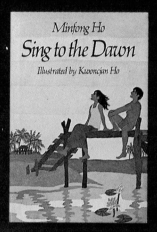

**Sing to the Dawn**
by Minfong Ho
Lothrop, 1975

**Corazon Aquino**
by Howard Chua-Eoan
Chelsea House, 1988

155

# ≈ M · E · E · T ≈
# FRANCISCO JIMÉNEZ

Sometimes Francisco Jiménez writes in English, and sometimes he writes in Spanish. "The language I use is determined by what period in my life I write about. Since Spanish was the dominant language during my childhood, I generally write about those experiences in Spanish."

Thus, Jiménez first wrote "The Circuit" in Spanish and then translated his work into English. But there was a problem—he could not always find an appropriate translation. Jiménez explains, "Language, especially the spoken word, carries with it an emotion or a feeling." The story's original title was "Cajas de Cartón," or "Cardboard Boxes." Jiménez recalls, "I didn't want to use the same title because 'Cardboard Boxes' didn't sound right to me. 'The Circuit' seemed to be a more appropriate English title."

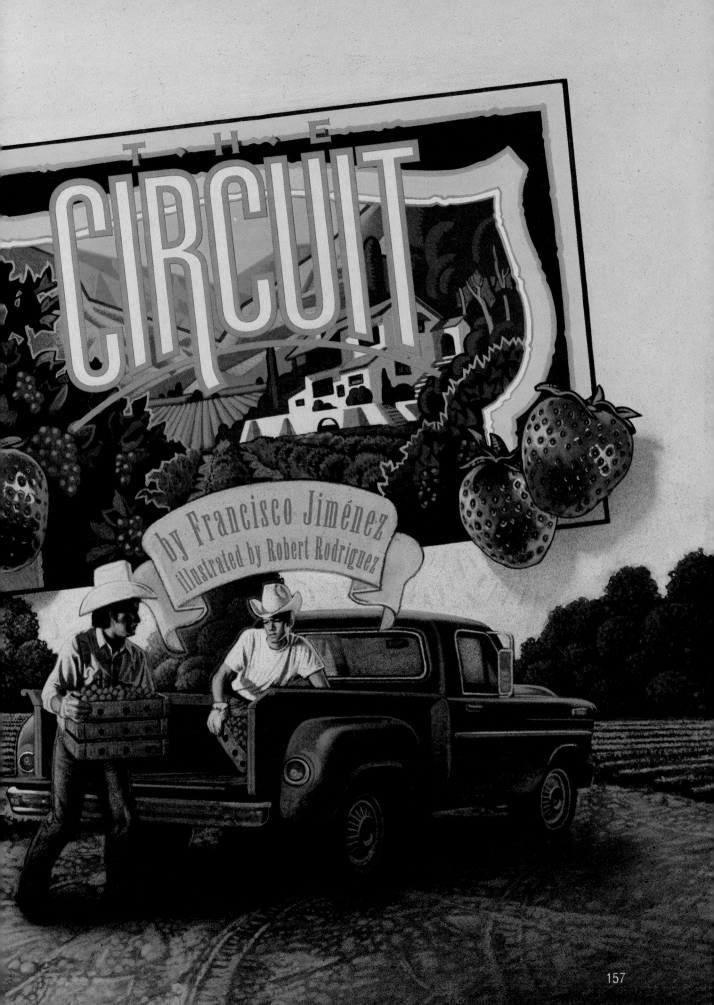

THE CIRCUIT

by Francisco Jiménez

illustrated by Robert Rodriguez

It was that time of year again. Ito, the strawberry share-cropper, did not smile. It was natural. The peak of the strawberry season was over and the last few days the workers, most of them braceros, were not picking as many boxes as they had during the months of June and July.

As the last days of August disappeared, so did the number of braceros. Sunday, only one—the best picker—came to work. I liked him. Sometimes we talked during our half-hour lunch break. That is how I found out he was from Jalisco, the same state in Mexico my family was from. That Sunday was the last time I saw him.

When the sun had tired and sunk behind the mountains, Ito signaled us that it was time to go home. "Ya esora," he yelled in his broken Spanish. Those were the words I waited for twelve hours a day, every day, seven days a week, week after week. And the thought of not hearing them again saddened me.

As we drove home Papá did not say a word. With both hands on the wheel, he stared at the dirt road. My older brother, Roberto, was also silent. He leaned his head back and closed his eyes. Once in a while he cleared from his throat the dust that blew in from outside.

Yes, it was that time of year. When I opened the front door to the shack, I stopped. Everything we owned was neatly packed in cardboard boxes. Suddenly I felt even more the weight of hours, days, weeks, and months of work. I sat down on a box. The thought of having to move to Fresno and know-ing what was in store for me there brought tears to my eyes.

That night I could not sleep. I lay in bed thinking about how much I hated this move.

A little before five o'clock in the morning, Papá woke everyone up. A few minutes later, the yelling and screaming of my little brothers and sisters, for whom the move was a great adventure, broke the silence of dawn. Shortly, the barking of the dogs accompanied them.

While we packed the breakfast dishes, Papá went outside to start the "Carcanchita." That was the name Papá gave his old '38 black Plymouth. He bought it in a used-car lot in Santa Rosa in the winter of 1949. Papá was very proud of his little jalopy. He had a right to be proud of it. He spent a lot of time looking at other cars before buying this one. When he finally chose the "Carcanchita," he checked it thoroughly before driving it out of the car lot. He examined every inch of the car. He listened to the motor, tilting his head from side to side like a parrot, trying to detect any noises that spelled car trouble. After being satisfied with the looks and sounds of the car, Papá then insisted on knowing who the original owner was. He never did find out from the car salesman, but he bought the car anyway. Papá figured the original owner must have been an important man because behind the rear seat of the car he found a blue necktie.

Papá parked the car out in front and left the motor running. "Listo," he yelled. Without saying a word, Roberto and I began to carry the boxes out to the car. Roberto carried the two big boxes and I carried the two smaller ones. Papá then threw the mattress on top of the car roof and tied it with ropes to the front and rear bumpers.

Everything was packed except Mamá's pot. It was an old large galvanized pot she had picked up at an army surplus store in Santa María the year I was born. The pot had many dents and nicks, and the more dents and nicks it acquired the more Mamá liked it. "Mi olla," she used to say proudly.

I held the front door open as Mamá carefully carried out her pot by both handles, making sure not to spill the cooked beans. When she got to the car, Papá reached out to help her with it. Roberto opened the rear car door and Papá gently placed it on the floor behind the front seat. All of us then climbed in. Papá sighed, wiped the sweat off his forehead with his sleeve, and said wearily: "Es todo."

As we drove away, I felt a lump in my throat. I turned around and looked at our little shack for the last time.

At sunset we drove into a labor camp near Fresno. Since Papá did not speak English, Mamá asked the camp foreman if he needed any more workers. "We don't need no more," said the foreman, scratching his head. "Check with Sullivan down the road. Can't miss him. He lives in a big white house with a fence around it."

When we got there, Mamá walked up to the house. She went through a white gate, past a row of rose bushes, up the stairs to the front door. She rang the doorbell. The porch light went on and a tall husky man came out. They exchanged a few words. After the man went in, Mamá clasped her hands and hurried back to the car. "We have work! Mr. Sullivan said we can stay there the whole season," she said, gasping and pointing to an old garage near the stables.

The garage was worn out by the years. It had no windows. The walls, eaten by termites, strained to support the roof full of holes. The dirt floor, populated by earth worms, looked like a gray road map.

That night, by the light of a kerosene lamp, we unpacked and cleaned our new home. Roberto swept away the loose dirt, leaving the hard ground. Papá plugged the holes in the walls with old newspapers and tin can tops. Mamá fed my little brothers and sisters. Papá and Roberto then brought in the mattress and placed it on the far corner of the garage. "Mamá, you and the little ones sleep on the mattress. Roberto, Panchito, and I will sleep outside under the trees," Papá said.

Early next morning Mr. Sullivan showed us where his crop was, and after breakfast, Papá, Roberto, and I headed for the vineyard to pick.

Around nine o'clock the temperature had risen to almost one hundred degrees. I was completely soaked in sweat and my mouth felt as if I had been chewing on a handkerchief. I walked over to the end of the row, picked up the jug of water

we had brought, and began drinking. "Don't drink too much; you'll get sick," Roberto shouted. No sooner had he said that than I felt sick to my stomach. I dropped to my knees and let the jug roll off my hands. I remained motionless with my eyes glued on the hot sandy ground. All I could hear was the drone of insects. Slowly I began to recover. I poured water over my face and neck and watched the dirty water run down my arms to the ground.

I still felt a little dizzy when we took a break to eat lunch. It was past two o'clock and we sat underneath a large walnut tree that was on the side of the road. While we ate, Papá jotted down the number of boxes we had picked. Roberto drew designs on the ground with a stick. Suddenly I noticed Papá's face turn pale as he looked down the road. "Here comes the school bus," he whispered loudly in alarm. Instinctively, Roberto and I ran and hid in the vineyards. We did not want to get in trouble for not going to school. The neatly dressed boys about my age got off. They carried books under their arms. After they crossed the street, the bus drove away. Roberto and I came out from hiding and joined Papá. "Tienen que tener cuidado," he warned us.

After lunch we went back to work. The sun kept beating down. The buzzing insects, the wet sweat, and the hot dry dust made the afternoon seem to last forever. Finally the mountains around the valley reached out and swallowed the sun. Within an hour it was too dark to continue picking. The vines blanketed the grapes, making it difficult to see the bunches. "Vámonos," said Papá, signaling to us that it was time to quit work. Papá then took out a pencil and began to figure out how much we had earned our first day. He wrote down numbers, crossed some out, wrote down some more. "Quince," he murmured.

When we arrived home, we took a cold shower underneath a waterhose. We then sat down to eat dinner around some wooden crates that served as a table. Mamá had cooked a special meal for us. We had rice and tortillas with "carne con chile," my favorite dish.

The next morning I could hardly move. My body ached all over. I felt little control over my arms and legs. This feeling went on every morning for days until my muscles finally got used to the work.

It was Monday, the first week of November. The grape season was over and I could now go to school. I woke up early that morning and lay in bed, looking at the stars and savoring the thought of not going to work and of starting sixth grade for the first time that year. Since I could not sleep, I decided to get up and join Papá and Roberto at breakfast. I sat at the table across from Roberto, but I kept my head down. I did not want to look up and face him. I knew he was sad. He was not going to school today. He was not going tomorrow, or next week, or next month. He would not go until the cotton season was over, and that was some-time in February. I rubbed my hands together and watched the dry, acid stained skin fall to the floor in little rolls.

When Papá and Roberto left for work, I felt relief. I walked to the top of a small grade next to the shack and watched the "Carcanchita" disappear in the distance in a cloud of dust.

Two hours later, around eight o'clock, I stood by the side of the road waiting for school bus number twenty. When it arrived I climbed in. Everyone was busy either talking or yelling. I sat in an empty seat in the back.

When the bus stopped in front of the school, I felt very nervous. I looked out the bus window and saw boys and girls carrying books under their arms. I put my hands in my pant pockets and walked to the principal's office. When I entered I heard a woman's voice say: "May I help you?" I was startled. I had not heard English for months. For a few seconds I remained speechless. I looked at the lady who waited for an answer. My first instinct was to answer her in Spanish, but I held back. Finally, after struggling for English words, I managed to tell her that I wanted to enroll in the sixth grade. After answering many questions, I was led to the classroom.

Mr. Lema, the sixth grade teacher, greeted me and assigned me a desk. He then introduced me to the class. I was so nervous and scared at that moment when everyone's eyes were on me that I wished I were with Papá and Roberto picking cotton. After taking roll, Mr. Lema gave the class the assignment for the first hour. "The first thing we have to do this morning is finish reading the story we began yesterday," he said enthusiastically. He walked up to me, handed me an English book, and asked me to read. "We are on page 125," he said politely. When I heard this, I felt my blood rush to my head; I felt dizzy. "Would you like to read?" he asked hesitantly. I opened the book to page 125. My mouth was dry. My eyes

began to water. I could not begin. "You can read later," Mr. Lema said understandingly.

For the rest of the reading period I kept getting angrier and angrier with myself. I should have read, I thought to myself.

During recess I went into the restroom and opened my English book to page 125. I began to read in a low voice, pretending I was in class. There were many words I did not know. I closed the book and headed back to the classroom.

Mr. Lema was sitting at his desk correcting papers. When I entered he looked up at me and smiled. I felt better. I walked up to him and asked if he could help me with the new words. "Gladly," he said.

The rest of the month I spent my lunch hours working on English with Mr. Lema, my best friend at school.

One Friday during lunch hour Mr. Lema asked me to take a walk with him to the music room. "Do you like music?" he asked me as we entered the building.

"Yes, I like corridos," I answered. He then picked up a trumpet, blew on it and handed it to me. The sound gave me goose bumps. I knew that sound. I had heard it in many corridos. "How would you like to learn how to play it?" he asked. He must have read my face because before I could answer, he added: "I'll teach you how to play it during our lunch hours."

That day I could hardly wait to get home to tell Papá and Mamá the great news. As I got off the bus, my little brothers and sisters ran up to meet me. They were yelling and screaming. I thought they were happy to see me, but when I opened the door to our shack, I saw that everything we owned was neatly packed in cardboard boxes.

*Francisco Jiménez finished his schooling and earned a doctorate from Columbia University in New York. He is now a professor at the University of Santa Clara in California, where he teaches Spanish language and literature.*

During World Wars I and II, Liberty and Victory gardens helped this country maintain its food supply. Once again, ingenious city dwellers are finding land and tilling their own gardens. Here, members from several Los Angeles families stand in the garden they created on an acre of land situated between two freeways.

Since the Spray brothers stopped using chemicals on their 650-acre Ohio farm 16 years ago, their farm produces 40 percent more than their neighbors!

Hundreds of years ago, Chinese farmers used ants to eat insects that were snacking on the leaves of their fruit trees; today, scientists have revived this method. In California's citrus groves, introducing natural enemies of the crop-destroying insects saved farmers half the cost of the chemical methods.

# DOWN ON THE NEW FARM

Food is the subject of poems, songs, and stories, and no wonder. Without it, we cannot live. Food has been sacred—early gatherers of yams always buried a part of the yam as an offering. What the gatherer probably didn't know was that she was also farming, since yams reproduce from a part of the root.

As people understood that seeds, when planted, grow into food, they began to settle down and purposely farm. They soon found natural ways to enrich the soil, prevent soil erosion, and control bothersome plant-eating bugs and  insects. But as agriculture became big business, farmers abandoned these natural methods. Fertilizers made from oil and chemicals that kill crop-eating bugs became the norm.

While not all chemical fertilizers and pesticides are harmful, farmers are beginning to return to the more organic ways of farming. They're creating chemical-free methods, bringing back forgotten plants that are a rich source of protein, and taking a new look at the wisdom of farmers from thousands of years ago.

*When vegetables are grown in water that contains nutrients, they thrive. Hydroponics (roughly translated from the Greek, the word means "water working") cuts down on the problems of bugs, fertilizer, and poor soil, and produces high-quality vegetables.*

*For eleven thousand years, Andean farmers have grown nuña beans. Now, North American farmers are beginning to grow these high-protein, low-fat beans, as well as many other grains and plants from ancient times.*

# Four Skinny Trees

## by Sandra Cisneros

They are the only ones who understand me.
I am the only one who understands them.
Four skinny trees with skinny necks and
pointy elbows like mine. Four who do not
belong here but are here. Four raggedy
excuses planted by the city. From our room
we can hear them, but Nenny just sleeps
and doesn't appreciate these things.

Their strength is secret. They send
ferocious roots beneath the ground.
They grow up and they grow down and
grab the earth between their hairy toes and
bite the sky with violent teeth and never
quit their anger. This is how they keep.

Let one forget his reason for being,
they'd all droop like tulips in a glass, each
with their arms around the other. Keep, keep,
keep, trees say when I sleep. They teach.

When I am too sad and too skinny to
keep keeping, when I am a tiny thing against
so many bricks, then it is I look at trees.
When there is nothing left to look at on this
street. Four who grew despite concrete.
Four who reach and do not forget to reach.
Four whose only reason is to be and be.

# Women

## Their Lives in Their Words
### by Doreen Rappaport

oday American women make up 45 percent of the work force. For most American women work is a necessity, as many are often the sole supporters of their families. It is predicted that by the year 2000, women will make up half the work force. Women have broken into previously closed occupations: one out of five lawyers and doctors are women, and these rates are increasing rapidly. Almost half the accountants and bus drivers are women. But in many occupations women have only token representation. Fewer than 4 percent of America's pilots, mechanics, construction workers, and firefighters are women. Only 3 percent of women hold top-management jobs in America's largest corporations. Though half the population, women are very underrepresented as political leaders.

In 1989 *The New York Times* polled American women to see how they felt about the changes in their lives brought about by working outside the home. Almost half the women said that women had sacrificed too much for their gains in the workplace. In most marriages, women come home after a day of work and begin their second job—cooking, housecleaning, food shopping, bill paying, and child care. Very few have husbands willing to assume housekeeping duties. Eighty-three percent of the working mothers interviewed said they were torn by having to juggle the demands of their jobs and the demands of family life. Many of these women feel stress, fatigue, and resentment over the lopsided division of labor at home but see no way of resolving the dilemma.

In the following interviews, high school girls express their feelings about being female and share their thoughts about their futures.

**Q: Was there any time in your life that being a girl hindered you?**

Yes, in the eighth grade. There was a patrol squad and the teachers only allowed boys to be on it. If you were a monitor, you either brought out the barricades around the school to protect the kids from cars or you stood by the school door and held it for the younger classes. Some monitors guarded the stairwells to maintain order. It just so happened that they only assigned boys to be monitors every year. Some friends of mine and I thought it wasn't fair and we asked the teachers why we couldn't be monitors. They didn't really have an explanation. They said, "It's always been like that, always been the boys' job." When our eighth grade graduated, they started assigning girls.

> **Seventeen-year-old Yuk Ming Liu is a junior in high school in New York City.**

**Q: What do you want to achieve in your life?**

I have many goals. Right now my main goal is to get into a good college, like one of the Ivy League schools. I'm split between the medical profession—becoming a psychiatrist, or doing something with languages. I want to continue studying Chinese. I'm also taking Latin, and might want to go into Classics. I want to marry but that will be after I'm set on a career and I know where I'm going. I'm still thinking about having kids but I'm not one hundred percent sure.

**Q: How will your life be similar/different from your mother's and grandmother's lives?**

My mother expects me to go to college. She had a chance to go to college when she was in Hong Kong. She was accepted but at that time the belief was that a woman didn't have to get a good education, all she had to do was finish high school and then look for a good husband and she would be fine. My mom has taught me that you should be settled before you get married, that you should make sure that you have some kind of foundation for yourself, and that's through getting a good education.

I'm going to be more liberal than my mom. When I was in grade school, she didn't let me go out anywhere—to friends' birthday parties, or even to the library—unless she was with me. I think she felt she had to protect me. We used to have play days after school when the kids got together to mingle; my mom never let me go to them. Now she's more loose and lets me go out once in a while to see a movie or be with friends. She's less strict with my brothers. My mom and I think differently. My mom grew up in a Chinese background. My background is a mixture of Chinese and American views.

My grandmother was born in China and now lives in Hong Kong. She went to school but I don't think she got past high school. Her life was harder than mine. When she was my age, women in China weren't treated equal to men.

### Q: If you plan to marry, how do you see your partnership with a man?

I think we'll both work. On weekends, we'll do things with the children. The first few years I might work part-time and be home with the kids. But after that we'll have babysitters—probably someone we know—during the week when we're both working. I wouldn't mind doing the cooking. I think the cleaning should be done by both of us. The decisions should be made collaboratively though I think that making decisions for the children will probably be my job. The husband's job should be to prevent his family from interfering from how we bring up our children. And the woman's job is to bring up the children the correct way.

### Q: What would you like women to achieve?

To get to know themselves. There are many women out there who are capable of doing so many things but they just let it go. They don't work at it. They have dreams but the dreams just float away. If you don't do something about the dream it does float away. I think women stop because they get discouraged. They stop pursuing their goals because the society says that girls shouldn't do this or that and they are easily influenced by this attitude. Some girls are lazy. There are other factors, too. Sometimes you're poor or the neighborhood you're brought up in isn't one that makes it easy for you to develop your skills. So a person has to really work to reach the top, to get out of the place they are in and get beyond.

**Q: What do you think is the biggest obstacle for women?**

The stereotyping of women. People say that they're too aggressive or they're not fit to do a man's job. Some women get really offended by these attitudes and try to change the person's view but some get discouraged when they hear these comments and their dreams start to fall apart slowly.

**Q: Was there any time in your life that being a girl hindered you?**

Not really. If I wanted to do something I could do it. If I wanted to run track being a girl didn't matter. I'm glad to be a girl.

**Q: What do you want to achieve in your life?**

**Seventeen-year-old Keana Bonds is a junior in high school in McComb, Mississippi.**

I want to go to college and study business management. I'm probably not going to stay and work in McComb. I'll probably go to Jackson where there are better jobs with better pay. I want to be married eventually, sometime in my twenties. I really don't want to rush into marriage when I get out of college. I want time to settle down and get a good job first.

**Q: How will your life be similar/different from your mother's and grandmother's lives?**

I'll be working hard like my mother did for my family. I'll be working at a job so I can give them things they need. I have my mother's ways. I'm softhearted like she is. I think I'll be stricter with my kids than my mother was with us. I don't want my kids to grow up thinking they have the control. My work will be different from my mother's. My mother works now as a clerk in a clothing store. She worked in a hospital for four years. I don't think I'll live in McComb when I'm married.

I'm like my grandmother, my father's mother. She was always on the positive side whatever the situation. I'm understanding and always there for people like she was.

**Q: If you plan to marry, how do you see your partnership with a man?**

I expect my husband to clean the house and not wait on me to do it. I expect him to take his share of the responsibility with the children and the bills and the house. I think I'll probably stay home awhile and then go back to work. If I'm at home my husband doesn't have to be there but when he's there, I want him to help. I'm sure I'll keep everything in order. I think I'd rather do the child care than have my husband do it because I think I'll be better at it. I think women are better at it than men.

**Q: What do you think is the biggest obstacle women face in achieving their goals?**

Sex discrimination is the biggest obstacle. Women can't get certain jobs like construction work. They can't become electricians. Only because they're women.

**Q: What would you like women to achieve?**

I want them to get higher-paying jobs. Men make more money than women do and I think it's unfair.

**Q: Was there any time in your life that being a girl hindered you?**

No, because when I was small I never saw being a girl as being different. I saw everyone as equals. We played the same games as boys did. My parents never discouraged me in doing anything. They told me, if you want to do it, you try to do your best.

**Q: What do you want to achieve in your life?**

I want to graduate from high school, go to the University of Texas in Austin, major in education, and teach first or second graders back here in the valley. I plan on getting married after I have a career and am financially set. I also plan on having a family.

Seventeen-year-old Elda D. Cantu is a junior in high school and lives in Mission, Texas.

**Q: How will your life be similar/different from your mother's and grandmother's lives?**

Both my mom and grandmother were teachers so in that sense my life will be similar. I'm going to use the values they've taught me for the rest of my life and in my career. They've taught me to achieve what you want. You can't be intimidated by anything. Down here in the valley the majority of people are Hispanic, and if I decide to venture off, maybe to New York, I can't be intimidated by being a minority. They've taught me to be proud of what I am.

I'm kind of old-fashioned. This generation may be materialistic but I'm not going to be trapped in that kind of world.

My grandmother was probably intimidated when she was my age because back then Hispanics weren't highly regarded. She was always thought of as a second-class citizen, though in her heart and within her family, she knew she wasn't.

**Q: If you plan to marry, how do you see your partnership with a man?**

Right now, I'm kind of scared about a marriage because I see so many of my parents' friends getting divorced and separated. If I do marry, I want a fifty-fifty relationship. I want to share finances, housework, responsibilities, problems, and child care.

**Q: What do you think is the biggest obstacle women face in achieving their goals?**

Intimidation by men is the biggest obstacle. Women are always being stereotyped as being second, behind men. If a woman is applying for the same job as a man, I think she might feel intimidated inside herself because she's scared of just not being able to compete with a man. Being a woman is a bigger obstacle for me than being Hispanic. Of course I'm proud to be a woman, but I'm more proud to be Hispanic. I won't let anyone put me down because I'm Hispanic.

**Q: What would you like women to achieve?**

I'd like to see a woman president. Women are just as capable as men. I think we came a great deal closer to that goal when Geraldine Ferraro ran for vice-president.

★ ★ ★

**Q: Was there any time in your life that being a girl hindered you?**

No. And I think there's a reason. Since my parents were both raised in a time when a lot of traditional ideas about how women should lead their lives were being shattered, they raised me to want my own life and make my own decisions. I'm not sure that they consciously decided they were going to instill a new set of values in me, different from the ones they grew up with, but they did. Since I was ten or so I've been

making a lot of big decisions for myself. I don't expect to be treated differently or discriminated against. If it's happened already, I haven't seen it.

**Q: What would you like to achieve in your life?**

I'd like to be an environmental journalist and I'd like to have a family, too. I don't think I can do both at the same time, because this occupation involves a lot of traveling. And aside from traveling, since I love environmental studies and writing, I would probably be immersed in my job, and when I have a family I would really like to give it my full attention. I don't think this has anything to do with being a woman. If whoever I marry decided that he would like to stay home and spend time with our children, then I'd be perfectly willing to go back to work to support the family. I could probably do both things but I want to give each my full involvement. From a practical angle, I may not be able to stop working because we may need the income but I'd certainly slow down when I have a family.

**Q: How will your life be similar/different from your mother's and grandmother's?**

My mother went to an all-girls' high school and grew up in a different time. This school had a greater impact on her than her era. She was never discriminated against at high school because it was all girls. So when women started becoming feminists, she didn't feel like she needed to assert herself in that way. She asserted herself by doing good work as a person, not a woman. She never expected anyone to treat her differently because she was a woman and neither do I.

My grandmother, my mother's mother, came over from Germany when she was in her teens. My grandfather came from Spain. They both had a lot of Old World values. I think that my grandmother would have liked to work but my grandfather didn't want her to because it would have hurt his pride. And I think that the difference between her life and what my life is and will be is huge. I can't ever imagine meeting a man who would think that way.

**Q: If you plan to marry, how do you see your partnership with a man?**

I think I already answered that question when I talked about my goals for my life.

**Q: What do you think is the biggest obstacle women face in achieving their goals?**

There are a lot of girls growing up in homes where their mothers both work and take care of all the housekeeping. I think this demonstrates that we still have a big hump to get over, in terms of men and women dividing up work equally. I think this is a really common situation because a lot of families now need both parents to work, but there's no definition of who's supposed to take care of the kids and all the other household duties. People are still falling back on tradition instead of making new definitions that equalize responsibilities at home between men and women.

**Q: What would you like women to achieve?**

I wish that women didn't feel that they had to be feminists. I wish women didn't have to know that discrimination exists. I think that if a woman is taught not to expect discrimination and is instilled with the sense that she can do anything she wants to do and that no one can stop her, then she can do it. That's not to say that discrimination isn't a real problem because it is. But I think women can overcome that problem by consistently showing that what they can do is no better or worse than what men can do.

★ ★ ★

**Q: Was there any time in your life that being a girl hindered you?**

Kind of. One time I wanted to play basketball in the high school school yard and there were a bunch of guys playing. I wanted to go over and play

180

but I felt like I would feel out of place and I wouldn't fit in, so I didn't go over.

**Q: What would you like to achieve in your life?**

I enjoy working with computers, specifically programming and organizing bank accounts. I plan to go to college and major in accounting and then get a job up here. I also want to get married and have a small family, one or two kids. I always thought I'd get married when I was about twenty-four. I want to travel all over the world, probably with my husband.

**Q: How will your life be similar/different from your mother's and grandmother's lives?**

Sixteen-year-old Angel Stimers is a junior in high school and lives in Claverack, New York.

My mother's father walked out of her life when she was very young so she grew up with one parent. I've been lucky to have two. My mother didn't have much money even though my grandmother worked. My mother never went to college and I plan to. My mother does cashier work and some bookkeeping. If she had had my opportunities, she might have been an accountant.

**Q: If you plan to marry, how do you see your partnership with a man?**

First off, I'd like my marriage to be based on trust. As far as raising children, I guess all kids say this, that they won't raise their kids like their parents did, but I think I probably will. I want shared responsibilities, but my husband will probably have the final say concerning problems and decisions about the children, the house, the car, like in my parents' marriage. I think it will be this way for me because that's how I've seen it. That's the only way I know. I intend to go back to work when my kids are about five years old.

**Q: What do you think is the biggest obstacle women face in achieving their goals?**

Men. They're always putting us down. They say women are supposed to stay home and cook and take care of the kids. Women have a right to go out there and make their own careers and do whatever they want to do. I've heard men teachers say these things. Even my father, and my grandfather, too. And when they say it, I try to argue back and they usually end up winning the argument. When I say, "What right do you have to put us down?" they answer, "The male species is dominant and more powerful." I always say it's not fair and they shouldn't judge us just because we're women or girls, but they don't listen.

**Q: What would you like women to achieve?**

I don't really know.

**Q: Was there any time in your life that being a girl hindered you?**

I remember when I was younger I had this impression that certain jobs were for men only and other jobs were for women only. As I entered junior high school, I began to realize then that more women were pursuing what they *wanted* to do, not what was expected of them. Sometimes I feel because of my traditions and how my mother and grandmother grew up, I'd have to follow what I was taught—a woman should stay home and be the keeper of the house and caretaker of the children. I [once] thought my choices were limited, but now I know they're not.

**Eighteen-year-old Esther Barela is a high school senior and lives in Zuni, New Mexico.**

**Q: What do you want to achieve in your life?**

I hope to become a pediatrician. I am very interested in the health field because I see a great need for doctors in my community. [Esther Barela is a member of the Zuni Pueblo, a Native American community.] I have been told time and time again that no matter who I am or where I come from, I can do just about anything in life. I have set my goals really high because I know it's going to be a hard journey and the things I learn along the way will help me grow to become the best I can.

### Q: How will your life be similar/different from your mother's and grandmother's lives?

I think my life will be different from theirs. My mother only graduated from high school. Then she went to a beauty school but she didn't finish because she had me. She never returned to school. Her work is usually as a clerk or cashier at a school. My grandmother didn't finish high school. She got married and lived on the reservation and brought up her kids there. Her life has been pretty confined to the reservation. I've probably gone more places in my eighteen years than my grandmother's gone in her sixty-four years.

My mother and grandmother take part in a lot of the traditional things of Zuni women. When we have traditional *kachina* dances, in which only the men dance, my mother and grandmother and the other women bake bread and cook foods. I don't do it. I don't know how to do it. I've asked my mother sometimes to teach me but I always seem too busy doing something else to learn.

I don't think I'm going to live on the reservation like they do. There are a lot of kids my age here who feel the same way. We have a hospital on the reservation. I might come back for my hospital residency but I'm not sure I'll stay.

### Q: If you plan to marry, how do you see your partnership with a man?

I do plan to marry; not soon, but in time enough to get my life together and settle down. I want to make a stable life for myself so that if a relationship or marriage doesn't work out, I can depend on myself instead of my spouse. I want my relationship with my future husband to be one of trust, honesty, and respect. I want to be able to pursue my goals and not have him feel possessive or that he can't trust me. I'd want my husband to have his independence too. I realize that this kind of relationship may be hard to find but it's only a matter of waiting for that right person.

**Q: What do you think is the biggest obstacle women face in achieving their goals? Are there any special obstacles you face being an American Indian?**

I think the biggest obstacle women face in achieving their goals is themselves. If a person doesn't believe in herself or himself, then she or he can't really get anywhere. I really do stress that it doesn't matter where you come from or what sex, color, or age you are; if you have enough faith in yourself and what you hope to accomplish, the sky's the limit.

**Q: What would you like women to achieve?**

I would like women to achieve all they've ever dreamed of. I see this being done more and more and I want it to continue. I hope women realize that they are just as important in this world as men are. When it comes to achieving one's life goals, it matters not what gender, race, color or age one is, but how much determination and drive one possesses.

# Meet Doreen *Rappaport*

★ ★ ★

**D**oreen Rappaport is a writer with a clear purpose. "I want to 'demythify' personal experience and historical events for young people," she has written. "I'm interested in the untold stories in history. . . . Young women need role models, . . . and all young people need to learn that life is more of a struggle than what is usually presented on television or in many history books."

Rappaport is especially concerned with reexamining history with an emphasis on women's experiences. She has created award-winning educational programs about women's history and is the author of *Trouble at the Mines* and *The Boston Coffee Party,* a book about a rebellion of women during the American Revolution.

# The Dream Keeper

*by Langston Hughes*

Bring me all of your dreams,
You dreamers,
Bring me all of your
Heart melodies
That I may wrap them
In a blue cloud-cloth
Away from the too-rough fingers
Of the world.

*Around Her* by Marc Chagall

# CONTENTS

# JUST US!

# TAKE A LUMP OF CLAY

Take a lump of clay,
Wet it, pat it,
Make a statue of you
And a statue of me.
Then shatter them, clatter them,
Add some water,
And break them and mold them
Into a statue of you
And a statue of me.
Then, in mine, there are bits of you
And in you there are bits of me.
Nothing shall ever keep us apart.

KUAN TAO SHENG
(SUNG DYNASTY)

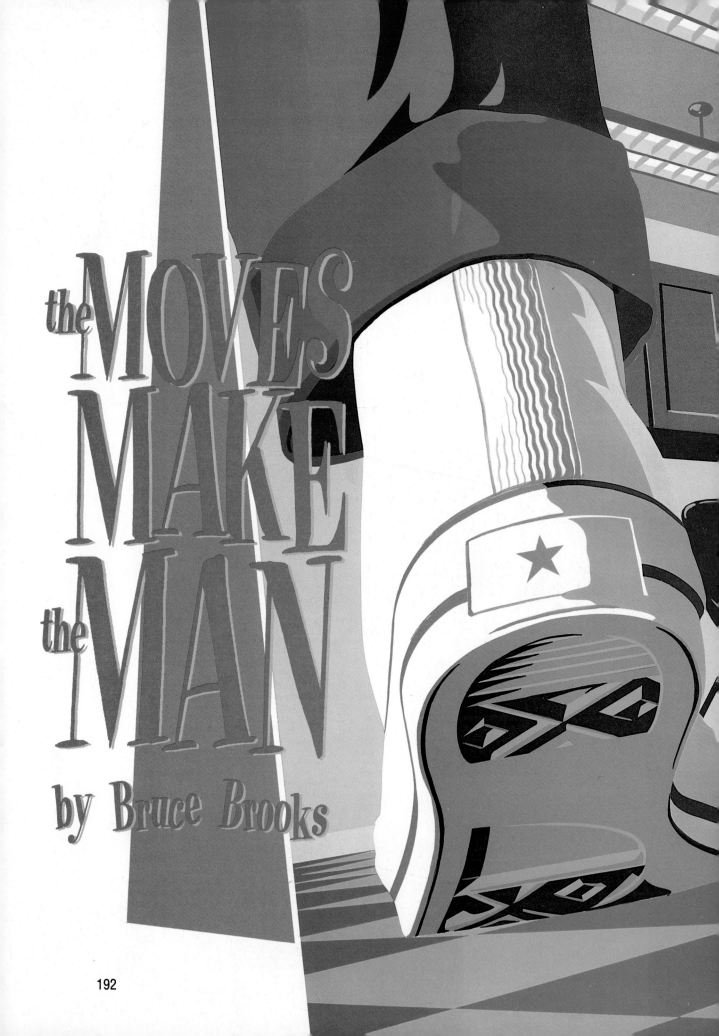

# the MOVES MAKE the MAN

by Bruce Brooks

ILLUSTRATED BY MARK RIEDY

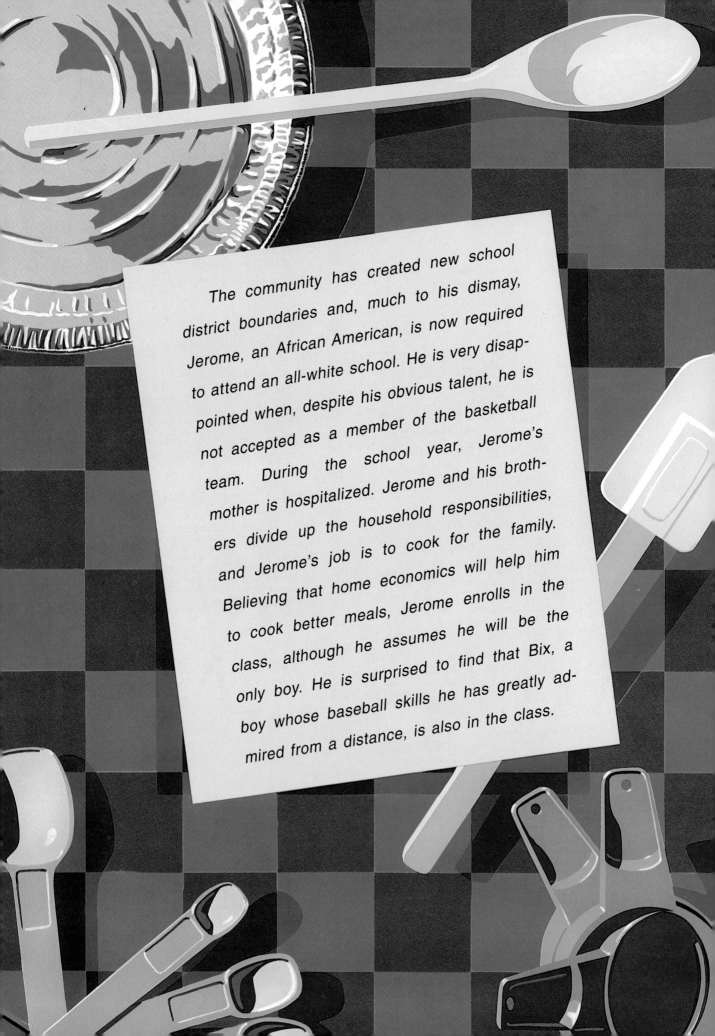

The community has created new school district boundaries and, much to his dismay, Jerome, an African American, is now required to attend an all-white school. He is very disappointed when, despite his obvious talent, he is not accepted as a member of the basketball team. During the school year, Jerome's mother is hospitalized. Jerome and his brothers divide up the household responsibilities, and Jerome's job is to cook for the family. Believing that home economics will help him to cook better meals, Jerome enrolls in the class, although he assumes he will be the only boy. He is surprised to find that Bix, a boy whose baseball skills he has greatly admired from a distance, is also in the class.

Over that weekend at home we ate mostly corn bread made from the box recipe and a canned ham our next door neighbor Mrs. Paul gave us, but I told the brothers about Home Ec and talked it up big, promising that the cook was going to fly come Monday night. I did not tell them about the apron jive. I wanted them to believe in Home Economics. Maybe then the stuff I made would not taste as bush, being officially taught stuff.

When I got to class on Monday, I did not look straight back at the table where I was to sit, but when I slung the eyes up for a charming smile at Miss Pimton who did not know where to look but not in my eyes, I could see out the corners that there was someone sitting there. I still did not look, turning toward the back and nodding at a couple of those dippy girls who giggled and fussed getting their polka dots on straight. But I started to feel a twiggle in my stomach.

I was feeling a little cocky, still. It was the same sort of feeling of having my onlyness broken that I had felt talking in the hall to the counselor. I did not like it, I knew it was foolish, but I could not help it and I knew I was not going to give that dude an easy time. Jerome can be cool and snappy when he is bad, and I felt like I was going to be bad. All the same, I was really pretty excited—here was a boy I would almost have to get to know, all alone like we were in that institute of wives for the future. I knew something was waiting for me back there in that kid, as I walked closer, swinging a cool check-out glance his way. But my cool fell right off my face, and I gaped. Sitting there, looking very different out of uniform but still the same kid without doubt, was the shortstop. What was it his momma called him? Bix. Bix Bix Bix. Bix for Braxton. Bix my baseball main man, my mystery opponent in phantom one on one, my new partner in cookery.

I expected him to recognize me and he did not, shooting me only a very timid don't-hurt-me look with a half smile like inviting me to be friendly, and then looking down again. Then I realized he could not have recognized me—he had never seen me before. This made me snooty again, like he someway SHOULD have got to know me while I was in the crowd watching him or something. Man, I was not thinking too clearly in the feelings that day.

I stared at him and he just looked down, feeling the stare and not wanting to meet it. I checked him out pretty thorough, and saw that he really was pretty different now, different from what I would have thought that Bix who gave me shivers pivoting on the double play and whipping that arm would be. First of all, I saw that kid as being sure of himself enough to look anybody in the eye and take the check-out proudly. Not this look-down dude here. Second, and maybe here I thought Egglestobbs' way for a moment, I thought he would be holding himself tight and high and clever on his feet, moving sure and fast and giving off that glow with all of his grace. But no, he slunk all down like the white basketball boys after I hit that boss shot, only he had no reason to. I had taken no shots yet.

He was a good looking kid, despite being a white boy with the usual problem of they have no good tone in the skin. He had thick light hair kind of long for most whites, but instead of hanging down it sort of bushed out, wavy enough not to be bristly. From that one glance I saw his eyes were very fine, round and big, the same light brown color as his hair which was a little odd but in a good way. I liked his eyebrows, very thick. I liked his cheek bones too, they stuck out like mine only higher and right now they were pale which most white people have red on them. The weirdest thing about the face was this pink flush in the forehead, not a scar or anything, just like what most whites get when they blush only in a different place and irregular. Later I found out he got it his first time up in a Little League game, age eight, when a twelve-year-old kid pitching beaned him smack in the thinker. But it only ever turned pink when he was ashamed or shy and never showed on the surface or at other times.

His clothes were naturally different from his spiffy uniform, but even so I expected they would be just as sharp. At first I thought he was just a mess in bad threads, but then I noticed that the clothes actually were good things. Nice cord pants and a yellow button-down like I like, and a tweed jacket, which would have looked fancy worn the right way with a little confidence. Nice duds. But right now they were only being used to carry around a very grand set of wrinkles, baby. This boy had not seen an iron in moons. What was wrong with his momma, she let him get out the house like this?

Then I felt a little tingle. His momma—what was he doing in Home Ec? I looked fast at his shoes. Leather loafers, all polished very nice. Wrinkly good clothes, polished good shoes. These added up, along with the counselor's talk the other day, and told me: something was wrong with this boy's mother too.

Here is how it figured. First, good threads. That went along with his momma, snazzy and decked out in full class to watch a ball game and yet not look silly either. Nice shoes, too. Now, what do you learn from polished shoes plus wrinkled clothes? Just this: a kid always polishes his own shoes, but his momma always irons his clothes. So if his shoes are done, it means he is still trying to look okay, well trained or whatever; but if his clothes are messy it means no momma at the ironing board, and nobody either to check his state of appearance be- fore he gets it out the door for school in the a.m. Hey—maybe this kid has no daddy too, I thought.

On the whole it was no wonder the girls treated him creepy. He was like a pup begging you not to kick him and

girls like that cannot resist getting a foot on such helplessness.

I sat down, and said, So, man, you going to be my partner?

I guess we are, he said. I mean, I guess I am.

You here to learn to sling the pots? He looked at me puzzled.

You know, I said, sling the pots, fling the pans—cook, man.

Oh, he said, sure. He grinned, then looked down. Sling the pots, fling the pans, he said. Or if not, open cans.

Hey, I said, that's not bad. Open those cans. Only we probably don't learn how to get into a can until next semester, after apron tying and rubber glove putting on and choosing the right smell of dish soap and a sponge to go with your nail polish.

He shrugged. He had livened up for a second, but now he was back to being pure fish. I looked up toward the front, sighing. He just

hunkered down. Between Miss Pimton and this dude, I might have a very trying time in old Home Ec.

Miss Pimton acted like she heard my thought, and set right out to obey. For she got out some tubs of water and a laundry basket full of torn up newspaper and smiled and said Okay girls, today, and tomorrow too, plenty of time, we are going to do patties.

Patties! squealed the girls, clapping their hands.

What do you think the newspapers are for? I asked Bix.

Newspaper patties? he said. I laughed, but he was right. For Miss Pimton made us come around her table and proceeded to show us how to make that perfect patty for the grill or broiler, only it was out of paper mache. Wet shredded newspaper, just right for the coals. Just right for tonight's supper at the Foxworthy household. Here we are, Maurice—you get last week's front page, and Henri, knowing your thing for football I have pattied up the sports section. Looked like fried eggs once more for the boys.

And I did not know, but when the next week we finally started on our first edible project, as Miss Pimton called it, I was in for the worst sight yet of White Man's Nonsense. I was never so amazed as when she told us what we were going to cook up. I mean, the usual jive like Communications of making something that seems important out of nothing is bad enough. But making something out of nothing and then EATING it . . .

$\frac{1}{2}$ cup milk

$\frac{1}{2}$ cup water (warm)

2 teaspoons cinnamon

1 cup sugar

$2\frac{1}{2}$ cups crushed Ritz crackers

1 pie crust

There you go. That's the ticket. Mix it all together, stick it in the oven, and you get yourself one official yummy Home Economic style Mock-Apple Pie. Dig it.

Mocking apples, man. Where did somebody get the idea that this was a good way to spend the day? Miss P thought it was pure genius. So did the girls. Imagine! Making something that looked and tasted a little bit like apple pie, only it was all completely fake! Hooray! How smart everybody in this world is!

I was groaning after it hit me that Miss Pimton was truly serious, but I was drowned out. Oh boy I bet that dumb old Buck Taylor will eat this up and never tell in a million years, or Sakes alive that high and mighty old Skeeter Darby won't he be fooled but good? All the girls clapped and begged could

they take some to their boyfriends, PLEASE? Miss Pimton loved it. She smiled like she was the queen giving the secrets of high life to all the people on feast day. Yes, she said, every team would prepare a pie, and they would get baked and we could take them to whomever we wanted. She looked at Bix and me when she said this with her eyes full of important meaning. I realized she was thinking we would actually take this tricky glop home and feed it to our poor starving families, bless our poor undernourished little hearts.

I couldn't stand that look, so I spoke up. What do I want to go fooling my brothers with a bunch of yellow crackers in water for? I said.

She looked startled. This food—

This is not food, I said. It's a costume. The only reason anybody even thinks about apple pie when they eat this is the cinnamon, I bet, because they are used to tasting cinnamon in real apple pie, and you are counting on fooling them on this little decoration taste alone. You're probably right, most of these dopes (I almost said Most of these white dopes but I held back but I think Miss Pimton knew, for she blushed something awful) will go no further than tasting the spice and saying Ah, this must be apple pie, because most dopey people judge too fast from the first thing they see anyway. So you put some little thing in to trick them, and it's enough. But you can't fool the body needing vitamins can you?

Miss Pimton blushed hard and cleared her throat very high several times. The girls were hanging open at the mouth and not yet recovered enough to look hateful at me, which they did soon enough. I was showing my true colors at last, what they knew I must be like all along, uppity and loud and rude.

Miss Pimton finally said, trying to be dignified and patient but sounding only quivery, Mock-Apple Pie, Jerome, is actually delicious in its own way.

More delicious than apple pie? snapped a voice beside me and I jumped and looked around and, whew, there he was! The shortstop was back! I mean, Bix had perked up his spine and stuck out his chin a bit and his cheeks were red and eyes flashing. He looked about ready to take a nasty one-hopper to his right backhand and whip it to first off the back foot beating the runner by six steps and killing the rally cold. I said, My man! very soft, and maybe he heard me but did not show it, looking very hard at Miss Pimton, not letting her off, almost that look that comes before a smile on his face. He knew he had her. So did she. She was bad surprised that he had waked up from being the puppy.

Well, I—

Come on. Is it tastier, more delicious, more scrumptious than old genuine apple pie, old Non-Mock-Apple-Pie?

I checked out the girls. They were gaping again, this time at Bix.

Well, Braxton, said Miss Pimton, fidgeting with her glasses on her nose, I suppose, no, that Mock-Apple Pie has not quite the richness of apple pie, but . . . for beginners—

Why make it, then?

Well . . . some people find that—

Are Ritz crackers more nourishing than apples?

Well, I don't believe, no, I could not think they are—

Are they less expensive? Do they save on the family grocery bill in these difficult times?

She mumbled. Man, he was pressing. He walked over and snatched the cracker box and brought it back to our table.

Seventy-six cents for ten ounces, he read. I think apples go for about twenty cents a pound. So Ritz crackers are not more economical for the home, are they?

I could not believe this was the same slouchy dude. Do it, baby, I said. The girls glared.

It appears that the crackers are a bit more costly, Miss Pimton admitted, all defeated.

So, he said. Not more scrumptious, not more nourishing, not cheaper. So why in the blue do we have to make this junk?

Everybody just sat there looking their own bad looks. Bix watched Miss

Pimton. The girls did too. Miss Pimton sort of cringed and frowned and glanced back at Bix from time to time. Nobody said anything. Finally, I said, I'll tell you why we have to make it.

Bix turned around, surprised but interested. Miss Pimton looked relieved and actually said Why? like she really wanted to know too. Then she blushed and tried to look like she just wanted to hear how silly my reason was. The girls were ready for more nonsense to scoff at.

It's simple, I said. We have to make this crummy pie just because we CAN make it. That's all. That's the rea-

son a lot of fools do a lot of things. Some joker thought of doing this one day, and he did it, and then it was on the books as something that COULD be done and so people have to keep on doing it.

Then I thought to myself, That is white man's disease, thinking you must do whatever you can dream up just because you're so smart. And it is black man's disease to wish they had the same inclination.

Everybody just sat for a few minutes, Miss Pimton looking about to

bawl, the girls starting to strut back and forth putting on their aprons and asking could they start please Miss P? because THEY really WANTED to make this YUMMY pie and couldn't wait to share it with their dearest loved ones, and now wouldn't she show them how to mash up these old crackers just right, please? And could they be daring and maybe use just a little extra cinnamon or sugar because that Mick Hogan just LOVED sweet things.

I looked around at Bix. He was watching the girls and Miss Pimton, frowning. He was not as hot and bright as a few minutes ago, still tough but hurt too, seeing that the girls were actually going to keep business going as usual. Already Miss Pimton was coming back to form, starting to warm up as she took a bowl from Matty Sue who was trying to look all clumsy and needing help, and commenced to show the dear girl a few key tricks probably her momma taught her about mashing crackers just right like they did in colonial times. Bix looked over at me. His eyes were all sunk, like as to say They have beaten us have they not, partner? I looked back at him hard and hot as like to say Not a bit, brother, not us, not with such a measly thing as a pie full of wet crackers. We stared into each other's eyes there for a long time, heat growing and light moving very sure between us, and it was great, grand in the chest and fluttery in the stomach

as we forgot everything else and took each other to each. I don't remember feeling the smile start to come on my face or noticing it start on his, but suddenly I felt my cheeks hurt and saw his smile too, and my eyes had those good tears that stay inside, his too, I think. We knew each other could do anything together.

Hey, he said, grinning very crafty.

I get you, I said.

As long as we got to make one of these mock jessies—

We got to make the very mockingest!

The most chock-full of mock!

The mock de la mock! I said, knowing French.

Get a bowl, he said, and keep an eye on my wrist work while I mash.

Only, I said, if you pay the closest attention to my handsome cinnamon technique.

Don't use too much, he said. Johnny Mack Fathead does not love cinnamon and may be offended.

And be watchful of the sugar, I said, for Arnold T. Stomachface is known to be not partial to sweets.

We laughed, and got the junk to make our pie. The girls had already started and were all gritting their teeth at work. They did not hear a word we said.

I was very happy. I had just gotten myself a best bud. I was positive about that, I really thought so.

# MEET Bruce Brooks

Some people dread moving, but Bruce Brooks always looked forward to it. He thought that moving to a new place was an opportunity to experiment with different aspects of his personality.

It was lucky that Brooks enjoyed moving because he moved regularly, back and forth between two homes. In one, he was a member of a small Washington, D.C., family. In the other, he was a member of a large, outgoing family based in a North Carolina town. The experience meant that he was "half-native and half-outsider everywhere."

To fit in easily, Brooks developed "an eye for detail, an ear for voices, a quickness to analyze how people do things and why, an almost desperately open mind, and a sense of strategy." Brooks utilized all of these talents when he wrote *The Moves Make the Man*. In creating Jerome's character, Brooks said, "I can speak as this kid speaks. . . . The voice arises entirely from who Jerome is."

In 1984, *The Moves Make the Man* was an American Library Association Notable Book and a Best Book for Young Adults; further recognition came in 1985 when it was chosen as a Newbery Honor Book and won a Boston Globe–Horn Book Award for fiction. Other award-winning novels by Brooks are *Midnight Hour Encores* and *No Kidding*.

# AfteR-DinNer Winners

Unlike Jerome's Mock-Apple Pie, many desserts truly are scrumptious, nourishing, and economical. Such desserts contain wholesome simple foods, such as fruit, eggs, milk, or whole grains. Meet three after-dinner winners that even a sports star could eat without guilt.

## Peanut Butter Bon Bons

1/4 cup peanut butter
1/2 cup skim milk
4 two-inch square graham crackers

1/4 cup raisins
1 teaspoon vanilla
1/4 teaspoon cinnamon

This recipe was adapted from *Delicious Ways to Lower Cholesterol* by Nedra P. Wilson and Susan M. Wood, published by Oxmoor House.

Soften and blend the peanut butter with 2 tablespoons of milk. Break the graham crackers into small pieces and add them to the peanut butter. Add remaining milk and other ingredients. Mix well. Use a teaspoon to scoop the peanut butter mixture and form each spoonful into a ball. Drop the balls onto wax paper or aluminum foil. Freeze until firm. You'll have enough for about 8 balls.

# Apple Crisp

6 tart apples
1 tablespoon sugar
1 tablespoon cinnamon
1/4 teaspoon ground cloves
1/2 cup packed brown sugar

1/4 cup nonfat dry milk
1/3 cup flour
1 cup rolled oats
4 tablespoons margarine

Preheat the oven to 350°. Peel, core, and slice the apples. Add the sugar, cinnamon, and cloves. Mix well and place in a deep casserole dish. Combine the brown sugar, milk, flour, and oats. Stir in the margarine until the mixture is crumbly. Sprinkle the mixture over the apples. Bake 45 minutes.

## Citrus Loaf

6 oranges
1 grapefruit
1 package lemon or lime gelatin

Peel the fruit and divide each into sections. Prepare the gelatin as directed on the package, but don't chill. Arrange a single layer of the fruit in a 9" x 5" pan. Pour in only enough gelatin to cover the fruit. Add another layer of fruit and more gelatin. Continue until all the fruit has been used. A final layer of gelatin should cover the fruit. Chill overnight. Dip pan quickly into warm water and flip over onto a plate.

These two recipes were adapted from *Eat Smart for a Healthy Heart Cookbook* by Denton A. Cooley, published by Barron's Educational Series, Inc.

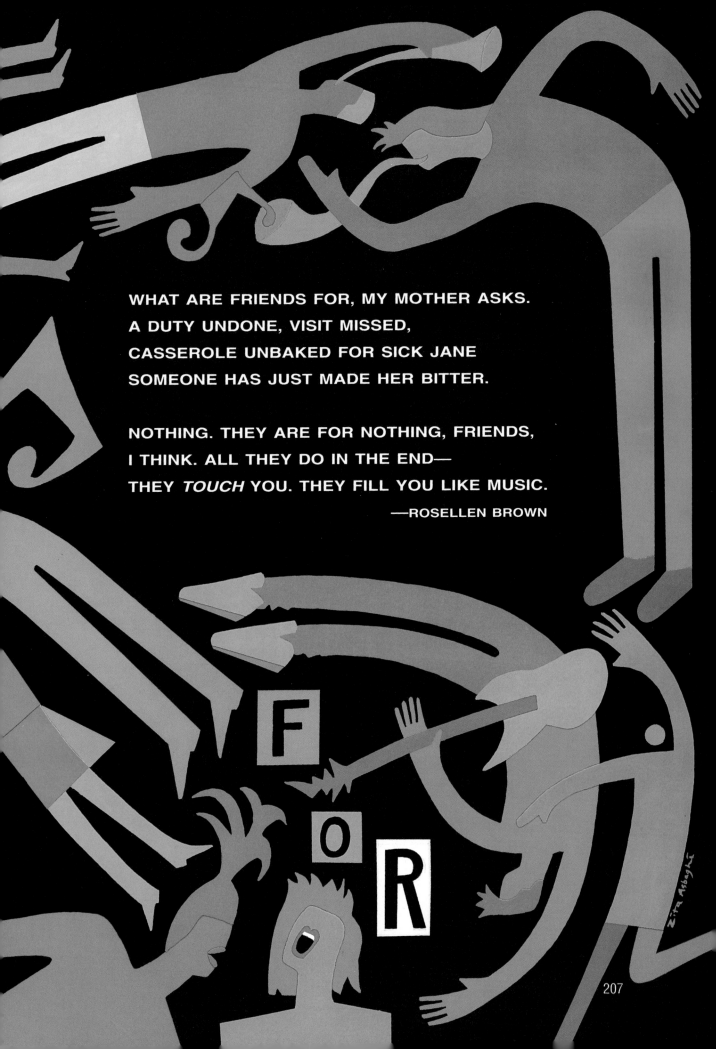

WHAT ARE FRIENDS FOR, MY MOTHER ASKS.
A DUTY UNDONE, VISIT MISSED,
CASSEROLE UNBAKED FOR SICK JANE
SOMEONE HAS JUST MADE HER BITTER.

NOTHING. THEY ARE FOR NOTHING, FRIENDS,
I THINK. ALL THEY DO IN THE END—
THEY *TOUCH* YOU. THEY FILL YOU LIKE MUSIC.
—ROSELLEN BROWN

# MEET *Jack Finney*

Menacing pod creatures who steal people's emotions and a man who finds love and happiness only by traveling back in time are only two of the strange fantasies imagined by Jack Finney, an author who is a bit of a mystery himself. His real name is Walter Braden Finney, and he was born in Milwaukee in 1911, but we know very little else about him. Finney chooses to communicate with the world primarily through his stories and novels.

Finney's first novel, *The Body Snatchers*, became the classic science fiction movie *The Invasion of the Body Snatchers*. His other best-selling novel, *Time and Again*, made time travel seem absolutely real to millions of readers. In addition, he has written many stories of mystery, fantasy, and science fiction, tales in which some strange or wonderful adventure suddenly becomes part of everyday life. He is famous for the kind of gripping plots that make people say, "I started this story and got so caught up that I couldn't put it down until I finished it ."

the

# LOVE
# LETTER

*by Jack Finney*

I've heard of secret drawers in old desks, of course; who hasn't? But the day I bought my desk I wasn't thinking of secret drawers, and I know very well I didn't have any least premonition or feel of mystery about it. I spotted it in the window of a secondhand store near my apartment and went in to look it over, and the proprietor told me where he got it. It came from one of the last of the big old mid-Victorian houses in Brooklyn; they were tearing it down over on Brock Place, a few blocks away, and he'd bought the desk along with some other furniture, dishes, glassware, light fixtures, and so on. But it didn't stir my imagination particularly; I never wondered or cared who might have used it long ago. I bought it and lugged it home because it was cheap and because it was small. I fastened the legless little wall desk to my living-room wall with heavy screws directly into the studding.

I'm 24 years old, tall and thin, and I live in Brooklyn to save money and work in Manhattan to make it. When you're 24 and a bachelor, you usually figure you'll be married before much longer, and since they tell me that takes money, I'm reasonably

ambitious and bring work home from the office every
once in a while. And maybe every couple of weeks or
so I write a letter to my folks in Florida. So I'd been
needing a desk; there's no table in my phone-booth
kitchenette, and I'd been trying to work at a wobbly
little end table I couldn't get my knees under.

So I bought the desk one Saturday afternoon
and spent an hour or more fastening it to the wall.
It was after six when I finished. I had a date that
night, and so I had time to stand and admire it for

only a minute or so. It was made of heavy wood, with a slant top like a kid's school desk, and with the same sort of space underneath to put things into. But the back of it rose a good two feet above the desk top and was full of pigeonholes like an old-style roll-top desk's. Underneath the pigeonholes was a row of three brass-knobbed little drawers. It was all pretty ornate, the drawer ends carved, some fancy scroll-work extending up over the back and out from the sides to help brace it against the wall. I dragged a chair up; sat down at the desk to try it for height; then got showered, shaved, and dressed and went over to Manhattan to pick up my date.

I'm trying to be honest about what happened, and I'm convinced that includes the way I felt when I got home around 2:00 or 2:30 that morning; I'm certain that what happened wouldn't have happened at all if I'd felt any other way. I'd had a good-enough time that evening; we'd gone to an early movie that wasn't too bad and then had dinner, a drink or so, and some dancing afterward. And the girl, Roberta Haig, is pretty nice—bright, pleasant, good-looking. But while I was walking home from the subway, the Brooklyn streets quiet and deserted, it occurred to me that although I'd probably see her again, I didn't really care whether I did or not. And I wondered, as I often had lately, whether there was something wrong with me, whether I'd ever meet a girl I desperately wanted to be with—the only way a man can get married, it seems to me.

So when I stepped into my apartment I knew I wasn't going to feel like sleep for a while. I was restless, half-irritated for no good reason, and I took off my coat and yanked down my tie, wondering whether I wanted a drink or some coffee. Then—I'd half forgotten about it—I saw the desk I'd bought that afternoon, and I walked over and sat down at it, thoroughly examining it for the first time.

I lifted the top and stared down into the empty space underneath it. Lowering the top, I reached into one of the pigeonholes, and my hand and shirt cuff came out streaked with old dust; the holes were a good foot deep. I pulled open one of the little brass-knobbed drawers, and there was a shred of paper in one of its corners, nothing else. I pulled the drawer all the way out and studied its construction, turning it in my hands; it was a solidly made, beautifully mortised little thing. Then I pushed my hand into the drawer opening; it went in to about the middle of my hand before my fingertips touched the back. There was nothing in there.

For a few moments I just sat at the desk, thinking vaguely that I could write a letter to my folks. And then it suddenly occurred to me that the little drawer in my hand was only half a foot long, while the pigeonholes just above the drawer extended a good foot back.

Shoving my hand into the opening again, exploring with my fingertips, I found a grooved indentation and pulled out the tiny secret drawer that lay in back of the first. For an instant I was excited at the glimpse of papers inside it. Then I felt a stab of disappointment as I saw what they were. There was a little sheaf of folded writing paper, plain white, but yellowed with age at the edges, and the sheets were all blank. There were three or four blank envelopes to match, and underneath them a small, round, glass bottle of ink; because it had been upside down, the cork remaining moist and tight in the bottle mouth, a good third of the ink had remained unevaporated still. Beside the bottle lay a plain, black wooden pen holder, the pen point reddish-black with old ink. There was nothing else in the drawer.

And then, putting the things back into the drawer, I felt the slight extra thickness of one blank envelope, saw that it was sealed, and ripped it open to

find the letter inside. The folded paper opened
stiffly, the crease permanent with age, and even before
I saw the date I knew this letter was old. The handwriting was obviously feminine, and beautifully clear—it's
called Spencerian, isn't it?—the letters perfectly formed
and very ornate, the capitals especially being a whirl of
dainty curlicues. The ink was rust-black, the date at the
top of the page was May 14, 1882, and reading it, I saw
that it was a love letter. It began:

*Dearest! Papa, Mamma, Willy and Cook are long re-
tired and to sleep. Now, the night far advanced, the house
silent, I alone remain awake, at last free to speak to you
as I choose. Yes, I am willing to say it! Heart of mine, I
crave your bold glance, I long for the tender warmth of
your look; I welcome your ardency, and prize it; for what
else should these be taken but sweet tribute to me?*

I smiled a little; it was hard to believe that people
had once expressed themselves in elaborate phrasings
of this kind, but they had. The letter continued, and I
wondered why it had never been sent:

*Dear one: Do not ever change your ways. Never
address me other than with what consideration my*

utterances should deserve. If I be foolish and whimsical, deride me sweetly if you will. But if I speak with seriousness, respond always with what care you deem my thoughts worthy. For, oh my beloved, I am sick to death of the indulgent smile and tolerant glance with which a woman's fancies are met. As I am repelled by the false gentleness and nicety of manner which too often ill conceal the wantonness they attempt to mask, I speak of the man I am to marry; if you could but save me from that!

But you cannot. You are everything I prize; warmly and honestly ardent, respectful in heart as well as in manner, true and loving. You are as I wish you to be—for

*you exist only in my mind. But figment though you are,
and though I shall never see your like, you are more
dear to me than he to whom I am betrothed.*

*I think of you constantly. I dream of you. I speak
with you, in my mind and heart; would you existed
outside them! Sweetheart, good night; dream of me, too.*

*With all my love, I am,
your Helen*

At the bottom of the page, as I'm sure she'd been
taught in school, was written, "Miss Helen Elizabeth
Worley, Brooklyn, New York," and as I stared down at
it now I was no longer smiling at this cry from the
heart in the middle of a long-ago night.

The night is a strange time when you're alone
in it, the rest of your world asleep. If I'd found that
letter in the daytime, I'd have smiled and shown it
to a few friends, then forgotten it. But alone here
now, a window partly open, a cool late-night freshness stirring the quiet air—it was impossible to think
of the girl who had written this letter as a very old
lady, or probably long since dead. As I read her
words, she seemed real and alive to me, sitting—or
so I pictured her—pen in hand at this desk, in a
long, white, old-fashioned dress, her young hair
piled on top of her head, in the dead of a night like
this, here in Brooklyn almost in sight of where I now
sat. And my heart went out to her as I stared down
at her secret, hopeless appeal against the world and
time she lived in.

I am trying to explain why I answered that
letter. There in the silence of a timeless spring night
it seemed natural enough to uncork that old bottle,
pick up the pen beside it, and then, spreading a
sheet of yellowing old notepaper on the desk top, to
begin to write. I felt that I was communicating with
a still-living young woman when I wrote:

*Helen: I have just read the letter in the secret drawer of your desk, and I wish I knew how I could possibly help you. I can't tell what you might think of me if there were a way I could reach you. But you are someone I am certain I would like to know. I hope you are beautiful, but you needn't be; you're a girl I could like, and maybe ardently, and if I did I promise you I'd be true and loving. Do the best you can, Helen Elizabeth Worley, in the time and place you are; I can't reach you or help you. But I'll think of you. And maybe I'll dream of you, too.*

*Yours,*

*Jake Belknap*

I was grinning a little sheepishly as I signed my name, knowing I'd read through what I'd written, then crumple the old sheet and throw it away. But I was glad I'd written it—and I didn't throw it away. Still caught in the feeling of the warm, silent night, it suddenly seemed to me that throwing my letter away would turn the writing of it into a meaningless and foolish thing, though maybe what I did seems more foolish still. I folded the paper, put it into one of the envelopes, and sealed it. Then I dipped the pen into the old ink and wrote "Miss Helen Worley" on the face of the envelope.

I suppose this can't be explained. You'd have to have been where I was and felt as I did to understand it, but I wanted to mail that letter. I simply quit examining my feelings and quit trying to be rational: I was suddenly determined to complete what I'd begun, just as far as I was able to go.

My parents sold their old home in New Jersey when my father retired two years ago, and now they live in Florida and enjoy it. And when my mother cleared out the old house I grew up in, she packed up and mailed me a huge package of useless things I was glad to have. There were class photographs dating from grammar school through college, old books I'd read as a kid, Boy Scout pins—a mass of junk of that sort, including a stamp collection I'd had in grade school. Now I found these things on my hall-closet shelf, in the box they'd come in, and I found my old stamp album.

It's funny how things can stick in your mind over the years; standing at the open closet door, I turned the pages of that beat-up old album directly to the stamps I remembered buying from another kid with 75¢ I had earned cutting grass. There they lay, lightly fastened to the page with a little gummed-paper hinge: a pair of mint-condition two-cent United States stamps, issued in 1869. And standing there in the hallway looking down at them, I once again got something of the thrill I'd had as a kid when I acquired them. It's a handsome stamp, square in shape, with an ornate border and a tiny engraving in the center: a rider on a galloping post horse. And for all I knew they might have been worth a fair amount of money by now, especially an unseparated pair of stamps. But back at the desk I pulled one of them loose, tearing carefully through the perforation; licked the back; and fastened it to the faintly yellowing old envelope.

I'd thought no further than that; by now, I suppose, I was in almost a kind of trance. I shoved the old ink bottle and pen into a hip pocket, picked up my letter, and walked out of my apartment.

Brock Place, three blocks away, was deserted when I reached it, the parked cars motionless at the curbs, the high, late moonlight softening the lines of the big concrete-block supermarket at the corner. Then, as I walked on, my letter in my hand, there stood the old house, just past a little shoe-repair shop. It stood far back from the broken cast-iron fence in the center of its wide weed-grown lot, black-etched in the moonlight, and I stopped on the walk and stood staring up at it.

The high-windowed old roof was gone, the interior nearly gutted, the yard strewn with splintered boards and great chunks of torn plaster. The windows and doors were all removed, the openings hollow in the clear wash of light. But the high old walls, last of all to go, still stood, tall and dignified in their old-fashioned strength and outmoded charm.

Then I walked through the opening where a gate had once hung, up the cracked and weed-grown brick pavement toward the wide old porch. And there on one of the ornate fluted posts, I saw the house number deeply and elaborately carved into the old wood. At the wide flat porch rail leading down to the walk, I brought out my ink and pen and copied the number carefully onto my envelope; "972," I printed under the name of the girl who had once lived here, "BROCK PLACE, BROOKLYN, N.Y." Then I turned toward the street again, my envelope in my hand.

There was a mailbox at the next corner, and I stopped beside it. But to drop this letter into that box, knowing in advance that it could go only to the dead-letter office, would again, I couldn't help feeling, turn the writing of it into an empty, meaningless act, and after a moment I walked on past the box, crossed the street, and turned right, suddenly knowing exactly where I was going.

I walked four blocks through the night, passing a hack stand with a single cab, its driver asleep with

his arms and head cradled on
the wheel, and a night watchman sitting on
a standpipe protruding from the building wall, smoking a pipe; he nodded as I passed, and I nodded in
response. I turned left at the next corner, walked half
a block more, then turned up onto the worn stone
steps of the Wister postal substation.

It must easily be one of the oldest postal sub-
stations in the borough, built, I suppose, not much
later than during the decade following the Civil War.
And I can't imagine that the inside has changed much
at all. The floor is marble, the ceiling high, the wood-
work dark and carved. The outer lobby is open at all
times, as are post-office lobbies everywhere, and as I
pushed through the old swinging doors I saw that it
was deserted. Somewhere behind the opaque blind
windows a light burned dimly far in the rear of the
post office, and I had an impression of subdued activity back there. But the lobby itself was dim and silent,

and as I walked across the worn stone of its floor, I knew I was seeing all around me precisely what Brooklynites had seen for no telling how many generations long dead.

The Post Office has always seemed an institution of vague mystery to me, an ancient and worn but still functioning mechanism that is not operated, but only tended by each succeeding generation of men to come along. It is a place where occasionally plainly addressed letters with clearly written return addresses go astray and are lost, to end up no one knows where for reasons impossible to discover, as the postal employee of whom you inquire will tell you. And its vague air of mystery, for me, is made up of stories—well, you've read them, too, from time to time, the odd little stories in your newspaper. A letter bearing a postmark of 1906 is delivered today—simply because inexplicably it arrived at some post office along with the other mail, with no explanation from anyone now alive. Or sometimes it's a postcard of greeting— from the Chicago World's Fair of 1893, maybe. And once, tragically, as I remember reading, it was an acceptance of a proposal of marriage offered in 1931— and received today, a lifetime too late, by the man who made it and who married someone else and is now a grandfather.

I pushed the worn brass plate open and dropped my letter into the silent blackness of the slot, and it disappeared forever with no sound. Then I turned and left to walk home with a feeling of fulfillment, of having done, at least, everything I possibly could in response to the silent cry for help I'd found in the secrecy of the old desk.

Next morning I felt the way almost anyone might. Standing at the bathroom mirror shaving, remembering what I'd done the night before, I grinned, feeling foolish but at the same time secretly pleased with myself. I was glad I'd written and solemnly mailed that letter, and now I realized why I'd put no return address on the envelope. I didn't want it to come forlornly back to me with NO SUCH PERSON, or whatever the phrase is, stamped on the envelope. There'd once been such a girl, and last night she still existed for me. And I didn't want to see my letter to her—rubber-stamped, scribbled on and unopened—to prove that there no longer was.

I was terrifically busy all the next week. I work for a wholesale-grocery concern; we got a big new account, a chain of supermarkets, and that meant extra work for everyone. More often than not I had lunch at my desk in the office and worked several evenings besides. I had dates the two evenings I was free. On Friday afternoon I was at the main public library in Manhattan, at Fifth Avenue and Forty-second, copying statistics from half a dozen trade publications for a memorandum I'd been assigned to write over the weekend on the new account.

Late in the afternoon the man sitting beside me at the big reading-room table closed his book, stowed away his glasses, picked up his hat from the table, and left. I sat back in my chair, glancing at my watch. Then I looked over at the book he'd left on the table. It was a big one-volume pictorial history of New York put out by Columbia University, and I dragged it over and began leafing through it.

I skimmed over the first sections on colonial and precolonial New York pretty quickly, but when the old sketches and drawings began giving way to actual photographs, I turned the pages more slowly. I leafed past the first photos, taken around the mid-century, and then past those of the Civil War period. But when

I reached the first photograph of the 1870s—it was a view of Fifth Avenue in 1871—I began reading the captions under each one.

I knew it would be too much to hope to find a photograph of Brock Place, in Helen Worley's time especially, and of course I didn't. But I knew there'd surely be photographs taken in Brooklyn during the 1880s, and a few pages farther on I found what I'd hoped I might. In clear, sharp detail and beautifully reproduced lay a big half-page photograph of a street less than a quarter mile from Brock Place, and staring down at it, there in the library, I knew that Helen Worley must often have walked along this very sidewalk. "Varney Street, 1881," the caption said. "A typical Brooklyn residential street of the period."

Varney Street today—I walk two blocks of it every night coming home from work—is a wasteland. I pass four cinder-packed used-car lots; a shabby concrete garage, the dead earth in front of it littered with rusting car parts and old tires; and a half dozen or so nearly paintless boardinghouses, one with a soiled card in its window reading MASSAGE. It's a nondescript, joyless street, and it's impossible to believe that there has ever been a tree on its entire length.

But there has been. There in sharp black-and-white, in the book on the table before me, lay Varney Street, 1881, and from the wide grass-covered parkways between the cut-stone curb and sidewalks, the thick old long-gone trees rose high on both sides to meet, intertwine, and roof the wide street with green. The photograph had been taken, apparently, from the street—it had been possible to do that then, in a day of occasional slow-trotting horses and buggies—and the camera was aimed at an angle to one side, toward the sidewalk and the big houses beyond it, looking down the walk for several hundred feet.

The old walk, there in the foreground under the great trees, appeared to be at least six feet wide, spacious enough easily for a family to walk down it four or five abreast—as families did, in those times, walk together down the sidewalks under the trees. And beyond the walk, widely separated and set far back across the fine old lawns, rose the great houses, the 10-, 12-, and 14-room family houses, two or more stories high, and with attics above them for children to play in and discover the relics of childhoods before them. Their windows were tall, and they were framed on the outside with ornamented wood. And in the solid construction of every one of those lost houses in that ancient photograph there had been left over the time, skill, money, and inclination to decorate their eaves with scrollwork—to finish a job with craftsmanship and pride. And time, too, to build huge wide porches on which families sat on summer evenings with palm-leaf fans.

Far down that lovely tree-sheltered street—out of focus and indistinct—walked the retreating figure of a long-skirted, puff-sleeved woman, her summer parasol open at her back. Of the thousands of long-dead girls it might have been, I knew this could not be Helen Worley. Yet it wasn't completely impossible, I told myself; this was a street, precisely as I saw it now, down which she must often have walked, and I let myself think that yes, this was she. Maybe I live in what is for me the wrong time, and I was filled now with the most desperate yearning to be there, on that peaceful street—to walk off, past the edges of the scene on the printed page before me, into the old and beautiful Brooklyn of long ago. And to draw near and overtake that bobbing parasol in the distance

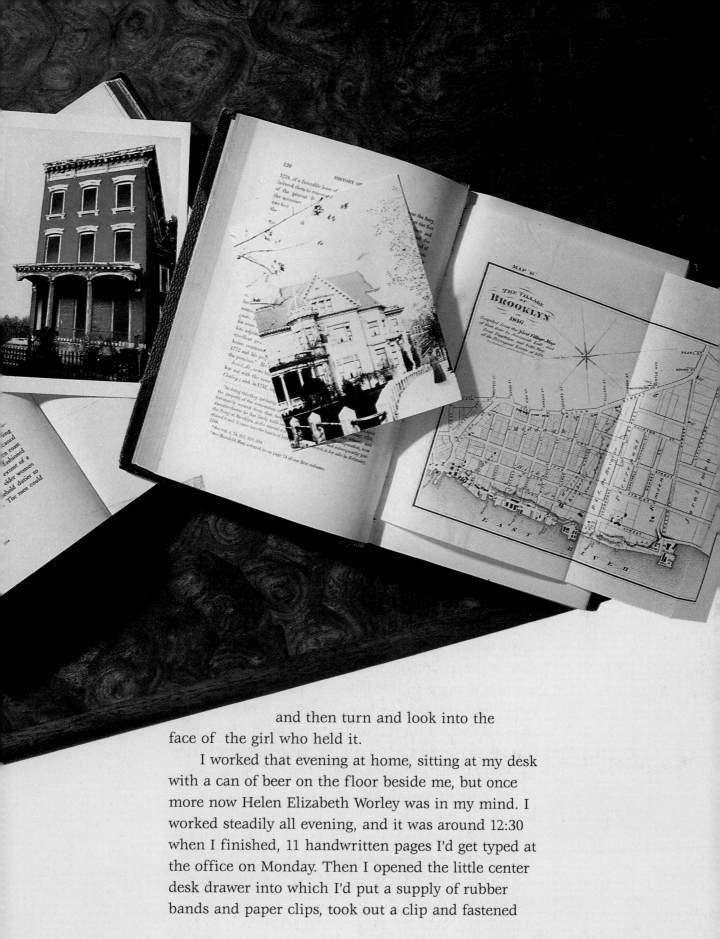

and then turn and look into the
face of the girl who held it.

I worked that evening at home, sitting at my desk
with a can of beer on the floor beside me, but once
more now Helen Elizabeth Worley was in my mind. I
worked steadily all evening, and it was around 12:30
when I finished, 11 handwritten pages I'd get typed at
the office on Monday. Then I opened the little center
desk drawer into which I'd put a supply of rubber
bands and paper clips, took out a clip and fastened

the pages together, and sat back in my chair, taking a swallow of beer. The little center desk drawer stood half open as I'd left it, and then, as my eye fell on it, I realized suddenly that of course it, too, must have another secret drawer behind it.

I hadn't thought of that. It simply hadn't occurred to me the week before, in my interest and excitement over the letter I'd found behind the first drawer of the row, and I'd been too busy all week to think of it since. But now I set down my beer, pulled the center drawer all the way out, reached behind it and found the little groove in the smooth wood I touched. Then I brought out the second secret little drawer.

I'll tell you what I think, what I'm certain of, though I don't claim to be speaking scientifically; I don't think science has a thing to do with it. The night *is* a strange time; things *are* different at night, as every human being knows somewhere deep inside him. And I think this: Brooklyn has changed over the decades; it is no longer the same place at all. But here and there, still, are little islands—isolated remnants of the way things once were. And the Wister postal substation is one of them; it has changed really not at all. And I think that at night—late at night, the world asleep, when the sounds of things as they are now are nearly silent, and the sight of things as they are now is vague in the darkness—the boundary between here and then wavers. At certain moments and places it fades. I think that there in the dimness of the old Wister post office, in the dead of night, lifting my letter to Helen Worley toward the old brass door of the letter drop—I think that I stood on one side of that slot in this year and that I dropped my letter, properly stamped, written and addressed in the ink and on the very paper of Helen Worley's youth, into the Brooklyn of 1882 on the other side of that worn old slot.

I believe that—I'm not even interested in proving it—but I believe it. Because now, from that second secret little drawer, I brought out the paper I found in it, opened it, and in rust-black ink on yellowing old paper I read:

*Please, oh, please—who are you? Where can I reach you? Your letter arrived today in the second morning post, and I have wandered the house and garden ever since in an agony of excitement. I cannot conceive how you saw my letter in its secret place, but since you did, perhaps you will see this one too. Oh, tell me your letter is no hoax or cruel joke! Willy, if it is you; if you have discovered my letter and think to deceive your sister with a prank, I pray you to tell me! But if it is not—if I now address someone who has truly responded to my most secret hopes—do not longer keep me ignorant of who and where you are. For I, too—and I confess it willingly—long to see you! And I, too, feel and am most certain of it, that if I could know you, I would love you. It is impossible for me to think otherwise.*

*I must hear from you again; I shall not rest until I do.*

*I remain, most sincerely,*
*Helen Elizabeth Worley*

After a long time, I opened the first little drawer of the old desk and took out the pen and ink I'd found there and a sheet of the note paper.

For minutes then, the pen in my hand, I sat there in the night staring down at the empty paper on the desk top; finally, then, I dipped the pen into the old ink and wrote:

*Helen, my dear: I don't know how to say this so it will seem even comprehensible to you. But I do exist, here in Brooklyn, less than three blocks from where you now read this. We are separated not by space, but by the years which lie between us. Now I own the desk which you once had, and at which you wrote the note I found in it. Helen, all I can tell you is that I answered that note, mailed it late at night at the old Wister station, and that somehow it reached you, as I hope this will too. This is no hoax! Can you imagine anyone playing a joke that cruel? I live in a Brooklyn, within sight of your house, that you cannot imagine. It is a city whose streets are now crowded with wheeled vehicles propelled by engines. And it is a city extending far beyond the limits you know, with a population of millions, so crowded there is hardly room any longer for trees. From my window as I write I can see—across Brooklyn Bridge, which is hardly changed from the way you, too, can see it now—Manhattan Island, and rising from it are the lighted silhouettes of stone-and-steel buildings more than one thousand feet high.*

*You must believe me. I live, I exist, many years after you read this; and I feel I have fallen in love with you.*

I sat for some moments staring at the wall, trying to figure out how to explain something I was certain was true. Then I wrote:

*Helen: There are three secret drawers in our desk. Into the first you put only the letter I found. You cannot now add something to that drawer and hope that it will reach me. For I*

*have already opened that drawer and found only the let-*
*ter you put there. Nothing else can now come down*
*through the years to me in that drawer, for you cannot*
*now alter what you have already done.*

*Into the second drawer, in 1882, you put the note*
*which lies before me, which I found when I opened that*
*drawer a few minutes ago. You put nothing else into it,*
*and now that, too, cannot be changed.*

*But I haven't opened the third drawer, Helen. Not*
*yet! It is the last way you can still reach me, and the last*
*time. I will mail this as I did before, then wait. In a week*
*I will open the last drawer.*

*Jake Belknap*

It was a long week. I worked and I kept busy daytimes, but at night I thought of hardly anything but the third secret drawer in my desk. I was terribly tempted to open it earlier, telling myself that whatever might lie in it had been put there decades before and must be there now, but I wasn't sure, and I waited.

Then, late at night, a week to the hour after I'd mailed my second letter at the old Wister post office, I pulled out the third drawer, reached in, and brought out the last secret drawer, which lay behind it. My hand was actually shaking, and for a moment I couldn't bear to look directly—something lay in the drawer—and I turned my head away. Then I looked.

I'd expected a long letter, very long, of many pages, her last communication with me, and full of everything she wanted to say. But there was no letter at all. It was a photograph, about three inches square, a faded sepia in color, mounted on heavy stiff cardboard, and with the photographer's name in tiny gold script down in the corner: *Brunner & Holland, Parisian Photography, Brooklyn, N.Y.*

The photograph showed the head and shoulders of a girl in a high-necked dark dress with a cameo brooch at the collar. Her dark hair was swept tightly back, covering the ears, in a style which no longer suits our ideas of beauty. But the stark severity of that dress and hair style couldn't spoil the beauty of the face that smiled out at me from that old photograph. It wasn't beautiful in any classic sense, I suppose. The brows were unplucked and somewhat heavier than we are used to. But it is the soft warm smile of her lips, and her eyes—large and serene as she looks out at me over the years—that make Helen Elizabeth Worley a beautiful woman. Across the bottom of her photograph she had written, "I will never forget." And as I sat there at the old desk, staring at what she had written, I understood that, of course, that was all there was to say— what else?—on this, the last time, as she knew, that she'd ever be able to reach me.

It wasn't the last time, though. There was one final way for Helen Worley to communicate with me over the years, and it took me a long time, as it must have taken her, to realize it. Only a week ago, on my fourth day of searching, I finally found it. It was late in the evening, and the sun was almost gone, when I found the old headstone among all the others stretching off in rows under the quiet trees. And then I read the inscription etched in the weathered old stone: *Helen Elizabeth Worley*—**1861—1934.** Under this were the words, **I NEVER FORGOT.**

And neither will I.

# Oranges

BY
GARY SOTO

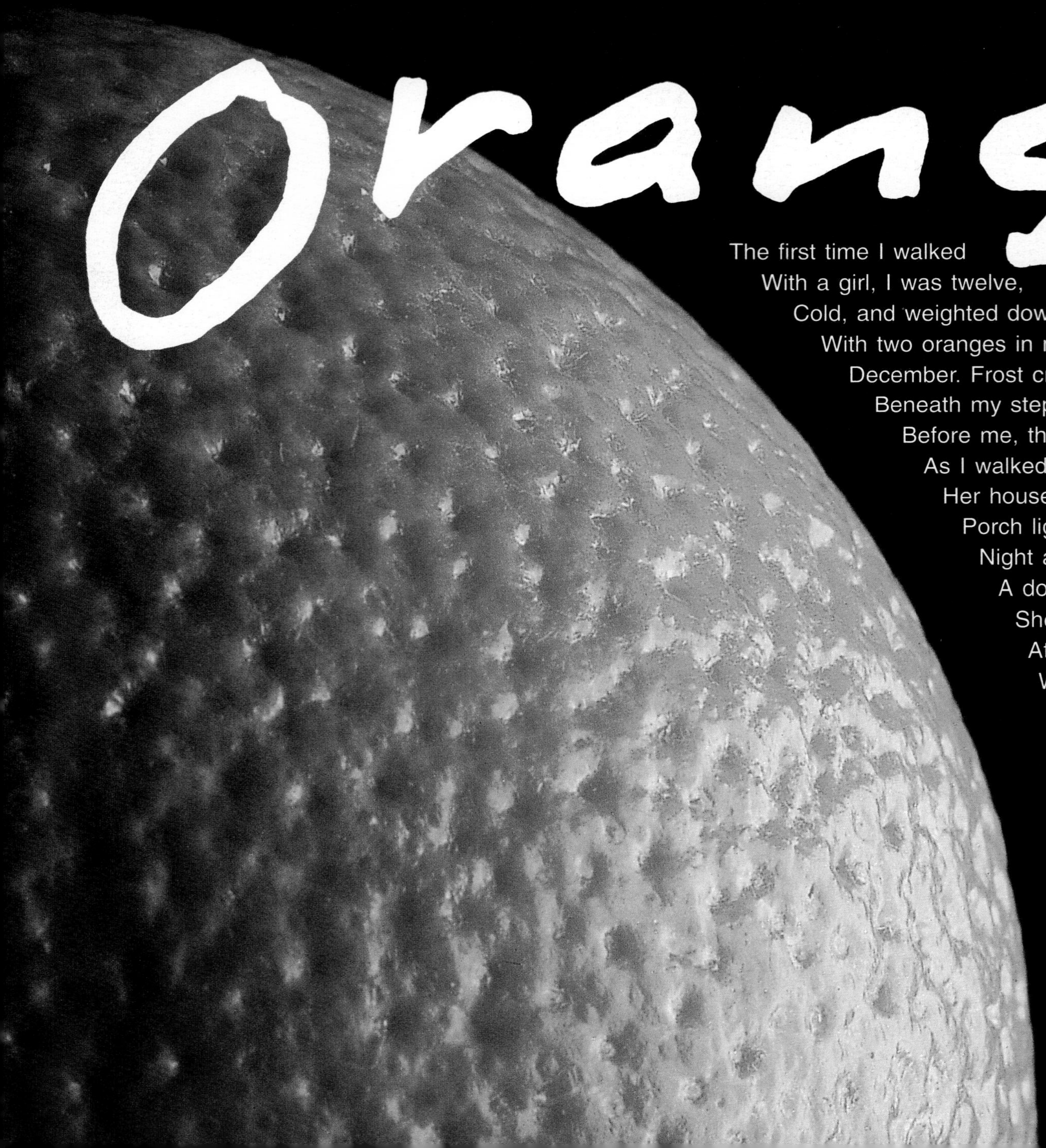

The first time I walked
With a girl, I was twelve,
Cold, and weighted down
With two oranges in my jacket.
December. Frost cracking
Beneath my steps, my breath
Before me, then gone,
As I walked toward
Her house, the one whose
Porch light burned yellow
Night and day, in any weather.
A dog barked at me, until
She came out pulling
At her gloves, face bright
With rouge. I smiled,
Touched her shoulder, and led
Her down the street, across
A used car lot and a line
Of newly planted trees,
Until we were breathing
Before a drugstore. We
Entered, the tiny bell
Bringing a saleslady
Down a narrow aisle of goods.
I turned to the candies
Tiered like bleachers,
And asked what she wanted—

Light in her eyes, a smile
Starting at the corners
Of her mouth. I fingered
A nickel in my pocket,
And when she lifted a chocolate
That cost a dime,
I didn't say anything.
I took the nickel from
My pocket, then an orange,
And set them quietly on
The counter. When I looked up,
The lady's eyes met mine,
And held them, knowing
Very well what it was all
About.

    Outside,
A few cars hissing past,
Fog hanging like old
Coats between the trees.
I took my girl's hand
In mine for two blocks,
Then released it to let
Her unwrap the chocolate.
I peeled my orange
That was so bright against
The gray of December
That, from some distance,
Someone might have thought
I was making a fire in my
hands.

233

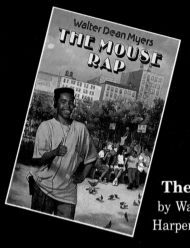

## The Mouse Rap

by Walter Dean Myers
Harper & Row, 1990

Ka-phoomp!  Ka-phoomp!  Da Doom Da Dooom!
Ka-phoomp!  Ka-phoomp!  Da Doom Da Dooom!
You can call me Mouse, 'cause that's my tag
I'm into it all, everything's my bag
You know I can run, you know I can hoop
I can do it alone, or in a group
My ace is Styx, he'll always do
Add Bev and Sheri, and you got my crew
My tag is Mouse, and it'll never fail
And just like a mouse I got me a tale

## Circus Dreams:
## The Making of a Circus Artist

by Kathleen Cushman  and Montana Miller
Little, Brown, 1990

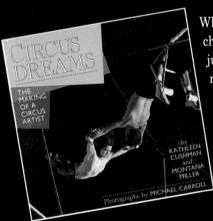

What you
choose to
juggle is as
much a
part
of the act
as how
you do it.

Through

234

Thick and Thin

# A CROWN OF WILD OLIVE

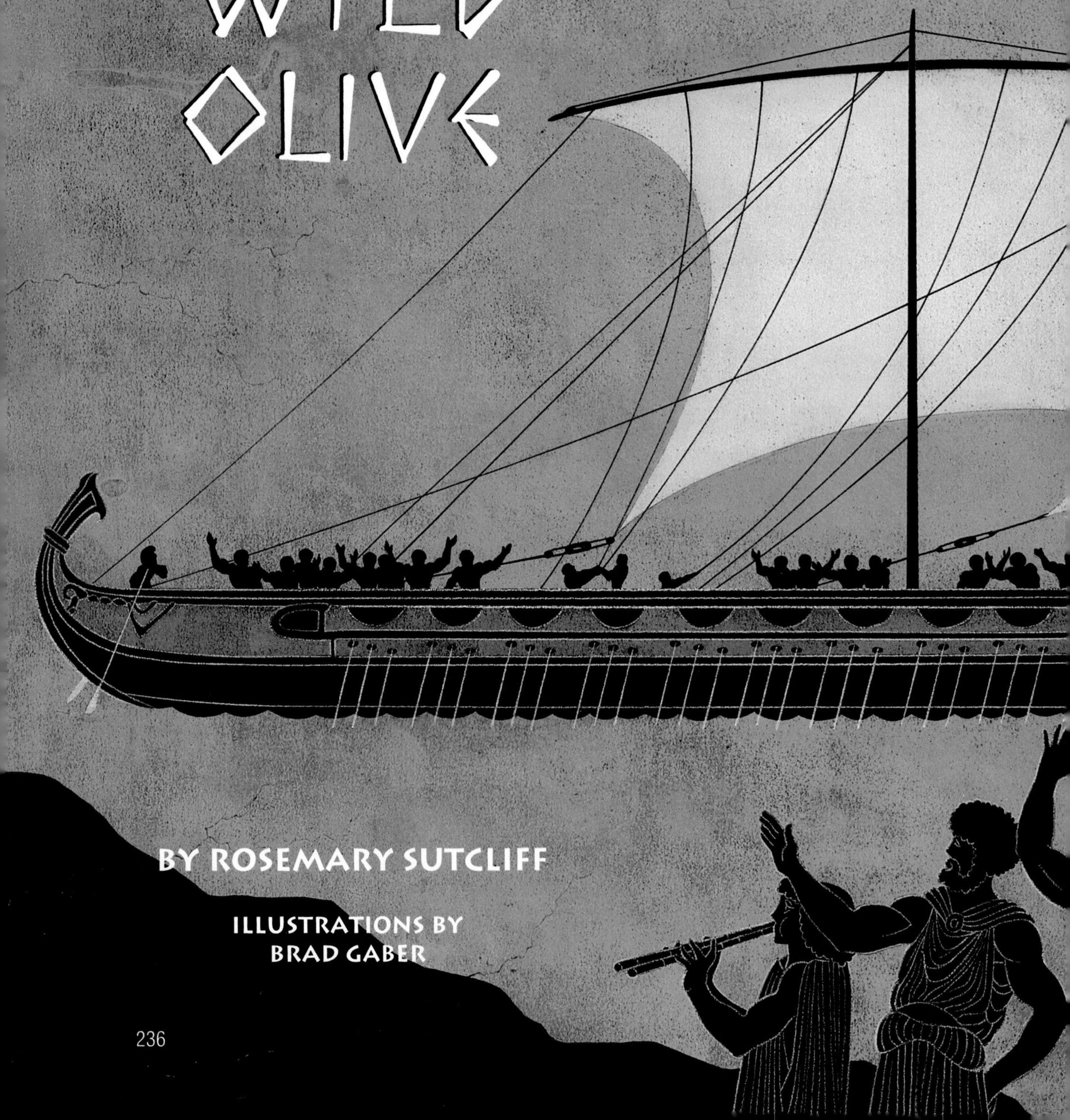

BY ROSEMARY SUTCLIFF

ILLUSTRATIONS BY
BRAD GABER

IT WAS STILL EARLY IN
THE DAY, BUT ALREADY
IT WAS GROWING HOT;
THE WHITE DRY HEAT
OF THE GREEK SUMMER
AND THE FAINT
OFF-SHORE WIND THAT
MADE IT BEARABLE HAD
BEGUN TO FEATHER
THE WATER, BREAKING
AND BLURRING THE
REFLECTIONS OF THE
GALLEYS LYING AT
ANCHOR IN PIRAEUS
HARBOUR.

Half Athens, it seemed, had crowded down to the port to watch the *Paralos,* the State Galley, sail for the Isthmus, taking their finest athletes on the first stage of their journey to Olympia.

Every fourth summer it happened; every fourth summer for more than three hundred years. Nothing was allowed to stand in the way, earthquake or pestilence or even war—even the long and weary war which, after a while of uneasy peace, had broken out again last year between Athens and Sparta.

Back in the spring the Herald had come, proclaiming the Truce of the Games; safe conduct through all lands and across all seas, both for the athletes and for those who went to watch them compete. And now, from every Greek state and from colonies and settlements all round the Mediterranean, the athletes would be gathering. . . .

Aboard the *Paralos* was all the ordered bustle of departure, ropes being cast off, rowers in their places at the oars. The Athenian athletes and their trainers with them had gathered on the afterdeck. Amyntas, son of Ariston, had drawn a little apart from the rest. He was the youngest there, still several months from his eighteenth birthday and somewhat conscious that he had not yet sacrificed his boy's long hair to Apollo, while the rest, even of those entered for the boys' events—you counted as a boy at Olympia until you were twenty—were already short-haired and doing their military service. A few of them even had scars gained in border clashes with the Spartans, to prove that their real place, whatever it might be on the race track or in the wrestling pit, was with the men. Amyntas envied them. He was proud that he had been picked so young to run for Athens in the Boys' Double Stade, the Four Hundred Yards. But he was lonely. He was bound in with all the others by their shared training; but they were bound together by something else, by another kind of life, other loyalties and shared experiences and private jokes, from which he was still shut out.

The last ropes holding ship to shore were being cast off now. Fathers and brothers and friends on the jetty were calling last moment advice and good luck wishes. Nobody called to Amyntas, but he turned and looked back to where his father stood among the crowd. Ariston had been a runner too in his day, before a Spartan spear wound had stiffened his left knee and spoiled his own hopes of an Olympic Olive

Crown. Everyone said that he and Amyntas were very alike, and looking back now at the slight dark man who still held himself like a runner, Amyntas hoped with a warm rush of pride, that they were right. He wished he had said so, before he came aboard; there were so many things he would have liked to have said, but he was even more tongue-tied with his father than he was with the rest of the world, when it came to saying the things that mattered. Now, as the last ropes fell away, he flung up his hand in salute, and tried to put them all into one wordless message. "I'll run the best race that's in me, Father—and if the Gods let me win it, I'll remember that I'm winning for us both."

Among the waving crowd, his father flung up an answering hand, as though he had somehow received the message. The water was widening between ship and shore; the Bos'n struck up the rowing time on his flute, and the rowers bent to their oars, sending the *Paralos* through the water towards the harbour mouth. Soon the crowd on shore was only a shingle of dark and coloured and white along the waterfront. But far off beyond the roofs of the warehouses and the covered docks, a flake of light showed where high over Athens the sunlight flashed back from the upraised spear-blade of the great Athene of the Citadel, four miles away.

They were out round the mole now, the one sail broke out from the mast, and they headed for the open gulf.

That night they beached the *Paralos* and made camp on the eastern-most point of the long island of Salamis; and not long past noon next day they went ashore at the Isthmus and took horse for Corinth on the far side, where a second galley was waiting to take them down the coast. At evening on the fifth day they rode down into the shallow valley where Olympian Zeus the Father of Gods and men had his sanctuary, and where the Sacred Games were celebrated in his honour.

What with the long journey and the strangeness of everything, Amyntas took in very little of that first evening. They were met and greeted by the Council of the Games, whose president made them a speech of welcome, after which the Chief Herald read them the rules. And afterwards they ate the evening meal in the athletes' mess; food that seemed to have no more taste nor substance than the food one eats in a dream. Then the dream blended away into a dark nothingness of sleep that took Amyntas almost before he had lain down on the narrow stretcher bed in the athletes' lodging, which would be his for the next month.

He woke to the first dappled fingers of sunlight shafting in through the doorway of his cell. They wavered and danced a little, as though broken by the shadows of tree branches. Somewhere further down the valley a cuckoo was calling, and the world was real again, and his, and new as though it had been born that morning. He rolled over, and lay for a few moments, his hands behind his head, looking up at the bare rafters; then shot off the bed and through the doorway in one swallow-dive of movement, to sluice his head and shoulders in the icy water trickling from the mouth of a stone bull into a basin just outside. He came up for air, spluttering and shaking the water out of his eyes. For a moment he saw the colonnaded court and the plane tree arching over the basin through a splintered brightness of flying droplets. And then suddenly, in the brightness, there stood a boy of about his own age, who must have come out of the lodging close behind him. A boy with a lean angular body, and a dark, bony face under a shock of hair like the crest of an ill-groomed pony. For a long moment they stood looking at each other. Then Amyntas moved aside to let the other come to the conduit.

As the stranger ducked his head and shoulders under the falling water, Amyntas saw his back. From shoulder to flank it was crisscrossed with scars, past the purple stage but not yet faded to the silvery white that they would be in a few years' time; pinkish scars that looked as though the skin was still drawn uncomfortably tight over them.

He must have made some betraying sound or movement, because the other boy ducked out from under the water, thrusting the wet russet hair back out of his eyes, and demanded curtly, "Have you never seen a Spartan back before?"

So that was it. Amyntas, like everyone else, had heard dark stories of Spartan boys flogged, sometimes to death, in a ritual test of courage, before the shrine of Artemis Orthia, the Lady of the Beasts.

"No," he said, "I am Athenian." And did not add that he hoped to see plenty of Spartan backs when once he had started his military service. It was odd, the cheap jibe came neatly into his head, and yet

he did not even want to speak it. It was as though here at Olympia, the Truce of the Games was not just a rule of conduct, but something in one's heart. Instead, he added, "And my name is Amyntas."

They seemed to stand confronting each other for a long time. The Spartan boy had the look of a dog sniffing at a stranger's fist and taking his own time to make sure whether it was friendly. Then he smiled; a slow, rather grave smile, but unexpectedly warm. "And mine is Leon."

"And you're a runner." Amyntas was taking in his build and the way he stood.

"I am entered for the Double Stade."

"Then we race against each other."

Leon said in the same curt tone, "May we both run a good race."

"And meanwhile,—when did you arrive, Leon?"

"Last night, the same as you."

Amyntas, who usually found it nearly as difficult to talk to strangers as he did to his own father, was surprised to hear himself saying, "Then you'll have seen no more of Olympia than I have. Shall we go and get some clothes on and have a look round?"

But by that time more men and boys were coming out into the early sunshine, yawning and stretching the sleep out of their muscles. And Amyntas felt a hand clamp down on his shoulder, and heard the voice of Hippias his trainer, "Oh no you don't, my lad! Five days' break in training is long enough, and I've work for you before you do any sightseeing!"

After that, they were kept hard at it, on the practice track and in the wrestling school that had the names of past Olympic victors carved on the colonnade walls. For the last month's training for the Games had to be done at Olympia itself; and the last month's training was hard, in the old style that did not allow for rest days in the modern fashion that most of the Athenian trainers favoured. Everything at Olympia had to be done the old way, even to clearing the stadium of its four years' growth of grass and weeds and spreading it with fresh sand. At other Crown Games, the work was done by paid labourers, but here, the contending athletes must do it themselves, to the glory of the Gods, as they had done it in the far-off days when the Games were new. Some of them grumbled a good deal and thought it was time that the Priests of Zeus and the Council of the Games brought their ideas up to date; but to Amyntas there seemed to be a sort of rightness about the thing as it was.

His training time was passed among boys from Corinth and Epidauros, Rhodes and Samos and Macedon. At first they were just figures in outline, like people seen too far off to have faces, whom he watched with interest at track work, at javelin or discus throwing or in the wrestling pit, trying to judge their form as he knew they were trying to judge his and each other's. But gradually as the early days went by, they changed into people with faces, with personal habits, and likes and dislikes, suffering from all the strains and stresses of the last weeks before the Games. But even before those first few days were over, he and the Spartan boy had drifted into a companionable pattern of doing things together. They would sluice each other down, squatting in the stone hip-baths in the washing room after practice, and scrape the mess of rubbing oil and sand off each other's backs—it took Amyntas a little while to learn to scrape the bronze blade of the strigil straight over the scars on Leon's back as though they were not there—and when they took their turn at scraping up the four years' growth of grass and sun-dried herbs from the stadium, they generally worked together, sharing one of the big rush carrying-baskets between them. And in the evenings, after the day's training was over, or in the hot noonday break when most people stretched themselves out in the shade of the plane trees for sleep or quiet talk, they seemed, more often than not, to drift into each other's company.

Once or twice they went to have a look at the town of tents and booths that was beginning to spring up all round the Sacred Enclosure and the Gymnasium buildings—for a Games Festival drew many people beside those who came to compete or to watch; merchants and wine sellers and fortune tellers, poets determined to get poems heard, horse dealers from Corinth and Cyrene, goldsmiths and leather-workers, philosophers gathering for the pleasure of arguing with each other, sword and fire swallowers, and acrobats who could dance on their hands to the soft notes of Phrygian pipes. But Leon did not much like the crowded noisy tent-ground; and most often they wandered down to the river that flung its loop about the south side of Olympia. It had shrunk now in the summer heat, to little more than a chain of pools in the middle of its pale dried-out pebbly bed; but there was shade under the oleander trees, and generally a whisper of moving air. And lying on the bank in the shade was free. It had dawned on Amyntas quite early that the reason Leon did not like the fairground was that he had no money. The Spartans did not use money, or at least, having decided that it was a bad thing, they had no coinage but iron bars so big and heavy that nobody could carry them about, or even keep a store at home that was worth enough to be any use. They were very proud of their freedom from wealth, but it made life difficult at a gathering such as this, when they had to mix with people from other states. Leon covered up by being extremely scornful of the gay and foolish things for sale in the merchants' booths, and the acrobats who passed the bowl round for contributions after their performance; but he was just that shade too scornful to be convincing. And anyway, Amyntas had none too much money himself, to get him through the month.

So they went to the river. They were down there one hot noontide something over a week after they had first arrived at Olympia; Amyntas lying on his back, his hands behind his head, squinting up into the dark shadow-shapes of the oleander branches against the sky; Leon sitting beside him with his arms round his updrawn knees, staring out into the dazzle of sunlight over the open riverbed. They had been talking runners' talk, and suddenly Amyntas said, "I was watching the Corinthian making his practice run this morning. I don't *think* we have either of us much to fear from him."

"The Rhodian runs well," said Leon, not bringing back his gaze from the white dance of sunlight beyond the oleanders.

"But he uses himself up too quickly. He's the kind that makes all the front running at first, and has nothing left for the home stretch. Myself, I'd say that red-headed barbarian from Macedon had the better chance."

"He's well enough for speed; and he knows how and when to use it. . . . What do you give for Nikomedes' chances?"

"Nikomedes?—The boy from Megara? It's hard to say. Not much, from the form he's shown so far; but we've only seen him at practice, and he's the sort that sometimes catches fire when it comes to the real thing. . . ."

There was a long silence between them, and they heard the churring of the grasshoppers, like the heat-shimmer turned to sound. And then Amyntas said, "I think you are the one I have most to fear."

And Leon turned his head slowly and looked down at him, and said, "Have you only just woken to that? I knew the same thing of *you,* three days ago."

And they were both silent again, and suddenly a little shocked. You might think that kind of thing, but it was best not to put it into words.

Leon made a quick sign with his fingers to avert ill luck; and Amyntas scrambled to his feet. "Come on, it's time we were getting back." They were both laughing, but a little breathlessly. Leon dived to his feet also, and shot ahead as they went up through the river-side scrub. But next instant, between one flying leap and the next, he stumbled slightly, and checked; then turned back, stooping to search for something among the dusty root-tangle of dry grass and camomile. Amyntas, swerving just in time to avoid him, checked also.

"What is it?"

"Something sharp. . . ." Leon pulled out from where it had lain half-buried, the broken end of a sickle blade that looked as though it might have lain there since the last Games. "Seems it's not only the Stadium that needs clearing up." He began to walk on, carrying the jagged fragment in his hand. But Amyntas saw the blood on the dry ground where he had been standing.

"You have cut your foot."

"I know," Leon said, and went on walking.

"Yes, I *know* you know. Let me look at it."

"It's only a scratch."

"All the same—show me."

Leon stood on one leg, steadying himself with a hand on Amyntas' shoulder, and turned up the sole of his foot. "Look then. You can hardly see it."

There was a cut on the hard brown sole, not long, but deep, with the blood welling slowly. Amyntas said in sudden exasperation, "Haven't you *any* sense? Oh we all know about the Spartan boy with the fox under his cloak, and nobody but you Spartans thinks it's a particularly clever or praiseworthy story; but if you get dirt into that cut, you'll like enough have to scratch from the race!"

Leon suddenly grinned. "Nobody but we Spartans understand that story. But about the dirt, you could be right."

"I could. And that bit of iron is dirty enough for a start. Best get the wound cleaned up, in the river before we go back to the Gymnasium. Then your trainer can take over."

So with Leon sitting on a boulder at the edge of the shrunken river, Amyntas set to work with ruthless thoroughness to clean the cut. He pulled it open, the cool water running over his hands, and a thin thread of crimson fronded away downstream. It would help clean the wound to let it bleed a little; but after a few moments the bleeding almost stopped. No harm in making sure; he ducked his head to the place, sucked hard and spat crimson into the water. Then he tore a strip from the skirt of his tunic; he would have commandeered Leon's

own—after all it was Leon's foot—but he knew that the Spartan boys
were only allowed to own one tunic at a time; if he did that, Leon
would be left without a respectable tunic to wear at the Sacrifices. He
lashed the thin brown foot tightly. "Now—put your arm over my shoulder and try to keep your weight off the cut as much as you can."

"Cluck, cluck, cluck!" said Leon, but he did as Amyntas said.

As they skirted the great open space of the Hippodrome, where
the chariot races would be held on the second day of the Games, they
came up with a couple of the Athenian contingent, strolling under the
plane trees. Eudorus the wrestler looked round and his face quickened
with concern, "Run into trouble?"

"Ran into the remains of a sickle blade someone left in the long grass," Amyntas said, touching the rusty bit of metal he had taken from Leon and stuck in his own belt. "It's near the tendon, but it's all right, so long as there's no dirt left in it."

"Near the tendon, eh? Then we'd best be taking no chances." Eudorus looked at Leon. "You are Spartan, I think?—Amyntas, go and find the Spartan trainer; I'll take over here." And then to Leon again, "Will you allow me to carry you up to the lodging? It seems the simplest way."

Amyntas caught one parting glimpse of Leon's rigid face as Eudorus lifted him, lightly as a ten-year-old, and set off towards the gymnasium buildings; and laughter caught at his stomach; but mixed with the laughter was sympathy. He knew he would have been just as furious in Leon's place. All this fuss and to-do over a cut that would have been nothing in itself—if the Games had not been only three weeks off.

He set off in search of the trainer.

In the middle of that night, Amyntas woke up with a thought already shaped and complete in his mind. It was an ugly thought, and it sat on his chest and mouthed at him slyly. "Leon is the one you have most to fear. If Leon is out of the race. . . ."

He looked at it in the darkness, feeling a little sick. Then he pushed it away, and rolled over on to his face with his head in his arms, and after a while he managed to go back to sleep again.

Next day, as soon as he could slip away between training sessions, he went out into the growing town of tents and booths, and found a seller of images and votive offerings, and bought a little bronze bull with silvered horns. It cost nearly all the money that he had to spare, so that he would not now be able to buy the hunting knife with silver inlay on the hilt, that had caught his fancy a day or two since. With the little figure in his hand, he went to the Sacred Enclosure, where, among altars shaded by plane trees, and statues of Gods and Olympic heroes, the great Temple of Zeus faced the older and darker house of Hera his wife.

Before the Temple of Zeus, the ancient wild olive trees from which the victors' crowns were made cast dapple-shade across the lower steps of the vast portico. He spoke to the attendant priest in the deep threshold shadows beyond.

"I ask leave to enter and make an offering."

"Enter then, and make the offering," the man said.

And he went through into the vastness of the Temple itself, where the sunlight sifting through under the acanthus roof tiles made a honeycomb glow that hung high in the upper spaces and flowed down the gigantic columns, but scarcely touched the pavement under foot, so that he seemed to wade in cool shadows. At the far end, sheathed in gold and ivory, his feet half lost in shadows, his head gloried with the dim radiance of the upper air, stern and serene above the affairs of mortal men, stood the mighty statue of the God himself. Olympian Zeus, in whose honour the Sacred Games had been held for more than three hundred years. Three hundred years, such a little while; looking up at the heart-stilling face above him, Amyntas wondered if the God had even noticed yet, that they were begun. Everything in the God's House was so huge, even time. . . . For a moment his head swam, and he had no means of judging the size of anything, even himself, here where all the known landmarks of the world of men were left behind. Only one thing, when he looked down at it, remained constant in size; the tiny bronze bull with the silvered horns that he held in his hand.

He went forward to the first of the Offering Tables before the feet of the gigantic statue, and set it down. Now, the tables were empty and waiting, but by the end of the festival, they would be piled with offerings; small humble ones like his own, and silver cups and tripods of gilded bronze to be taken away and housed in the Temple treasury. On the eve of the Games they would begin to fill up, with votive offerings made for the most part by the athletes themselves, for their own victory, or the victory of a friend taking part in a different event. Amyntas was not making the offering for his own victory, nor for Leon's. He was not quite sure why he was making it, but it was for something much more complicated than victory in the Double Stade. With one finger still resting on the back of the little bronze bull, he sent up the best prayer he could sort out from the tangle of thoughts and feelings within himself. "Father of all things, Lord of these Sacred Games, let me keep a clean heart in this, let me run the best race that is in me, and think of nothing more."

Outside again, beyond the dapple-shade of the olive trees, the white sunlight fell dazzling across his eyes, and the world of men, in which things had returned to their normal size, received him back; and he knew that Hippias was going to be loudly angry with him for having missed a training session. But unaccountably, everything, including Hippias' anger, seemed surprisingly small.

Leon had to break training for three days, at least so far as track-work was concerned; and it was several more before he could get back into full training; so for a while it was doubtful whether he would be able to take his place in the race. But with still more than a week to go, both his trainer and the Doctor-Priest of Asklepius declared him fit, and his name remained on the list of entrants for the Double Stade.

And then it was the first day of the Festival; the day of solemn dedication, when each competitor must go before the Council to be looked over and identified, and take the Oath of the Games before the great bronze statue of Zeus of the Thunderbolts.

The day passed. And next morning before it was light, Amyntas woke to hear the unmistakable, unforgettable voice of the crowds gathering in the Stadium. A shapeless surf of sound, pricked by the sharper cries of the jugglers and acrobats, and the sellers of water and honeycakes, myrtle and victors' ribbons calling their wares.

This was the day of the Sacred Procession; the Priests and Officials, the beasts garlanded for sacrifice, the athletes marching into the waiting Stadium, while the Herald proclaimed the name and state of each one as he passed the rostrum. Amyntas, marching in with the Athenians, heard his own name called, and Leon's, among names from Samos and Cyrene, Crete and Corinth and Argos and Megara. And he smelled the incense on the morning air, and felt for the first time, under his swelling pride in being Athenian, the thread of his own Greekness interwoven with the Greekness of

all those others. This must have been, a little, the thing their Great Grandfathers had felt when they stood together, shield to shield, to hurl back the whole strength of invading Persia, so that they might remain free. That had been in a Games year, too. . . .

The rest of that day was given over to the chariot and horse races; and that night Amyntas went to his sleeping cell with the thunder of hooves and wheels still sounding somewhere behind his ears. He seemed to hear it in his dreams all night, but when he woke in the morning, it had turned into the sound that he had woken to yesterday, the surf-sound of the gathering crowd. But this morning it had a new note for him, for this was the Day, and the crowd that was gathering out there round the Stadium was his crowd, and his belly tightened and the skin prickled at the back of his neck as he heard it.

He lay for a few moments, listening, then got up and went out to the conduit. Leon came out after him as he had done that first morning of all, and they sluiced down as best they could. The water barely dribbled from the mouth of the stone bull now, for with the vast gathering of people, and the usual end-of-summer drought, the water shortage was getting desperate, as it always did by the time the Festival days arrived.

"How is the foot?" Amyntas asked.

"I can't remember where the cut was, unless I look for it."

They stood looking at each other, the friendship that they had never put into words trying to find some way to reach across from one to the other.

"We cannot even wish each other luck," Amyntas said at last, helplessly.

And Leon said, almost exactly as he had said it at their first meeting, "May both of us run a good race."

They reached out and touched hands quickly and went their separate ways.

The next time they saw each other, they were waiting oiled and naked for the track, with the rest of the Double Stade boys just outside the arched way into the Stadium. The Dolichus, the long distance race, and the Stade had been run, each with its boys' race immediately after. Now the trumpet was sounding to start the Double Stade. Amyntas' eyes went to meet Leon's, and found the Spartan boy's slightly frowning gaze waiting for him. He heard the sudden roar of the crowd, and his belly lifted and tightened. A little stir ran through the waiting boys; the next time the starting trumpet sounded, the next time the crowd gave that roar, it would be for them. Hippias was murmuring last-minute advice into Amyntas' ear, but he did not hear a word of it. . . . He was going out there before all those thousands upon thousands of staring eyes and yelling mouths, and he was going to fail. Not just fail to win the race, but *fail*. His belly was churning now, his heart banging away right up in his throat so that it almost choked him. His mouth was dry and the palms of his hands were wet; and the beginnings of panic were whimpering up in him. He looked again at Leon, and saw him run the tip of his tongue over his lips as though they were suddenly dry. It was the first time he had ever known the Spartan boy to betray anything of what was going on inside him; and the sight gave him a sense of companionship that somehow steadied him. He began to take deep quiet breaths, as he had been taught, and the rising panic quietened and sank away.

The voice of the crowd was rising, rising to a great roar; the Men's Double Stade was over. He heard the Herald crying the name of the winner, and another roar from the crowd; and then the runners were coming out through the arched entrance; and the boys pressed back to let them past, filthy with sweat and sand and oil. Amyntas looked at the face of the man with the victor's ribbons knotted round his head and arms, and saw that it was grey and spent and oddly peaceful.

"Now it's us!" someone said; and the boys were sprinting down the covered way, out into the open sun-drenched space of the Stadium.

The turf banks on either side of the broad track, and the lower slopes of the Kronon Hill that looked down upon it were packed with a vast multitude of onlookers. Half-way down on the right-hand side, raised above the tawny grass on which everybody else sat, were the benches for the Council, looking across to the white marble seat opposite, where the Priestess of Demeter, the only woman allowed at the Games, sat as still as though she herself were carved from marble, among all the jostling, swaying, noisy throng. Men were raking over the silver sand on the track. The trumpeter stood ready.

They had taken their places now behind the long white limestone curbs of the starting line. The Umpire was calling: "Runners! Feet to the lines!"

Amyntas felt the scorching heat of the limestone as he braced the ball of his right foot into the shaped groove. All the panic of a while back had left him, he felt light, and clear headed, and master of himself. He had drawn the sixth place, with Leon on his left and the boy from Megara on his right. Before him the track stretched white in the sunlight, an infinity of emptiness and distance.

The starting trumpet yelped; and the line of runners sprang forward like a wave of hunting dogs slipped from the leash.

Amyntas was running smoothly and without hurry. Let the green front-runners push on ahead. In this heat they would have burned themselves out before they reached the turning post. He and Leon were running neck and neck with the red-headed Macedonian. The Rhodian had gone ahead now after the front-runners, the rest were still bunched. Then the Corinthian made a sprint and passed the boy from Rhodes, but fell back almost at once. The white track was reeling back underfoot, the turning post racing towards them. The bunch had thinned out, the front-runners beginning to drop back already; and as they came up towards the turning post, first the boy from Macedon, and then Nikomedes catching fire at last, slid into the lead, with Amyntas and Leon close behind them. Rounding the post, Amyntas skidded on the loose sand and Leon went ahead; and it was then, seeing the lean scarred back ahead of him, that Amyntas lengthened his stride, knowing that the time had come to run. They were a quarter of the way down the home lap when they passed Nikomedes; the Megaran boy had taken fire too late. They were beginning to overhaul the redhead; and Amyntas knew in his bursting heart that unless something unexpected happened, the race must be between himself and Leon. Spartan and Macedonian were going neck and neck now; the position held for a few paces, and then the redhead gradually fell behind. Amyntas was going all out, there was pain in his breast and belly and in the backs of his legs, and he did not know where his next breath was coming from; but still the thin scarred back was just ahead. The crowd were beginning to give tongue, seeing the two come through to the front; a solid roar of sound that would go on rising now until they passed the finishing post. And then suddenly Amyntas knew that something was wrong; Leon was labouring a little, beginning to lose the first keen edge of his speed. Snatching a glance downward, he saw a fleck of crimson in the sand. The cut had re-opened.

His body went on running, but for a sort of splinter of time his head seemed quite apart from the rest of him, and filled with an unmanageable swirl of thoughts and feelings. Leon might have passed the top of his speed anyway, it might be nothing to do with his foot— But the cut *had* re-opened. . . . To lose the race because of a cut foot. . . . It would be so easy not to make that final desperate effort that his whole body was crying out against. Then Leon would keep his lead. . . . And at the same time another part of himself was remembering his father standing on the quayside at Piraeus as the *Paralos* drew away—crying out that he was not running only for himself but for Athens, his City and his people. . . . A crown of wild olive would be the greatest thing that anyone could give to his friend. . . . It would be to insult Leon to let him win . . . you could not do that to your friend. . . . And then, like a clean cold sword of light cutting through the swirling tangle of his thoughts, came the knowledge that greater than any of these things were the Gods. These were the Sacred Games, not some mere struggle between boys in the gymnasium. For one fleeting instant of time he remembered himself standing in the Temple before the great statue of Zeus, holding the tiny bronze bull with the silvered horns. "Let me run the best race that is in me, and think of nothing more."

He drove himself forward in one last agonizing burst of speed, he was breathing against knives, and the roar of the blood in his ears drowned the roar of the crowd. He was level with Leon—and then there was nothing ahead of him but the winning post.

The onlookers had crowded right down towards it; even above the howl of the blood in his head he heard them now, roar on solid roar of sound, shouting him in to victory. And then Hippias had caught him as he plunged past the post; and he was bending over the trainer's arm, bending over the pain in his belly, snatching at his breath and trying

not to be sick. People were throwing sprigs of myrtle, he felt them flicking and falling on his head and shoulders. The sickness eased a little and his head was clearing; he began to hear friendly voices congratulating him; and Eudorus came shouldering through the crowd with a coloured ribbon to tie round his head. But when he looked round for Leon, the Spartan boy had been swept away by his trainer. And a queer desolation rose in Amyntas and robbed his moment of its glory.

Afterwards in the changing room, some of the other boys came up to congratulate him. Leon did not come; but when they had cleaned off the sand and oil and sweat, and sluiced down with the little water that was allowed them, Amyntas hung about, sitting on the well kerb outside while the trainer finished seeing to his friend's foot. And when Leon came out at last, he came straight across to the well, as though they had arranged to meet there. His face was as unreadable as usual.

"You will have cooled off enough by now, do you want to drink?" Amyntas said, mainly because somebody had to say something; and dipped the bronze cup that always stood on the well kerb in the pail that he had drawn.

Leon took the cup from him and drank, and sat down on the well kerb beside him. As Amyntas dipped the cup again and bent his head to drink in his turn, the ends of the victor's ribbon fell forward against his cheek, and he pulled it off impatiently, and dropped it beside the well.

"Why did you do that?" Leon said.

"I shall never be sure whether I won that race."

"The judges are not often mistaken, and I never heard yet of folk tying victors' ribbons on the wrong man."

Amyntas flicked a thumb at Leon's bandaged foot. "You know well enough what I mean. I'll never be sure whether I'd have come first past the post, if that hadn't opened up again."

Leon looked at him a moment in silence, then flung up his head and laughed. "Do you really think that could make any difference? It would take more than a cut foot to slow me up, Athenian!—You ran the better race, that's all."

It was said on such a harsh, bragging note that in the first moment Amyntas felt as though he had been struck in the face. Then he wondered if it was the overwhelming Spartan pride giving tongue, or simply Leon, hurt and angry and speaking the truth. Either way, he was too tired to be angry back again. And which ever it was, it seemed that Leon had shaken it off already. The noon break was over, and the trumpets were sounding for the Pentathlon.

"Up!" Leon said, when Amyntas did not move at once. "Are you going to let it be said that your own event is the only one that interests you?"

They went, quickly and together, while the trainer's eye was off them, for Leon was under orders to keep off his foot. And the people cheered them both when they appeared in the Stadium. They seldom cared much for a good loser, but Leon had come in a close second, and they had seen the blood in the sand.

The next day the heavyweight events were held; and then it was the last day of all, the Crowning Day. Ever after, Amyntas remembered that day as a quietness after great stress and turmoil. It was not, in truth, much less noisy than the days that had gone before. The roaring of the Stadium crowds was gone; but in the town of tents the crowds milled to and fro. The jugglers with knives and the eaters of fire shouted for an audience and the merchants cried their wares; and within the Sacred Enclosure where the winners received their crowns and made their sacrifices before the Temples of Zeus and Hera, there were the flutes and the songs in praise of the victors, and the deep-voiced invocations to the Gods.

But in Amyntas himself, there was the quiet. He remembered the Herald crying his name, and the light springy coolness of the wild olive crown as it was pressed down on his head; and later, the spitting light of pine torches under the plane trees, where the officials and athletes were feasting. And he remembered most, looking up out of the torchlight, and seeing, high and remote above it all, the winged tripods on the roof of the great Temple, outlined against the light of a moon two days past the full.

The boys left before the feasting was over; and in his sleeping cell Amyntas heard the poets singing in praise of some chariot team, and the applause, while he gathered his few belongings together, ready for tomorrow's early start, and stowed his olive crown among them. Already the leaves were beginning to wilt after the heat of the day. The room that had seemed so strange the first night, was familiar now; part of himself; and after tonight it would not know him anymore.

Next morning in all the hustle of departure, he and Leon contrived to meet and slip off for a little on their own.

The whole valley of Olympia was a chaos of tents and booths being taken down, merchants as well as athletes and onlookers making ready for the road. But the Sacred Enclosure itself was quiet, and the gates stood open. They went through, into the shade of the olive trees before the Temple of Zeus. A priest making the morning offering at a side altar looked at them; but they seemed to be doing no harm, and to want nothing, so he let them alone. There was a smell of frankincense in the air, and the early morning smell of last night's heavy dew on parched ground. They stood among the twisted trunks and low-hanging branches, and looked at each other and did not know what to say. Already they were remembering that there was war between Athens and Sparta, that the Truce of the Games would last them back to their own states, but no further; and the longer the silence lasted, the more they remembered.

From beyond the quiet of the Enclosure came all the sounds of the great concourse breaking up; voices calling, the stamping of impatient horses. "By this time tomorrow everyone will be gone," Amyntas said at last. "It will be just as it was before we came, for another four years."

"The Corinthians are off already."

"Catching the cool of the morning for those fine chariot horses," Amyntas said, and thought, There's so little time, why do we have to waste it like this?

"One of the charioteers had that hunting knife with the silver inlay. The one you took a fancy to. Why didn't you buy it after all?"

"I spent the money on something else." For a moment Amyntas was afraid that Leon would ask what. But the other boy only nodded and let it go.

He wished suddenly that he could give Leon something, but there was nothing among his few belongings that would make sense in the Spartan's world. It was a world so far off from his own. Too far to reach out, too far to call. Already they seemed to be drifting away from each other, drifting back to a month ago, before they had even met. He put out a hand quickly, as though to hold the other boy back for one more moment, and Leon's hand came to meet it.

"It has been good. All this month it has been good," Leon said.

"It has been good," Amyntas agreed. He wanted to say, "Until the next Games, then." But manhood and military service were only a few months away for both of them; if they did meet at another Games, there would be the faces of dead comrades, Spartan or Athenian, between them; and like enough, for one of them or both, there might be no other Games. Far more likely, if they ever saw each other again, it would be over the tops of their shields.

He had noticed before how, despite their different worlds, he and Leon sometimes thought the same thing at the same time, and answered each other as though the thought had been spoken. Leon said in his abrupt, dead-level voice, "The Gods be with you, Amyntas, and grant that we never meet again."

They put their arms round each other's necks and strained fiercely close for a moment, hard cheekbone against hard cheekbone.

"The Gods be with you, Leon."

And then Eudorus was calling, "Amyntas! Amyntas! We're all waiting!"

And Amyntas turned and ran—out through the gateway of the Sacred Enclosure, towards where the Athenian party were ready to start, and Eudorus was already coming back to look for him.

As they rode up from the Valley of Olympia and took the tracks towards the coast, Amyntas did not look back. The horses' legs brushed the dry dust-grey scrub beside the track, and loosed the hot aromatic scents of wild lavender and camomile and lentisk upon the air. A yellow butterfly hovered past, and watching it out of sight, it came to him suddenly, that he and Leon had exchanged gifts of a sort, after all. It was hard to give them a name, but they were real enough. And the outward and visible sign of his gift to Leon was in the little bronze bull with the silvered horns that he had left on the Offering Table before the feet of Olympian Zeus. And Leon's gift to him. . . . That had been made with the Spartan's boast that it would take more than a cut foot to slow him up. He had thought at the time that it was either the harsh Spartan pride, or the truth spoken in anger. But he understood now, quite suddenly, that it had been Leon giving up his own private and inward claim to the olive crown, so that he, Amyntas, might believe that he had rightfully won it. Amyntas knew that he would never be sure of that, never in all his life. But it made no difference to the gift.

The track had begun to run downhill, and the pale dust-cloud was rising behind them. He knew that if he looked back now, there would be nothing to see.

# MEET
# ROSEMARY
# SUTCLIFF

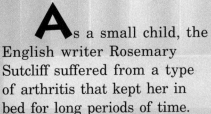

**A**s a small child, the English writer Rosemary Sutcliff suffered from a type of arthritis that kept her in bed for long periods of time. For entertainment, her mother often read stories to her—especially folk tales, myths, and legends. Sutcliff enjoyed listening to her mother read so much that she refused to learn to read for herself. Not until she was ten years old and able to go to school did she read on her own.

Never an enthusiastic student, Sutcliff left school when she was fourteen to study art. At first, she supported herself by painting miniature portraits. But the work was dull, and she began to write for her own pleasure. Sutcliff recalls, "It was a delight, a way of escape. . . ."

Like "A Crown of Wild Olive," most of Sutcliff's stories are set in the past. "I love trying to piece together historical background and to catch the right smell of the period," she says.

Sutcliff's many awards show how successful she is at making the past come alive. Her award-winning books include *The Mark of the Horse Lord, Blood Feud,* and *Tristan and Iseult.*

# Let the Games Begin

You're sitting in a stadium filled with thousands of people. You look up and see flags from almost every nation in the world surrounding the huge arena. An amplified voice proclaims the opening of the games, and then the parade and ceremony of the Olympics begin. At no other time does so much of the world share cheers, tears, smiles, and embraces. And the memories linger. . . .

Did you know that the five rings on the flag represent the continents of Eurasia, Africa, North America, South America, and Australia? They are interlocked to show the sporting friendships among nations. The five colors of the rings were chosen because each country's flag contains at least one of the colors.

Do you remember the doves being released above the stadium? What an exciting way to be reminded of the spirit of peace and freedom that unites all participants in the Olympics!

The torch, ignited in Greece, is carried across the world by relay runners until it reaches the site of the Games. There it is used to light the Olympic flame.

The heart of the Olympics has always been its athletes and their teams. Imagine competing with more than eight thousand athletes from one hundred countries! All contestants in the Olympics receive a diploma and a medal as a reward for their efforts, but the best earn a Gold, Silver, or Bronze Medal.

Whether or not athletes win a coveted medal, they are proud to participate in the games. Pierre de Coubertin, the creator of the modern Olympics, expressed it well when he stated that "the most important thing in the Olympic games is not to win but to take part, just as the most important thing in life is not the triumph but the struggle. The essential thing is not to have conquered but to have fought well."

# REMEMBER ME TO HARLEM SQUARE

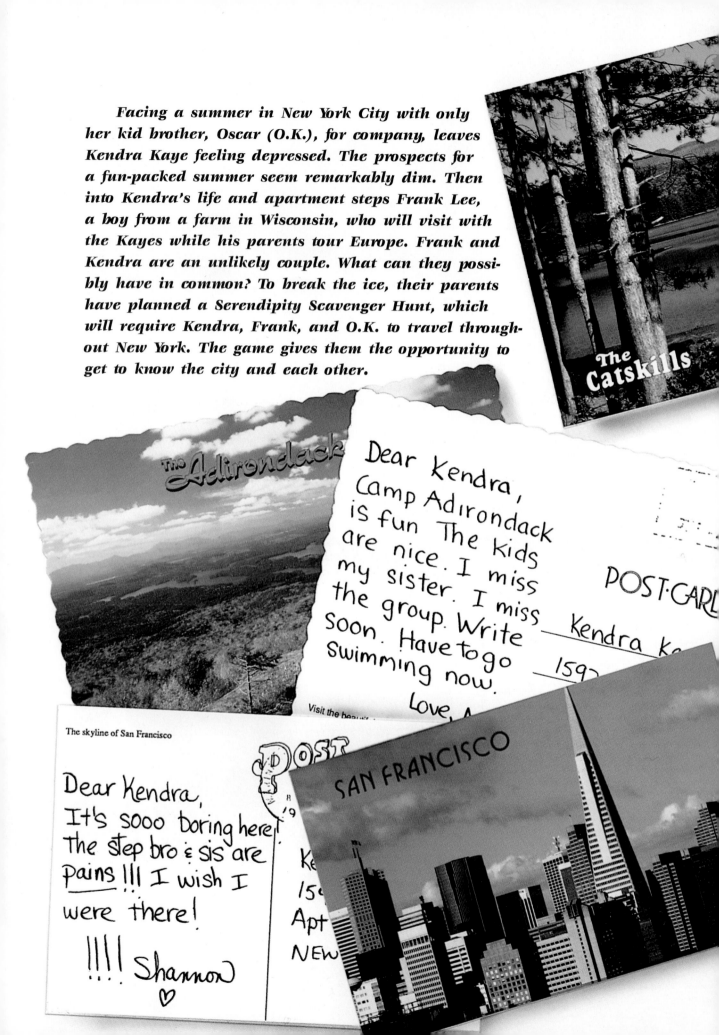

Facing a summer in New York City with only her kid brother, Oscar (O.K.), for company, leaves Kendra Kaye feeling depressed. The prospects for a fun-packed summer seem remarkably dim. Then into Kendra's life and apartment steps Frank Lee, a boy from a farm in Wisconsin, who will visit with the Kayes while his parents tour Europe. Frank and Kendra are an unlikely couple. What can they possibly have in common? To break the ice, their parents have planned a Serendipity Scavenger Hunt, which will require Kendra, Frank, and O.K. to travel throughout New York. The game gives them the opportunity to get to know the city and each other.

The Catskills

The Adirondack

Dear Kendra,
Camp Adirondack is fun The kids are nice. I miss my sister. I miss the group. Write soon. Have to go swimming now.
Love,

POST·CARD

Kendra K
159

Visit the beau

The skyline of San Francisco

POST

SAN FRANCISCO

Dear Kendra,
It's sooo boring here! the step bro & sis are pains !!! I wish I were there!
!!!! ... !! Shannon
♡

Ke
159
Apt
NEW

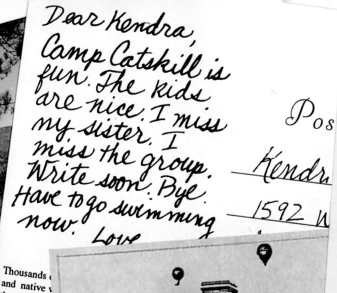

Dear Kendra,
Camp Catskill is
fun. The kids
are nice. I miss
my sister. I
miss the group.
Write soon. Bye.
Have to go swimming
now. Love

*Pos*

Kendr...

1592 W...

Thousands ...
and native ...
the Catskills ...

Dear Kendra,
Paris is Beautiful!
But I'm so homesick
I could die. Wish
you were here.
Write immediately.
XXXX Teri

TO:        KENDRA
FROM:    BETHANY
RE:        A MAJOR PROBLEM

    Yesterday, my father's new
production got a TERRIBLE review
in "The N.Y. Times."
    Yesterday the phone bill arrived.
We're still wiping my father
off the ceiling.
    TODAY, my long distance phone
calls have been limited to two a
week . . . and they can't be our normal
hour long talks.
    We're going to have to start writing
each other. What a nightmare!
    Life can be so tragic sometimes.
    It's a shame that "The N.Y. Times"
doesn't publish parent reviews by kids.

Frantically yours,
Bethany

Reading each letter twice, I really miss the group.

I wonder how Bonnie is doing. Something tells me
that she's not going to be much of a letter writer.

O.K. comes into the kitchen. "You know the letter that Frank
just got—the one that stinks of perfume?"

I nod, very curious, but try to act as if I'm not. "What about it?"

"Well, he's in the bedroom and asked to be left alone while he
reads it."

"Oh," I say.

O.K. continues. "I asked him what the big S.W.A.K. means.
That's when he asked for privacy."

"Was he mean when he said it?" This is the seventh day of the
Scavenger Hunt and I still don't have Frank figured out.

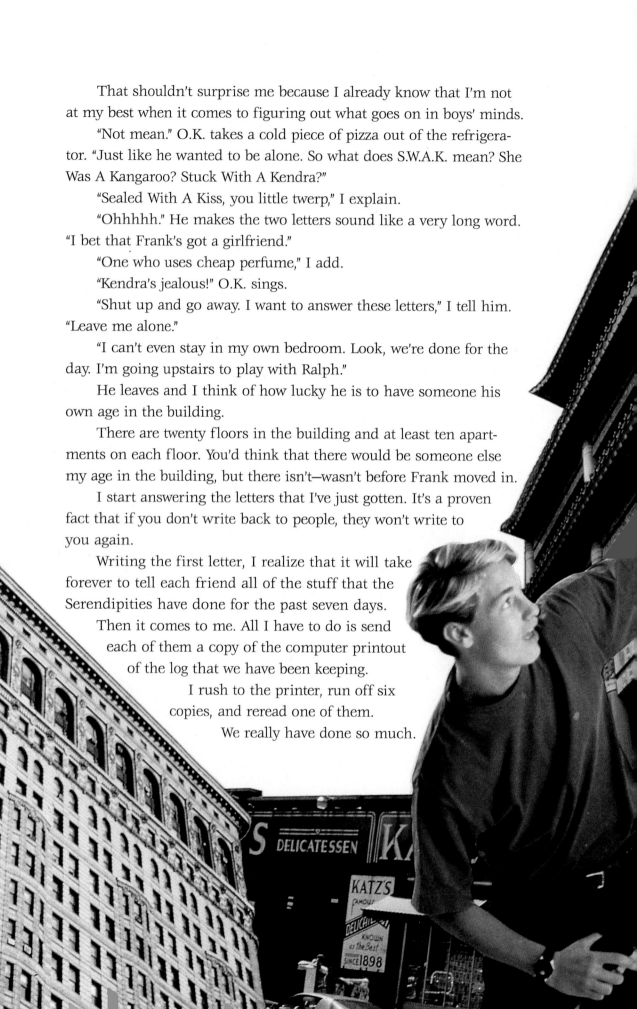

That shouldn't surprise me because I already know that I'm not at my best when it comes to figuring out what goes on in boys' minds.

"Not mean." O.K. takes a cold piece of pizza out of the refrigerator. "Just like he wanted to be alone. So what does S.W.A.K. mean? She Was A Kangaroo? Stuck With A Kendra?"

"Sealed With A Kiss, you little twerp," I explain.

"Ohhhhh." He makes the two letters sound like a very long word. "I bet that Frank's got a girlfriend."

"One who uses cheap perfume," I add.

"Kendra's jealous!" O.K. sings.

"Shut up and go away. I want to answer these letters," I tell him. "Leave me alone."

"I can't even stay in my own bedroom. Look, we're done for the day. I'm going upstairs to play with Ralph."

He leaves and I think of how lucky he is to have someone his own age in the building.

There are twenty floors in the building and at least ten apartments on each floor. You'd think that there would be someone else my age in the building, but there isn't—wasn't before Frank moved in.

I start answering the letters that I've just gotten. It's a proven fact that if you don't write back to people, they won't write to you again.

Writing the first letter, I realize that it will take forever to tell each friend all of the stuff that the Serendipities have done for the past seven days.

Then it comes to me. All I have to do is send each of them a copy of the computer printout of the log that we have been keeping.

I rush to the printer, run off six copies, and reread one of them.

We really have done so much.

# Serendipity Log

*DAY 1*

Parents (the Kayes, heretofore referred to as "The Ks") drive Serendipities all over the city on Sunday. Special stops on Lower East Side: Chinatown. Ate knishes at Yonah Shimmel. Ate salami, pastrami, corned beef sandwiches at Katz's.

THIS CITY IS AMAZING. Frank Lee (FL)

CAN I HELP IT IF I GET CAR SICK? Oscar Kaye (OK)

WHY DO I ALWAYS HAVE TO SIT NEXT TO O.K. IN CARS? IT'S NOT FAIR. Kendra Kaye (KK)

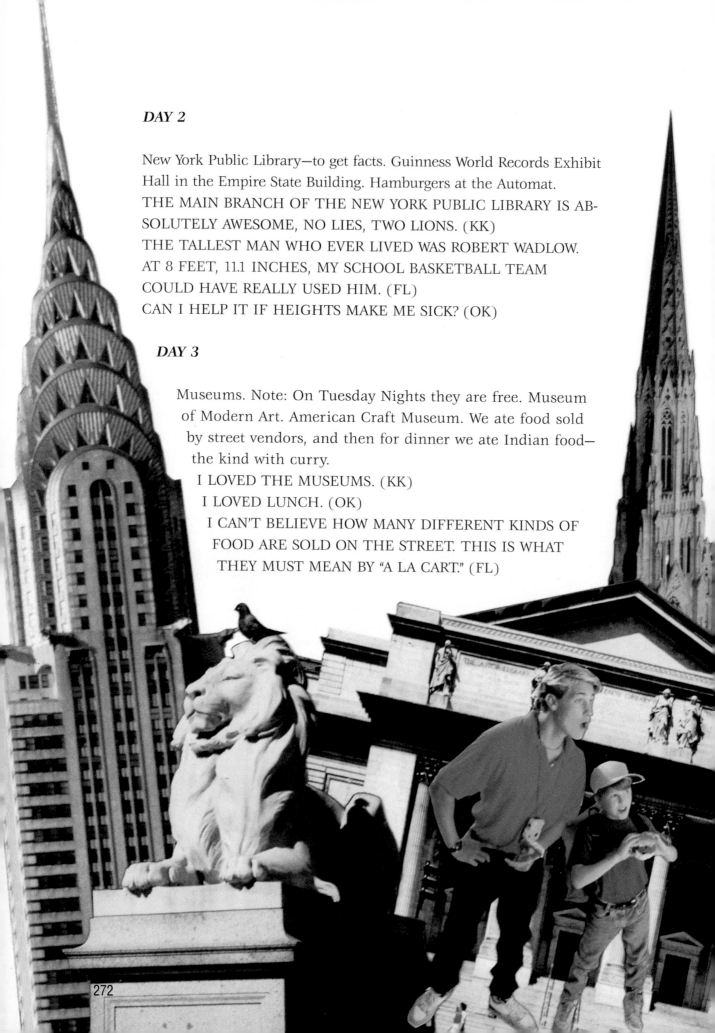

**DAY 2**

New York Public Library—to get facts. Guinness World Records Exhibit Hall in the Empire State Building. Hamburgers at the Automat.
THE MAIN BRANCH OF THE NEW YORK PUBLIC LIBRARY IS ABSOLUTELY AWESOME, NO LIES, TWO LIONS. (KK)
THE TALLEST MAN WHO EVER LIVED WAS ROBERT WADLOW. AT 8 FEET, 11.1 INCHES, MY SCHOOL BASKETBALL TEAM COULD HAVE REALLY USED HIM. (FL)
CAN I HELP IT IF HEIGHTS MAKE ME SICK? (OK)

**DAY 3**

Museums. Note: On Tuesday Nights they are free. Museum of Modern Art. American Craft Museum. We ate food sold by street vendors, and then for dinner we ate Indian food— the kind with curry.
I LOVED THE MUSEUMS. (KK)
I LOVED LUNCH. (OK)
I CAN'T BELIEVE HOW MANY DIFFERENT KINDS OF FOOD ARE SOLD ON THE STREET. THIS IS WHAT THEY MUST MEAN BY "A LA CART." (FL)

**DAY 4**

Museum of Holography. St. Patrick's Cathedral. TKTS (Broadway at 47th Street), where you can buy tickets to a lot of shows for half price, but you have to stand in a long line. We got tickets to *A Chorus Line*. Pizza.

HOLOGRAPHY MEANS WHOLE MESSAGE. 3D WITH LASERS. MAYBE SOMEDAY I'LL BE A HOLOGRAPHER. (OK)

*A CHORUS LINE* WAS TERRIFIC. (KK)

NEW YORK IS AMAZING. I WISH IT WERE CLOSER TO WISCONSIN. (FL)

**DAY 5**

Radio City Music Hall. The Rockettes. A movie. Rockefeller Center.

THIS PLACE IS DEFINITELY NOT LIKE CINEMA 3 AT OUR MALL. (FL)

WHAT'S A MALL? JUST KIDDING. WE GO TO THEM SOME-TIMES IN NEW JERSEY. I THOUGHT THAT WATCHING THE ROCKETTES WAS A REAL KICK. (KK)

I LIKED THE POPCORN. (OK)

### DAY 6

Metropolitan Museum of Art.
THIS PLACE IS SO TERRIFIC. (KK)
INCREDIBLE. (FL)
I AGREE. (OK)

### DAY 7

The Ks go with us. Statue of Liberty. American
Museum of Immigration (located at base
of statue), Ellis Island. Dinner: pasta at
Bazzini's Restaurant.
A GREAT DAY. THE FERRY BOAT
RIDE WAS FUN. WE LEARNED A LOT
BUT IT WAS FUN ANYWAY. (KK)
I AGREE. (FL)
I WONDER IF THE STATUE OF LIBERTY
USES UNDERARM DEODORANT. (OK)

Frank walks into the kitchen.

Looking up, I smile and say, "Hi."

What I really want to say is: So what's in the letter? Who wrote it to you? Does she really wear that perfume or does she use it as bathroom freshener? Is she pretty? Do you like her better than you like me?

I say none of those things, however.

Frank nods hello, walks to the refrigerator, opens it up, and looks for something, which he doesn't seem able to find.

He starts to walk around the room, looking in cabinets.

My mother told him to feel at home in the kitchen. Obviously he does.

"Are you looking for something special? Maybe I know where it is," I offer.

He shakes his head. "I don't think that what I'm looking for is going to be that easily found."

I figure out that he's not really looking for anything, that he's just doing something to be doing something—anything. When I get upset I act like that, but I didn't think anyone else did.

As he paces around the room, I realize that this is the first time that we've been alone. For seven days, the three of us have been Serendipities together.

When I don't know what to say, sometimes I chatter. This is one of those times. "So the summer's going to be fun, huh? We'll even get to go to the TV studio to watch *All My Children* being taped. It's really lucky that Dee, who lives in this building, is a lighting director on the show and that she's so nice and is getting us passes and giving us the tour. And then we can walk over to Lincoln Center, which is just around the corner from the studio, and then maybe we'll get the dreaded sushi meal over with. So what do you think?"

"Kendra," Frank says. "Have you ever been in love—really in love?"

I guess that when you ask Frank what he thinks, you've got to be prepared to hear what he's really thinking.

I want to seem sophisticated, really sure of myself, a woman of the world. Because sometimes I feel like such a kid around Frank.

"Yes," I say, and think of Jeremy. "Actually, no. I've been in strong like, but not in real love."

He starts to say something and we hear the door open.

It's too noisy to be parents.

O.K. and Ralph come in and head immediately for the refrigerator.

Our refrigerator is a giant magnet that draws people to it.

Bad timing for the kids to show up right now.

Actually, O.K. is known for his bad timing. He should have been born in the next century so that I wouldn't have to deal with him.

"Let's go for a walk." I look at Frank.

O.K. turns around. "Sure."

"No," I say firmly. "Just Frank and me."

O.K. falls to the ground. "Life is unfair. Alas. Alack. Woe is us."

Frank steps over his body. "Let's go."

We leave the apartment and go down in the elevator.

I'm dying to find out what Frank was going to say, but the elevator man starts talking. "So what do you think of those Mets? Aren't they the greatest? Have you had a chance to get over to Shea Stadium yet and see them play?"

"Joe." I sigh. "Frank just got here a little while ago, and anyway—not everyone is interested in a silly baseball game."

"Silly," Joe says. "Kendra. How can you say that?"

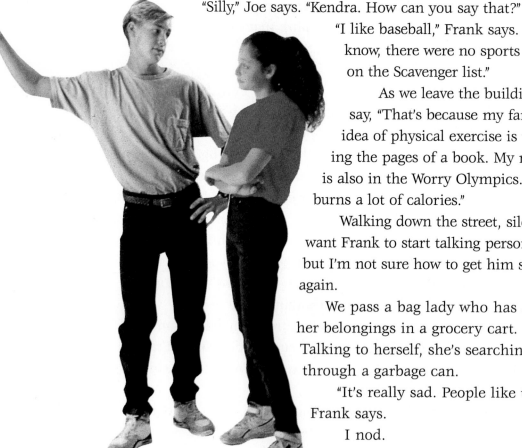

"I like baseball," Frank says. "You know, there were no sports things on the Scavenger list."

As we leave the building, I say, "That's because my family's idea of physical exercise is turning the pages of a book. My mother is also in the Worry Olympics. That burns a lot of calories."

Walking down the street, silently, I want Frank to start talking personally, but I'm not sure how to get him started again.

We pass a bag lady who has all of her belongings in a grocery cart. Talking to herself, she's searching through a garbage can.

"It's really sad. People like that," Frank says.

I nod.

In New York City, there are a lot of homeless people. It gets so that I don't even notice them, which is so awful to say. Now that Frank's here, I see them differently, through his eyes, and then through my own eyes and my own heart.

It is so sad.

My family always contributes to charity to help the homeless.

Lately I've been thinking about doing something on my own to help people out in the City. When school starts again, I'll be a volunteer tutor in one of the special programs in my neighborhood—as long as I don't have to help with math.

I'm beginning to realize how much I get from the City and now I want to give something back.

As we cross the street to go to Central Park, Frank points at a stretch limo. "That's the longest, biggest car I've ever seen."

I glance at it. Limos are another thing I hardly ever notice in New York City.

It's a strange city, with so much richness and so much poverty.

Frank says, "You know, back home I never saw a limo. There are some big expensive cars, yes—but not something like that with a chauffeur. But then, back home I see a lot of tractors, and I haven't seen one here."

"I've never ever seen a tractor—not in person," I say.

We walk into the park.

Frank says, "Sometimes I feel like I've been dropped onto another planet. You'd feel that way too if you came to visit our farm. It's so different."

He gets quiet again.

"Let's go over there." I point to an empty space under a tree.

He nods and we sit down.

There's quiet again.

There used to be a lot of quiet times with Jeremy. However, I never had the feeling that much was going on in his brain when he was silent. With Frank, I get the feeling there are layers and levels.

I pick a blade of grass.

Finally Frank speaks. "Look, I don't know where to begin or what I want to say. This really isn't easy for me. Back home I don't have the kind of friends that I tell personal things to, so I guess I just have to start. So here goes." He takes a deep breath. "A lot has happened this year. Actually, some of it's been going on for a long time. For years my parents didn't get along. I knew they were heading for a divorce. In some ways, I hated it. Other times, I hoped for it. They'd fight over keeping the farm. Dad really loves it, but Mom wants to live in a big city. And even though they've both inherited a lot of money, the farm is becoming a drain."

Frank seems far away for a minute, and then he goes on. "Believe it or not, it gets worse. About a year ago, the doctors told my father that he had cancer. So for the past year he's been fighting that—going to hospitals, getting chemotherapy. My mother really helped him, stayed with him at the hospital. Now they think that maybe he has it licked and my parents want to get away and relax. Mom said that they want to rekindle the romance in their marriage." He makes a face. "Sometimes I think that's going to take an arsonist."

He smiles, and then gets serious again. "During that whole time, I was left alone a lot. They took all those trips to the hospital. There was this guy who was sort of a house sitter, but he really took care of the farm and mostly left me alone. It was good, because I got involved with someone and liked not being checked up on. Mary Alice is her name."

The one who writes S.W.A.K. all over her envelopes and pours tacky cheap perfume on them, I think, tearing a blade of grass into tiny strips.

Continuing, he says, "Mary Alice is three years older. She just graduated from high school and we got really close last year. I didn't feel so alone after we started going out. She's someone you can talk to and she listens—like you do, Kendra. And she's very mature."

While he goes on about how nice and pretty and wonderful she is, I try to sort out what I'm feeling. Jealous, maybe. Curious, yes. What did they do together? Hearing about Frank's "older woman" makes me feel like a kid.

Frank says, "Anyway, when the doctors told my father that he was all right, my parents came back and saw how serious it was between Mary Alice and me. They wanted it to end. They said that she was too old, too experienced, and that I was just a kid. They weren't around much for a year, and then they thought they could come back and run my life. There was a lot of fighting all the time. Finally, my mother took me aside and said that the fighting was upsetting

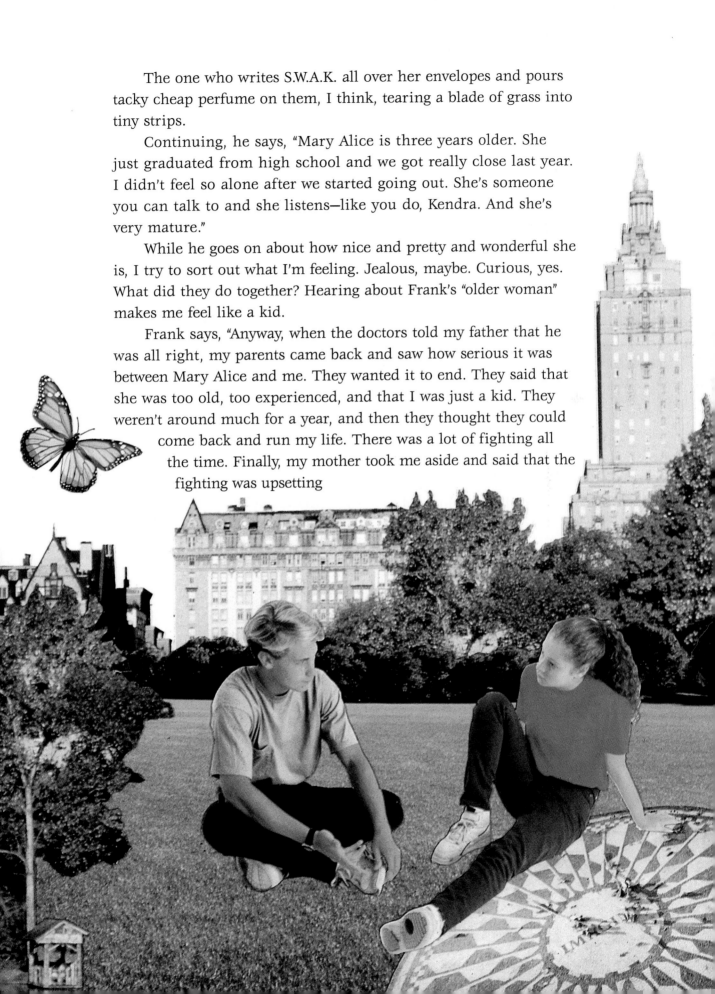

my father too much and she was afraid it would make him sick again."

And I thought my mother gave guilt trips.

He looks very sad. "They said I should go to Europe with them—that they wouldn't leave me behind and that they wouldn't go if I stayed there. They said that they really needed the vacation. I didn't know what to do, you know. I'm only fifteen and that's not old enough to quit school and get a job. And I know that would be dumb to do. Running away wouldn't help, either. Mary Alice thought I could come live at her house, but her parents didn't like that idea."

I think about how much Frank's been through, what a survivor he is and also about how sad he is, and wonder what I can do to help him.

"So," he says, "we decided that I would stay in New York while they're in Europe and then, when we go back, we'll see what happens. They think the problem is going to vanish, but I still love Mary Alice, so the problem's not going to vanish."

He looks sad and angry. "I had to give in on this. What if my father dies? They're not sure that this isn't just remission, a break, and I wanted him and Mom to have a chance to try to be happy. I thought that if I'm reasonable, then when they come back, maybe they'll be reasonable too."

Frank just sits quietly, looking down at the ground.

Who would have thought that someone so cute, with so much going for him, would have so many problems.

I really do have to remember not to judge people so much on surface stuff. My parents are always telling me that.

I also think that I have to give up any thoughts that maybe Frank and I will be boyfriend and girlfriend.

Something tells me that this is the time to be his friend.

I think he really needs one.

# MEET PAULA DANZIGER

After Paula Danziger was injured in an accident in which a drunk driver slammed into her car, she began to feel that perhaps she had no control over her own life. "The last time I felt that way was when I was a kid. When you're a kid," she has said, "everyone seems to be in charge, to have the right to tell you what to do, how to feel . . . I wanted to confront all of that."

Soon after her accident, Danziger began to write books for young adults. For many of her stories, Danziger drew upon her own life. *The Cat Ate My Gymsuit*, her first book, grew out of her memories of the stormy relationship she had with her father, her discouraging failures in gym class, and her younger brother's habit of stuffing his teddy bear with orange pits.

This mixture of lifelike characters, funny dialog, and the theme of coping with problems in contemporary life makes Paula Danziger's books extremely popular with young adults. These books include *The Cat Ate My Gymsuit, The Pistachio Description, Can You Sue Your Parents for Malpractice?* and *The Divorce Express.* In commenting about her work, Danziger says, "So here I am a full-time writer, a 'grown-up' who chooses to write about kids. I've made this choice because I think that kids and adults share a lot of the same feelings and thoughts."

# friend

BY GWENDOLYN BROOKS

Walking with you
shuts off shivering.
Here we are.
Here we are.

I am with you to share and to bear and to care.

This is warm.
I want you happy, I want you warm.

Your Friend for our forever is what I am.
Your Friend in thorough thankfulness.

It is the evening of our love.
Evening is hale and whole.
Evening shall not go out.
Evening is comforting flame
Evening is comforting flame.

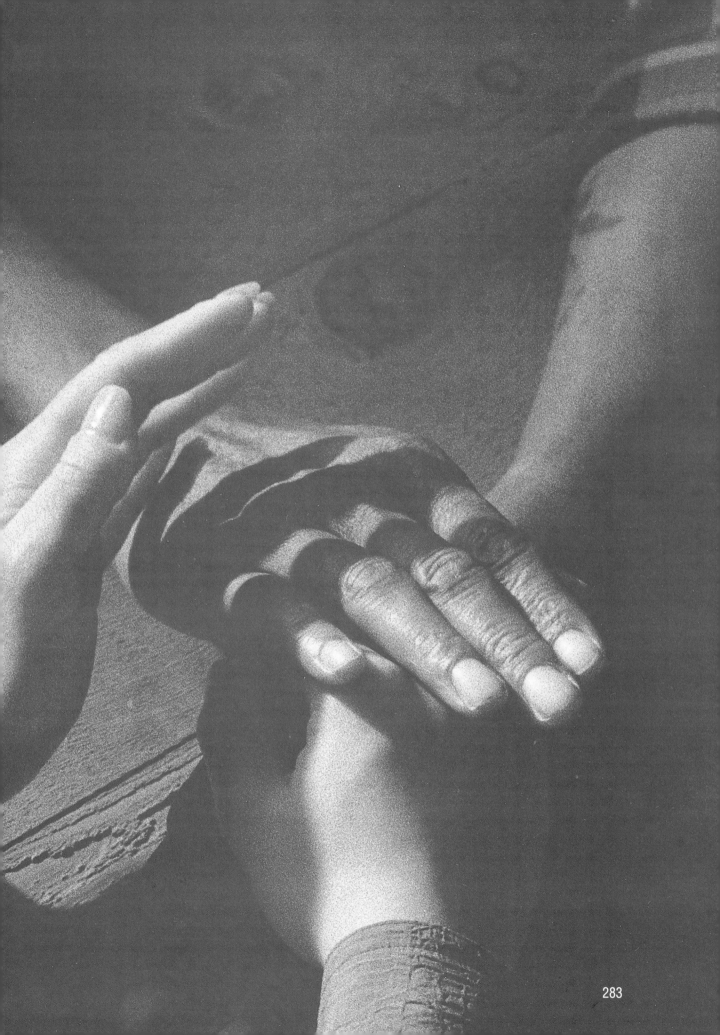

# CONTENTS

Getting the Message

"Then you should say what you mean," the March Hare went on.

"I do," Alice hastily replied; "at least—at least I mean what I say—that's the same thing, you know."

"Not the same thing a bit!" said the Hatter. "Why, you might just as well say that 'I see what I eat' is the same thing as 'I eat what I see'!"

LEWIS CARROLL
from *Alice's Adventures in Wonderland*

# CHECKOUTS

by Cynthia Rylant                    illustrated by Mark Chickinelli

**H**er parents had moved her to Cincinnati, to a large house with beveled glass windows and several porches and the *history* her mother liked to emphasize. You'll love the house, they said. You'll be lonely at first, they admitted, but you're so nice you'll make friends fast. And as an impulse tore at her to lie on the floor, to hold to their ankles and tell them she felt she was dying, to offer anything, anything at all, so they might allow her to finish growing up in the town of her childhood, they firmed their mouths and spoke from their chests and they said, It's decided.

They moved her to Cincinnati, where for a month she spent the greater part of every day in a room full of beveled glass windows, sifting through photographs of the life she'd lived and left behind. But it is difficult work, suffering, and in its own way a kind of art, and finally she didn't have the energy for it anymore, so she emerged from the beautiful house and fell in love with a bag boy at the supermarket. Of course, this didn't happen all at once, just like that, but in the sequence of things that's exactly the way it happened.

She liked to grocery shop. She loved it in the way some people love to drive long country roads, because doing it she could think and relax and wander. Her parents wrote up the list and handed it to her and off she went without complaint to perform what they regarded as a great sacrifice of her time and a sign that she was indeed a very nice girl. She had never told them how much she loved grocery shopping, only that she was "willing" to do it. She had an intuition which told her that her parents were not safe for sharing such strong, important facts about herself. Let them think they knew her.

Once inside the supermarket, her hands firmly around the handle of the cart, she would lapse into a kind of reverie and wheel toward the produce. Like a Tibetan monk in solitary meditation, she calmed to a point of deep, deep happiness; this feeling came to her, reliably, if strangely, only in the supermarket.

Then one day the bag boy dropped her jar of mayonnaise and that is how she fell in love.

He was nervous—first day on the job—and along had come this fascinating girl, standing in the checkout line with the unfocused stare one often sees in young children,

her face turned enough away that he might take several full looks at her as he packed sturdy bags full of food and the goods of modern life. She interested him because her hair was red and thick, and in it she had placed a huge orange bow, nearly the size of a small hat. That was enough to distract him, and when finally it was her groceries he was packing, she looked at him and smiled and he could respond only by busting her jar of mayonnaise on the floor, shards of glass and oozing cream decorating the area around his feet.

She loved him at exactly that moment, and if he'd known this perhaps he wouldn't have fallen into the brown depression he fell into, which lasted the rest of his shift. He believed he must have looked the jackass in her eyes, and he envied the sureness of everyone around him: the cocky cashier at the register, the grim and harried store manager, the bland butcher, and the brazen bag boys who smoked in the warehouse on their breaks. He wanted a second chance. Another chance to be confident and say witty things to her as he threw tin cans into her bags, persuading her to allow him to help her to her car so he might learn just a little about her, check out the floor of the car for signs of hobbies or fetishes and the bumpers for clues as to beliefs and loyalties.

But he busted her jar of mayonnaise and nothing else worked out for the rest of the day.

Strange, how attractive clumsiness can be. She left the supermarket with stars in her eyes, for she had loved the way his long nervous fingers moved from the conveyor belt to the bags, how deftly (until the mayonnaise) they had picked up her items and placed them into her bags. She had loved the way the hair kept falling into his eyes as he leaned over to grab a box or a tin. And the tattered brown shoes he wore with no socks. And the left side of his collar turned in rather than out.

The bag boy seemed a wonderful contrast to the perfectly beautiful house she had been forced to accept as her home, to the *history* she hated, to the loneliness she had become used to, and she couldn't wait to come back for more of his awkwardness and dishevelment.

Incredibly, it was another four weeks before they saw each other again. As fate would have it, her visits to the supermarket never coincided with his schedule to bag. Each time she went to the store, her eyes scanned the checkouts at once, her heart in her mouth. And each hour he worked, the bag boy kept one eye on the door, watching for the red-haired girl with the big orange bow.

**Y**et in their disappointment these weeks there was a kind of ecstasy. It is reason enough to be alive, the hope you may see again some face which has meant something to you. The anticipation of meeting the bag boy eased the girl's painful transition into her new and jarring life in Cincinnati. It provided for her an anchor amid all that was impersonal and unfamiliar, and she spent less time on thoughts of what she had left behind as she concentrated on what might lie ahead. And for the boy, the long and often tedious hours at the supermarket which provided no challenge other than that of showing up the following workday . . . these hours became possibilities of mystery and romance for him as he watched the electric doors for the girl in the orange bow.

**A**nd when finally they did meet up again, neither offered a clue to the other that he, or she, had been the object of obsessive thought for weeks. She spotted him as soon as she came into the store, but she kept her eyes strictly in front of her as she pulled out a cart and wheeled it toward the produce. And he, too, knew the instant she came through the door—though the orange bow was gone, replaced by a small but bright yellow flower instead—and he never once turned his head in her direction but watched her from the corner of his vision as he tried to swallow back the fear in his throat.

t is odd how we sometimes deny ourselves the very pleasure we have longed for and which is finally within our reach. For some perverse reason she would not have been able to articulate, the girl did not bring her cart up to the bag boy's checkout when her shopping was done. And the bag boy let her leave the store, pretending no notice of her.

This is often the way of children, when they truly want a thing, to pretend that they don't. And then they grow angry when no one tries harder to give them this thing they so casually rejected, and they soon find themselves in a rage simply because they cannot say yes when they mean yes. Humans are very complicated. (And perhaps cats, who have been known to react in the same way, though the resulting rage can only be guessed at.)

The girl hated herself for not checking out at the boy's line, and the boy hated himself for not catching her eye and saying hello, and they most sincerely hated each other without having ever exchanged even two minutes of conversation.

ventually—in fact, within the week—a kind and intelligent boy who lived very near her beautiful house asked the girl to a movie and she gave up her fancy for the bag boy at the supermarket. And the bag boy himself grew so bored with his job that he made a desperate search for something better and ended up in a bookstore where scores of fascinating girls lingered like honeybees about a hive. Some months later the bag boy and the girl with the orange bow again crossed paths, standing in line with their dates at a movie theater, and, glancing toward the other, each smiled slightly, then looked away, as strangers on public buses often do, when one is moving off the bus and the other is moving on.

# Meet Cynthia Rylant

"It took me about seven books to feel like a writer. But I know now that's what I am," Cynthia Rylant has said. Now she has more than seventeen books to her credit, including the novels *A Fine White Dust,* a Newbery Honor Book, and *A Kindness,* which was named an American Library Association Best Book for Young Adults.

Rylant initially believed that she had "nothing to write about" because her life was so ordinary. Yet it was that very ordinary family life and the years she spent as a child in West Virginia that provided her with the material for her stories and shaped her unique writer's voice. "I came from people who worked very, very hard and whose lives were never simple nor easy. In my books I try to touch on how hard life can be sometimes, but always, always show that for everything we lose, we will get something back."

Most of Rylant's characters are teenagers or young children. "I like writing about child characters," she says, "because they have more possibilities. They can get away with more love, more anger, more fear than adult characters. They can be more moving. I like them more. I sympathize with them more."

A COUPLE OF KOOKS
and Other Stories
about Love by
Cynthia Rylant

Cynthia Rylant
A FINE WHITE DUST

The idea that the pun is "the lowest form of humor" is usually held by people who aren't clever enough to think of one. In fact, the pun has proved irresistible to writers from Aristotle to Shakespeare to Lewis Carroll. Even Cynthia Rylant couldn't resist using a pun in the title of her story "Checkouts."

## Jester One-Track Mind

In olden times, there was a king whose court jester punned endlessly. Growing sick of the constant puns, the king finally ordered the jester to be hanged. At the last minute, just as the jester was being tied to the royal noose, the king had a change of heart and declared that the jester would be spared if he would agree never to make another pun. The jester thought it over and said, "Well, no noose is good news." And so he was hanged.

## Having a Bad Spell

During the first round of his class's spelling bee, little Stevie was asked to spell the word *weather*. He thought for a moment and then spelled out, "W-A-H-T-I-O-U-R." His teacher looked at him in amazement and said, "Stevie, that's the worst spell of weather we've had around here for years!"

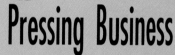

## Pressing Business

At first the tailor hemmed and hawed at being button-holed, but then he replied, "I don't want to skirt the issue; we're taking a uniform cut. I try to pleats my customers; I seam to tweed them right. But right now business is only sew-sew—if we don't tie up more orders, I'll hat to clothes down!"

## The Pun Is Here to Slay

If you've ever tried to tell a pun, you already know that the best puns are the ones that always conjure up groans from your audience. Sometimes the best puns are the really *bad* ones. And, hey, remember: As bad as your puns are—they could always be verse!

# PETS

**BY JACCI COLE**

## If Only They Could Talk

**T**he small collie pup ran frantically back and forth between the house and the little girl out in the field. It ran into the house whimpering and barking, waited a moment, and then ran outside again. Outside, the pup licked the face of the crying girl, barked a few times, and ran to the house once more. In the house the collie became more insistent. It grabbed the pant leg of the girl's father and pulled him from his chair.

Out in the field, the crying girl tried again to free her leg trapped in the fence. She heard the barking dog and looked up. She was not surprised to see her father running beside the dog; she had known her pup would help her.

# TALKING PETS

Every so often that story comes up when I visit my father. To this day, he still brags about our collie Lassie who "saved" me from the clutches of a chain link fence. "That dog was more than smart," he'll say. "She could talk. She told me that day my little girl was in trouble."

Has something like this ever happened to you?

If you believe your pet can "talk" to you, you're not alone. "Ninety percent of all pet owners regularly chat with their dogs, cats, and birds," researcher Richard Wolkomir states in a recent study. "And 73 percent are convinced their pets talk back."

It seems that if we're exploring animal communication, we don't have to look very far! "Pet owners know animals have an eloquent vocabulary of yawns, yips, wags, whines, scratches, back rolls, and withering glares when dinner is late," Wolkomir continues. "Interpreting these signals, owners can speak for their pets."

My father didn't always believe our dog "talked." She was like most dogs, always running in and out of the house barking and being a nuisance. Why then did he follow her to the field that day when I was caught in the fence? Did he think her barking meant "Follow me!"? Did he know I was in trouble? No, he did not. In truth, he followed her because her barking was so insistent that he became curious. Only after finding me did he realize that she had been trying to tell him something important. Today if someone were to ask my father if dogs can communicate with people, he would say they can.

# TRADITION AND ANIMAL COMMUNICATION

People have been debating the issue of animal communication for centuries. Some believe strongly in the communication abilities of animals while others scoff.

In ancient Ethiopia people elected a dog as their king. By growling or wagging his tail, this king would express his opinions, unfavorable or favorable, on whatever matter he was asked to decide. Even today in Lapland, some people think black cats are reincarnated relatives; that is, their relatives' spirits are in the cats. The cats' opinions are asked whenever family matters are involved.

Jewish folklore has it that if a cat washes itself, guests will soon arrive. In ancient England people looked to their cats' tails to forecast the weather: If the tail pointed toward the fire, they got ready for a cold spell. If the cat licked its tail, they prepared for rain.

Are these really examples of animals trying to communicate, or are they silly superstitions? Before you laugh at our ancestors, think about today's family pet. "It seems we are now going through a pet revolution," says researcher Boris M. Levinson. "We in modern times have elevated the pet to a being on a par with man." We do more than just pet and play with them—we talk with them as we would our best friends.

"Pet owners know animals have an eloquent vocabulary of yawns, yips, wags, whines, scratches, back rolls, and withering glares when dinner is late. Interpreting these signals, owners can speak for their pets."

*Science writer*
*Richard Wolkomir*

"Dogs have their own social reasons for acting the way they do but we have our own reasons for interpreting their behavior in a symbolic fashion."

*Veterinarian Bruce Fogle*

# SPECIAL FRIENDS

Why do some people talk with their pets? Researcher Michael Robin talked with young people about their pets and found a special kind of closeness and communication. "My dog is very special to me," said one sixteen-year-old girl. "When I was little I used to go to her and pet her when I was depressed and crying. She seemed to understand. You could tell by the look in her eyes." Said a sixteen-year-old boy about his dog: "He was there to talk anytime I needed him. We were very close. I mean I would talk and he would look at me as though he understood every word I said."

Are these animals communicating with their owners? Some people would say yes. The pets gave these young people what they needed most: companionship and someone to talk to. As some communication specialists explain, a two-sided conversation isn't essential for communication.

In fact, most agree that listening well is one important part of good communication.

In addition, animal experts state that most animals *do* communicate in their own ways. They do a lot of non-verbal communication—that is, communication through noises and movements instead of words. For example, when family members have been gone all day, the family pet will tell his people, "I'm sure happy to see you again" with a wag of the tail, a rub on the leg, or a jump and a bark.

Pets also tell their people when they want attention. Researcher Sharon L. Smith noted that petting isn't something that people do only when they feel like it. "Even though it was the person who touched the dog," she reports, "the dog participated consistently by remaining within reach" and by nosing or pawing the person to get more petting.

# PET INTELLIGENCE?

Most pet owners feel their pets are intelligent, and many believe that they communicate intelligently. But how is a person to know if his pet is a smart communicator? Naturalist Bil Gilbert states, "When we speak of an 'intelligent' or 'good' dog, we generally mean one who is especially responsive to humans, has exceptional talent for understanding what we expect of him, and for making himself understood to us—a good communicator."

Gilbert thinks most dogs are smart because they have to communicate in two languages! With other dogs, they exchange information through smell, body language, and vocal noises. These communication skills are similar to those of wolves but not as well developed. To communicate with people, dogs have to learn another language—human signs and gestures. According to Gilbert, a dog inherits its ability to understand other dogs. But with people, dogs have to *learn* and *remember* the signs people use. For instance, dogs can learn a command such as "sit" or "stay," but they don't understand it until it is taught to them. They do not inherit the ability to understand people and people language.

Nor can they learn to talk to another dog in people language. For example, "fetch" is a simple command a person can teach a dog. But a dog is not able to give another dog a signal to "fetch."

However, most dogs can be good communicators. Perhaps it's because of centuries of domestication (being taught to live with people) that dogs seem to be born with a desire to respond to people. Gilbert believes, "Dogs seem far more anxious to communicate with their human companions than they do with other dogs." This willingness to communicate with people may be the reason for the enduring partnership and friendship between dogs and humans.

Cats seem to be more subtle in their attempts to communicate. According to cat-watcher Patricia Moyes, they communicate "by means of body language" more than with sounds. They give messages to people and to other animals mostly with the tail and ears, but the whole body can be used to express some moods.

For instance, a happy, contented cat carries its tail high and straight like a banner. But a sad or disappointed cat has a droopy tail. "In a more subtle way," Moyes says, "both tail and ears are used to react when a cat knows that he is the subject of human conversation. He will sit or crouch with his back to you, but at the mention of his name, the tip of the tail will twitch and one ear will quiver."

So, is this a cat's attempt to communicate with us? Moyes says yes, and she gives another example: "A cat who flattens his ears backward rather than sideways is bent on mischief. He will run away from you, his ears back and his buttocks swinging, dancing on the tips of his toes. . . . The fact that cats will signal their intentions so obviously leads me to conclude that part of the fun is to attract human attention and invite pursuit." In other words, this is a cat's way of saying, "Come play with me!"

Cats also have several clear ways of communicating with other cats. Moyes says, "The lick is the most basic experience of a cat's life because the rasp of his mother's rough tongue is the first sensation a newborn kitten experiences." Though licking is used for grooming and cleaning, it is also a means for communicating comfort to other cats.

Moyes says that cats don't usually vocalize much when communicating with other cats; they do their talking with their bodies. However, during courtship and mating the male cat will croon softly and gently to the female. And we have all heard the ear-piercing screeches of the fighting rival males!

Our pets, no doubt, save most of their meowing to communicate with us. Moyes believes that different kinds of meows have different meanings. Some of the different meows she has identified are: the welcome—a series of short, chirruping mews, each running from high to low tones; the demand—a high-pitched, sustained, incessantly repeated noise; and the information meow—a series of fairly short but unhurried meows, often interspersed with purring.

# CAN WE UNDERSTAND CAT COMMUNICATION?

Can we really understand a cat's meow? According to animal lover Laura Flores, we can if we take the time to listen. She has one cat who will climb into the cupboard where his food is and "call" to her to come feed him.

Her other cat uses a more subtle approach. She and this cat play a game she says the cat invented because "he knows what bugs me." She says she can be sitting at her kitchen table eating dinner and reading the paper. "My cat is sitting at my feet watching me, but I ignore him. But this cat is really smart. He knows I hate to be stared at. He never says a word; he never moves. He just sits there and stares."

Is this communication? Flores seems to think so. Although figuring this cat out took a while, she believes they now know how to "tell" each other what they want to say. She states, "You just have to be patient when they're talking. Cats are so conceited, they like to take a long time; they like an audience."

Another cat owner, Penny Doehrmann, disagrees. She likes cats; they're fun to have around and they're good for catching mice. But talk to her cat? No way! "Cats aren't people and I'm not a cat. If I want to talk to somebody, I'll get on the phone!"

# COMMUNICATION BETWEEN PETS AND PEOPLE

There are those who remain convinced that animal communication with people is a bunch of hooey. Psychologist Aaron H. Katcher agrees. He thinks communication between pets and people is limited because of the pets. People can learn and move beyond their natural origins. They can change and adapt to new circumstances. But the dog, for instance, "stays fixed in his dual role, neither wolf nor person." In other words, due to domestication, dogs can't communicate well with others of their kind and certainly not well with their wild cousin, the wolf. And though they're great companions, they can't really talk with people either, says Katcher.

But don't say that when you're close to Michael W. Fox. He points to the pet communication people don't yet understand. "For example," he says, "one morning a Siamese cat in Philadelphia began to call loudly and incessantly at 10 a.m. the morning after the evening before when its companion, an aged German shepherd, was rushed to the veterinary hospital. The veterinarian called at 11 a.m. that morning to tell the owner that the dog had died on the operating table at 10 a.m. The owner had already been prepared for this loss by her cat's strange behavior. But how did the cat know?" However it knew, it communicated the sad news in the only way it knew how.

"Our debt to [pets] is unmeasurable, for we have learned and are still learning from them to become more fully human: responsible and compassionate."

Michael W. Fox, director of the Humane Society of the United States

"The dog does not teach a child responsibility; the parents teach a child responsibility using the dog as a stimulus or reward."

Psychologist Aaron H. Katcher

Pet Talk

"[Experience] has led me to believe without doubt that many creatures do possess a good deal of intelligence. Though their languages, their principles, their basic way of life are all different from ours, that does not give me the right to discount their ability to think or to act on thought."

*Photojournalist Bill Thomas*

"We tend to call a dog or a chimp or an elephant 'intelligent' because it learns quickly to do what humans teach it. Perhaps we should say instead that the animal is very adaptable."

*Author Emily Hahn, Look Who's Talking!*

# PETS AS THERAPISTS

Part of the mystery of animals is the way they can comfort and change us. Researcher Ange Condoret tells this story of an autistic child. A person who is autistic lives in his or her own fantasy world with no contact with the real people around her. This child, Bethsabee, "refused all physical contact," Condoret says. "She retreated from all of her classmates. She could not bear to be held by the hand and certainly not to be kissed or hugged."

Then one day one of the classroom pets, a dove, opened its wings in front of Bethsabee, and flew. A magical thing happened to the girl: "Her gaze left the world of objects to follow the flight of the bird; she awkwardly mimicked the motions of flight with her hands; when the dove flew again, she blushed, looked fixedly at the animal, and uttered new sounds, 'que-que,' as if trying to talk to the bird. Her gaze, the way she was holding her head, and her gestures expressed for the first time a will to communicate with this living, flying being."

What did the bird communicate to Bethsabee to help her discover the world around her? It remains a mystery. But Condoret declares, "Animals have the capacity to draw out a set of emotional and verbal behaviors from very young children" that help them learn to speak. This dove somehow brought about a wonderful change in Bethsabee. Within a few months she was beginning to talk, was playing with other children, and even let her friends kiss her. Perhaps pets, as gentle teachers, can show us that there are many ways to communicate with them and with other people.

But Aaron H. Katcher thinks we give animals too much credit as teachers. "It is an idle fiction to believe that a dog teaches us or our children anything. Information that changes us is given through words," he insists, "and the dog has no words." Katcher goes on to say that pets like the dog "may excite . . . but the dog teaches nothing, save the simple games that one learns to play with dogs."

313

# TOWARD GREATER UNDERSTANDING

All of this is beside the real point of animal/human communication, says researcher Boris Levinson. The problem is, "We have tried to teach an animal companion our language, our way of communication, rather than trying to learn his."

In our attempts to "talk with the animals," we may be overlooking a great deal. It's obvious that animals don't possess the ability to talk as we do, but they should be given more credit for the efforts they make. We should use our greater understanding of ourselves and them to bridge the gap in animal/human communication.

With some of the animals we study and watch, their interest in people and their desire to communicate is evident. We have a long history of companionship with dogs and cats. Yet our ability to communicate with them still has limitations. Perhaps we are too arrogant in the way we think of animals. If we could see the world through their eyes, how would we be changed?

# MEMO

## Meet JACCI COLE

As a young girl, Jacci Cole was saved from the steely grip of a chain-link fence by her responsive pet collie. That incident, which is described in "Pets: If Only They Could Talk," also precipitated a lifelong interest in pet communication. As the owner of three cats, Cole has had a great many opportunities to test opposing viewpoints about the ways in which animals communicate. Because she wishes to remain an objective reporter, Cole has not taken sides in the ongoing controversy. When she isn't writing a book, Jacci Cole runs a free-lance editing business, raises children, paints, and hunts for wild mushrooms.

315

# Unsatisfied Yearning

Down in the silent hallway
    Scampers the dog about,
And whines, and barks, and scratches,
    In order to get out.

Once in the glittering starlight,
    He straightway doth begin
To set up a doleful howling
    In order to get in!

*Richard Kendall Munkittrick*

# AFTER THE BEEP

## The Westing Game
by Ellen Raskin ▪ Avon, 1984

Then one day (it happened to be the Fourth of July), a most uncommon-looking delivery boy rode around town slipping letters under the doors of the chosen tenants-to-be. The letters were signed Barney Northrup.

The delivery boy was sixty-two years old, and there was no such person as Barney Northrup.

**Poetspeak**
by Paul Janeczko ▪ Bradbury, 1983

Poems are best delivered fast, sharp, smart and tellingly. They can help you realize something you could not understand before—they can illuminate the spirit with long forgotten beauties and uglies—

*Poetspeak:*
In their work, about their work
A selection by Paul B. Janeczko

# MEET Jean Craighead George

When Jean Craighead George was invited to visit a scientist in Alaska who was studying a wolf pack, she didn't hesitate. "I can see wild wolves?" she replied. "I'm going!"

Within a few days, George and her son had set up camp on the wild tundra of Alaska's McKinley National Park. Using a special spy scope, she settled down to watch the daily comings and goings of twelve wolves and their magnificent leader.

Two incidents in particular made a lasting impression on the author—one was of the dominant wolf with his pack; the other was of a young Eskimo girl seen walking alone across the tundra. Those images "haunted me for a year or more," George has said. She brought the images together in *Julie of the Wolves,* her powerful novel that won the Newbery Medal in 1973. A few years later, the book was chosen as one of the ten best American children's books of the past two hundred years!

George's writing career has spanned many years and has produced more than forty books; among them is the Newbery Honor Book *My Side of the Mountain* and its sequel, *On the Far Side of the Mountain.*

320

# JULIE
## of the Wolves

**By Jean Craighead George**
**Illustrated by Kris Wiltse**

Miyax pushed back the hood of her sealskin parka and looked at the Arctic sun. It was a yellow disc in a lime-green sky, the colors of six o'clock in the evening and the time when the wolves awoke. Quietly she put down her cooking pot and crept to the top of a dome-shaped frost heave, one of the many earth buckles that rise and fall in the crackling cold of the Arctic winter. Lying on her stomach, she looked across a vast lawn of grass and moss and focused her attention on the wolves she had come upon two sleeps ago. They were wagging their tails as they awoke and saw each other.

Her hands trembled and her heartbeat quickened, for she was frightened, not so much of the wolves, who were shy and many harpoon-shots away, but because of her desperate predicament. Miyax was lost. She had been lost without food for many sleeps on the North Slope of Alaska. The barren slope stretches for three hundred miles from the Brooks Range to the Arctic Ocean, and for more than eight hundred miles from the Chukchi to the Beaufort Sea. No roads cross it; ponds and lakes freckle its immensity. Winds scream across it, and the view in every direction is exactly the same. Somewhere in this cosmos was Miyax; and the very life in her body, its spark and warmth, depended upon these wolves for survival. And she was not so sure they would help.

Miyax stared hard at the regal black wolf, hoping to catch his eye. She must somehow tell him that she

was starving and ask him for food. This could be done she knew, for her father, an Eskimo hunter, had done so. One year he had camped near a wolf den while on a hunt. When a month had passed and her father had seen no game, he told the leader of the wolves that he was hungry and needed food. The next night the wolf called him from far away and her father went to him and found a freshly killed caribou. Unfortunately, Miyax's father never explained to her how he had told the wolf of his needs. And not long afterward he paddled his kayak into the Bering Sea to hunt for seal, and he never returned.

She had been watching the wolves for two days, trying to discern which of their sounds and movements expressed goodwill and friendship. Most animals had such signals. The little Arctic ground squirrels flicked their tails sideways to notify others of their kind that they were friendly. By imitating this signal with her forefinger, Miyax had lured many a squirrel to her hand. If she could discover such a gesture for the wolves she would be able to make friends with them and share their food, like a bird or a fox.

Propped on her elbows with her chin in her fists, she stared at the black wolf, trying to catch his eye. She had chosen him because he was much larger than the others, and because he walked like her father, Kapugen, with his head high and his chest out. The black wolf also possessed wisdom, she had observed. The pack looked to him when the wind carried strange scents or the birds cried nervously. If he was alarmed, they were alarmed. If he was calm, they were calm.

Long minutes passed, and the black wolf did not look at her. He had ignored her since she first came upon them, two sleeps ago. True, she moved slowly and quietly, so as not to alarm him; yet she did wish he would see the kindness in her eyes. Many animals could tell the difference between hostile hunters and friendly people by merely looking at them. But the big black wolf would not even glance her way.

A bird stretched in the grass. The wolf looked at it. A flower twisted in the wind. He glanced at that. Then the breeze rippled the wolverine ruff on Miyax's parka and it glistened in the light. He did not look at that. She waited. Patience with the ways of nature had been instilled in her by her father. And

so she knew better than to move or shout. Yet she must get food or die. Her hands shook slightly and she swallowed hard to keep calm.

**M**iyax was a classic Eskimo beauty, small of bone and delicately wired with strong muscles. Her face was pearl-round and her nose was flat. Her black eyes, which slanted gracefully, were moist and sparkling. Like the beautifully formed polar bears and foxes of the north, she was slightly short-limbed. The frigid environment of the Arctic has sculptured life into compact shapes. Unlike the long-limbed, long-bodied animals of the south that are cooled by dispensing heat on extended surfaces, all live things in the Arctic tend toward compactness, to conserve heat.

The length of her limbs and the beauty of her face were of no use to Miyax as she lay on the lichen-speckled frost heave in the midst of the bleak tundra. Her stomach ached and the royal black wolf was carefully ignoring her.

"*Amaroq, ilaya,* wolf, my friend," she finally called. "Look at me. Look at me."

She spoke half in Eskimo and half in English, as if the instincts of her father and the science of the *gussaks,* the white-faced, might evoke some magical combination that would help her get her message through to the wolf.

Amaroq glanced at his paw and slowly turned his head her way without lifting his eyes. He licked his shoulder. A few matted hairs sprang apart and twinkled individually. Then his eyes sped to each of the three adult wolves that made up his pack and finally to the five pups who were sleeping in a fuzzy mass near the den entrance. The great wolf's eyes softened at the sight of the little wolves, then quickly hardened into brittle yellow jewels as he scanned the flat tundra.

Not a tree grew anywhere to break the monotony of the gold-green plain, for the soils of the tundra are permanently frozen. Only moss, grass, lichens, and a few hardy flowers take root in the thin upper layer that thaws briefly in summer. Nor do many species of animals live in this rigorous land, but those creatures that do dwell here exist in bountiful numbers. Amaroq watched a large cloud of Lapland longspurs wheel up into the sky, then alight in the grasses. Swarms of crane flies, one

324

of the few insects that can survive
the cold, darkened the tips of the
mosses. Birds wheeled, turned, and
called. Thousands sprang up from the
ground like leaves in a wind.

The wolf's ears cupped forward
and tuned in on some distant message from the tundra. Miyax tensed
and listened, too. Did he hear some
brewing storm, some approaching
enemy? Apparently not. His ears relaxed and he rolled to his side. She
sighed, glanced at the vaulting sky,
and was painfully aware of her
predicament.

Here she was, watching wolves—she, Miyax, daughter of Kapugen, adopted child of Martha, citizen of the United States, pupil at the Bureau of Indian Affairs School in Barrow, Alaska, and thirteen-year-old wife of the boy Daniel. She shivered at the thought of Daniel, for it was he who had driven her to this fate. She had run away from him exactly seven sleeps ago, and because of this she had one more title by gussak standards—the child divorcée.

The wolf rolled to his belly.

"Amaroq," she whispered. "I am lost and the sun will not set for a month. There is no North Star to guide me."

Amaroq did not stir.

"And there are no berry bushes here to bend under the polar wind and point to the south. Nor are there any birds I can follow." She looked up. "Here the birds are buntings and longspurs. They do not fly to the sea twice a day like the puffins and sandpipers that my father followed."

The wolf groomed his chest with his tongue.

"I never dreamed I could get lost, Amaroq," she went on, talking out loud to ease her fear. "At home on Nunivak Island where I was born, the plants and birds pointed the way for wanderers. I thought they did so everywhere . . . and so, great black Amaroq, I'm without a compass."

It had been a frightening moment when two days ago she realized that the tundra was an ocean of grass on which she was circling around and around. Now as that fear overcame her again she closed her eyes. When she opened them her heart skipped excitedly. Amaroq was looking at her!

"*Ee-lie*," she called and scrambled to her feet. The wolf arched his neck and narrowed his

eyes. He pressed his ears forward. She waved. He drew back his lips and showed his teeth. Frightened by what seemed a snarl, she lay down again. When she was flat on her stomach, Amaroq flattened his ears and wagged his tail once. Then he tossed his head and looked away.

**D**iscouraged, she wriggled backward down the frost heave and arrived at her camp feet first. The heave was between herself and the wolf pack and so she relaxed, stood up, and took stock of her home. It was a simple affair, for she had not been able to carry much when she ran away; she took just those things she would need for the journey—a backpack, food for a week or so, needles to mend clothes, matches, her sleeping skin, and ground cloth to go under it, two knives, and a pot.

She had intended to walk to Point Hope. There she would meet the *North Star*, the ship that brings supplies from the States to the towns on the Arctic Ocean in August when the ice pack breaks up. The ship could always use

dishwashers or laundresses, she had heard, and so she would work her way to San Francisco where Amy, her pen pal, lived. At the end of every letter Amy always wrote: "When are you coming to San Francisco?" Seven days ago she had been on her way—on her way to the glittering, white, postcard city that sat on a hill among trees, those enormous plants she had never seen. She had been on her way to see the television and carpeting in Amy's school, the glass buildings, traffic lights, and stores full of fruits; on her way to the harbor that never froze and the Golden Gate Bridge. But primarily she was on her way to be rid of Daniel, her terrifying husband.

She kicked the sod at the thought of her marriage; then shaking her head to forget, she surveyed her camp. It was nice. Upon discovering the wolves, she had settled down to live near them in the hope of sharing their food, until the sun set and the stars came out to guide her. She had built a house of sod, like the summer homes of the old

Eskimos. Each brick had been cut with her *ulo,* the half-moon shaped woman's knife, so versatile it can trim a baby's hair, slice a tough bear, or chip an iceberg.

Her house was not well built for she had never made one before, but it was cozy inside. She had windproofed it by sealing the sod bricks with mud from the pond at her door, and she had made it beautiful by spreading her caribou ground cloth on the floor. On this she had placed her sleeping skin, a moosehide bag lined with soft white rabbit skins. Next to her bed she had built a low table of sod on which to put her clothes when she slept. To decorate the house she had made three flowers of bird feathers and stuck them in the top of the table. Then she had built a fireplace outdoors and placed her pot beside it. The pot was empty, for she had not found even a lemming to eat.

Last winter, when she had walked to school in Barrow, these mice-like rodents were so numerous they ran out from under her feet wherever she stepped. There were thousands and thousands of them until December, when they suddenly vanished. Her teacher said that the lemmings had a chemical similar to antifreeze in their blood, that kept them active all winter when other

little mammals were hibernating. "They eat grass and multiply all winter," Mrs. Franklin had said in her singsong voice. "When there are too many, they grow nervous at the sight of each other. Somehow this shoots too much antifreeze into their bloodstreams and it begins to poison them. They become restless, then crazy. They run in a frenzy until they die."

Of this phenomenon Miyax's father had simply said, "The hour of the lemming is over for four years."

Unfortunately for Miyax, the hour of the animals that prey on the lemmings was also over. The white fox, the snowy owl, the weasel, the jaeger, and the siskin had virtually disappeared. They had no food to eat and bore few or no young. Those that lived preyed on each other. With the passing of the lemmings, however, the grasses had grown high again and the hour of the caribou was upon the land. Healthy fat caribou cows gave birth to many calves. The caribou population increased, and this in turn increased the number of wolves who prey on the caribou. The abundance of the big deer of the north did Miyax no good, for she had not brought a gun on her trip. It had never occurred to her that she would not reach Point Hope before her food ran out.

A dull pain seized her stomach. She pulled blades of grass from their sheaths and ate the sweet ends. They were not very satisfying, so she picked a handful of caribou moss, a lichen. If the deer could survive in winter on this food, why not she? She munched, decided the plant might taste better if cooked, and went to the pond for water.

As she dipped her pot in, she thought about Amaroq. Why had he bared his teeth at her? Because she was young and he knew she couldn't hurt him? No, she said to herself, it was because he was speaking to her! He had told her to lie down. She had even understood and obeyed him. He had talked to her not with his voice, but with his ears, eyes, and lips; and he had even commended her with a wag of his tail.

She dropped her pot, scrambled up the frost heave and stretched out on her stomach.

"Amaroq," she called softly, "I understand what you said. Can you understand me? I'm hungry— very, very hungry. Please bring me some meat."

The great wolf did not look her way and she began to doubt her reasoning. After all, flattened ears and a tail-wag were scarcely a conversation. She dropped her forehead against the lichens and rethought what had gone between them.

"Then why did I lie down?" she asked, lifting her head and looking at Amaroq. "Why did I?" she called to the yawning wolves. Not one turned her way.

Amaroq got to his feet, and as he slowly arose he seemed to fill the sky and blot out the sun. He was enormous. He could swallow her without even chewing.

"But he won't," she reminded herself. "Wolves do not eat people. That's gussak talk. Kapugen said wolves are gentle brothers."

The black puppy was looking at her and wagging his tail. Hopefully, Miyax held out a pleading hand to him. His tail wagged harder. The mother rushed to him and stood above him sternly. When he licked her cheek apologetically, she pulled back her lips from her fine white teeth. They flashed as she smiled and forgave her cub.

"But don't let it happen again," said Miyax sarcastically, mimicking her own elders. The mother walked toward Amaroq.

"I should call you Martha after my stepmother," Miyax whispered. "But you're much too beautiful. I shall call you Silver instead."

Silver moved in a halo of light, for the sun sparkled on the guard hairs that grew out over the dense underfur and she seemed to glow.

The reprimanded pup snapped at a crane fly and shook himself. Bits of lichen and grass spun off his fur. He reeled unsteadily, took a wider stance, and looked down at his sleeping sister. With a yap he jumped on her and rolled her to her feet. She whined. He barked and picked up a bone. When he was sure she was watching, he ran down the slope with it. The sister tagged after him. He stopped and she grabbed the bone, too. She pulled; he pulled; then he pulled and she yanked.

Miyax could not help laughing. The puppies played with bones like Eskimo children played with leather ropes.

"I understand *that*," she said to the pups. "That's tug-o-war. Now how do you say, 'I'm hungry'?"

Amaroq was pacing restlessly along the crest of the frost heave as

if something were about to happen. His eyes shot to Silver, then to the gray wolf Miyax had named Nails. These glances seemed to be a summons, for Silver and Nails glided to him, spanked the ground with their forepaws and bit him gently under the chin. He wagged his tail furiously and took Silver's slender nose in his mouth. She crouched before him, licked his cheek and lovingly bit his lower jaw. Amaroq's tail flashed high as her mouthing charged him with vitality. He nosed her affectionately. Unlike the fox who met his mate only in the breeding season, Amaroq lived with his mate all year.

Next, Nails took Amaroq's jaw in his mouth and the leader bit the top of his nose. A third adult, a

small male, came slinking up. He got down on his belly before Amaroq, rolled trembling to his back, and wriggled.

"Hello, Jello," Miyax whispered, for he reminded her of the quivering gussak dessert her mother-in-law made.

She had seen the wolves mouth Amaroq's chin twice before and so she concluded that it was a ceremony, a sort of "Hail to the Chief." He must indeed be their leader for he was clearly the wealthy wolf; that is, wealthy as she had known the meaning of the word on Nunivak Island. There the old Eskimo hunters she

had known in her childhood thought the riches of life were intelligence, fearlessness, and love. A man with these gifts was rich and was a great spirit who was admired in the same way that the gussaks admired a man with money and goods.

The three adults paid tribute to Amaroq until he was almost smothered with love; then he bayed a wild note that sounded like the wind on the frozen sea. With that the others sat around him, the puppies scattered between them. Jello hunched forward and Silver shot a fierce glance at him. Intimidated, Jello pulled his ears together and back. He drew himself down until he looked smaller than ever.

Amaroq wailed again, stretching his neck until his head was high above the others. They gazed at him affectionately and it was plain to see that he was their great spirit, a royal leader who held his group together with love and wisdom.

Any fear Miyax had of the wolves was dispelled by their affection for each other. They were friendly animals and so devoted to

Amaroq that she needed only to be accepted by him to be accepted by all. She even knew how to achieve this—bite him under the chin. But how was she going to do that?

She studied the pups hoping they had a simpler way of expressing their love for him. The black puppy approached the leader, sat, then lay down and wagged his tail vigorously. He gazed up at Amaroq in pure adoration, and the royal eyes softened.

Well, that's what I'm doing! Miyax thought. She called to Amaroq. "I'm lying down gazing at you, too, but you don't look at *me* that way!"

When all the puppies were wagging his praises, Amaroq yipped, hit a high note, and crooned. As his voice rose and fell, the other adults sang out and the puppies yipped and bounced.

The song ended abruptly. Amaroq arose and trotted swiftly down the slope. Nails followed, and behind him ran Silver, then Jello. But Jello did not run far. Silver turned and looked him straight in the eye. She pressed her ears forward aggressively and lifted her tail. With that, Jello went back to the puppies and the three sped away like dark birds.

Miyax hunched forward on her elbows, the better to see and learn. She now knew how to be a good

puppy, pay tribute to the leader, and even to be a leader by biting others on the top of the nose. She also knew how to tell Jello to baby-sit. If only she had big ears and a tail, she could lecture and talk to them all.

Flapping her hands on her head for ears, she flattened her fingers to make friends, pulled them together and back to express fear, and shot them forward to display her aggression and dominance. Then she folded her arms and studied the puppies again.

The black one greeted Jello by tackling his feet. Another jumped on his tail, and before he could discipline either, all five were upon him. He rolled and tumbled with them for almost an hour; then he ran down the slope, turned, and stopped. The pursuing pups plowed into him, tumbled, fell, and lay still. During a minute of surprised recovery there was no action. Then the black pup flashed his tail like a semaphore signal and they all jumped on Jello again.

**M**iyax rolled over and laughed aloud. "That's funny. They're really like kids."

When she looked back, Jello's tongue was hanging from his mouth and his sides were heaving. Four of the puppies had collapsed at his feet and were asleep. Jello flopped down, too, but the black pup still looked around. He was not the least bit

tired. Miyax watched him, for there was something special about him.

He ran to the top of the den and barked. The smallest pup, whom Miyax called Sister, lifted her head, saw her favorite brother in action and, struggling to her feet, followed him devotedly. While they romped, Jello took the opportunity to rest behind a clump of sedge, a moisture-loving plant of the tundra. But hardly was he settled before a pup tracked him to his hideout and pounced on him. Jello narrowed his eyes, pressed his ears forward, and showed his teeth.

"I know what you're saying," she called to him. "You're saying, 'lie down.'" The puppy lay down, and Miyax got on all fours and looked for the nearest pup to speak to. It was Sister.

"Ummmm," she whined, and when Sister turned around she narrowed her eyes and showed her white teeth. Obediently, Sister lay down.

"I'm talking wolf! I'm talking wolf!" Miyax clapped, and tossing her head like a pup, crawled in a happy

circle. As she was coming back she saw all five puppies sitting in a row watching her, their heads cocked in curiosity. Boldly the black pup came toward her, his fat backside swinging as he trotted to the bottom of her frost heave, and barked.

"You are *very* fearless and *very* smart," she said. "Now I know why you are special. You are wealthy and the leader of the puppies. There is no doubt what you'll grow up to be. So I shall name you after my father Kapugen, and I shall call you Kapu for short."

Kapu wrinkled his brow and turned an ear to tune in more acutely on her voice.

"You don't understand, do you?"

Hardly had she spoken than his tail went up, his mouth opened slightly, and he fairly grinned.

"Ee-lie!" she gasped. "You do understand. And that scares me." She perched on her heels. Jello whined an undulating note and Kapu turned back to the den.

Miyax imitated the call to come home. Kapu looked back over his shoulder in surprise.

She giggled. He wagged his tail and jumped on Jello.

She clapped her hands and settled down to watch this language of jumps and tumbles, elated that she was at last breaking the wolf code. After a long time she decided they were not talking but rough-housing, and so she started home. Later she changed her mind. Roughhousing was very important to wolves. It occupied almost the entire night for the pups.

"Ee-lie, okay," she said. "I'll learn to roughhouse. Maybe then you'll accept me and feed me." She pranced, jumped, and whimpered; she growled, snarled, and rolled. But nobody came to roughhouse.

Sliding back to her camp, she heard the grass swish and looked up to see Amaroq and his hunters sweep around her frost heave and stop about five feet away. She could smell the sweet scent of their fur.

The hairs on her neck rose and her eyes widened. Amaroq's ears went forward aggressively and she remembered that wide eyes meant fear to him. It was not good to show him she was afraid. Animals attacked the fearful. She tried to narrow them, but remembered that was not right either. Narrowed eyes were mean. In desperation she recalled that Kapu had moved

forward when challenged. She pranced right up to Amaroq. Her heart beat furiously as she grunt-whined the sound of the puppy begging adoringly for attention. Then she got down on her belly and gazed at him with fondness.

The great wolf backed up and avoided her eyes. She had said something wrong! Perhaps even offended him. Some slight gesture that meant nothing to her had apparently meant something to the wolf. His ears shot forward angrily and it seemed all was lost. She wanted to get up and run, but she gathered her courage and pranced closer to him. Swiftly she patted him under the chin.

The signal went off. It sped through his body and triggered emotions of love. Amaroq's ears flattened and his tail wagged in friendship. He could not react in any other way to the chin pat, for the roots of this signal lay deep in wolf history. It was inherited from generations and generations of leaders before him. As his eyes softened, the sweet odor of ambrosia arose from the gland on the top of his tail and she was drenched lightly in wolf scent. Miyax was one of the pack.

# who's afraid of the BIG BAD WOLF?

Remember the first time you heard the word wolf? Maybe it was in a story like "The Three Little Pigs" or "Little Red Riding Hood." Whatever tale it was, chances are that the wolf was the bad guy in the story. Perhaps almost everything you've ever seen or heard about wolves was bad until you read about them in Julie of the Wolves.

Here is a sprinkling of some of the fascinating facts that naturalists have learned about wolves.

**WOLVES** *are very friendly with other members of their own pack,* but they will attack wolves they do not know. A wolf forms nearly all of its friendships when it is still a pup. That's one reason why wolves almost never leave their packs.

**WOLF** *packs are small.* Most only have about eight members, and packs rarely get any larger than fifteen members. The main reason for this is that wolves can kill only one animal at a time, and the carcass must supply food for the entire pack.

**WOLVES** *often travel many miles to find food,* so their hunting grounds may cover as much as a thousand square miles. Even a place as big as Yellowstone National Park does not have room for more than about one hundred wolves.

**WOLVES howl for several reasons.** A call from the leader is the easiest way to bring the pack together, especially when they become separated during a hunt. Howling is also a way to warn other wolves to stay away from the pack's territory. Most of the time, however, wolves howl for the pure joy of it. When one begins, the rest happily join in.

**WOLVES will eat rabbits, beavers, and even mice,** but they prefer to hunt large mammals like moose and deer. These mammals are larger than the wolves and can kill with their hoofs and antlers. If they choose to stand and fight, the wolves may leave them alone. The wolves catch the weakest animals, often those that are sick or dying. This helps to maintain a balance in animal populations.

**WOLVES in Yellowstone National Park were killed years ago** by the United States government because nearby ranchers were afraid of losing sheep and cattle. But when the wolves were gone, the elk no longer had any natural enemies, and soon there were too many of them. The food supply was too limited to feed all the elk. Many elk and other plant-eating animals starved to death. The Park Service plans to bring wolves back to Yellowstone in order to restore the balance of nature.

337

# THE WOLF

When the pale moon hides and the wild wind wails,
And over the tree-tops the nighthawk sails,
The gray wolf sits on the world's far rim,
And howls: and it seems to comfort him.

The wolf is a lonely soul, you see,
No beast in the wood, nor bird in the tree,
But shuns his path; in the windy gloom
They give him plenty, and plenty of room.

So he sits with his long, lean face to the sky
Watching the ragged clouds go by.
There in the night, alone, apart,
Singing the song of his lone, wild heart.

Far away, on the world's dark rim
He howls, and it seems to comfort him.

*by Georgia Roberts Durston*

# SEEING EARTH FROM SPACE

BY PATRICIA LAUBER

Satellites have expanded possibilities for
sending and receiving messages. Now
it is possible not only to transmit
information from one part of the earth to
another, but also from Earth to space and back.
The results have transformed the way
we view our planet.

## REMOTE SENSING

Space photography is called remote sensing because
it is a way of learning about a target, such as the earth,
without touching it. There are many kinds of remote sensing.
Among them are ones found in the human body. You use yours
every day of your life.

Is a radiator hot? To find out, you don't touch it. You hold
your hands out toward it. If there is heat, nerve endings in your
skin will sense it. That is one kind of human remote sensing.

Eyesight, or vision, is a much more important kind.
To use it, you need light.

White light is a mixture of colors. You see this when
the sun's white light breaks up into a band of colors and
makes a rainbow in the sky. You see it when white light
passes through a prism. The light breaks up into a band of
colors known as a spectrum.

Light travels in waves, and each color has its own wave-
length. When the sun's white light shines on a buttercup,
the flower absorbs most of the wavelengths, but it reflects
the yellow ones. And so you see a yellow flower. A purple plum
is reflecting a mixture of red and violet wavelengths. A brown
dog is reflecting a mixture of red, orange, and yellow ones.

Like the human eye, a camera takes in reflected light. Used with black-and-white or color film, a camera records the kinds of things that the eye sees.

Red wavelengths are the longest that the human eye can detect. So red is the last color we see in the spectrum. But there is color beyond red, color with longer wavelengths. It is in the part of the spectrum called the infrared, meaning "below red." If we could see in the infrared, we would see color beyond red in every rainbow, color we cannot even imagine.

If we could detect even longer infrared wavelengths, we would see something else. After sunset, we would see a dim glow, the glow of heat being given off.

**Agena Docking Vehicle**

Sunlight warms the earth's surface by day. The heat is absorbed by oceans, deserts, rocks, trees, and everything else on the surface. Some of the heat is radiated back into the atmosphere as infrared energy. If we could see these infrared wavelengths, the landscape would glow at night.

Although human eyes cannot sense infrared, there are ways of detecting it. One is to use film that senses infrared. There are also electronic sensors that detect infrared. They are carried on satellites—the Landsat series launched by the United States and satellites launched by other countries. The sensors scan the earth beneath them. They measure the light reflected by the earth, both the wavelengths we see and the infrared. The sensors are another kind of remote sensing.

Sensors record their measurements as numbers, using a scale of 0 to 255. The numbers are radioed to Earth, where computers put them together and make pictures. Bright false colors are added to make details stand out and to let us see what was recorded in infrared.

Some of the pictures, or images, look like photographs; some don't. But all provide far more information than the eye alone could do.

This Landsat picture was made using information sensed and recorded in green, red, and infrared wavelengths. It shows California's Salton Sea, which looks like a big footprint, and the Imperial Valley, which stretches southward. In the valley's warm, dry climate crops grow year-round, irrigated with water from the Colorado River. Healthy green plants reflect infrared strongly; they appear as bright red in this false-color image. Thinner vegetation is pink. Clear water is black. Windblown sand from the neighboring desert is white. The checkerboard pattern shows that some fields have ripening crops (red and pink) and some are lying fallow, or resting (blue-gray).

Because of a difference in the way farming is done, the border between the United States and Mexico appears as a straight line across the Imperial Valley. It is one of the few national boundaries on Earth that can be seen from space.

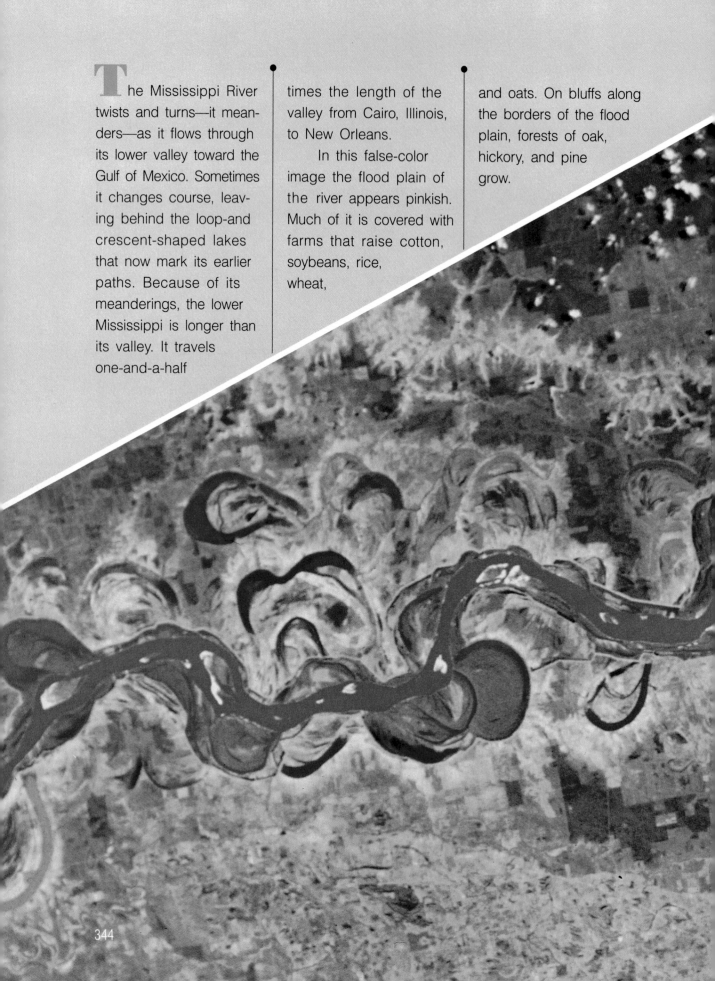

The Mississippi River twists and turns—it meanders—as it flows through its lower valley toward the Gulf of Mexico. Sometimes it changes course, leaving behind the loop-and crescent-shaped lakes that now mark its earlier paths. Because of its meanderings, the lower Mississippi is longer than its valley. It travels one-and-a-half times the length of the valley from Cairo, Illinois, to New Orleans.

In this false-color image the flood plain of the river appears pinkish. Much of it is covered with farms that raise cotton, soybeans, rice, wheat, and oats. On bluffs along the borders of the flood plain, forests of oak, hickory, and pine grow.

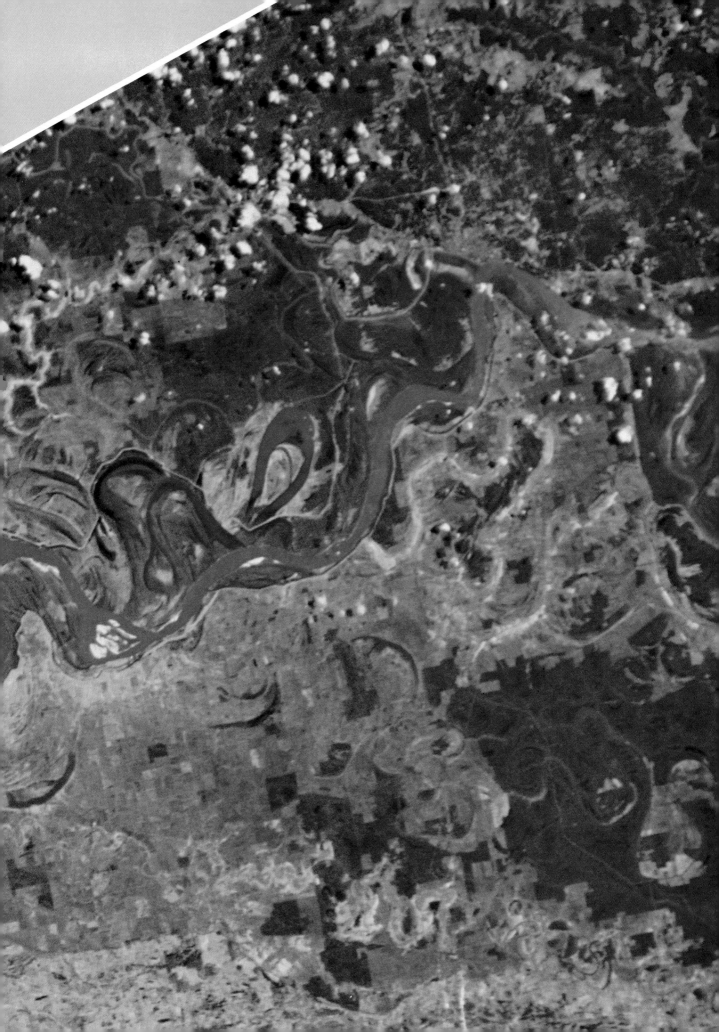

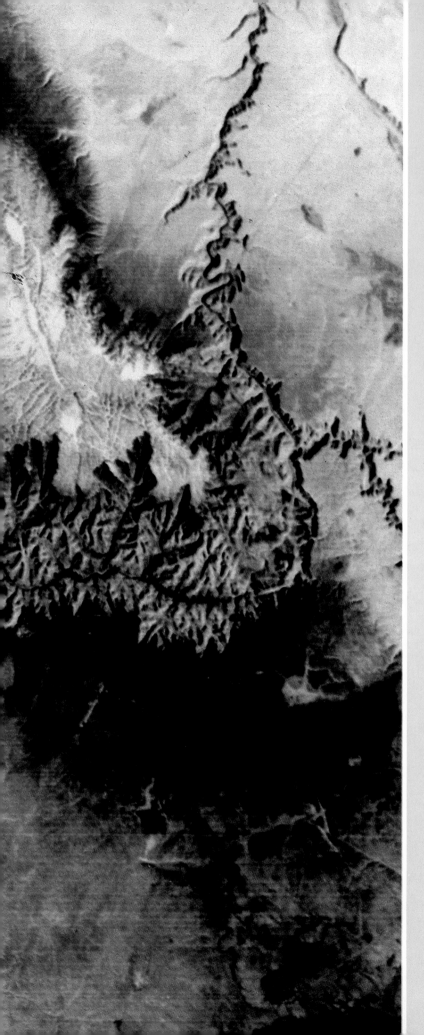

Looking like a scar on the face of the earth, the Grand Canyon twists its way across Arizona in this Landsat picture. This part of the canyon is about a mile deep and 12 miles wide from rim to rim. Its layered rock walls reveal some 2 billion years of Earth's history. The racing Colorado River, which carves the canyon deeper and deeper, is later stopped and pooled by Hoover Dam and Lake Mead.

Radar is still another kind of remote sensing. Unlike the Landsat sensors, it does not measure light reflected from the earth. Instead, it sends out its own radio waves and microwaves. It beams them toward its target and detects their echoes. The strength of the echoes is recorded and used to make maps or pictures. Because it does not use light, radar works both day and night. And because its waves pass through clouds, it can be used when skies are overcast.

One of the space shuttles flew over Montreal, Quebec, at a time when most of the city was covered by clouds. Information from its radar was used to make this false-color image. The St. Lawrence River, above, is shown in black, as are the smaller rivers. You can see the bridges that cross them. Buildings and pavements appear pink and blue. Land that is being cultivated is dark green. Plant life that grows wild is lighter green. The big green oval to the left of the St. Lawrence is Mount Royal.

The same shuttle flew over the high plateau of northern Peru, below. Its radar showed these folded, layered rocks, some 70 million years old. False colors have been used to highlight different kinds of rock. The wormlike black line in the center of the picture is a river that feeds into the Amazon.

Remote sensing shows us the earth in new and often surprising images. For scientists who use the images, they open up ways of studying the earth that have never existed before.

As it orbits, a satellite regularly passes over the same parts of Earth. And so its images let scientists trace what happens as the seasons change. They can, for example, predict flooding by studying winter snowfalls and spring meltings. And they can make cloud-free pictures of any region by piecing together images from different times of year. That was how they obtained this false-color image of Italy. In it, plant life appears in shades of red. Cities and barren areas are blue-gray. Mountains stand out clearly. And the volcano Mount Etna, its sides dark with lava, can be seen on the island of Sicily, off the toe of the boot.

The view from space helps many kinds of scientists. Geographers have discovered mountains and lakes that did not appear on their maps. They have found a previously unknown

island off the coast of Labrador and a reef in the Indian Ocean. They have mapped mountain ranges, deserts, and Arctic lands.

In earlier times, oceanographers could only study the oceans from ships. It was long, slow work. The oceans were huge, covering more than 70 percent of Earth's surface, and the ships were small. Now these scientists can also study the oceans

through pictures from space. They can see large features that they could not see from ships. They can track currents, such as the Gulf Stream, that play a major part in climate. They can track the masses of tiny plants that form the base of food chains in the oceans. They can see and follow details in ways that used to be impossible.

They can, for example, follow the swirling rings of water thrown off by currents, such as these eddies in the Mediterranean Sea. Eddies can be 200 miles in diameter and travel hundreds of miles over several years. By stirring up the water, eddies speed up the spread of heat from tropical areas. They are also important to the life of the sea, because they carry minerals used by plants in making their food.

**S**easat was a United States satellite that failed after a few months. It was designed to study the oceans—roughness, the patterns of currents, water temperature, the speed of surface winds, sea ice. One of its instruments was a radar altimeter, which meas- ured the height of the satellite above the ocean. Seasat sent out a beam of radio waves. When they hit the surface of the water, they were reflected back to the altimeter and recorded.

The results were a surprise: The surface of the ocean rises and falls with the rise and fall of the seabed beneath it. If you could smooth out all the waves, you would see that the ocean surface has hills and valleys. They mark places where there are under- sea mountains and trenches. Where there is a big seamount, for

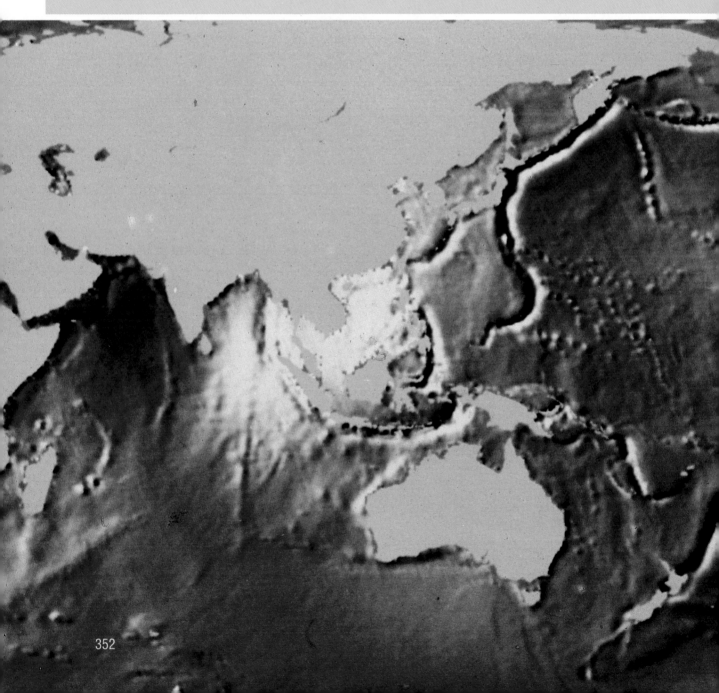

example, there is extra gravity. The seamount pulls a little extra water toward itself. The extra water makes a gentle hill a few feet high. Above a valley or a trench, there is a dip in the surface. And so a map of the ocean surface is also a map of the ocean floor.

This map shows several deep ocean trenches. They are places where plates of the earth's crust are colliding. The leading edge of one plate slides under the other and turns down, creating a trench.

The map also shows the Mid-Atlantic Ridge, a range of undersea volcanic mountains. The range runs down the middle of the Atlantic Ocean and continues around the world, like the seam on a baseball. Here molten rock wells up from inside the earth and is added to the trailing edges of plates.

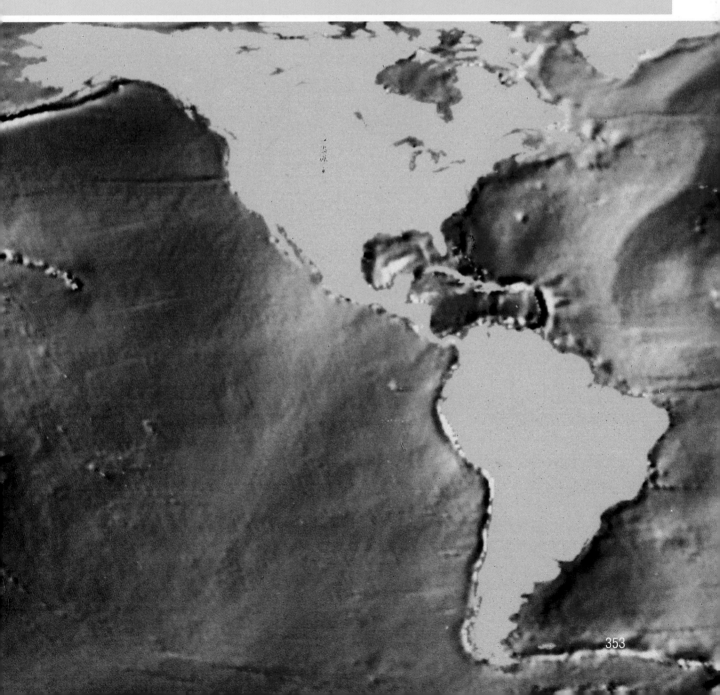

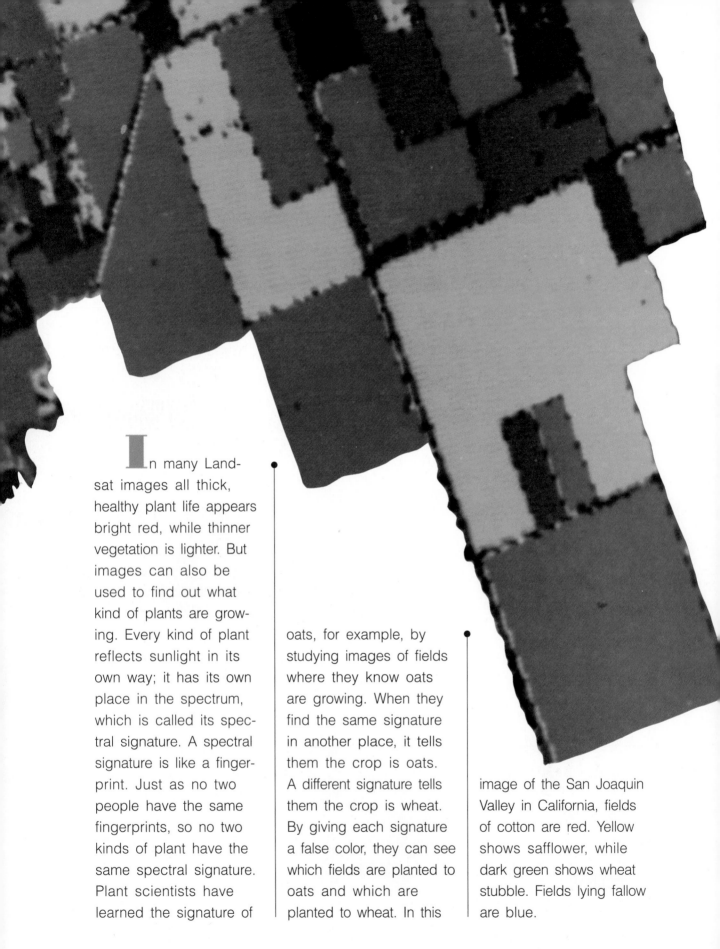

In many Landsat images all thick, healthy plant life appears bright red, while thinner vegetation is lighter. But images can also be used to find out what kind of plants are growing. Every kind of plant reflects sunlight in its own way; it has its own place in the spectrum, which is called its spectral signature. A spectral signature is like a fingerprint. Just as no two people have the same fingerprints, so no two kinds of plant have the same spectral signature. Plant scientists have learned the signature of oats, for example, by studying images of fields where they know oats are growing. When they find the same signature in another place, it tells them the crop is oats. A different signature tells them the crop is wheat. By giving each signature a false color, they can see which fields are planted to oats and which are planted to wheat. In this image of the San Joaquin Valley in California, fields of cotton are red. Yellow shows safflower, while dark green shows wheat stubble. Fields lying fallow are blue.

Shuttle astronauts photographed this strange scene while passing over the Saudi Arabian desert. The pattern of perfect circles told them they were seeing something man-made. It turned out to be farmland. Each circle marked a piece of desert irrigated by a sprinkler that pumped water from underground and broadcast it in a circle.

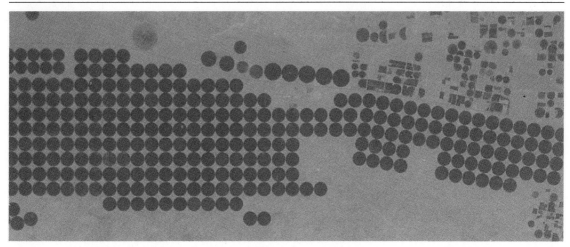

The astronauts' film showed all plant life in one color. Landsat detected far more when it passed over Garden City, Kansas. Here, too, are the circles that tell how the crops are watered. But the Landsat image also tells what the crops are.

The time of year is December. White shows where corn has been harvested and its stubble left on the ground. Red shows that healthy winter wheat is growing. Fields that are black and white have been left fallow to build moisture in the soil.

By noting small differences in spectral signatures, plant scientists can tell a newly planted crop from a ripe crop. They can tell whether plants are healthy. They can even tell if unhealthy plants are suffering from a disease or being attacked by pests.

Geologists use images from space to study places that are far away or hard to explore by land. The image on this page shows Death Valley in southeastern California. It is the lowest point in the Americas, dropping 282 feet below sea level, and the driest, hottest part of the United States. The false-color image shows that almost no plants grow in the region. Red appears only on top of the Panamint Mountains, where a forest grows, and in a few small spots where crops can be irrigated. The image also shows the courses of streams that sometimes run down the slopes of the Panamint Mountains, spread out into fans, and drop the sediment that they were carrying.

Using images from space, geologists have discovered faults in the earth's crust—long cracks that mark places where earthquakes may occur. These are places where dams, power plants, pipelines, factories, and houses should not be built. Geologists also use images to search for minerals. Sometimes they look for the kind of landforms where oil, for example, is likely to be found. Sometimes they look for traces of minerals at the surface. Just as each kind of plant has its own spectral signature, so does each kind of mineral. Seen in the infrared, sandstone is different from shale, tin from copper. With the help of such clues, geologists have discovered copper, nickel, zinc, and uranium in the United States, tin in Brazil, copper in Mexico.

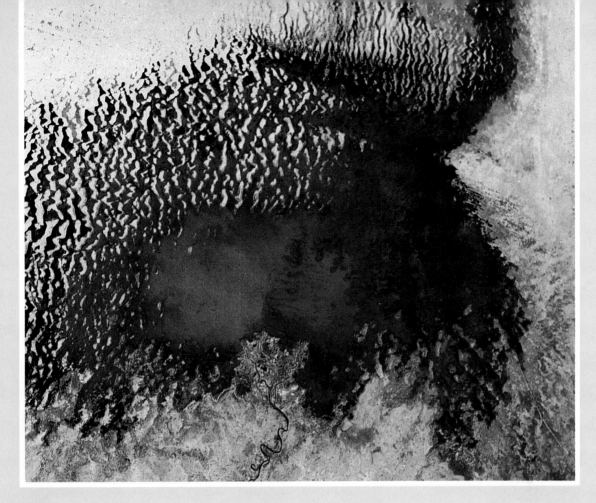

Scientists who study droughts and food supplies use images from space to track changes. Astronaut photographs, for example, show the effect of drought in northern Africa, where the rains have failed year after year. Lake Chad, in Chad and Nigeria, is a once-giant body of water. When first photographed from space, it covered about 7,000 square miles. In this photograph, taken twenty years later, it has shrunk to 1,000 square miles. Ancient dunes, long covered by lake waters, can now be seen. They appear both as dunes and as islands.

The growth of the Sahara Desert along its southern edge can also be traced. Here too the rains have failed, year after year. But the greater problem is that the land cannot support the number of people who live on it. Farmers till poorer and poorer land. They do not let fields lie fallow and rest. They fell trees for firewood or building materials, and without trees to hold the soil in place, winds carry it away. Cattle, goats, and camels strip the land of low-growing plants. The exposed soil bakes hard in the sun and loses its ability to take in and store water. When rain does come, water runs off quickly or evaporates. Sand blows in and buries the plants that remain. And so dry lands become desert—and are added to the Sahara.

oday the Sahara is the world's largest desert. But this part of North Africa has not always been dry. It has been a place where rains fell, rivers flowed, plants grew, and animals and people could live.

Scientists have known this for a number of years, but an unexpected piece of evidence came to light from shuttle radar.

In 1981 the shuttle Columbia was passing over a region of the Sahara where rain falls about once every fifty years. Its radar passed through several feet of loose, dry sand and echoed off bedrock. Images showed a network of ancient riverbeds, some wider than today's Nile. The find was of

great interest to archeologists, scientists who study ancient civilizations and peoples. Several expeditions set out overland and dug down to the riverbeds. They found shells of a land snail that can live only in a moist, tropical climate. They found stones shaped into points at one end, which may have been used as axes or weapons or for hunting. By dating their finds, scientists have discovered three periods when people lived in these river valleys: 212,000, 141,000, and 45,000 years ago.

The picture shows a radar image of the riverbed placed on a Landsat image of the Sahara.

## MEET PATRICIA LAUBER

Can you imagine an eye that tirelessly circles the earth, creating detailed photographs of everything in its path? Patricia Lauber relied on just such an eye—a communications satellite—to provide the information for her book *Seeing Earth from Space.* It was her own vision, however, that selected and described the stunning photos, providing us with an amazing view of our own small planet.

Ms. Lauber's writer's eye has an extraordinary field of vision. She has written more than eighty books—fiction and nonfiction—that focus on topics as diverse as the Ice Age, runaway fleas,

cowboys, and the Loch Ness monster. She gets her ideas "from everywhere—from things I read, from things people tell me about, from things I see about me, from things I experience. The important aspect is that they must interest me very much, because then I want to share them with other people and so I write about them."

Her award-winning *Journey to the Planets* uses the recent photos from unmanned space probes to paint a fascinating picture of the solar system. Her book that describes a volcano, *Volcano: The Eruption and Healing of Mount St. Helens,* was awarded a Newbery Honor Medal.

# Fireflies

by Paul Fleischman

| | |
|---|---|
| Light | Light |
| | is the ink we use |
| Night | Night |
| is our parchment | |
| | We're |
| | fireflies |
| fireflies | flickering |
| flitting | |
| | flashing |
| fireflies | |
| glimmering | fireflies |
| | gleaming |
| glowing | |
| Insect calligraphers | Insect calligraphers |
| practicing penmanship | |
| | copying sentences |
| Six-legged scribblers | Six-legged scribblers |
| of vanishing messages, | |
| | fleeting graffiti |
| Fine artists in flight | Fine artists in flight |
| adding dabs of light | |
| | bright brush strokes |
| Signing the June nights | Signing the June nights |
| as if they were paintings | as if they were paintings |
| | We're |
| flickering | fireflies |
| fireflies | flickering |
| fireflies. | fireflies. |

# CONTENTS

REACH OUT

You can fall down
by yourself
but to get up
you need a friend's hand.

YIDDISH PROVERB

# BEYOND THE DIVIDE

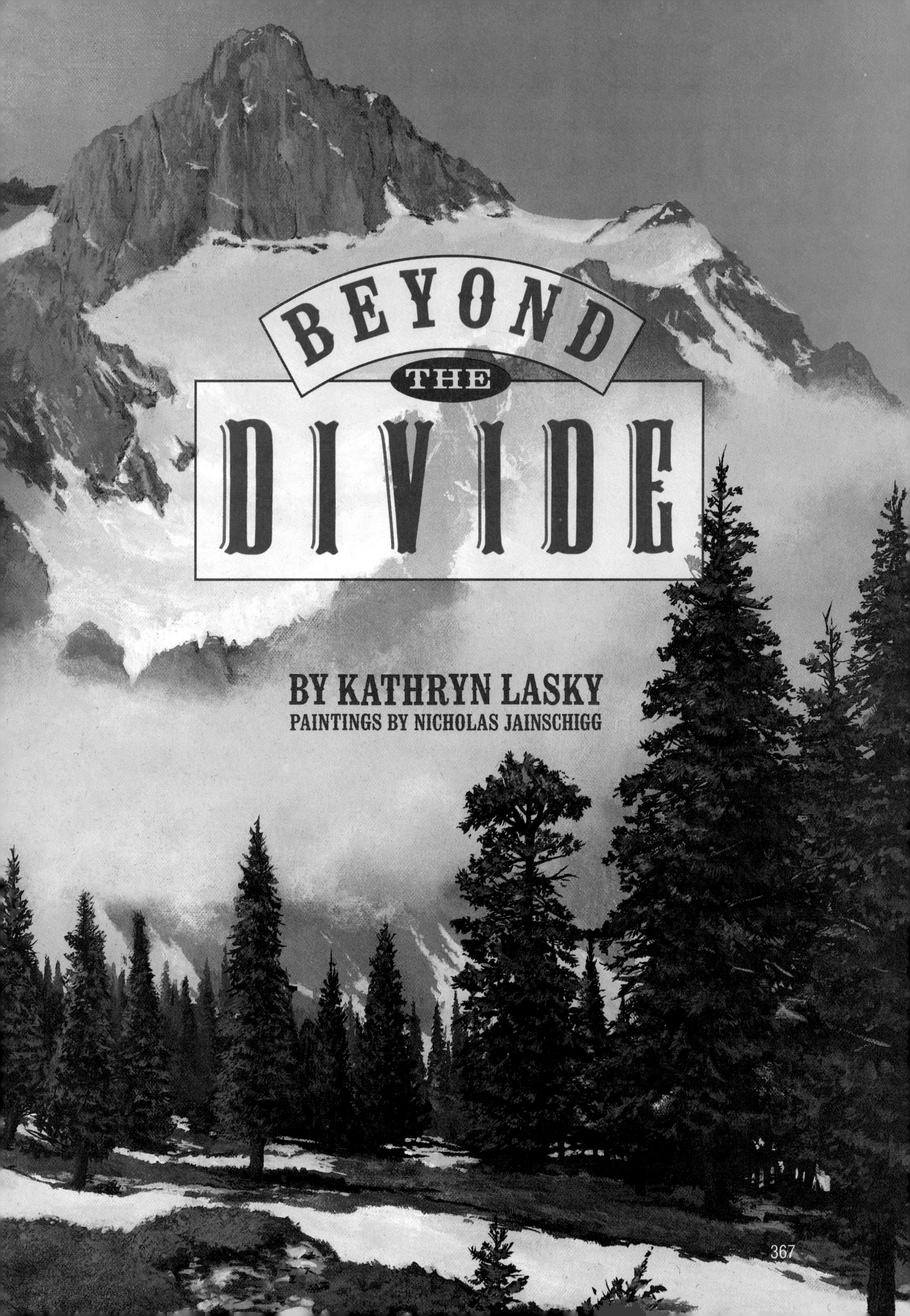

### THE

# DIVIDE

## BY KATHRYN LASKY

PAINTINGS BY NICHOLAS JAINSCHIGG

IN 1849, GOLD IS DISCOVERED IN CALIFORNIA, AND MERIBAH SIMON AND HER FATHER LEAVE THEIR AMISH COMMUNITY IN PENNSYLVANIA TO JOIN ONE OF THE MANY WAGON TRAINS HEADING WEST. DURING THEIR JOURNEY, MERIBAH'S FATHER BECOMES ILL, AND THEY ARE ABANDONED BY THE WAGON TRAIN. JOHN GOODNOUGH COMES TO THEIR AID. ULTIMATELY MERIBAH'S FATHER DOES NOT SURVIVE THE HARSH WINTER AND THE HARD-SHIPS OF THE TRAIL. LEAVING MERIBAH SHELTERED IN A CAVE WITH SOME PROVISIONS, GOODNOUGH SETS OFF TO FIND HELP. A SUCCESSION OF BLIZZARDS DELAYS HIS RETURN.

## January 1, 1850
### The cave on the gorge between the Deer and Mill creeks

In a grove of oaks she dug down under the snow for the acorns. Some were rotten from the dampness, but she found a number of good ones. Nearby she also found hazelnuts and buck-eyes. Spotting a small winter bird pecking at a pine cone for its nuts, she decided to try some of these also. Although autumn was the time for gathering nuts and many of Meribah's appeared rotten, she had found ways of peeling away the bad parts, drying them slowly in the heat of warm ashes, and then roasting them, to make them palatable. She headed now on her snowshoes for a grove of birch trees that she remembered.

The snow was becoming softer and more difficult to walk on. She stopped on a bare crest of hill to take off the hood that she had made from the pelt of the squirrel that Goodnough had shot. The snow had never been able to gather on the wind-swept crest, but an ice lip had formed on its edge. Meribah looked at the glis-tening rim of ice. Ice burn, she thought as she saw the patches of scorched grass be-neath the ice. She had seen this before on the ridges of the gorge, which were often swept bare of snow by the wind. The ice acted as a magnifying glass to scorch whatever grew beneath it. The nurturing warmth of the

sun was turned into a fire by the ice. What was supposed to nourish instead consumed. It was an odd act of nature that fascinated Meribah.

As she stared down at the icy crest, something caught her eye. Bright and red as jewels, they sparkled under the ice on a cushion of scorched grass. "Raspberries!" she cried, and dropped to her knees. She took out her knife and chipped through the ice. Raspberries for her birthday. The berries were plump and ripe. In another hour they would have been burned. There were perhaps three handfuls, which she ate right there. They were not meant to be saved. They were meant to be eaten there, straddling that thin silver rim of ice at the top of a new world. With the sweet juice of a miracle in her mouth, Meribah looked out toward the march of snowy peaks.

⚡

That night by her fire she thought about the raspberries. She could still taste their sweetness. No summer berry would ever taste as sweet. She would always have the taste of these, clinging and more real than a memory. She began to think about things that cling. Her father, he was gone, but yet she lived with him, seeing his face, hearing his voice. It was as if he were still there with her, a presence streaming through the minutes of her life like a current in a river. Miracles, Meribah decided, were not meant to be pondered too hard or studied too deeply. They just happened, and one felt blessed by them.

The next morning the sun poured into the cave, and Meribah, feeling warm and still blessed, looked over at her substantial cache of nuts. She decided that perhaps she should replenish the woven basket in the tree hollow. She set out immediately after her breakfast of acorn mush sprinkled with pine nuts, a new flavor that she liked as much as the acorns.

The snow nearly reached the lower edge of the tree hollow, but the basket was still there. Meribah had not realized before how lovely the basket was. Not only was it tightly woven but beautifully shaped into an

almost perfect oval with elaborate designs. When she reached into it to put in her acorns, she gasped. The basket had been refilled, and this time there were more camass roots and dried apples! This was meant to be pondered.

There had been evidence of Indians everywhere between Mill Creek and Deer Creek. Especially since she had left the tent to come to the cave, Meribah had seen many signs—obsidian chips from toolmaking, heavy flat stones used for grinding. She had even taken one such stone back to the cave to grind her own acorns. She was surprised not that there were Indians but that a sign had been made to her. As little as Meribah had seen earlier of the California Indians, just after they had crossed Fandango Pass, she realized that these Indians were different from the ones of the plains. She and Goodnough had talked about these differences. The Pitt River Indians, which included the Mill Creeks of this region and those to the north and east where the Pitt River originated, were neither painted nor befeathered.

They seemed to blend in with the forests and rugged terrain in which they lived. Unlike the Plains Indians, they sought no contact with the emigrants for either trade or confrontation. Withdrawal seemed to be their pattern. Very rarely was a Mill Creek ever seen by a white person, and yet they seemed to have the run of the gorges, the hills, and the forests between the Mill and Deer creeks. Meribah was stunned now as she stood holding the dried apples and camass roots in her hands. A clear sign had been given, a contact of sorts had been made. What did it mean?

Each day the basket was replenished in a small way—a root, a piece of dried deer meat or salmon, some nuts. Meribah continued to look for her own food sources. She did not feel it right to take everything from the basket or to become reliant solely on her secret benefactor. The notion of total reliance on anyone except herself was becoming an alien one to Meribah. But she did continue to visit the tree hollow almost daily—never, however, catching a glimpse of the

basket's replenisher. Between the basket and Meribah's own successes in finding nuts, food was not the problem that it had been several weeks before.

There were, however, two other problems. The first was that of making fire. Meribah had fifteen matches left for starting her fire. She tried hard to keep the coals going, but when she was out gathering, they often died. Meribah knew no other way to start a fire than by striking a match. She had heard that Indians rubbed sticks together until they smoked or sparks flew, but to Meribah this seemed like a magic reserved for Indians alone.

The second problem was loneliness. As Meribah's hunger diminished, her sense of loneliness increased. Questions of survival had occupied most of Meribah's time. As she grew more proficient at the tasks of survival and more a master of her cave-forest world, she had more time to think about things other than keeping her stomach full, her body warm, and the cave safe from predators. Meribah came to realize that simply to survive was not enough for her. There were periods of loneliness, of need for human conversation, that were as acute as hunger pangs. She missed her father, and she missed Goodnough. Their conversations had blazed as warmly as any fire. She yearned to share a thought, a word, a sunset, with another person, not just any person, but one who could respond in kind.

To Meribah's mind, the first problem was more solvable. There had to be another way to start a fire, and she was determined to do it one mid-January morning as she looked out the cave and saw a light drizzle veiling the forest and gorge, for she was sure it would take more than a single match to start her fire. She really had to give the Indian method a try. There was all to gain and no matches to lose. Perhaps it was not so magical. Meribah began rubbing some dry kindling sticks together. After five minutes she had a small pile of finely shredded wood. After ten minutes she had two broken sticks, and she was considerably irritated. What would

she do! There had to be a way of starting a fire without matches. She picked up two more sticks. She would change her rhythm and the length of her strokes. She had not rubbed ten strokes before the sticks snapped. "Darn!" she muttered. She looked up out of the cave and grimaced.

It might have been a full fifteen seconds that Meribah stared out the cave pondering the problem when she realized suddenly that there was another human being staring back. Her first problem was unsolved; her second one, the incredible loneliness that gnawed like hunger, might be over.

The young woman seemed to have grown out of the trees, which she stood among so noiselessly. Her copper skin, her skirt of shredded bark, the dark fur cape, all made her indistinguishable from the textures and colors of the forest. Meribah hardly breathed as she looked upon the Indian woman. She was human, yet she seemed to be of another order. The woman was at the cave opening. Her damp woody fragrance washed over Meribah, and Meribah felt her own heart beat wildly. At last she was not alone! Meribah savored that human face, the first she had seen in almost two months, as a starving person would savor food. The Indian woman's face was bathed in Meribah's joyous gaze.

The woman looked about the cave. Her eyes settled on a flat piece of wood. She picked it up. Then sorting through Meribah's kindling, she picked out a straight stick of cedar. She dropped to her knees by the fire pit and motioned for Meribah to sit beside her. From a small fur pouch the woman took an obsidian knife with a pointed end. She quickly gouged out a socket a quarter of an inch deep in the flat piece of wood. She notched the edge of the socket and cut a shallow channel between it and the edge of the flat piece of wood. Meribah watched with rapt attention as the woman deftly chiseled and refashioned the wood. When she finally finished, she looked up and smiled.

"*Muehli,*" she said, pointing to the wood piece. It was the first word that Meribah

had heard spoken by another human being since the last day at the tent. The sound was exquisite in her ears—a soft, honeyed oval of a sound. She wished that the woman would say it again. She leaned toward the Indian and tried to repeat it. *"Moo–"*

*"Muehli,"* the woman said once more, and tapped the wood.

*"Muehli?"* said Meribah.

The woman smiled and nodded vigorously. Meribah wondered what the word meant. Was it "wood," or did it mean the gouge in the wood? Meribah touched another cedar stick. *"Muehli?"* she asked.

*"K'ui, k'ui."* The woman shook her head. *"Ishi! Ishi!"* she said, holding the stick.

*"Ishi?"* Meribah was confused.

The woman took the flat piece in her left hand and the stick in her right hand. *"Muehli."* She spoke the word and held out her left hand toward Meribah. *"Ishi,"* she said, putting the other hand forward. One was called *muehli* and the other was called *ishi*, but they were both wood. Was she referring to the shape of the wood or the kind?

The woman was now tapping her chest lightly and saying the word *muehli* again. She pointed toward Meribah and said the word.

Meribah was still befuddled. Was this the woman's name? Was she supposed to say her name too? "Meribah!" she said, pointing to herself.

The woman now looked perplexed. *"K'ui, k'ui."* She shook her head again as if to say that this wasn't Meribah's name. *"Muehli!"* She pointed to Meribah. *"Muehli!"* She pointed to herself. Suddenly Meribah understood. "Woman!" she exclaimed. "Yes! You're woman! I'm woman!"

The Indian woman nodded excitedly and now repeated the English word fairly closely and held up the flat piece of wood.

"And *ishi!* Man!" Meribah grasped the stick.

The woman nodded again. Then she put the two pieces together. *"Siwini,"* she said. She pointed to the other pieces of wood in Meribah's kindling pile.

"Wood!" Meribah whispered, and then repeated the woman's word for it: *"Siwini."*

The woman again nodded and directed Meribah to watch. She took some pine needles from a pouch and then crumbled some bark from a log and placed it in the notch and along the channel of the flat piece as well as on the ground near the channel's runoff. Squatting, she held both ends of the flat piece of wood steady against the ground with her feet. Then she placed the cedar stick upright, the larger end in the socket. Holding the stick between her palms, she began to rub them together back and forth in opposite directions. With each motion the stick rotated to the right and then the left. Her hands bore down, pressing the twirling stick into the socket. Small bits of wood were ground off the sides of the socket, making a wood powder. Meribah's eyes widened as she saw the powder turn brown and begin to smoke. The woman twirled the stick faster, coaxing the smoke from the powder. The powder turned darker and darker, and more smoke came. The accumulating wood powder began to seep down the channel to the edge of the flat piece of wood. The woman worked even faster, keeping the stick in a twirling fury until a tiny spark glowed in the powdered wood. The spark formed just at the notch of the socket, where it traveled down the channel to the tinder at its end on the ground.

*"Auna!"* the woman exclaimed as the first lick of flame consumed the pine needles. She added some more and blew gently on the newborn fire.

It had taken the woman less than ten minutes to make the fire. But Meribah felt as if she had been in some dream world, witnessing a most extraordinary fantasy, for the last half-hour. It had been barely that long since she had looked up from her own pathetic efforts at firemaking and spotted the woman. Since that moment it seemed to Meribah that the entire world had changed. Fire had been made. New words had been spoken. And, most extraordinary of all, she was no longer alone.

Research is a very important part of the writing process for Kathryn Lasky. Although her fiction and nonfiction works are filled with carefully compiled facts and details, she says, "In writing I am searching for the story among the truths, the facts, the lies, and the realities. . . . Facts are quite cheap, but real stories are rare and expensive."

Once she has the facts, Lasky then works hard to imagine the thoughts and feelings of the characters whose adventure she wishes to tell. In *Beyond the Divide,* the vivid descriptions of Meribah's struggle to survive re-create an experience from another time for the reader. When Lasky speaks of her goals as a writer, she says, "I really do not care if readers remember a single fact. What I do hope is that they come away with a sense of joy—indeed celebration—about something they have sensed of the world in which they live."

Lasky has received much praise for her versatility in depicting various historical situations and for her ability to capture moods. Her award-winning books include *Sugaring Time,* a Newbery Honor Book; *The Weaver's Gift;* and *The Bone Wars.*

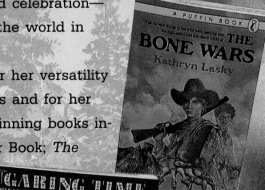

# GIFTS OF LIFE

## STAYING HEALTHY

Because citrus fruits were scarce, Europeans often suffered from a lack of vitamin C. They suffered from a disease called scurvy. Unable to find a cure, they turned to the Hurons, who drank a tonic made from the bark and needles of an evergreen tree, probably hemlock or pine, that helped people recover from the disease. Scientists have since discovered that this tonic is very rich in vitamin C.

## SIDE DISHES, TOO

Corn on the cob, corn chowder, corn bread, corn pone, succotash, hominy grits—how many other corn dishes can you name? European settlers learned from Native Americans how to cultivate and cook corn, as well as the many other vegetables, such as beans, pumpkins, and squash, that grew at that time only in North America.

How often have you munched on popcorn at the movies, enjoyed fried clams, taken vitamins, or soothed some aching muscles with a cooling salve? When you have, all you had to do was go out and buy these items.

But how did people manage in a time before stores existed? You may be surprised to know that the early European settlers in America enjoyed many of these same treats and treatments—all thanks to the help and generosity of the numerous Native American nations who knew how to live off the land. Here are a few of the gifts from nature that Native Americans gave to the Europeans.

## WHAT'S FOR DINNER?

*Ask people in any seaside community, and they are sure to tell you that nothing beats a clambake, where clams are slowly steamed out-of-doors in a bed of seaweed. Early European settlers in New England, however, believed that clams were poisonous, until the Narragansets taught them how to bake the clams with seaweed in an earthen oven.*

## MAKE IT BETTER, PLEASE

*The shelves of your local pharmacy are filled with salves and antibiotic ointments. Many such treatments originated among the Native Americans, who taught the European settlers how to use the roots, bark, and leaves of plants. Oil of wintergreen, for example, was found to ease the pain and swelling of sprains and bruises. Petroleum was refined into a jellylike substance to protect wounds. These and other medicines became quite popular with the settlers and saved many lives*

# MIRACLE HILL

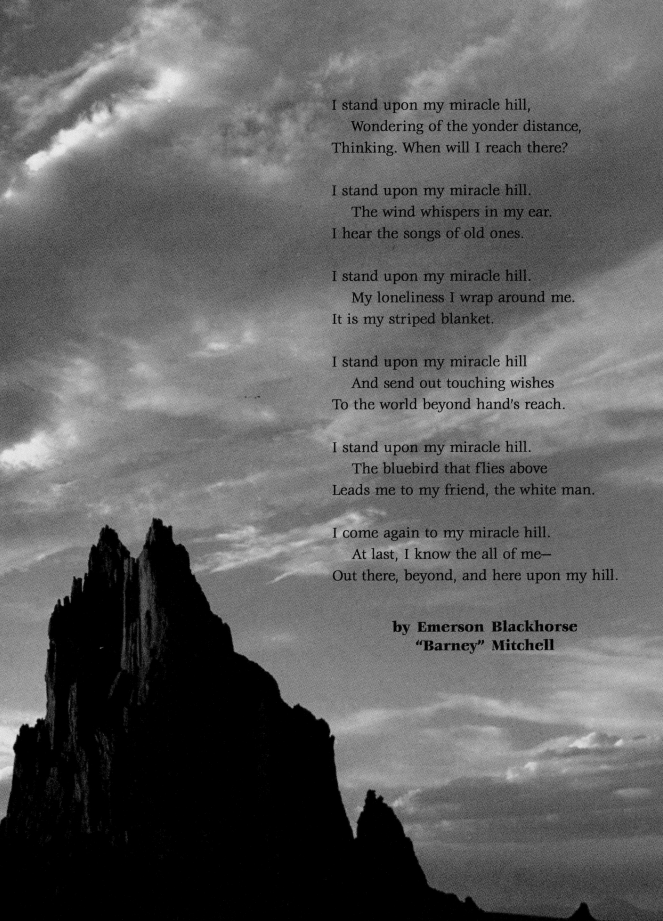

I stand upon my miracle hill,
    Wondering of the yonder distance,
Thinking. When will I reach there?

I stand upon my miracle hill.
    The wind whispers in my ear.
I hear the songs of old ones.

I stand upon my miracle hill.
    My loneliness I wrap around me.
It is my striped blanket.

I stand upon my miracle hill
    And send out touching wishes
To the world beyond hand's reach.

I stand upon my miracle hill.
    The bluebird that flies above
Leads me to my friend, the white man.

I come again to my miracle hill.
    At last, I know the all of me—
Out there, beyond, and here upon my hill.

**by Emerson Blackhorse
"Barney" Mitchell**

Shiprock Pinnacle on the
Navajo reservation in New Mexico

# meet *José Torres*

José Torres, a former world light heavyweight boxing champion, pulls no punches when it comes to sharing his views about his own life as well as the prospects for today's Hispanic teenagers. Although he grew up in a poor barrio in Puerto Rico, he refused to allow these circumstances to knock him down. As a boxer he learned that "you cannot surrender to fear, but you *can* use it as a kind of fuel."

In "A Letter to a Child Like Me," Torres discusses how he used that fuel to overcome poverty and a lack of education. His articles have appeared in many magazines and newspapers, including the *New York Daily News* and *El Diario*; his book about Muhammad Ali, *Sting Like a Bee*, has been translated into nine languages.

**illustrated by** *Marty Gunsaulus*

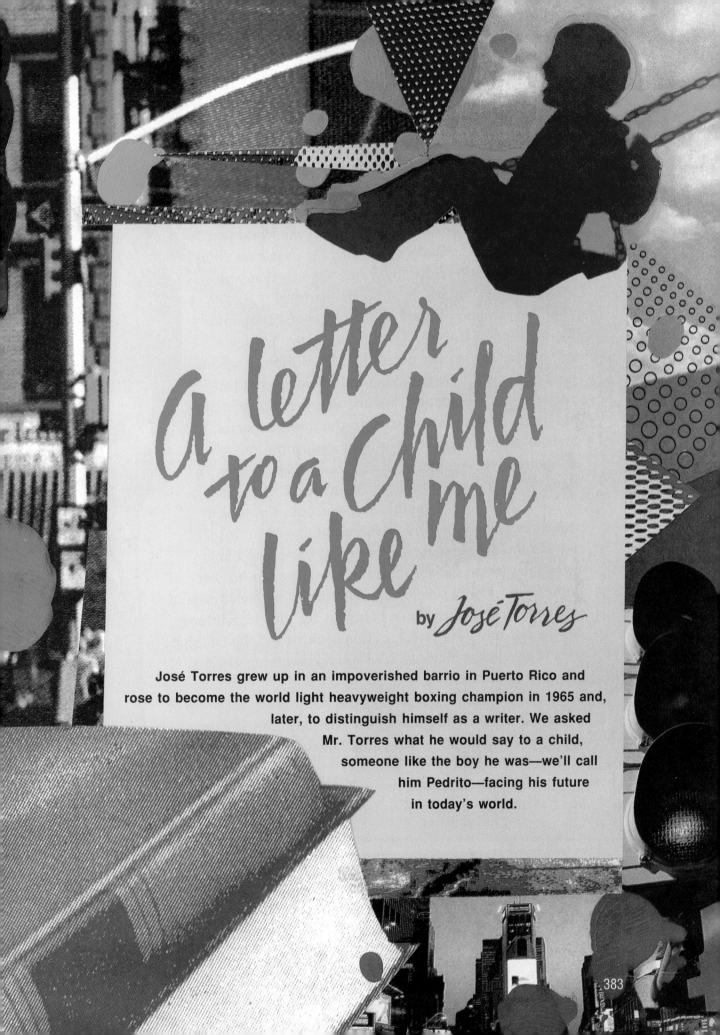

# A letter to a child like me

by José Torres

José Torres grew up in an impoverished barrio in Puerto Rico and rose to become the world light heavyweight boxing champion in 1965 and, later, to distinguish himself as a writer. We asked Mr. Torres what he would say to a child, someone like the boy he was—we'll call him Pedrito—facing his future in today's world.

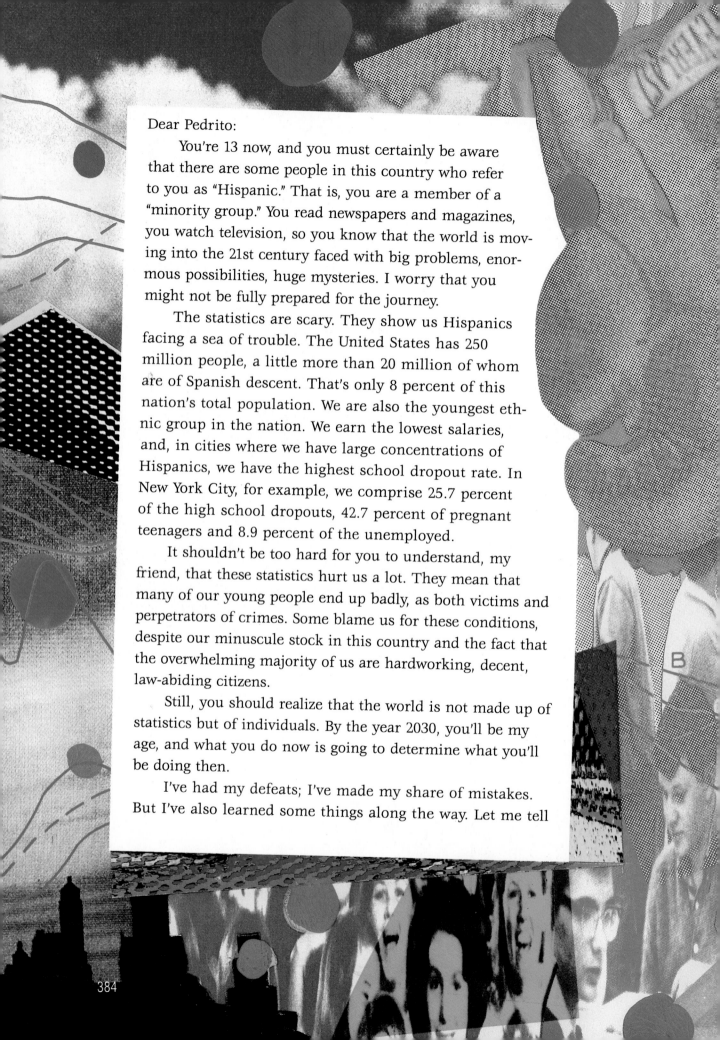

Dear Pedrito:

    You're 13 now, and you must certainly be aware that there are some people in this country who refer to you as "Hispanic." That is, you are a member of a "minority group." You read newspapers and magazines, you watch television, so you know that the world is moving into the 21st century faced with big problems, enormous possibilities, huge mysteries. I worry that you might not be fully prepared for the journey.

    The statistics are scary. They show us Hispanics facing a sea of trouble. The United States has 250 million people, a little more than 20 million of whom are of Spanish descent. That's only 8 percent of this nation's total population. We are also the youngest ethnic group in the nation. We earn the lowest salaries, and, in cities where we have large concentrations of Hispanics, we have the highest school dropout rate. In New York City, for example, we comprise 25.7 percent of the high school dropouts, 42.7 percent of pregnant teenagers and 8.9 percent of the unemployed.

    It shouldn't be too hard for you to understand, my friend, that these statistics hurt us a lot. They mean that many of our young people end up badly, as both victims and perpetrators of crimes. Some blame us for these conditions, despite our minuscule stock in this country and the fact that the overwhelming majority of us are hardworking, decent, law-abiding citizens.

    Still, you should realize that the world is not made up of statistics but of individuals. By the year 2030, you'll be my age, and what you do now is going to determine what you'll be doing then.

    I've had my defeats; I've made my share of mistakes. But I've also learned some things along the way. Let me tell you about a few of them. You didn't ask for this advice, but I'm going to give it to you anyway.

Let's start with a fundamental human problem, and I don't mean race or religion or origin. I mean fear. Fright, my young friend, may be the first serious enemy you have to face in our society. It is the most destructive emotional bogeyman there is. Cold feet, panic, depression and violence are all symptoms of fear—when it's out of control. But this feeling, ironically, can also trigger courage, alertness, objectivity. You must learn not to try to rid yourself of this basic human emotion but to manipulate it for your own advantage. You cannot surrender to fear, but you *can* use it as a kind of fuel. Once you learn to control fear—to make it work for you—it will become one of your best friends.

I learned this the hard way. I was a boxer. I became a world champion, but on my way up the ladder, I found Frankie "Kid" Anslem, a tough young Philadelphian made of steel. The match proceeded, to my increasing dismay, with me hitting and Anslem smiling. At one point, I remember, I let go a particularly devastating left hook/right cross combination. It landed flush on his jaw, but he simply riposted with a smile—and some hard leather of his own.

Suddenly, I found myself struggling for my life. I was afraid. For two rounds—the eighth and ninth—Anslem and I seemed contestants in an evil struggle. My punches

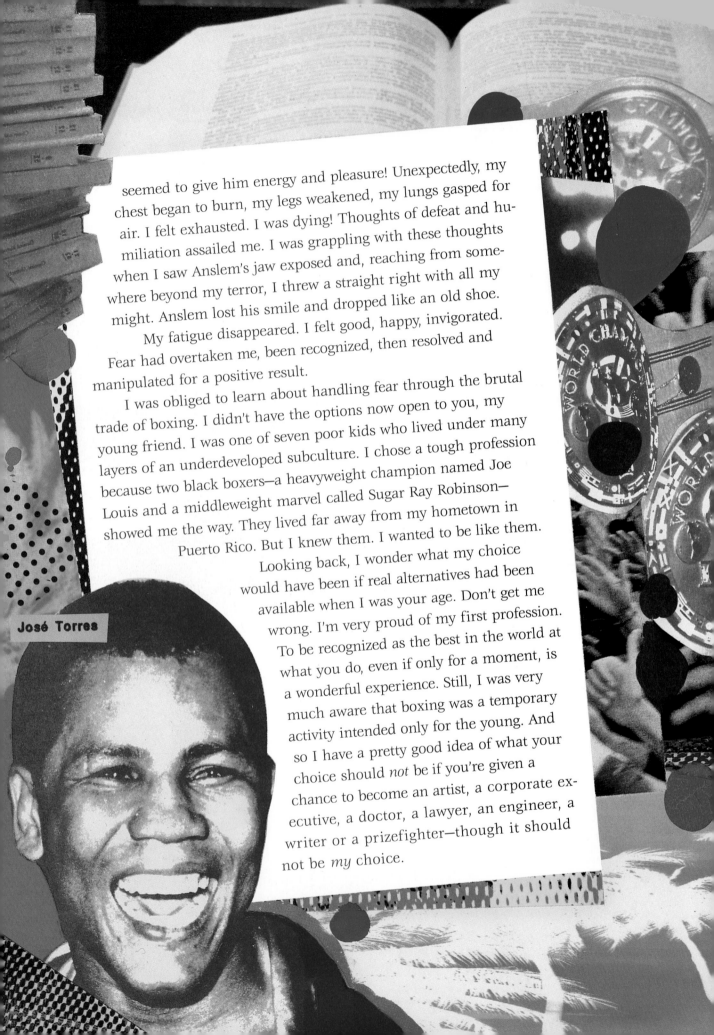

seemed to give him energy and pleasure! Unexpectedly, my chest began to burn, my legs weakened, my lungs gasped for air. I felt exhausted. I was dying! Thoughts of defeat and humiliation assailed me. I was grappling with these thoughts when I saw Anslem's jaw exposed and, reaching from somewhere beyond my terror, I threw a straight right with all my might. Anslem lost his smile and dropped like an old shoe.

My fatigue disappeared. I felt good, happy, invigorated. Fear had overtaken me, been recognized, then resolved and manipulated for a positive result.

I was obliged to learn about handling fear through the brutal trade of boxing. I didn't have the options now open to you, my young friend. I was one of seven poor kids who lived under many layers of an underdeveloped subculture. I chose a tough profession because two black boxers—a heavyweight champion named Joe Louis and a middleweight marvel called Sugar Ray Robinson—showed me the way. They lived far away from my hometown in Puerto Rico. But I knew them. I wanted to be like them.

Looking back, I wonder what my choice would have been if real alternatives had been available when I was your age. Don't get me wrong. I'm very proud of my first profession. To be recognized as the best in the world at what you do, even if only for a moment, is a wonderful experience. Still, I was very much aware that boxing was a temporary activity intended only for the young. And so I have a pretty good idea of what your choice should *not* be if you're given a chance to become an artist, a corporate executive, a doctor, a lawyer, an engineer, a writer or a prizefighter—though it should not be *my* choice.

José Torres

Whatever your ambition, you must educate yourself. School is a great gift our society offers you. It provides the key to your future. You must accept this gift, not disdain it. School is where you'll learn about your country and your world and your life in both. You'll also discover the conflicts and contradictions of history. You'll unlock the treasure chest of the world's literature and begin to sense the beauty of music and art. You'll acquire the tools of abstract thinking, of science and mathematics—and the computer, perhaps the primary instrument of the world you will inherit.

At home, you should learn about compassion and dignity and care. You should realize that the workings of an individual heart and soul can be as important as the histories of the great battles, military generals, dictators and kings. Most of all, you should learn that it's *you* who are responsible for your future.

There's a basic principle you should never forget: Don't be ruled by other people's low expectation of you! It almost happened to me. I grew up in Playa de Ponce, a small barrio in the southern part of Puerto Rico, an island 100 miles long and 35 miles wide with a dense population today of more than 3.3 million—1000 human beings per square mile. I was only 5 when I first noticed the American military men—many of them tall, blond and blue-eyed—wearing a variety of uniforms, roaming the streets of my neighborhood and picking up the prettiest girls. They seemed to own Playa de Ponce. Their

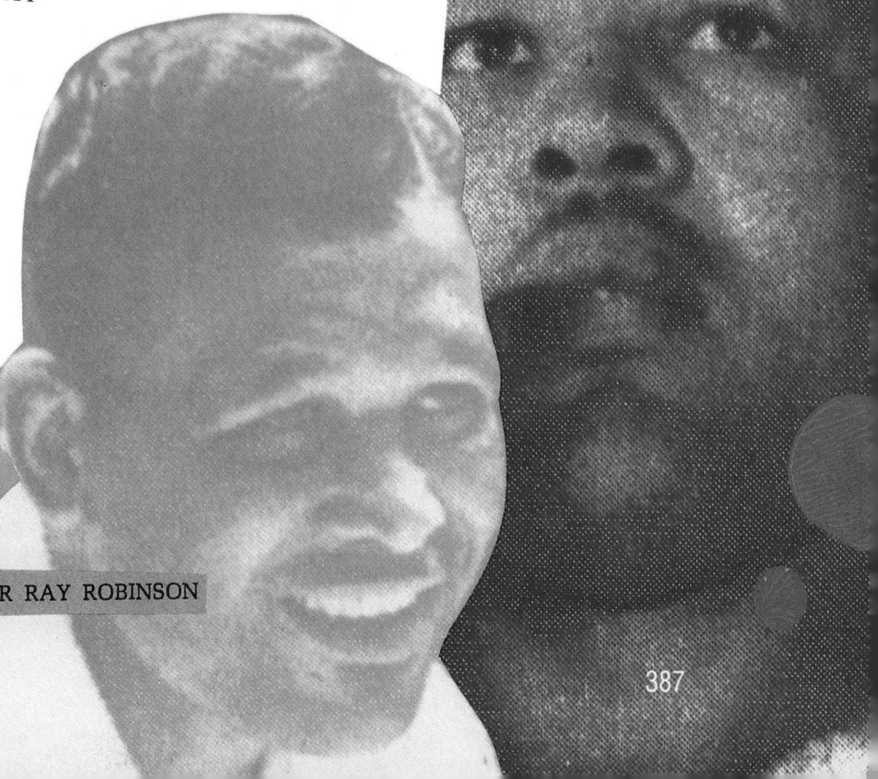

Joe Louis

SUGAR RAY ROBINSON

387

attitude in the streets and their country's constant military victories, which we witnessed at the movie houses, became symbols of these young men's "obvious superiority." By comparison we Puerto Ricans felt limited, inadequate.

To catch up, I volunteered to serve in the U.S. Army as soon as I became of age. And, for some mysterious reason, I joined its boxing team. My first four opponents were two compatriots and two black men from the Virgin Islands, all of whom I had no trouble disposing of. But just before my fifth fight—against one of those tall, blond, blue-eyed "superior" American soldiers—doubts started to creep into my mind. Yet, despite my worries, after three rounds of tough boxing, I overcame. I won! I had discovered the equality of the human race.

Your best defense against the ignorance of bigots and haters is pride in your own heritage. That is why you must learn your own history. Do it now—don't wait until you're in college. You don't need teachers. Go to the library. Ask your parents and relatives and friends.

Be proud of your ethnicity and language. Don't be afraid to use it. Don't give in to the stupidity of those know-nothings who insist that one language is better than two or three. You should know, and be proud, that in the Western Hemisphere more people speak Spanish than English; that Español was the language of the hemisphere's first university—the Santo Tomás de Aquino University in the Dominican Republic, founded in 1538—and of the books in its first library. When you discover the long and honorable tradition to which you belong, your pride will soar.

Sammy Davis Jr.

Reggie Jackson

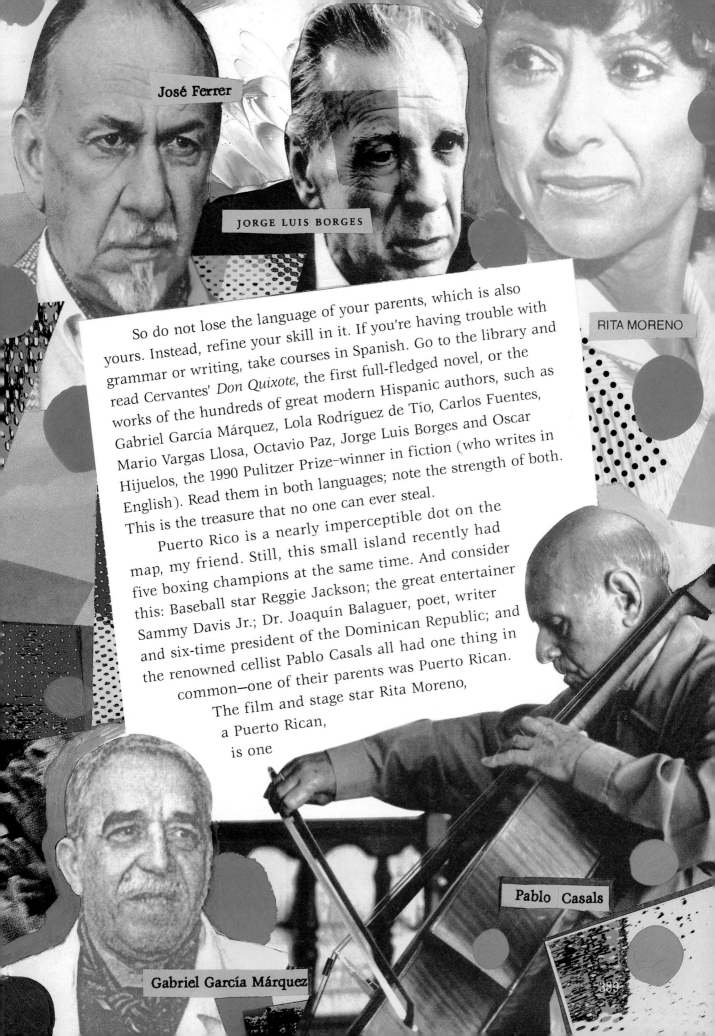

José Ferrer

JORGE LUIS BORGES

RITA MORENO

So do not lose the language of your parents, which is also yours. Instead, refine your skill in it. If you're having trouble with grammar or writing, take courses in Spanish. Go to the library and read Cervantes' *Don Quixote*, the first full-fledged novel, or the works of the hundreds of great modern Hispanic authors, such as Gabriel García Márquez, Lola Rodríguez de Tío, Carlos Fuentes, Mario Vargas Llosa, Octavio Paz, Jorge Luis Borges and Oscar Hijuelos, the 1990 Pulitzer Prize–winner in fiction (who writes in English). Read them in both languages; note the strength of both. This is the treasure that no one can ever steal.

Puerto Rico is a nearly imperceptible dot on the map, my friend. Still, this small island recently had five boxing champions at the same time. And consider this: Baseball star Reggie Jackson; the great entertainer Sammy Davis Jr.; Dr. Joaquín Balaguer, poet, writer and six-time president of the Dominican Republic; and the renowned cellist Pablo Casals all had one thing in common—one of their parents was Puerto Rican.

The film and stage star Rita Moreno,
a Puerto Rican,
is one

Pablo Casals

Gabriel García Márquez

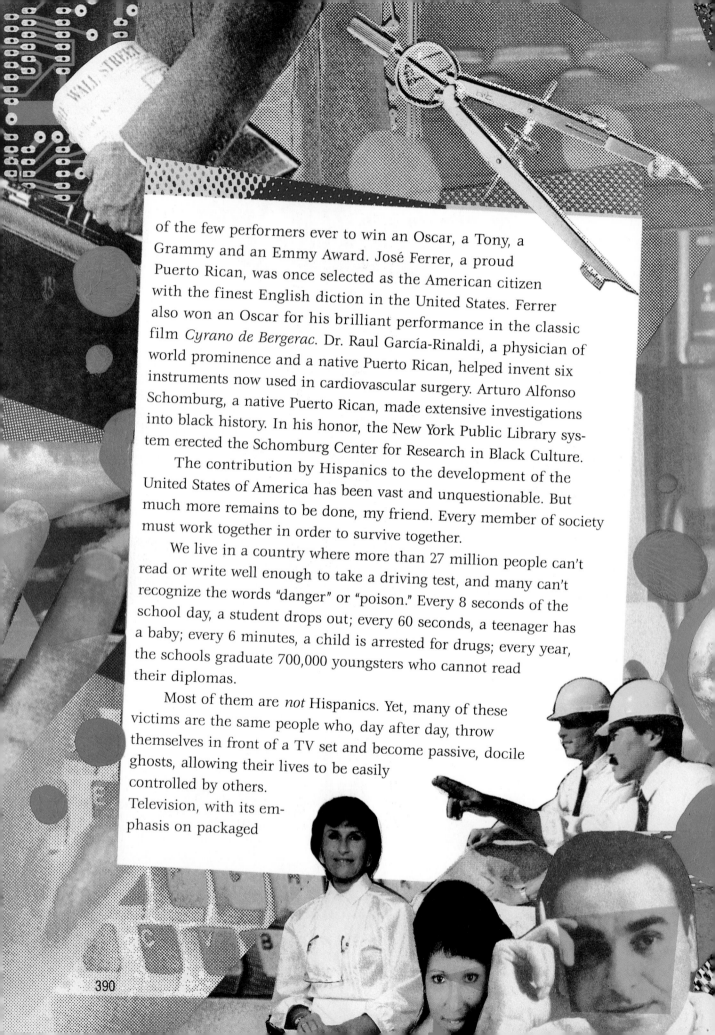

of the few performers ever to win an Oscar, a Tony, a Grammy and an Emmy Award. José Ferrer, a proud Puerto Rican, was once selected as the American citizen with the finest English diction in the United States. Ferrer also won an Oscar for his brilliant performance in the classic film *Cyrano de Bergerac*. Dr. Raul García-Rinaldi, a physician of world prominence and a native Puerto Rican, helped invent six instruments now used in cardiovascular surgery. Arturo Alfonso Schomburg, a native Puerto Rican, made extensive investigations into black history. In his honor, the New York Public Library system erected the Schomburg Center for Research in Black Culture.

The contribution by Hispanics to the development of the United States of America has been vast and unquestionable. But much more remains to be done, my friend. Every member of society must work together in order to survive together.

We live in a country where more than 27 million people can't read or write well enough to take a driving test, and many can't recognize the words "danger" or "poison." Every 8 seconds of the school day, a student drops out; every 60 seconds, a teenager has a baby; every 6 minutes, a child is arrested for drugs; every year, the schools graduate 700,000 youngsters who cannot read their diplomas.

Most of them are *not* Hispanics. Yet, many of these victims are the same people who, day after day, throw themselves in front of a TV set and become passive, docile ghosts, allowing their lives to be easily controlled by others. Television, with its emphasis on packaged

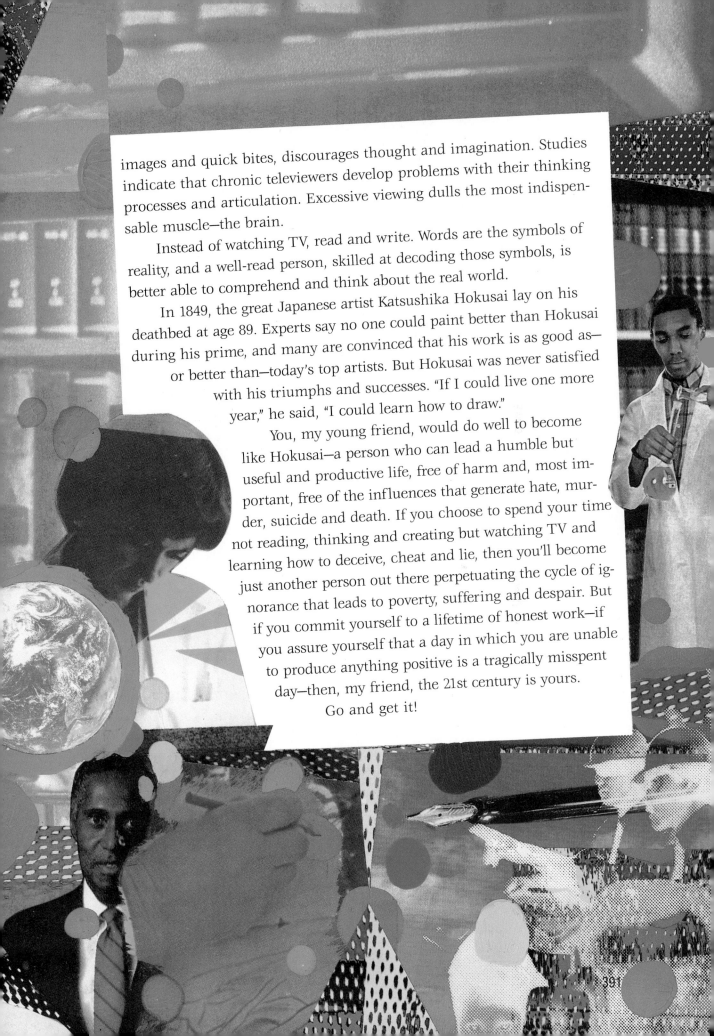

images and quick bites, discourages thought and imagination. Studies indicate that chronic televiewers develop problems with their thinking processes and articulation. Excessive viewing dulls the most indispensable muscle—the brain.

Instead of watching TV, read and write. Words are the symbols of reality, and a well-read person, skilled at decoding those symbols, is better able to comprehend and think about the real world.

In 1849, the great Japanese artist Katsushika Hokusai lay on his deathbed at age 89. Experts say no one could paint better than Hokusai during his prime, and many are convinced that his work is as good as—or better than—today's top artists. But Hokusai was never satisfied with his triumphs and successes. "If I could live one more year," he said, "I could learn how to draw."

You, my young friend, would do well to become like Hokusai—a person who can lead a humble but useful and productive life, free of harm and, most important, free of the influences that generate hate, murder, suicide and death. If you choose to spend your time not reading, thinking and creating but watching TV and learning how to deceive, cheat and lie, then you'll become just another person out there perpetuating the cycle of ignorance that leads to poverty, suffering and despair. But if you commit yourself to a lifetime of honest work—if you assure yourself that a day in which you are unable to produce anything positive is a tragically misspent day—then, my friend, the 21st century is yours.

Go and get it!

BY AMIRI BARAKA (LEROI JONES)

# YOUNG

AN ASANTE SILK KENTE CLOTH FROM GHANA

FIRST, FEEL, THEN FEEL, THEN
READ, OR READ, THEN FEEL, THEN
FALL, OR STAND, WHERE YOU
ALREADY ARE. THINK
OF YOUR SELF, AND THE OTHER
SELVES . . . THINK
OF YOUR PARENTS, YOUR MOTHERS
AND SISTERS, YOUR BENTSLICK
FATHER, THEN FEEL, OR
FALL, ON YOUR KNEES
IF NOTHING ELSE WILL MOVE YOU,

THEN READ
AND LOOK DEEPLY
INTO ALL MATTERS
COME CLOSE TO YOU
CITY BOYS—
COUNTRY MEN

MAKE SOME MUSCLE
IN YOUR HEAD, BUT
USE THE MUSCLE
IN YR HEART

SOUL

# *From the Heart*

## SUMMER OF MY GERMAN SOLDIER

by Bette Greene
Bantam, 1974

"It's truly extraordinary," he said. "Who would believe it? 'Jewish girl risks all for German soldier.' Tell me, Patty Bergen—" his voice became soft, but with a trace of hoarseness— "why are you doing this for me?"

## ANNE FRANK: THE DIARY OF A YOUNG GIRL

by Anne Frank
Simon & Schuster, 1972

It's an odd idea for someone like me to keep a diary; not only because I have never done so before, but because it seems to me that neither I—nor for that matter anyone else—will be interested. . . . Still, what does that matter? I want to write, but more than that, I want to bring out all kinds of things that lie buried deep in my heart.

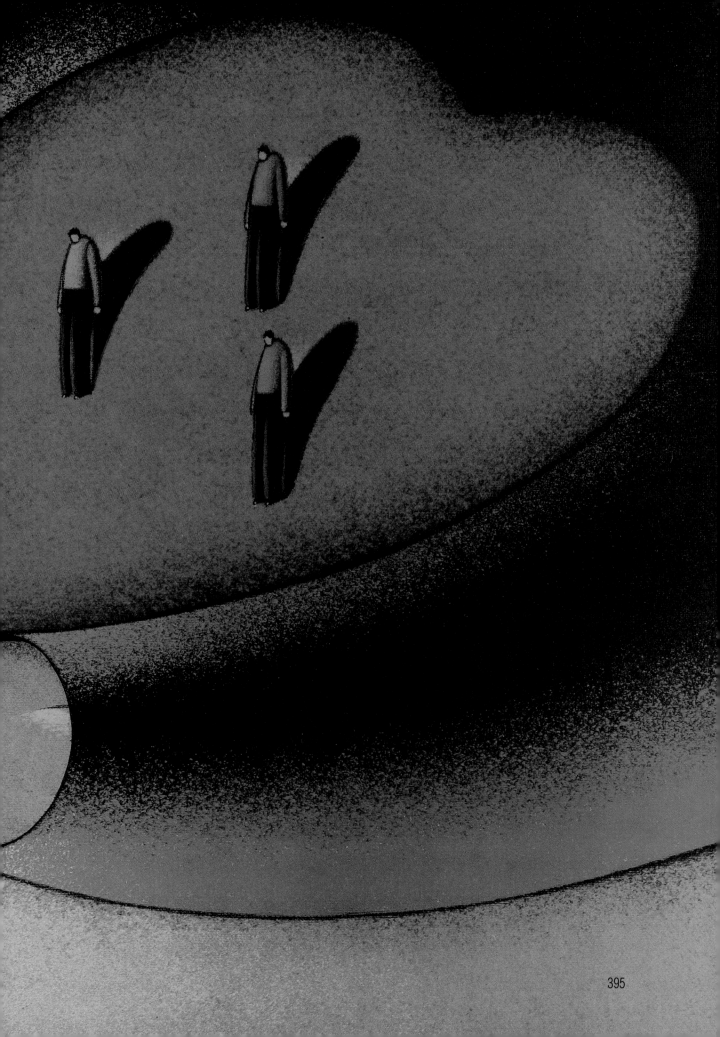

# *Anne Frank*

## THE STORY OF THE WOMAN WHO

## MEET MIEP GIES

When Miep Gies joined the firm owned by Otto Frank, she did not realize how tightly their lives would become intertwined. The Nazis' invasion of Holland and their subsequent roundup of the Dutch Jews forced Frank and his family into hiding. Gies not only helped the Franks to move into their secret hiding place, but she also visited them twice daily, bringing with her scarce food and news of the outside world.

"So many people in Holland did the same thing we did," says Gies of the help she and others gave to the Franks. "We are not heroes. We only did our human duty. We helped people who needed our help."

It was Gies who discovered Anne's now-famous diary a few hours after the police raided the Franks' hidden rooms. She gave it to Otto Frank, still unread, on the day he learned of his daughters' deaths. Gies still remembers the Anne who was "always friendly, smiling, always ready to help."

# Remembered

## HELPED TO HIDE THE FRANK FAMILY

**BY MIEP GIES WITH ALISON LESLIE GOLD**

*The German occupation of the Netherlands in the spring of 1940 marked the beginning of five years of hardship for the Dutch people. Curfews were imposed, food was rationed, and free speech suppressed. German soldiers patrolled the streets and entered homes and offices at will. • Dutch Jews suffered the most. One by one, all their freedoms were revoked. They could not, for example, hold jobs, attend schools of their choice, or ride streetcars or use bicycles for transportation. They could not even walk the streets freely. In 1942, it became mandatory for all Jews—men, women, and children—to wear a six-pointed yellow star as identification on their clothing. • In 1933, Otto Frank hired Miep Gies to work in his firm. Gradually, both Miep and her husband, Henk, established a strong relationship with the entire Frank family. Frank, increasingly aware that Jews were no longer safe in Holland, confided to Miep his intentions to hide his family in a secret attic above his offices. He asked for Miep's help. To aid Jewish people was extremely dangerous, but Miep did not hesitate.*

---

It was the first Sunday in July, a warm summer night. Henk and I, Mrs. Samson, and the others had eaten our evening meal and were all engaged in our various activities. For me, Sunday evening meant doing small things to get ready for a new workweek.

These days anything unusual was immediately upsetting, and when there came an insistent ringing of our bell, tension rose in the apartment at the sound. Our eyes darted from one to another. Quickly, Henk went to the door and I followed him. There stood Herman van Daan in quite an agitated condition. Henk and I spoke quietly to him, not wanting to upset Mrs. Samson and her family.

"Come right away," Van Daan entreated in a hushed but urgent voice. "Margot Frank has received a postcard ordering her to appear for forced-labor shipment to Germany. She's been ordered to bring a suitcase with winter things. The Franks have decided to go immediately into hiding. Can you come right now to take a few things that they'll need in hiding? Their preparations aren't complete, you see."

"We will come," Henk told him. We put on our raincoats. To be seen carrying bags and packages would be too dangerous; we could hide much under our baggy old raincoats. It might appear odd to be wearing raincoats on a warm, dry summer night, but it was better than having bags full of possessions in our arms.

Henk made some explanation to Mrs. Samson so as not to alarm her and the others, and we left with Mr. van Daan. When Mr. Frank had confided in me about the hiding plan, I had that very night told Henk about our conversation. Without discussion, Henk had affirmed his unconditional assistance to the Franks and agreed that the plan was a sound one. But neither of us had expected the Franks to go into hiding this soon. Walking quickly but not hurrying, in order not to attract attention, we went toward the Merwedeplein. On the way, Van Daan told us that Mr. Frank had just told his girls about the hiding plan but not where the hiding place was.

*Me in 1933*

"You can imagine," he explained, "they're in a state of great confusion. There's so much to do and so little time, and their damned lodger seems to be hanging about, making it all quite difficult."

Walking to the Franks', I suddenly felt a great sense of urgency for my friends. Conscripting a sixteen-year-old girl for forced labor was a new abomination the Germans were inflicting on the Jews. Yes, I thought, the sooner our friends got safely out of sight, the better. And how many more young girls like Margot have they conscripted? Girls with no father like Mr. Frank and no hiding plan? Girls who must be horribly frightened tonight. With these thoughts, I had to force myself not to run the rest of the way to the Merwedeplein.

When we arrived at the Frank apartment, few words were exchanged. I could feel their urgency, an undercurrent of near-panic. But I could see that much needed to be organized and prepared. It was all too terrible. Mrs. Frank handed us piles of what felt like children's clothes and shoes.

I was in such a state myself that I didn't look. I just took and took as much as I could, hiding the bunches of things the best way I could under my coat, in my pockets, under Henk's coat, in his pockets. The plan was that I'd bring these things to the hiding place at some later date when our friends were safely inside.

With our coats bursting, Henk and I made our way back to our rooms and quickly unloaded what we'd had under our coats. We put it all under our bed. Then, our coats empty again, we hurried back to the Merwedeplein to get another load.

Because of the Franks' lodger, the atmosphere at the Frank apartment was muted and disguised. Everyone was making an effort to seem normal, not to run, not to raise a voice. More things were handed to us. Mrs. Frank bundled, and sorted quickly, and gave to us as we again took and took. Her hair was escaping from her tight bun into her eyes. Anne came in, bringing too many things; Mrs. Frank told her to take them back. Anne's eyes were like saucers, a mixture of excitement and terrible fright.

Henk and I took as much as we could, and quickly left.

Early the next day, Monday, I woke to the sound of rain.

Before seven thirty, as we had arranged the night before, I had ridden my bicycle to the Merwedeplein. No sooner had I reached the front stoop than the door of the Franks' apartment opened and Margot emerged. Her bike was standing outside. Margot had not handed her bicycle in as ordered. Mr. and Mrs. Frank were inside, and Anne, wide-eyed in a nightgown, hung back inside the doorway.

I could tell that Margot was wearing layers of clothing. Mr. and Mrs. Frank looked at me. Their eyes pierced mine.

I made an effort to be assuring. "Don't worry. The rain is very heavy. Even the Green Police won't want to go out in it. The rain will provide a shelter."

"Go," Mr. Frank instructed us, taking a look up and down the square. "Anne and Edith and I will come later in the morning. Go now."

Without a backward glance, Margot and I pushed our bicycles onto the street. Quickly, we pedaled away from the Merwedeplein, going north at the first turning. We pedaled evenly, not too fast, in order to appear like two everyday working girls on the way to work on a Monday morning.

Not one Green Policeman was out in the downpour. I took the big crowded streets from the Merwedeplein to Waalstraat, then to the left to Noorder Amstellaan to Ferdinand Bolstraat, Vijzelstraat to Rokin, Dam Square, Raadhuisstraat, finally turning onto the Prinsengracht, never so glad before to see our cobbled street and murky canal.

All the way we had not said one word. We both knew that from the moment we'd mounted our bicycles we'd become criminals. There we were, a Christian and a Jew without the yellow star, riding on an illegal bicycle. And at a time when the Jew was ordered to report for a forced-labor brigade about to leave for parts unknown in Hitler's Germany. Margot's face showed no intimidation. She betrayed nothing of what she was feeling inside. Suddenly we'd become two allies against the might of the German beast among us.

Not a soul was about on the Prinsengracht. After opening the door, we carried our bicycles into the storeroom, then we left the room and shut the door. I opened the next door to the office and shut the door against the rain. We were soaked through to the skin. I could see that Margot was suddenly on the verge of crumbling.

I took her arm and led her past Mr. Frank's office and up the stairway to the landing that led to the hiding place. It was approaching the time that the others would be coming to work. I was now afraid that someone would come, but I kept silent.

Margot was now like someone stunned, in shock. I could feel her shock now that we were inside. As she opened the door, I gripped her arm to give her courage. Still, we said nothing. She disappeared be-

hind the door and I took my place in the front office.

My heart too was thumping. I sat at my desk wondering how I could get my mind onto my work. The pouring summer rain had been our shelter. Now one person was safe inside the hiding place. Three more had to be protected by the rain.

Mr. Koophuis arrived at work and took Margot's bicycle somewhere that I didn't know. Soon after he left I could hear the warehouseman arriving, stamping the water off his shoes.

Late in the morning I heard Mr. and Mrs. Frank and Anne coming through the front office door. I had been waiting for that moment and quickly joined them and hurried them along past Mr. Kraler's office up the stairway to the door of the hiding place. All three of them were quite wet. They were carrying a few things, and all had yellow stars sewn onto their clothes. I opened the door for them and shut it when they had vanished inside.

In the afternoon when no one was around and all was quiet, I went upstairs to that door myself and disappeared into the hiding place, closing the door tight behind me.

Entering the rooms for the first time, I was surprised by what I saw. In total disorder were sacks and boxes and furnishings, piles of things. I could not imagine how all these things had been brought up to the hiding place. I had not once noticed anything being brought in. Perhaps it had been brought at night, or on Sundays when the office was closed.

On this floor there were two quite small rooms. One was rectangular with a window, and the other long and thin, also with a window. The rooms were wood-paneled, the wood painted a dark green, the wallpaper old and yellowish and peeling in places. The windows were covered by thick, white, makeshift curtains. There was a toilet in a large room, with a dressing area off to the side.

Up a steep flight of old wooden steps was a large room with sink and stove and cabinets. Here too the windows were covered with curtains. Off this large room was another rickety stairway to an attic and storage area. The steps to the attic cut through a tiny garret-type room, again filled with piles and sacks of things.

Mrs. Frank and Margot were like lost people, drained of blood, in

*The entrance to the hiding place*

403

conditions of complete lethargy. They appeared as though they couldn't move. Anne and her father were making efforts to create some order out of the multitude of objects, pushing, carrying, clearing. I asked Mrs. Frank, "What can I do?"

She shook her head. I suggested, "Let me bring some food?"

She acquiesced. "A few things only, Miep — maybe some bread, a little butter; maybe milk?"

The situation was very upsetting. I wanted to leave the family alone together. I couldn't begin to imagine what they must be feeling to have walked away from everything they owned in the world—their home; a lifetime of gathered possessions; Anne's little cat, Moortje. Keepsakes from the past. And friends.

They had simply closed the door of their lives and had vanished from Amsterdam. Mrs. Frank's face said it all. Quickly, I left them.

*Anne's combing shawl and a photo of Otto Frank on a desk that had belonged to the Franks and which Mr. Frank gave to me before he died*

# Anne Frank

## THE DIARY OF A YOUNG GIRL

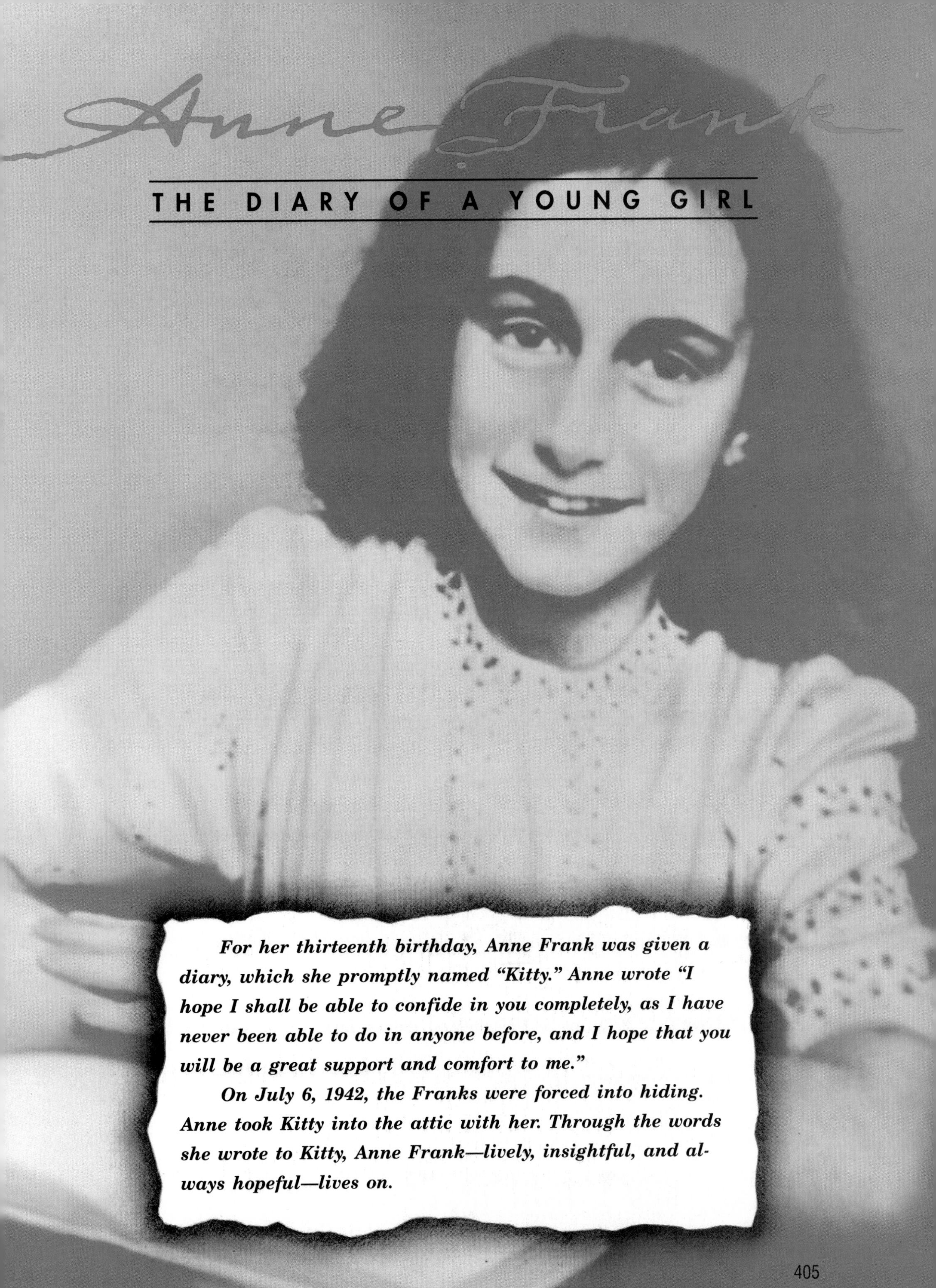

*For her thirteenth birthday, Anne Frank was given a diary, which she promptly named "Kitty." Anne wrote "I hope I shall be able to confide in you completely, as I have never been able to do in anyone before, and I hope that you will be a great support and comfort to me."*

*On July 6, 1942, the Franks were forced into hiding. Anne took Kitty into the attic with her. Through the words she wrote to Kitty, Anne Frank—lively, insightful, and always hopeful—lives on.*

In the following diary entries, Anne describes from her own perspective the events that Miep recalls in the excerpt from her book *Anne Frank Remembered*.

*Wednesday, 8 July, 1942*

Dear Kitty,

Years seem to have passed between Sunday and now. So much has happened, it is just as if the whole world had turned upside down. But I am still alive, Kitty, and that is the main thing, Daddy says.

Yes, I'm still alive, indeed, but don't ask where or how. You wouldn't understand a word, so I will begin by telling you what happened on Sunday afternoon.

At three o'clock (Harry had just gone, but was coming back later) someone rang the front doorbell. I was lying lazily reading a book on the veranda in the sunshine, so I didn't hear it. A bit later, Margot appeared at the kitchen door looking very excited. "The S.S. have sent a call-up notice for Daddy," she whispered. "Mummy has gone to see Mr. Van Daan already." (Van Daan is a friend who works with Daddy in the business.) It was a great shock to me, a call-up; everyone knows what that means. I picture concentration camps and lonely cells—should we allow him to be doomed to this? "Of course he won't go," declared Margot, while we waited together. "Mummy has gone to the Van Daans to discuss whether we should move into our hiding place tomorrow. The Van Daans are going with us, so we shall be seven in all." Silence. We couldn't talk anymore, thinking about Daddy, who, little knowing what was going on, was visiting some old people in the Joodse Invalide; waiting for Mummy, the heat and suspense, all made us very overawed and silent.

Suddenly the bell rang again. "That is Harry," I said. "Don't open the door." Margot held me back, but it was not necessary as we heard Mummy and Mr. Van Daan downstairs, talking to Harry, then they came in and closed the door behind them. Each time the bell went, Margot or I had to creep softly down to see if it was Daddy, not opening the door to anyone else.

Margot and I were sent out of the room. Van Daan wanted to talk to Mummy alone. When we were alone together in our bedroom, Margot told me that the call-up was not for Daddy, but for her. I was more frightened than ever and began to cry. Margot is sixteen; would they really take girls of that age away alone? But thank goodness she won't go, Mummy said so herself; that must be what Daddy meant when he talked about us going into hiding.

Into hiding—where would we go, in a town or the country, in a house or a cottage, when, how, where . . . ?

These were questions I was not allowed to ask, but I couldn't get them out of my mind. Margot and I began to pack some of our most vital belongings into a school satchel. The first thing I put in was this diary, then hair curlers, handkerchiefs, schoolbooks, a comb, old letters; I put in the craziest things with the idea that we were going into hiding. But I'm not sorry, memories mean more to me than dresses.

At five o'clock Daddy finally arrived, and we phoned Mr. Koophuis to ask if he could come around in the evening. Van Daan went and fetched Miep. Miep has been in the business with Daddy since 1933 and has become a close friend, likewise her brand-new husband, Henk. Miep came and took some shoes, dresses, coats, underwear, and stockings away in her bag, promising to return in the evening. Then silence fell on the house; not one of us felt like eating anything, it was still hot and everything was very strange. We let our large upstairs room to a certain Mr. Goudsmit, a divorced man in his thirties, who appeared to have nothing to do on this particular evening; we simply could not get rid of him without being rude; he hung about until ten o'clock. At eleven o'clock Miep and Henk Van Santen arrived. Once again, shoes, stockings, books, and under-clothes disappeared into Miep's bag and Henk's deep pockets, and at eleven-thirty they too disappeared. I was dog-tired and although I knew that it would be my last night in my own bed, I fell asleep immediately and didn't wake up until Mummy called me at five-thirty the next morning. Luckily it was not so hot as Sunday; warm rain fell steadily all day. We put on heaps of clothes as if we were going to the North Pole, the sole reason being to take clothes with us. No Jew in our situation would have dreamed of going out with a suitcase full of clothing. I had on two vests, three pairs of pants, a dress, on top of that a skirt, jacket, summer coat, two pairs of stockings, lace-up shoes, woolly cap, scarf, and still more; I was nearly stifled before we started, but no one inquired about that.

Margot filled her satchel with schoolbooks, fetched her bicycle, and rode off behind Miep into the un-known, as far as I was concerned. You see I still didn't know where our secret hiding place was to be. At seven-thirty the door closed behind us. Moortje, my little cat, was the only creature to whom I said farewell. She would have a good home with the

*Margot Frank, 1940*

neighbors. This was all written in a letter addressed to Mr. Goudsmit.

There was one pound of meat in the kitchen for the cat, breakfast things lying on the table, stripped beds, all giving the impression that we had left helter-skelter. But we didn't care about impressions, we only wanted to get away, only escape and arrive safely, nothing else. Continued tomorrow.

Yours, Anne

The house where Anne was born

Thursday, 9 July, 1942

Dear Kitty,

So we walked in the pouring rain, Daddy, Mummy, and I, each with a school satchel and shopping bag filled to the brim with all kinds of things thrown together anyhow.

We got sympathetic looks from people on their way to work. You could see by their faces how sorry they were they couldn't offer us a lift; the gaudy yellow star spoke for itself.

Only when we were on the road did Mummy and Daddy begin to tell me bits and pieces about the plan. For months as many of our goods and chattels and necessities of life as possible had been sent away and they were sufficiently ready for us to have gone into hiding of our own accord on July 16. The plan had had to be speeded up ten days because of the call-up, so our quarters would not be so well organized, but we had to make the best of it. The hiding place itself would be in the building where Daddy has his office. It will be hard for outsiders to understand, but I shall explain that later on. Daddy didn't have many people working for him: Mr. Kraler, Koophuis,

Miep, and Elli Vossen, a twenty-three-year-old typist who all knew of our arrival. Mr. Vossen, Elli's father, and two boys worked in the warehouse; they had not been told.

I will describe the building: there is a large warehouse on the ground floor which is used as a store. The front door to the house is next to the warehouse door, and inside the front door is a second doorway which leads to a staircase. There is another door at the top of the stairs, with a frosted glass window in it, which has "Office" written in black letters across it. That is the large main office, very big, very light, and very full. Elli, Miep, and Mr. Koophuis work there in the daytime. A small dark room containing the safe, a wardrobe, and a large cupboard leads to a small somewhat dark second office. Mr. Kraler and Mr. Van Daan used to sit here, now it is only Mr. Kraler. One can reach Kraler's office from the passage, but only via a glass door which can be opened from the inside, but not easily from the outside.

From Kraler's office a long passage goes past the coal store, up four steps and leads to the showroom of the whole building: the private office. Dark, dignified furniture, linoleum and carpets on the floor, radio, smart lamp, everything first-class. Next door there is a roomy kitchen with a hot-water faucet and a gas stove. Next door the W.C. That is the first floor.

A wooden staircase leads from the downstairs passage to the next floor. There is a small landing at the top. There is a door at each end of the landing, the left one leading to a storeroom at the front of the house and to the attics. One of those really steep Dutch staircases runs from the side to the other door opening on to the street.

The right-hand door leads to our "Secret Annexe." No one would ever guess that there would be so many rooms hidden behind that plain gray door. There's a little step in front of the door and then you are inside.

There is a steep staircase immediately opposite the entrance. On the left a tiny passage brings you into a room which was to become the Frank family's bed-sitting-room, next door a smaller room, study and bedroom for the two young ladies of the family. On the right a little room without windows containing the washbasin and a small W.C. compartment, with another door leading to Margot's and my room. If you go up the next flight of stairs and open the door, you are simply amazed that there could be such a big light room in such an old house by the canal. There is a gas stove in this room (thanks to the fact that it was used as a laboratory) and a sink. This is now the kitchen for the Van Daan couple, besides being general living room, dining room, and scullery.

A tiny little corridor room will become Peter Van Daan's apartment. Then, just as on the lower landing, there is a large attic. So there you are, I've introduced you to the whole of our beautiful "Secret Annexe."

*Yours, Anne*

Floor plan of the annex

Anne in 1992

# The DUTCH RESISTANCE

## THE HEART OF HEROISM

DEUTSCHE

Wer für Hitler kämpft,
kämpft, gegen das eigen
Volk!
Legt die Waffen nieder

USING A HIDDEN CAMERA, A
MEMBER OF THE DUTCH UNDER-
GROUND TAKES A PHOTOGRAPH
THROUGH A HOLE IN HER HANDBAG.

At the beginning of May 1940, the small nation of Holland was overrun by the German army. Even though their nation had been defeated, the Dutch people did not give up. They continued to fight back against the Nazis in countless ways. Thousands of Dutch troops went into hiding, organizing themselves into military action groups; and many thousands more Dutch civilians, like Miep and Henk Gies, heroically risked their lives to protect the Jewish citizens of Holland and to resist the Nazi occupation.

At first, the resistance was disorganized, but as the Nazi occupation of Holland intensified, so too did the resistance. In 1942, when the Nazis ordered all Dutch Jews to wear yellow stars, many non-Jewish Dutch citizens voluntarily wore yellow stars as an act of solidarity. When the Nazis began to deport Dutch Jews to concentration camps later that year, a nationwide underground network sprang into action. Risking their own lives, they smuggled Jews into hiding throughout the country, from urban attics and basements to rural barns, chicken houses, and storage huts. Sometimes their schemes were as bold as they were ingenious—as when members of the underground donned stolen Nazi uniforms, handcuffed their Jewish comrades, and marched them to safety past German soldiers. Overall, some twenty-five-thousand Dutch Jews went into hiding, and although many—like the Frank family—were eventually caught and sent to concentration camps, by the end of the war, more than fifteen thousand lives had been saved.

The Dutch resistance also engaged in clandestine military actions aimed at disrupting the Nazi occupation. Throughout Holland, the underground assassinated dozens of leading Nazi officials and their Dutch sympathizers. Sometimes a large measure of bluff was involved: Weaponry was so scarce that often the commandos were reduced to carrying toy guns during these raids.

Holland was eventually freed by the Allied troops in May 1945, almost five years after the Nazi invasion. During that time, the Dutch showed how a nation can find its heart in the heroic act of standing together and saying No.

A DUTCH FARMER STANDS BESIDE THE FAKE STORAGE HUT HE USED TO CONCEAL JEWS DURING THE WAR.

*Thurgood Marshall*

EQUAL JUST

EQUAL JUST

Lisa Aldred

# JUSTICE UNDER LAW

On the cold morning of December 8, 1953, attorney Thurgood Marshall climbed a flight of white marble steps in Washington, D.C. Halfway up the stairs, the tall, dark-skinned lawyer glanced upward. He could see four familiar words carved across the front of the huge white building: Equal Justice Under Law. Marshall intended to make those words a reality.

Striding between the imposing columns, Marshall entered the vast sanctum of the United States Supreme Court. He laid his bulging briefcase on the table and drew a deep breath. Today, Marshall would offer his final arguments in the most important case of his distinguished career. If he won, the United States Supreme Court would rule that America's long-entrenched, segregated school systems were unconstitutional. If he lost, most of America's black children would continue to receive second-rate educations in substandard, ill-equipped schools.

Marshall's case, entitled *Brown v. Board of Education of Topeka,* was a consolidation of five separate lawsuits. Challenging the legality of their local school boards, black students and their parents had brought suits in Delaware, the District of Columbia, Kansas, South Carolina, and Virginia. The case of Virginia's 16-year-old Barbara Rose Johns was typical of the others. Dissatisfied with the only school open to her and other black students—a tar-paper shack lacking proper heat or other facilities—Johns had led 450 classmates in a strike that climaxed in legal action against the school board of Prince Edward County.

The South Carolina case involved gas station attendant Harry Briggs, a navy veteran from Clarendon County. Seeking improved school conditions for his 5 children, Briggs had joined 19 other black parents in a suit against the county's segregated school system. As a result, Briggs and his wife had lost their jobs and their credit at the local bank.

Defeated in each of the five locations, the black students and parents appealed to the Supreme Court. Because the Kansas case—in which Topeka parent Oliver Brown sued his city's school board—came first alphabetically, the five clustered cases came to be known as *Brown.* The case presented the court with a question of vital importance to millions of Americans: Is government-enforced school segregation unconstitutional?

When the segregation cases came before the Supreme Court, legal counsel, directed by attorney Thurgood Marshall, was supplied by the National Association for the Advancement of Colored People (NAACP). Founded in 1909, the NAACP—whose membership was biracial—had spent decades fighting racial discrimination and segregation. In its early years, the NAACP concentrated on obtaining black suffrage (the right to vote), eliminating lynching and other mob violence against blacks, and promoting integration in housing and public places.

By the early 1930s, NAACP officials realized that blacks could never achieve social and economic equality without educational equality, and the organization made improved schooling for blacks a top priority. Thurgood Marshall had joined the organization in 1934. Now, in 1953, the 45-year-old attorney hoped for a major victory in what had been a long, grueling struggle.

Marshall hoped to win the *Brown* case by demolishing the "separate but equal" doctrine established by *Plessy v. Ferguson*. A celebrated Supreme Court case of 1896, *Plessy* began when a black man, Homer Adolph Plessy, refused to ride in the "Jim Crow" (segregated) car of a train passing through Louisiana. (The popular minstrel shows of the 19th century often featured white actors who wore blackface makeup and danced to the refrain, "Jump, Jim Crow!" The term Jim Crow, used as a patronizing name for black people, was also applied to post–Civil War segregation laws.)

Charged with violating a state law that required racial segregation in public facilities, Plessy was convicted by a Louisiana judge (Ferguson). When Plessy's lawyer appealed the conviction before the United States Supreme Court, he argued that enforced

Marshall prepares to argue the most important case of his career: *Brown v. Board of Education of Topeka*. At stake in the 1952–54 U.S. Supreme Court case, which was a consolidation of five separate lawsuits challenging racial segregation in public schools, was the future of black education in the United States.

separation of the two races violated the Constitution's Fourteenth Amendment, which guarantees all citizens "the equal protection of the laws."

The Fourteenth Amendment was ratified in 1868, five years after President Abraham Lincoln's Emancipation Proclamation legally ended slavery in the South. The amendment was designed to guarantee newly freed blacks the same legal rights and privileges as whites. But the Supreme Court, in its 1896 *Plessy* decision, upheld the Louisiana segregation law, ruling that separate but "equal" facilities satisfied the amendment's "equal protection" guarantee.

Although the court's decision technically applied only to the Louisiana law, it established a *precedent* (a legal decision that serves as a rule or pattern for future, similar cases). When the Supreme Court establishes a precedent, the nation's lower courts are bound to follow it unless it is overturned by the Supreme Court itself. Because consistency is very important to a legal system, precedents are seldom overturned.

*Plessy* opened the gates for a flood of new Jim Crow laws—statutes that required racial separation in both private residential areas and public facilities. By 1900, blacks in many states were restricted to Jim Crow drinking fountains, railroad cars, movie theater sections, hospitals, and schools. Despite the *Plessy* ruling, few state or local governments enforced the equality of the institutions and services available to blacks.

Guided by the separate-but-equal precedent, county and state courts routinely dismissed antisegregation suits; black students could legally be compelled to attend segregated schools if these institutions were judged equal to the schools reserved for white students. The judgments, of course, were made by people committed to preserving the separation of the races. Segregation had become the law of the land.

To help him prepare his arguments in *Brown v. Board of Education of Topeka,* Marshall recruited dozens of experts: lawyers, constitutional scholars, sociologists, psychiatrists, anthropologists, and educators. Under Marshall's guidance, the team scrutinized all aspects of the Fourteenth Amendment, examined every available study of children's learning patterns, and pored over research on the history and psychological effects of segregation on youngsters of both races.

The Supreme Court agreed to hear the *Brown* case in its 1952 session. During the 1952 hearing, Marshall asserted that the whole weight of social science demonstrated that black and white children possessed equal learning potential. He pointed out that school segregation had no reasonable basis and that it had a devastating effect on black children, decreasing their motivation to learn, lowering their self-esteem, and blighting their futures.

The court's nine justices found Marshall's arguments impressive, but legal precedents were heavily stacked against the NAACP's position. Deciding that the issue bore further consideration, the justices scheduled a rehearing, which began on December 7, 1953. Now, on December 8, Thurgood Marshall would offer his final arguments in the case.

When Marshall entered the courtroom, spectators, both black and white, filled every seat. Eager to witness history, many had waited outside in the

Most of the South's black schools—overcrowded, understaffed, and ill equipped—stood in sharp contrast to its white schools, where classes were smaller, teachers more numerous and highly trained, and buildings better supplied and maintained.

bitter cold since before daybreak. The crowd's excited murmurs ceased when the marshal of the court stepped forward and, in ringing tones, pronounced the ancient ritual words: "The honorable the Chief Justice, the Associate Justices of the Supreme Court of the United States. Oyez, oyez, oyez! All persons having business before the honorable the Supreme Court of the United States are advised to draw near and give their attention, for the Court is now sitting, and God save the United States and this honorable Court."

Everyone present stood and faced the long, highly polished bench at the front of the courtroom. Then the red velvet curtains behind the bench parted; nine black-robed men stepped forward and seated themselves in high-backed leather chairs.

Marshall eyed his opponent, John W. Davis. Tall, pale, and aristocratic in bearing, the 80-year-old Davis was known as the nation's leading constitutional lawyer. As a law student, Thurgood Marshall had sometimes skipped classes to hear Davis argue before the Supreme Court. By 1953, Davis had argued 140 cases before the high court. Marshall himself had participated in 15 Supreme Court cases, but *Brown* had brought him face-to-face with the formidable Davis for the first time.

Like Marshall, Davis argued *Brown* for moral rather than financial reasons. (His only payment for defending the South's segregated school systems, in fact, was a silver tea service, presented by the South Carolina legislature.) Davis believed segregation was not only fair but necessary. Marshall, of course, believed exactly the opposite, but he nevertheless respected the older attorney: John W. Davis was a force to be reckoned with, and Marshall knew it. Presenting his final points on the *Brown* case the day before, Davis had argued brilliantly. Although he referred to his notes more frequently than in the past, the elderly attorney had lost none of his eloquence. With his mane of snow-white hair and his formal, old-fashioned suit, he cut an impressive figure in the courtroom.

Davis regarded the separate-but-equal doctrine as a basic principle of American life. A time comes, he said, when such a principle "has been so often announced, so confidently relied upon, so long continued, that it passes the limits of judicial discretion and disturbance." Davis had no doubt that equality had been achieved in the segregated school system. "I am reminded," he said, "and I hope it won't be treated as a reflection on anybody—of Aesop's fable of the dog and the meat: The dog, with a fine piece of meat in his mouth, crossed a bridge and saw [his] shadow in the stream and plunged in for it and lost both substance and shadow. Here is equal education, not promised, not prophesied, but present. Shall it be thrown away on some fancied question of racial prestige?"

Thurgood Marshall stepped up to the bar to make his final rebuttal. "I got the feeling on hearing the discussion yesterday that when you put a white child in a school with a whole lot of colored children, the child would fall apart or something," he said. "Everybody knows that is not true. These same kids in Virginia and South Carolina—and I have seen them do it—they play in the streets together, they play on their farms together, they go down the road together, they separate to go to school, they come out of school and play ball together. They have to be separated in school."

Marshall declared that school segregation laws were deliberately designed to oppress black people. The only way the Supreme Court could uphold them, he asserted, would be "to find that for some reason Negroes are inferior to all other human beings." Ending his argument, he said, "The only thing [segregation] can be is an inherent determination that the people who were formerly in slavery, regardless of anything else, shall be kept as near that stage as is possible. And now is the time, we submit, that this Court should make it clear that that is not what our Constitution stands for."

After the lawyers completed their arguments, the justices followed their standard procedure, conferring about the case in secret session. Five months later—on May 17, 1954—they reassembled at their great mahogany

Crowning the imposing Washington, D.C., building of the U.S. Supreme Court is the motto Equal Justice Under Law. But until the 1950s, when Marshall successfully argued that segregation was unconstitutional, many Americans acted as though the motto read *Separate But Equal Justice Under Law.*

As the U.S. Supreme Court's pronouncement that "separate educational facilities are inherently unequal" makes headlines around the world, a mother and daughter celebrate the May 1954 overthrow of public school segregation with a visit to the Supreme Court building.

bench. As Chief Justice Earl Warren prepared to read the Court's opinion in *Brown v. Board of Education,* spectators leaned forward in silence. Wire-service reporters started filing their dispatches from the press table. At 12:57 P.M., the Associated Press wire carried a bulletin: "Chief Justice Warren today began reading the Supreme Court's decision in the public school desegregation cases. The court's ruling could not be determined immediately." The alarm went off in every newsroom in America. The nation waited.

But instead of delivering a crisp summary of the decision, Warren embarked on a long, discursive text. He referred to the evidence of psychologists, sociologists, and educators on the effects of segregation on black students. He discussed *Plessy v. Ferguson* and the Fourteenth Amendment's equal protection guarantee; thus far, he said, no precedent existed for the application of that guarantee to school segregation. After citing a number of earlier cases and outlining the history of black education in America, Warren called education "the most important function of state and local governments."

An hour after he started, the chief justice had yet to reveal the court's ruling. Warren, wired the AP correspondent at 1:12, "had not read far enough in the court's opinion for newsmen to say that segregation was being struck down as unconstitutional."

Finally, at 1:20 P.M., Warren reached the crucial question: "Does segregation of children in public schools solely on the basis of race . . . deprive the children of the minority group of equal educational opportunities?"

Warren paused for a split second. Then he said, "We believe that it does." He continued: "To separate [black children] from others . . . solely because of their race generates a feeling of inferiority . . . that may affect their hearts and minds in a way unlikely ever to be undone."

Approaching the end of the decision, Warren read, "We conclude . . ." Then he paused, raised his eyes from the document, and added, "unanimously." A shock wave seemed to sweep the courtroom. The justice continued, ". . . that in the field of public education the doctrine of 'separate but equal' has no place. Separate educational facilities are inherently unequal."

Stop-press bulletins flashed across the land. Radio and TV stations interrupted their programming. The Voice of America network beamed the news across the world in 34 languages: The Supreme Court of the United States of America had declared school segregation unconstitutional. Word of the decision reached Thurgood Marshall and his colleague Roy Wilkins in the New York office of the NAACP. Decades of struggle had finally paid off in victory. Silently, the two campaign veterans embraced.

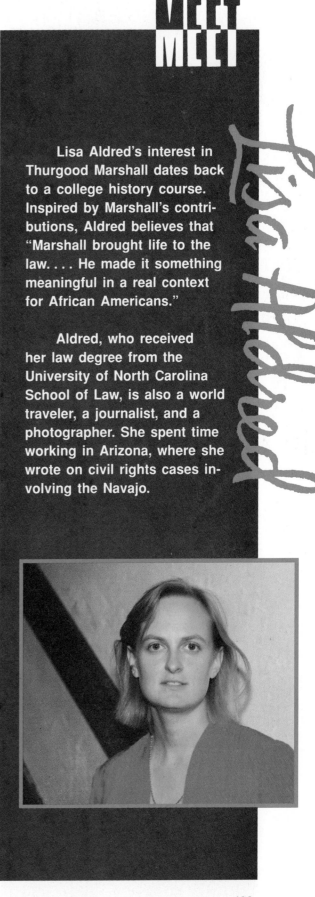

# MEET
## Lisa Aldred

Lisa Aldred's interest in Thurgood Marshall dates back to a college history course. Inspired by Marshall's contributions, Aldred believes that "Marshall brought life to the law. . . . He made it something meaningful in a real context for African Americans."

Aldred, who received her law degree from the University of North Carolina School of Law, is also a world traveler, a journalist, and a photographer. She spent time working in Arizona, where she wrote on civil rights cases involving the Navajo.

# Thurgood Marshall

# THE MAN AND HIS LEGACY

AT AGE 82, HIS TALL, BEARISH FIGURE NOW STOOPED, HIS EYES DIMMED BY BIFOCALS, THE RETIRING SUPREME COURT JUSTICE THURGOOD MARSHALL PAUSED FOR A MOMENT TO CONSIDER THE LEGACY HE HAD LEFT BEHIND. "I DON'T KNOW WHAT LEGACY I LEFT," HE FINALLY TOLD HIS VISITOR. "I LEAVE THAT TO THE PEOPLE."

In fact, Thurgood Marshall's heroic legacy seems very clear. When he first began practicing law in Baltimore in 1933, African-American children were not allowed to attend school with whites, public facilities were completely segregated by race, and African Americans were often denied basic Constitutional rights, such as the right to vote and the right to receive a fair trial. By the time Marshall retired from the Supreme Court in 1991, this institutionalized racism had been eliminated. And perhaps no other American—with the exception of Dr. Martin Luther King, Jr.— was as influential in achieving all this as was Thurgood Marshall himself.

Although his victory in the *Brown v. Board of Education* decision is his most famous, Thurgood Marshall spent much of his lifetime arguing—and winning—landmark cases. His success was the product not only of a remarkable legal mind, but also of a courageous spirit, for often he had to practice law under the threat of violence. One time, for instance, after helping to acquit twenty-five African-American men who were wrongly accused of murder in Tennessee, Marshall was arrested while driving away from the courthouse, accused of drunk driving, and driven back into town by the police. Then, he was told to walk across the street to the magistrate's office by himself. Marshall refused, saying, "You're not going to be able to say you shot me in the back while I was trying to escape." He forced the police to drive him to the local judge, who threw out the drunk driving charge.

Marshall also won important legal cases that helped African Americans to fight discrimination in housing, to enroll in previously all-white graduate schools, and to vote in state primaries. Much of the time, he did his arguing before the U.S. Supreme Court. In all, he argued thirty-two cases before the Supreme Court and won fully twenty-nine of them.

Eventually, however, he found himself not just arguing before the Court, but serving on it. In 1967, President Lyndon Johnson nominated Thurgood Marshall for the position of Supreme Court justice; he was the first African-American ever to hold that post.

On the Court, Thurgood Marshall was known for his bluntness and his sharp style of questioning. His stern visage and occasionally gruff exterior, though, camouflage a personality that is actually warm and easygoing. Regular visitors to the Supreme Court cannot remember another justice as open and approachable as Marshall was, nor one as informal in his manner. (Marshall liked to greet Chief Justice Warren Burger by saying, "What's shakin', Chiefie baby?") He is also a great fan of jazz, a renowned chef, and an avid watcher of old Western movies. (He was once quoted as saying, "I'm still waiting to see one showing where the Indians win.")

After announcing his retirement from the Supreme Court, he was asked what type of justice he would like to see replace him. With the same simplicity, honesty, and directness that characterized his entire career, Marshall replied with just one word: "Me."

"I'VE BEEN TO THE MOUNTAIN TOP"

# BY MARTIN LUTHER KING, JR.

We have been forced to a point where we're going to have to grapple with the problems that men have been trying to grapple with through history, but the demands didn't force them to do it. Survival demands that we grapple with them. Men, for years now, have been talking about war and peace. But now no longer can they just talk about it. It is no longer a choice between violence and nonviolence in this world, it's nonviolence or nonexistence.

That is where we are today. And also in the human rights revolution, if something isn't done, and in a hurry, to bring the colored peoples of the world out of their long years of poverty, their long years of hurt and neglect, the whole world is doomed.

. . . If I lived in China or even Russia, or any totalitarian country, maybe I could understand some of these illegal injunctions. Maybe I could understand the denial of certain basic First Amendment privileges, because they hadn't committed themselves to that over there. But somewhere I read of the freedom of assembly. Somewhere I read of the freedom of speech. Somewhere I read of the freedom of the press. Somewhere I read that the greatness of America is the right to protest for right. And so, just as I say, we aren't going to let any dog or water hose turn us around. We aren't going to let any injunction turn us around. We are going on.

. . . Let us rise up tonight with a greater readiness. Let us stand with a greater determination. And let us move on in these powerful days, these days of challenge, to make America what it ought to be. We have an opportunity to make a better nation. And I want to thank God, once more, for allowing me to be here with you.

. . . I don't know what will happen now. We've got some difficult days ahead. But it really doesn't matter with me now, because I've been to the mountain top. And I don't mind. Like anybody, I would like to live a long life; longevity has its place. But I'm not concerned about that now. I just want to do God's will. And He's allowed me to go up to the mountain. And I've looked over. And I've seen the promised land. I may not get there with you. But I want you to know tonight that we as a people will get to the promised land. And I'm happy tonight, I'm not worried about anything. I'm not fearing any man. Mine eyes have seen the glory of the coming of the Lord.

**APRIL 3, 1968 MEMPHIS, TENNESSEE**
**An excerpt from the last speech given by Dr. King**

# CONTENTS

FINDING YOUR WAY

It isn't the destination that counts. It is the journey. That is what life is. A journey. Make it the right way and you will fill it correctly with days. Pay attention to the journey.

GARY PAULSEN
from *Dogsong*

430

**THE**

**M.C. Higgins,**

**THE**

Illustrated by Larry Winborg

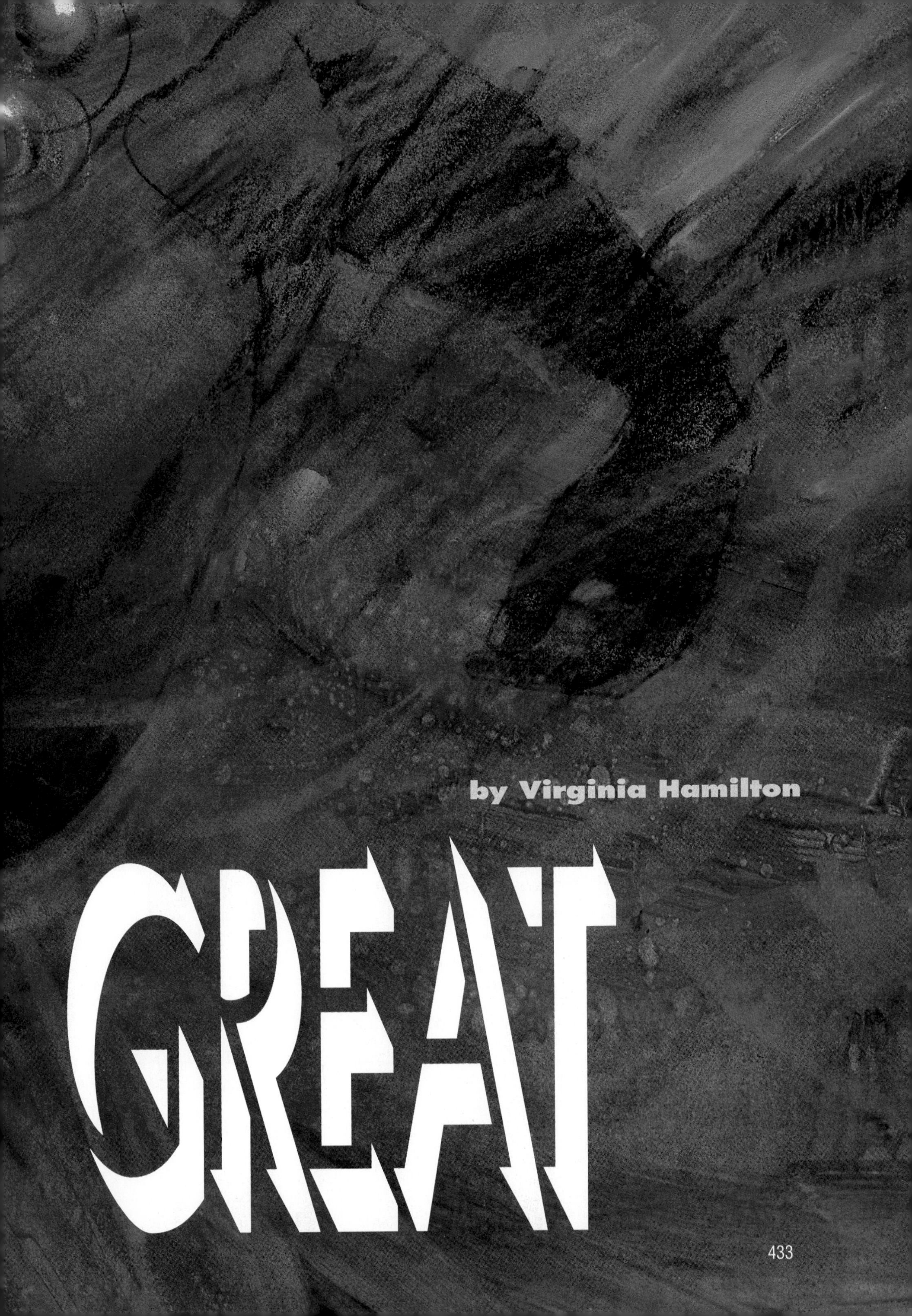

by Virginia Hamilton

# GREAT

ayo Cornelius Higgins, known as "M.C.," lives with his mother and father, his two brothers, Harper and Lennie Pool, and his sister, Macie, on Sarah's Mountain. M.C. loves to sit atop the gleaming forty-foot steel pole that stands in the front yard of his home. From the top of the pole, he can see the surrounding countryside. One day he notices that a young woman has set up a tent at the edge of the lake where he and the other children take their morning swim. When he meets her for the first time, he introduces himself as "M.C. Higgins, the Great."

"M.C., the Great?" she said.

"Yea." He grinned.

"Why 'the Great'?" she asked him.

"'Cause I can swim the best and everything."

"Everything, what?"

"You stick around and you'll see," he said easily.

n an instant he had plunged into the lake to begin a perfect breast stroke. In water, all of the awkwardness of a youth standing on land left him. With his knowledge and skill in it, he made no unnecessary move. His powerful arms shot upward, then outward and rearward, as he cut through the lake like some bold sea creature. His back turned gold from the sun glistening on it.

Hemmed in by mountains, surrounded by tall pines, the dark surge of the lake was magical. Fascinated, the girl watched it and the way M.C. cut through it, until she could no longer resist. She backed away, turned and disappeared into her tent. When she came out again, M.C. and the children were down at the far end of the lake.

She wore wrinkled, pink shorts and a faded man's shirt with sleeves cut away. She had tied the shirttails in a knot at her waist. M.C. thought she was about as nice-looking as she could be. But rather than strike out into the water from where she was, she came around the shore.

"Come on in," they shouted at her.

She preferred to walk down to the end of the beach. There she leaned on the rocks and plunged a foot in the water. "That's cold!" she said, looking pleased that they had invited her.

"Not underneath," Macie said. "Just on the top. You get in, and it's real warm."

M.C. said something to his brothers, and then: "Don't let Macie . . . I'm going through."

Head first, he upended himself and vanished beneath the surface. The water grew still again as if he had never been there. Macie rode on Harper's back until he grabbed the rocks and shook her off. Once he had climbed up on them, he gave Macie a hand. Lennie Pool followed.

The girl watched the water but it remained smooth and dark.

"What's your name?" Macie said, curious all of a sudden.

The girl smiled at Macie. But then her eyes flicked back to the lake where M.C. had gone under. She began to walk back and forth, her hands on her hips.

The children watched her.

"What's
he doing down
there?" she asked
them.

They said nothing.

"I don't think he's coming up,
you'd better do something."

Macie broke their silence with a giggle. "He's
not even down there," she said. "Just over and behind
these rocks." She led the way around the edge of the rocks.
Harper and Lennie went, too, and cautiously the girl followed.

On the other side lay a surprise. It was an opening in the
rocks. No one who didn't know would suspect it was there.
The rocks fell back in a small clearing where there was a silent
pool with grassy banks.

The children stopped at the edge. Macie turned brightly to
the girl and smiled.

M.C. surged up from the center of the pool in a great splash.
He sucked in air as though he would never again get enough
of it, as the girl covered her mouth to stifle a scream.

The kids laughed at her. "It's a water tunnel," Harper told
her in his soft, urgent voice. He told how the tunnel went
under the rocks beneath the water at the edge of the lake
and ended at the pool.

"Only M.C. can travel it," Macie said. "We ain't allowed.
The kids from town don't even know there's a tunnel."

"You wouldn't know it, either, if you hadn't caught me doing
it once," M.C. said. "Better keep the sense never to try it, too."

"How do you hold your breath so long?" The girl, talking to
M.C. as though he were older, showing respect for him now.

He pulled himself up on the grassy bank and wiped water
out of his eyes. He had to smile. She kneeled next to him, her
fear of him and the children gone.

Proud
he'd done some-
thing she never ex-
pected he could do. And she
had come from somewhere by
herself in a car. But he could be by
himself, too. He could travel through water
like nobody. First he thought of lying, to tell her
he could hold his breath longer than anyone. The kids
would know.

Finally he said, "It's not so long. I came up before you all ever got here. Hear you coming, and I just went under and waited. Then I splash up like I was out of breath."

She didn't seem to mind he had played a trick. "It's dark in the tunnel?" she asked him. Her face so close, he could see tiny bumps he hadn't noticed before.

Shyly, he looked at his feet hanging in the water. "It's gray light, kind of," he said. "This pool is at the end of the tunnel. Sunlight drifts in and gets faded, I guess. But I see a little. It's ghostly, though, when fishes slide over your skin."

She cringed with the picture of it. Watching her, Macie shivered with delight.

His eyes on the pool, M.C. sensed the girl watching him. Felt himself reaching out for her, the way he often reached out when he sat next to Jones. His skin itched and came alive with little things he seemed to know about her. She might travel alone, but every minute she was scared being by herself. The impression came to him, swift and certain.

Already he felt attuned to the girl, less self-conscious at having her so near.

He rubbed his arms and neck until the itching went away. Tiredness settled in the knot on his forehead in a dull ache that came and went. He wasn't feeling quite himself this morning. Yet he didn't want to go and leave her.

"What's your name?" he asked.

She shrugged. "No use of saying names."

"I told you our names," he said.

"I could tell you a name and you wouldn't know if it was really mine."

"Where do you come from then?"

"Same thing," she said. "You wouldn't know if I came from where I said."

"Then why not tell?"

She said nothing. She looked at him and quickly away, as if she wanted to speak out, but couldn't. Soon she was looking from the pool to the rocks and back to the pool.

She did this several times before it came to M.C. what was on her mind.

"A water tunnel won't be like a pool," he told her, "or even a lake."

She nodded, staring at the rocks.

"A pool or even a lake is simple. Water will lift you," he said.

She sat still, with just her head turning to look at him and then away.

"But tunnel is a bottleneck. No place to take off the pressure; or maybe pressure's not the trouble. It's just a tight place without a top, and you can get sick to your stomach."

A long silence in which she said nothing.

"How long can you hold your breath?" M.C. asked her.

"What?"

"If you travel that tunnel," he said. "How long can you go with no breathing?"

Wide-eyed, she stared at him. "As long as anybody." All at once she breathed hugely, holding the air in.

Macie and the boys scrambled close to see. Everything was still. The girl's eyes began to pop and tear. She held out while none of them moved, until at last her breath burst through her teeth. She fell back, panting.

"That was long!" Harper said.

"Maybe forty-five seconds," M.C. said. "Not long enough."

The girl sat up again.

"Try it once more," M.C. said.

"You don't think I can do it," she said.

"I'm not thinking a thing. It just has to be longer," he said. "Long enough to reach the pool."

"Well, I don't know," she said, her voice edgy. She searched M.C.'s face.

"If you're worried, don't try it," he said.

Then she was smirking at him. "Sure think you're something, don't you?" she said. "I saw you on that pole. Not just with the fire, but in the daylight. Sitting up there with nothing to do and no place to do it!"

Her anger shot through him. It hurt him and he didn't know what to say. He hadn't meant anything bad by what he said.

"The tunnel is fun," he said quietly, "but you have to have the lungs to hold out."

The girl sucked in her breath again. M.C. kept his eyes on the pool. He didn't want to be watching her if this time she failed. He tried just to feel when the time was long enough. But in spite of himself, he began counting in his head.

When he knew she would have to breathe, he turned to her. Still she held out. Tendons and veins stood out on her neck. Her eyes were squeezed shut. Her cheeks and mouth were twisted in an awful face.

She exploded, bursting with air and squirming on the ground, trying to breathe again. Uncomfortably, M.C. turned his face away.

"You did it!" Macie yelled. Lennie Pool grinned and Harper clapped his hands.

"M.C., she did it!" Macie screeched. "Didn't she?"

He nodded at Macie to let all of them know.

But he was wondering if he had forgotten something he should have remembered to ask.

Never taken someone through that tunnel, he thought. Maybe I shouldn't.

"Are you going to swim it right now?" Macie asked the girl.

But she couldn't answer. She seemed to be having that cold, sickening feeling that came from holding your breath too long. M.C. knew this. Drying sweat caused his skin to itch again.

"We maybe can swim it later on," he said. "Give you plenty of time . . ."

The girl shot up from the ground. Even though she looked weak, she stood with her hands firmly on her hips. "You think I can't do it." Her eyes snapped at him.

M.C. couldn't get himself loose from those eyes, they were so pretty. Slowly he got to his feet.

There grew a silence between them that separated them from the children. They stood close together, watching each other.

"You have to do just as I say," M.C. told her.

"Why?"

"'Cause I know how to get through."

She thought a moment. "Okay," she said.

They were in a world all their own, where she was older but he was the leader. He knew why she had to try the tunnel.

Not because I've done it. 'Cause I'm the only one.

He turned and led the way over the rocks to the lake. The girl followed close on his heels.

The lake lay as serene and peaceful as when they had left it. Way down at the other end was the ridge. In between the ridge and the rocky end where now he and the girl crouched was the tent, like an intruder in the sun. All around them were pines, undergrowth, greens and browns closing in the magical shimmer of the lake.

He and the girl hung onto rocks just above the waterline. The children were clinging a foot above them.

"The tunnel's right down there," M.C. told her. "About eight to ten feet down. Maybe twelve feet long and that's a couple of body lengths." He paused, looking out over the lake. "Now I lead," he told her. "I lead and we hold together like this." With his right hand, he took hold of her left arm, forcing her to balance herself with her back against the rocks. "Hold on to my arm just above the wrist."

"Like this?" She grabbed his arm with fingers stronger than he'd expected. So close to her, he felt shy but calm.

"We jump here, we get more power," he told her. "We get down faster but it has to be done just right."

"How?" she said.

M.C. didn't know how. He was figuring it all out as he went along, working fast in his head the best way to jump and the quickest way to get through the tunnel.

"Best way is . . . if I jump backward and you jump frontward." He spoke carefully. "See, I hit and go in facing the tunnel. I have your left arm and you are pulled over. You follow in just in back of me. Now. In the tunnel, you have your right arm free and I have my left." They would use their free arms to push them through if they had to, and they could kick with their feet.

"Tunnel sides are moss," he said. "Push off from them when you bump them. It'll feel slimy but it won't hurt."

"Okay," she said.

"Pay no mind to fishes," he went on. "Most times, they're but just a few. They don't do nothing but get out of your way."

She nodded. M.C. could feel her tension through her arm.

"You all ready?" Macie asked from above them.

M.C. looked at the girl. "I'm ready," she said.

"You have to hold out for most of a minute."

"I can do it," she said.

"If you lose air, just stay calm," M.C. said. "I can get us out."

"I said I can do it!"

Her anger cut through him again, making him ashamed, he didn't know why.

"Macie, you count it off," he said grimly.

"She always get to do something," Harper said.

"He told *me,* now shut," Macie said.

"Stay out of the water. Wait for us at the pool. Now," M.C. said.

"Ready!" Macie yelled. "Get yourself set. . . ."

The girl grew rigid.

"You have to stay calm," M.C. told her. He held her arm as tightly as he could without hurting her. Her fingers dug into his wrist.

"Watch your nails!" he warned. They both sucked in air.

"Go, y'all!"

They leaped out and plunged. They hit the water at the same time but M.C. went under first because he was heavier. The girl turned facing him before her head went under. That was good, but pulling her after him slowed M.C. It seemed to take forever to get down to the tunnel level. Water closed in on them. Sounds became muffled and then no sound at all. They were alone as never before. And there was nothing for M.C. to do but get it over with.

M.C. liked nothing better than being in the deep, with sunlight breaking into rays of green and gold. Water was a pressure of delicious weight as he passed through it, down and down. It was as if feeling no longer belonged to him. The water possessed it and touched along every inch of him.

He pulled out of his downward fall at the sight of the gaping tunnel opening. He no longer felt the girl next to him. He knew she was there with him by the impression she made on the deep.

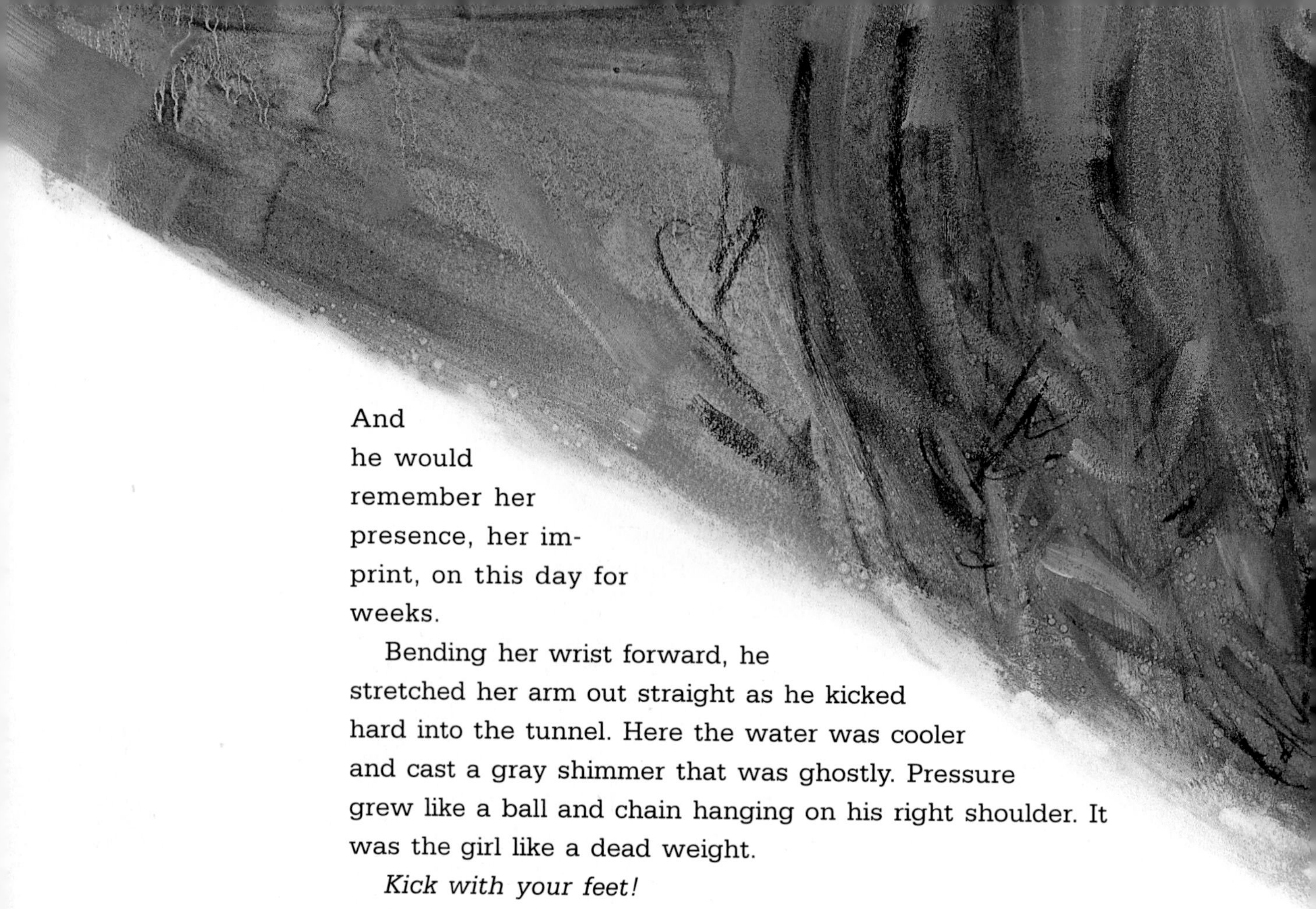

And
he would
remember her
presence, her im-
print, on this day for
weeks.

Bending her wrist forward, he
stretched her arm out straight as he kicked
hard into the tunnel. Here the water was cooler
and cast a gray shimmer that was ghostly. Pressure
grew like a ball and chain hanging on his right shoulder. It
was the girl like a dead weight.

*Kick with your feet!*

With a powerful scissoring of his legs, he tried to swim midway between the ceiling and bottom of the tunnel.

*Push off with your hand!*

Her dead pressure dragged him down. His knees banged
hard against the bottom. His back hit the tunnel side as he
realized she was struggling to get away. Fractions of seconds
were lost as he tried twisting her arm to pull her body into
line. Fishes slid over his skin, tickling and sending shivers
to his toes. They must have touched the girl. For he had no
moment to brace himself as she shot up on her back toward
the ceiling.

*Won't make it.*

Horror, outrage stunned him. He had taken for granted
the one thing he should have asked her. For the want of a
question, the tunnel would be a grave for both of them.

She kicked futilely against the tunnel side and rose above
him, twisting his arm straight up.

*Yank, like Macie will pull down on a balloon.*

If he could get the girl turned over, they might have a
chance. But his breath seemed to be gone.

*Not a
grave, it's a
tunnel.*

In his lungs, empti-
ness was pain. But the will
not to fail was there in his burning chest, in his free arm pushing hard
against the deep. His legs were still loose
and working. Then a sudden surge of strength,
like a second wind.

*Be M.C. Higgins, the Great.*

He yanked the balloon down—he mustn't break the string.
At the same time he propelled himself forward, knowing she
would follow as she turned over.

An awful pounding in his head snapped his brain open. M.C.
shot out of the tunnel like a cork from a jug of cider. And arching his back, he swung mightily with his right arm.

*Dark balloon to the light above.*

He hadn't the strength to hurl her to the surface. But he was right behind her. Before she could struggle down again, he was there, pulling at her. She opened her mouth in a pitiful attempt to breathe. He pounded her back, hoping to dislodge water. And held her close a split second to calm her. She was rigid.

*Girl, don't drown.*

Swiftly he caught her ankles and tossed her up over his head. She broke the surface. He was there, feeling sweet air just when he would have to open his mouth or have his lungs collapse.

M.C. fought against dizziness, aware he had his hand on her neck in a bruising clasp to hold her up. He had to let go or break it.

The girl was gagging, trying to breathe. He heard his own breath in a harsh, raw heaving. He was daydreaming a distant cheering. Then he saw the children, feet jumping up and down on the grassy bank. A swirl of rocks before he realized the girl was sinking. He must have let her go. But he had the sense to catch her again around the waist.

Still M.C. Still the leader. He had taken her through the tunnel and they were back in the world together. Still all the blame was his. But he could fix it. Could keep the children from knowing about her.

Moaning cry, coughing, she clung to him.

"No." He knocked her hands away. With just the pressure of his arm and shoulder on her back, he forced her flat out. As though she were dog-paddling, he glided her into the land. The feet jumping on the grassy bank fell back and were still.

Macie stood there on the bank, closest to M.C.'s head.

"She's weak," he said to Macie. "See if you can help pull her some . . . my wind is gone."

Macie clasped the girl's arms. M.C. had her by the waist. Halfway out of the water, she kicked M.C. away. She slithered and kneed her way over the bank. On the grass, she hunched into a ball, and struggling to breathe, closed her eyes.

*Dark balloon.*

M.C. climbed out and crawled a distance to collapse on his back. He was away from the girl, with the children between them, but he kept his eye on her. They were close together in his mind, where a vision had started. Day after day, they swam the lake. Hour upon hour, they sunned themselves on the shore.

M.C.'s chest wouldn't stop its heave and fall. His mouth watered with stomach bile as the pounding ache spread out across his forehead.

None of them moved. For a long while neither Harper nor Macie asked a single question. Lennie Pool never did say much.

M.C. felt as if every muscle were trying to get out of his skin. He was sick with exhaustion. But light out of the sky bore into him, warming and relaxing him. It was a healing band on his eyelids. As the ache in his forehead moved off, tunnel and water filled his mind. His eyes shot open, blinding the awful memory.

Seeing that M.C. was awake, Macie came over to him. "You did it!" she said happily. "Were you scared?"

He knew he would vomit if he tried to talk. He swallowed hard.

"You sure took your time. Was it any trouble?" Macie went on.

"Just took it easy," he said finally.

The girl brought up pool water she had swallowed. Half an hour later, she sat up shakily on her knees. In a slow, mechanical sweep, she brushed grass and twigs from her drying clothes.

M.C. raised his head. "You all right?" he asked her.

When she stood, the children stood with her. M.C. was on his feet as well, as though he moved only when she moved.

Slowly she seemed to change. He watched her grow stronger, throwing her head back, thrusting out her chin.

"I went all the way through that tunnel," she said, smiling vaguely. "I could have drowned—I can't even swim a lick."

The children gaped at her. Shocked, they turned to M.C.

"And you took her down?" Macie gasped. "You took her clear through . . . you didn't even know!"

The kids began to giggle, jostling one another, with the girl looking solemnly on.

M.C. felt the heat of shame rising in his neck. Only this one secret between them, but the girl wouldn't have it. She made him stand there with the kids laughing at him. He stared at his hands, at the jagged nails which he bit down to the skin while sitting on his pole.

"I can't stand a lying kid," the girl said.

Worse than a slap in the face, but he said evenly, "I'm not any kid. And I didn't lie."

"You told your sister we took it easy," she said, smirking at him.

"*I* took it easy," he said. "If I hadn't, you wouldn't be here, girl."

The children stared at him soberly now. The girl looked uncertain.

"It's no joke not to tell somebody you can't swim," he said.

"Somebody didn't ask me," she said sullenly.

"Didn't need to ask—you should've told me!"

"I just wanted to see it. I didn't know it was going to be so *long*."

"So you want to see something and we almost drown?" He was shaking now with the memory of the tunnel. "Ever think of somebody but yourself?"

The girl shrank back. Uncomfortably, they watched her. M.C. hadn't meant to make her appear stupid. But she was quick to apologize.

"I'm sorry," she said simply. "You told me you were some M.C., the Great. . . ."

The look she gave him, as if she knew only he could have saved her, made him feel proud. He had to smile. "You have some good nerve. A lot of real good nerve," he said at last.

# MEET Virginia Hamilton

**V**irginia Hamilton has tried "every source of occupation imaginable, from singer to bookkeeper." Luckily for literature, she "stumbled into . . . writing for young people" and has been producing award-winning books ever since.

Hamilton's characters are survivors. Most of them are young African Americans who, like M.C. Higgins, face important challenges and who find the inner strength and talent to do what they must do. She says, "My stories are little pieces of me."

Her mother's father escaped slavery to settle in Yellow Springs, Ohio. Hamilton lives and writes on land that was once part of her family's farm. She knows that area well. Several of her novels—*M.C. Higgins, the Great; The House of Dies Drear;* and *Willie Bea and the Time the Martians Landed*—are set in rural Ohio.

Ironically, Hamilton never intended to write for young people. One day a friend reminded her about a children's story she had written in college. As Hamilton recalls, "That children's story became *Zeely,* my first book." Hamilton learned her craft so well that, in 1975, *M.C. Higgins, the Great* was the first book to win both the Newbery Medal and the National Book Award for Children's Literature. She re-ceived the Hans Christian Andersen Award in 1992.

# DIVE RIGHT IN

Holding your breath for a long time hurts, as M.C. Higgins knows. Imagine holding your breath for more than three minutes or swimming for five days straight! As these world record holders show, being the best takes courage, endurance, and great willpower.

## KIDS SWIM THE ENGLISH CHANNEL

Thomas Gregory swam from France to England in just under 12 hours. At the time, September 1988, he was one month short of his twelfth birthday and the youngest person ever to swim the English Channel. The youngest girl to swim the Channel was twelve-year-old Samantha Claire Bruce. In 1983, she swam from England to France in 15 hours 27 minutes.

## SWIMMING THE GREAT LAKES

Vicki Keith, a Canadian swimmer, swam all five Great Lakes in 1988, becoming the first person ever to do so. She also holds the women's world record for length-of-time swimming. She swam (in a swimming pool) for 5 days, 9 hours, and 45 minutes straight and covered 78 miles (126 km)!

## THE DEEPEST DIVE

Jacques Mayol of France holds the record for the deepest dive without any breathing apparatus. In December 1983, he dove 344 feet (105 m), spending over 3 minutes underwater holding his breath. Rossana Majorca of Italy achieved the women's deepest dive in July 1987, when she dove 246 feet (75 m) off the shore of Sicily.

## A WALK ON THE WET SIDE

David Kiner of New York "walked" 155 miles (249 km) down the Hudson River from Albany to New York City in June 1987. It took him 5½ days at an average of 1.17 miles (1.88 km) per hour. Here he is, showing off his 11-foot water-ski shoes and double-bladed paddle. David doesn't hold the record for this odd sport, though. In 1983, Fritz Weber "walked" 185 miles (298 km) on the Main River in Germany at an average of 4 miles per day.

# BLUE
## A JOURNEY INTO AMERICA
# HIGHWAYS
### BY WILLIAM LEAST HEAT-MOON  ILLUSTRATED BY TERRY HOFF

At a time when America
was not yet ribboned by
superhighways, road maps
were printed in two colors:
red for the main routes
and blue for the back
roads. Armed with one of
these old maps, and trav-
eling on only the smallest
back roads—or blue high-
ways—William Least
Heat-Moon begins a spe-
cial 13,000-mile journey
into the heartland of
America. Yearning to fill
his life with new meaning,
Heat-Moon impulsively
packs his van, Ghost
Dancing, and sets out to
discover forgotten towns so
small that they are not
even named on the map.
He crosses through dozens
of these quaint towns:
Philadelphia in Mississippi,
Dimebox in Texas, and
Tuba City in Arizona are
just a few.

Nameless, Tennessee,
marks another stop on his
eventful trip.

Had it not been raining hard that morning on the Livingston square, I never would have learned of Nameless, Tennessee. Waiting for the rain to ease, I lay on my bunk and read the atlas to pass time rather than to see where I might go. In Kentucky were towns with fine names like Boreing, Bear Wallow, Decoy, Subtle, Mud Lick, Mummie, Neon; Belcher was just down the road from Mouthcard, and Minnie only ten miles from Mousie.

I looked at Tennessee. Turtletown eight miles from Ducktown. And also: Peavine, Wheel, Milky Way, Love Joy, Dull, Weakly, Fly, Spot, Miser Station, Only, McBurg, Peeled Chestnut, Clouds, Topsy, Isoline. And the best of all, Nameless. The logic! I was heading east, and Nameless lay forty-five miles west. I decided to go anyway.

The rain stopped, but things looked saturated, even bricks. In Gainesboro, a hill town with a square of businesses around the Jackson County Courthouse, I stopped for directions and breakfast. There is one almost infallible way to find honest food at just prices in blue-highway America: count the wall calendars in a cafe.

No calendar: Same as an interstate pit stop.
One calendar: Preprocessed food assembled in New Jersey.
Two calendars: Only if fish trophies present.
Three calendars: Can't miss on the farm-boy breakfasts.
Four calendars: Try the ho-made pie too.
Five calendars: Keep it under your hat, or they'll franchise.

One time I found a six-calendar cafe in the Ozarks, which served fried chicken, peach pie, and chocolate malts, that left me searching for another ever since. I've never seen a seven-calendar place. But old-time travelers—road men in a day when cars had running boards and lunchroom windows said AIR COOLED in blue letters with icicles dripping from the tops—those travelers have told me the golden legends of seven-calendar cafes.

To the rider of back roads, nothing shows the tone, the voice of a small town more quickly than the breakfast grill or the five-thirty tavern. Much of what the people do and believe and share is evident then. The City Cafe in Gainesboro had three calendars that I could

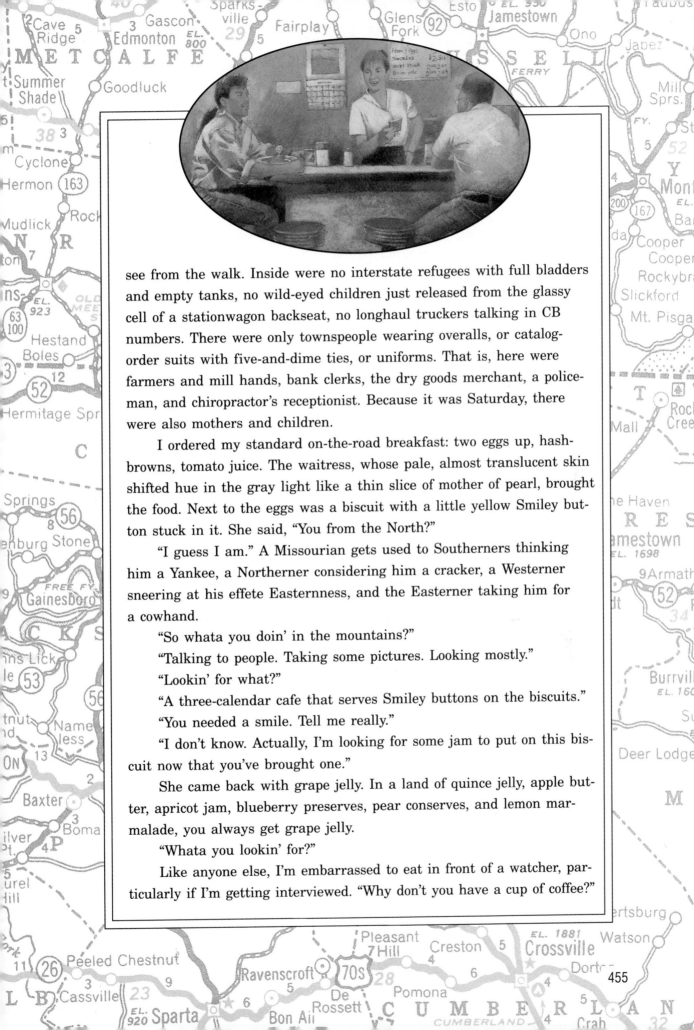

see from the walk. Inside were no interstate refugees with full bladders and empty tanks, no wild-eyed children just released from the glassy cell of a stationwagon backseat, no longhaul truckers talking in CB numbers. There were only townspeople wearing overalls, or catalog-order suits with five-and-dime ties, or uniforms. That is, here were farmers and mill hands, bank clerks, the dry goods merchant, a police-man, and chiropractor's receptionist. Because it was Saturday, there were also mothers and children.

I ordered my standard on-the-road breakfast: two eggs up, hash-browns, tomato juice. The waitress, whose pale, almost translucent skin shifted hue in the gray light like a thin slice of mother of pearl, brought the food. Next to the eggs was a biscuit with a little yellow Smiley but-ton stuck in it. She said, "You from the North?"

"I guess I am." A Missourian gets used to Southerners thinking him a Yankee, a Northerner considering him a cracker, a Westerner sneering at his effete Easternness, and the Easterner taking him for a cowhand.

"So whata you doin' in the mountains?"

"Talking to people. Taking some pictures. Looking mostly."

"Lookin' for what?"

"A three-calendar cafe that serves Smiley buttons on the biscuits."

"You needed a smile. Tell me really."

"I don't know. Actually, I'm looking for some jam to put on this bis-cuit now that you've brought one."

She came back with grape jelly. In a land of quince jelly, apple but-ter, apricot jam, blueberry preserves, pear conserves, and lemon mar-malade, you always get grape jelly.

"Whata you lookin' for?"

Like anyone else, I'm embarrassed to eat in front of a watcher, par-ticularly if I'm getting interviewed. "Why don't you have a cup of coffee?"

"Cain't right now. You gonna tell me?"

"I don't know how to describe it to you. Call it harmony."

She waited for something more. "Is that it?" Someone called her to the kitchen. I had managed almost to finish by the time she came back. She sat on the edge of the booth. "I started out in life not likin' anything, but then it grew on me. Maybe that'll happen to you." She watched me spread the jelly. "Saw your van." She watched me eat the biscuit. "You sleep in there?" I told her I did. "I'd love to do that, but I'd be scared spitless."

"I don't mind being scared spitless. Sometimes."

"I'd love to take off cross country. I like to look at different license plates. But I'd take a dog. You carry a dog?"

"No dogs, no cats, no budgie birds. It's a one-man campaign to show Americans a person can travel alone without a pet."

"Cain't travel without a dog!"

"I like to do things the hard way."

"Shoot! I'd take me a dog to talk to. And for protection."

"It isn't traveling to cross the country and talk to your pug instead of people along the way. Besides, being alone on the road makes you ready to meet someone when you stop. You get sociable traveling alone."

She looked out toward the van again. "Time I get the nerve to take a trip, gas'll cost five dollars a gallon."

"Could be. My rig might go the way of the steamboat." I remembered why I'd come to Gainesboro. "You know the way to Nameless?"

"Nameless? I've heard of Nameless. Better ask the amlance driver in the corner booth." She pinned the Smiley on my jacket. "Maybe I'll see you on the road somewhere. His name's Bob, by the way."

"The ambulance driver?"

"The Smiley. I always name my Smileys—otherwise they all look alike. I'd talk to him before you go."

"The Smiley?"

"The amlance driver."

And so I went looking for Nameless, Tennessee, with a Smiley button named Bob.

**"I** don't know if I got directions for where you're goin'," the ambulance driver said. "I *think* there's a Nameless down the Shepardsville Road."

"When I get to Shepardsville, will I have gone too far?"

"Ain't no Shepardsville."

"How will I know when I'm there?"

"Cain't say for certain."

"What's Nameless look like?"

"Don't recollect."

"Is the road paved?"

"It's possible."

Those were the directions. I was looking for an unnumbered road named after a nonexistent town that would take me to a place called Nameless that nobody was sure existed.

Clumps of wild garlic lined the county highway that I hoped was the Shepardsville Road. It scrimmaged with the mountain as it tried to stay on top of the ridges; the hillsides were so steep and thick with oak, I felt as if I were following a trail through the misty treetops. Chickens, doing more work with their necks than legs, ran across the road, and, with a battering of wings, half leapt and half flew into the lower branches of oaks. A vicious pair of mixed-breed German shepherds raced along trying to eat the tires. After miles, I decided I'd missed the town—assuming there truly *was* a Nameless, Tennessee. It wouldn't be the first time I'd qualified for the Ponce de Leon Believe Anything Award.

I stopped beside a big man loading tools in a pickup. "I may be lost."

"Where'd you lose the right road?"

"I don't know. Somewhere around nineteen sixty-five."

"Highway fifty-six, you mean?"

"I came down fifty-six. I think I should've turned at the last junction."

"Only thing down that road's stumps and huckleberries, and the berries ain't there in March. Where you tryin' to get to?"

"Nameless. If there is such a place."

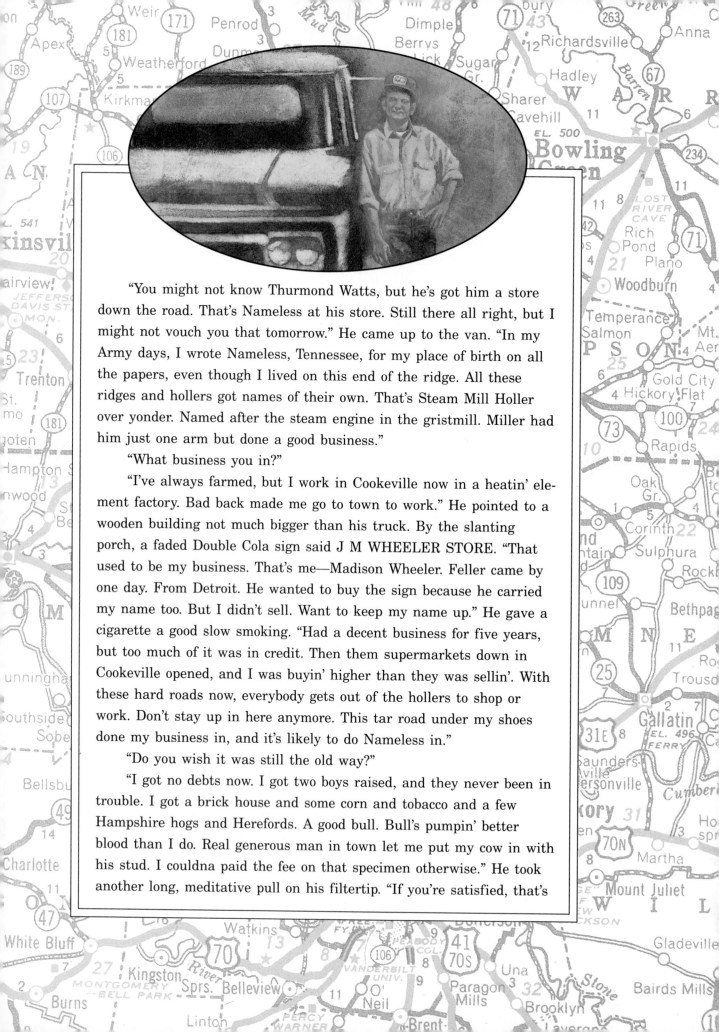

"You might not know Thurmond Watts, but he's got him a store down the road. That's Nameless at his store. Still there all right, but I might not vouch you that tomorrow." He came up to the van. "In my Army days, I wrote Nameless, Tennessee, for my place of birth on all the papers, even though I lived on this end of the ridge. All these ridges and hollers got names of their own. That's Steam Mill Holler over yonder. Named after the steam engine in the gristmill. Miller had him just one arm but done a good business."

"What business you in?"

"I've always farmed, but I work in Cookeville now in a heatin' element factory. Bad back made me go to town to work." He pointed to a wooden building not much bigger than his truck. By the slanting porch, a faded Double Cola sign said J M WHEELER STORE. "That used to be my business. That's me—Madison Wheeler. Feller came by one day. From Detroit. He wanted to buy the sign because he carried my name too. But I didn't sell. Want to keep my name up." He gave a cigarette a good slow smoking. "Had a decent business for five years, but too much of it was in credit. Then them supermarkets down in Cookeville opened, and I was buyin' higher than they was sellin'. With these hard roads now, everybody gets out of the hollers to shop or work. Don't stay up in here anymore. This tar road under my shoes done my business in, and it's likely to do Nameless in."

"Do you wish it was still the old way?"

"I got no debts now. I got two boys raised, and they never been in trouble. I got a brick house and some corn and tobacco and a few Hampshire hogs and Herefords. A good bull. Bull's pumpin' better blood than I do. Real generous man in town let me put my cow in with his stud. I couldna paid the fee on that specimen otherwise." He took another long, meditative pull on his filtertip. "If you're satisfied, that's all they are to it. I'll tell you, people from all over the nation—Florida, Mississippi—are comin' in here to retire because it's good country. But our young ones don't stay on. Not much way to make a livin' in here anymore. Take me. I been beatin' on these stumps all my life, tryin' to farm these hills. They don't give much up to you. Fightin' rocks and briars all the time. One of the first things I recollect is swingin' a briar blade—filed out of an old saw it was. Now they come in with them crawlers and push out a pasture in a day. Still, it's a grudgin' land— like the gourd. Got to hard cuss gourd seed, they say, to get it up out of the ground."

The whole time, my rig sat in the middle of the right lane while we stood talking next to it and wiped at the mist. No one else came or went. Wheeler said, "Factory work's easier on the back, and I don't mind it, understand, but a man becomes what he does. Got to watch that. That's why I keep at farmin', although the crops haven't ever throve. It's the doin' that's important." He looked up suddenly. "My apologies. I didn't ask what you do that gets you into these hollers."

I told him. I'd been gone only six days, but my account of the trip already had taken on some polish.

He nodded. "Satisfaction is doin' what's important to yourself. A man ought to honor other people, but he's got to honor what he believes in too."

As I started the engine, Wheeler said, "If you get back this way, stop in and see me. Always got beans and taters and a little piece of meat."

Down along the ridge, I wondered why it's always those who live on little who are the ones who ask you to dinner.

**N**ameless, Tennessee, was a town of maybe ninety people if you pushed it, a dozen houses along the road, a couple of barns, same number of churches, a general merchandise store selling Fire Chief gasoline, and a community center with a lighted volleyball court. Behind the center was an open-roof, rusting metal privy with PAINT

ME on the door; in the hollow of a nearby oak lay a full pint of Jack Daniel's Black Label. From the houses, the odor of coal smoke.

Next to a red tobacco barn stood the general merchandise with a poster of Senator Albert Gore, Jr., smiling from the window. I knocked. The door opened partway. A tall, thin man said, "Closed up. For good," and started to shut the door.

"Don't want to buy anything. Just a question for Mr. Thurmond Watts."

The man peered through the slight opening. He looked me over. "What question would that be?"

"If this is Nameless, Tennessee, could he tell me how it got that name?"

The man turned back into the store and called out, "Miss Ginny! Somebody here wants to know how Nameless come to be Nameless."

Miss Ginny edged to the door and looked me and my truck over. Clearly, she didn't approve. She said, "You know as well as I do, Thurmond. Don't keep him on the stoop in the damp to tell him." Miss Ginny, I found out, was Mrs. Virginia Watts, Thurmond's wife.

I stepped in and they both began telling the story, adding a detail here, the other correcting a fact there, both smiling at the foolishness of it all. It seems the hilltop settlement went for years without a name. Then one day the Post Office Department told the people if they wanted mail up on the mountain they would have to give the place a name you could properly address a letter to. The community met; there were only a handful, but they commenced debating. Some wanted patriotic names, some names from nature, one man recommended in all seriousness his own name. They couldn't agree, and they ran out of names to argue about. Finally, a fellow tired of the talk; he didn't like the mail he received anyway. "Forget the durn Post Office," he said. "This here's a nameless place if I ever seen one, so leave it be." And that's just what they did.

Watts pointed out the window. "We used to have signs on the road, but the Halloween boys keep tearin' them down."

"You think Nameless is a funny name," Miss Ginny said. "I see it plain in your eyes. Well, you take yourself up north a piece to Difficult or Defeated or Shake Rag. Now them are silly names."

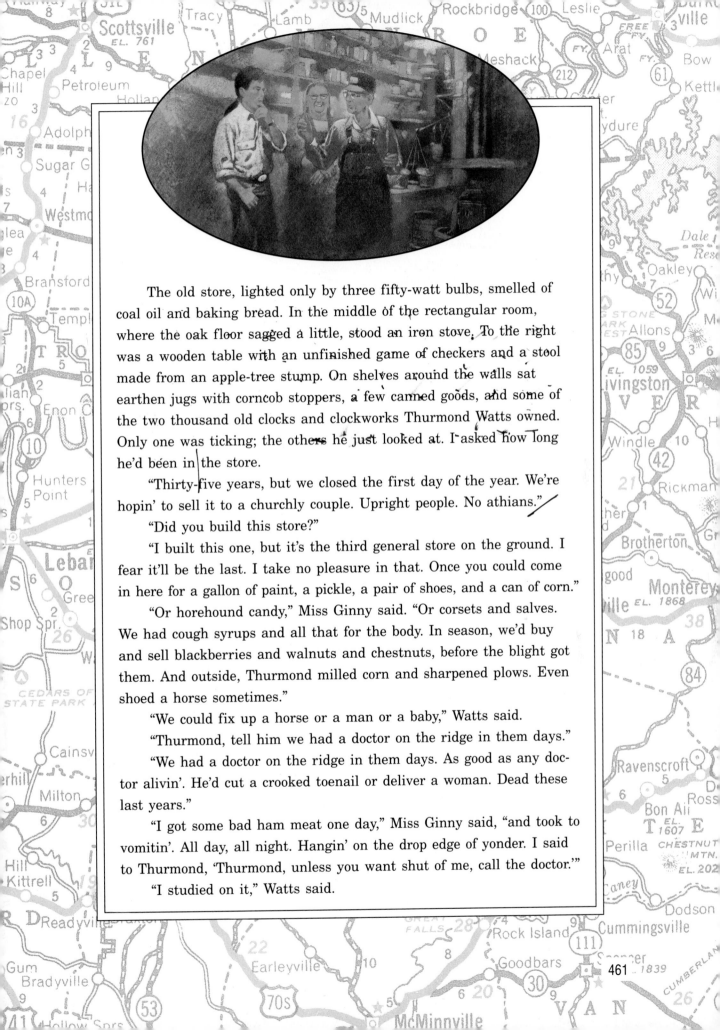

The old store, lighted only by three fifty-watt bulbs, smelled of coal oil and baking bread. In the middle of the rectangular room, where the oak floor sagged a little, stood an iron stove. To the right was a wooden table with an unfinished game of checkers and a stool made from an apple-tree stump. On shelves around the walls sat earthen jugs with corncob stoppers, a few canned goods, and some of the two thousand old clocks and clockworks Thurmond Watts owned. Only one was ticking; the others he just looked at. I asked how long he'd been in the store.

"Thirty-five years, but we closed the first day of the year. We're hopin' to sell it to a churchly couple. Upright people. No athians."

"Did you build this store?"

"I built this one, but it's the third general store on the ground. I fear it'll be the last. I take no pleasure in that. Once you could come in here for a gallon of paint, a pickle, a pair of shoes, and a can of corn."

"Or horehound candy," Miss Ginny said. "Or corsets and salves. We had cough syrups and all that for the body. In season, we'd buy and sell blackberries and walnuts and chestnuts, before the blight got them. And outside, Thurmond milled corn and sharpened plows. Even shoed a horse sometimes."

"We could fix up a horse or a man or a baby," Watts said.

"Thurmond, tell him we had a doctor on the ridge in them days."

"We had a doctor on the ridge in them days. As good as any doctor alivin'. He'd cut a crooked toenail or deliver a woman. Dead these last years."

"I got some bad ham meat one day," Miss Ginny said, "and took to vomitin'. All day, all night. Hangin' on the drop edge of yonder. I said to Thurmond, 'Thurmond, unless you want shut of me, call the doctor.'"

"I studied on it," Watts said.

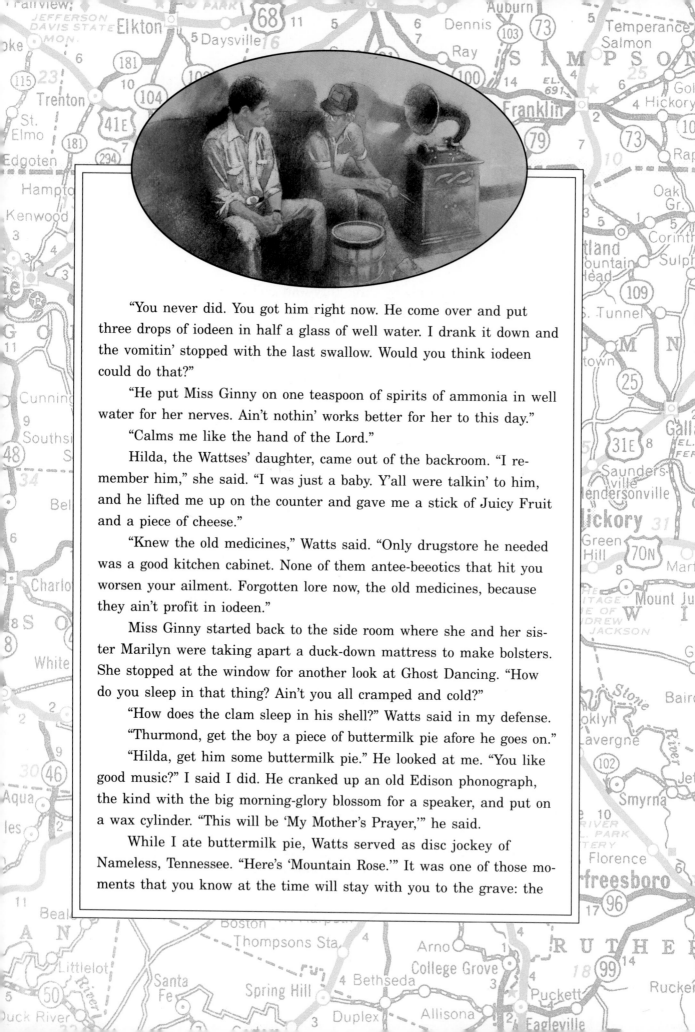

"You never did. You got him right now. He come over and put three drops of iodeen in half a glass of well water. I drank it down and the vomitin' stopped with the last swallow. Would you think iodeen could do that?"

"He put Miss Ginny on one teaspoon of spirits of ammonia in well water for her nerves. Ain't nothin' works better for her to this day."

"Calms me like the hand of the Lord."

Hilda, the Wattses' daughter, came out of the backroom. "I remember him," she said. "I was just a baby. Y'all were talkin' to him, and he lifted me up on the counter and gave me a stick of Juicy Fruit and a piece of cheese."

"Knew the old medicines," Watts said. "Only drugstore he needed was a good kitchen cabinet. None of them antee-beeotics that hit you worsen your ailment. Forgotten lore now, the old medicines, because they ain't profit in iodeen."

Miss Ginny started back to the side room where she and her sister Marilyn were taking apart a duck-down mattress to make bolsters. She stopped at the window for another look at Ghost Dancing. "How do you sleep in that thing? Ain't you all cramped and cold?"

"How does the clam sleep in his shell?" Watts said in my defense.

"Thurmond, get the boy a piece of buttermilk pie afore he goes on."

"Hilda, get him some buttermilk pie." He looked at me. "You like good music?" I said I did. He cranked up an old Edison phonograph, the kind with the big morning-glory blossom for a speaker, and put on a wax cylinder. "This will be 'My Mother's Prayer,'" he said.

While I ate buttermilk pie, Watts served as disc jockey of Nameless, Tennessee. "Here's 'Mountain Rose.'" It was one of those moments that you know at the time will stay with you to the grave: the sweet pie, the gaunt man playing the old music, the coals in the stove glowing orange, the scent of kerosene and hot bread. "Here's 'Evening Rhapsody.'" The music was so heavily romantic we both laughed. I thought: It is for this I have come.

Feathered over and giggling, Miss Ginny stepped from the side room. She knew she was a sight. "Thurmond, give him some lunch. Still looks hungry."

Hilda pulled food off the woodstove in the backroom: home-butchered and canned whole-hog sausage, home-canned June apples, turnip greens, cole slaw, potatoes, stuffing, hot cornbread. All delicious.

Watts and Hilda sat and talked while I ate. "Wish you would join me."

"We've ate," Watts said. "Cain't beat a woodstove for flavorful cookin'."

He told me he was raised in a one-hundred-fifty-year-old cabin still standing in one of the hollows. "How many's left," he said, "that grew up in a log cabin? I ain't the last surely, but I must be climbin' on the list."

Hilda cleared the table. "You Watts ladies know how to cook."

"She's in nursin' school at Tennessee Tech. I went over for one of them football games last year there at Coevul." To say *Cookeville,* you let the word collapse in upon itself so that it comes out "Coevul."

"Do you like football?" I asked.

"Don't know. I was so high up in that stadium, I never opened my eyes."

Watts went to the back and returned with a fat spiral notebook that he set on the table. His expression had changed. "Miss Ginny's *Deathbook.*"

The thing startled me. Was it something I was supposed to sign? He opened it but said nothing. There were scads of names written in a tidy hand over pages incised to crinkliness by a ballpoint. Chronologically, the names had piled up: wives, grandparents, a still-born infant, relatives, friends close and distant. Names, names. After each, the date of *the* unknown finally known and transcribed. The last entry bore yesterday's date.

"She's wrote out twenty years' worth. Ever day she listens to the hospital report on the radio and puts the names in. Folks come by to check a date. Or they just turn through the books. Read them like a scrapbook."

Hilda said, "Like Saint Peter at the gates inscribin' the names."

Watts took my arm. "Come along." He led me to the fruit cellar under the store. As we went down, he said, "Always take a newborn baby upstairs afore you take him downstairs, otherwise you'll incline him downwards."

The cellar was dry and full of cobwebs and jar after jar of home-canned food, the bottles organized as a shopkeeper would: sausage, pumpkin, sweet pickles, tomatoes, corn relish, blackberries, peppers, squash, jellies. He held a hand out toward the dusty bottles. "Our tomorrows."

Upstairs again, he said, "Hope to sell the store to the right folk. I see now, though, it'll be somebody offen the ridge. I've studied on it, and maybe it's the end of our place." He stirred the coals. "This store could give a comfortable livin', but not likely get you rich. But just gettin' by is dice rollin' to people nowadays. I never did see my day guaranteed."

When it was time to go, Watts said, "If you find anyone along your way wants a good store—on the road to Cordell Hull Lake—tell them about us."

I said I would. Miss Ginny and Hilda and Marilyn came out to say goodbye. It was cold and drizzling again. "Weather to give a man the weary dismals," Watts grumbled. "Where you headed from here?"

"I don't know."

"Cain't get lost then."

Miss Ginny looked again at my rig. It had worried her from the first as it had my mother. "I hope you don't get yourself kilt in that durn thing gallivantin' around the country."

"Come back when the hills dry off," Watts said. "We'll go lookin' for some of them round rocks all sparkly inside."

I thought a moment. "Geodes?"

"Them's the ones. The county's properly full of them."

# MEET WILLIAM LEAST HEAT-MOON

At a time in his life when he was feeling very confused, William Least Heat-Moon "took to the open road," setting out in his van to explore the back roads of America. He was searching for "places where change did not mean ruin and where time and men and deeds connected." Heat-Moon's three-month journey took him to small towns such as Nameless, Tennessee, and Looking Glass, Oregon. And his experiences on the road became the highly acclaimed best-seller *Blue Highways*.

Heat-Moon, also known as William Trogdon, is of English, Irish, and Osage descent. His mixed heritage was another inspiration for his journey.

He searched for his own identity and place in American life, while letting the people he met tell him their own stories. "A good traveler has to improvise as he goes," Heat-Moon says. "He has to take what each journey gives, good or bad."

*Blue Highways* received the Christopher Award and was named one of the best books of 1983 by *The New York Times* and *Time* magazine. Least Heat-Moon's latest book is *PrairyErth,* a profile of people and places in Kansas.

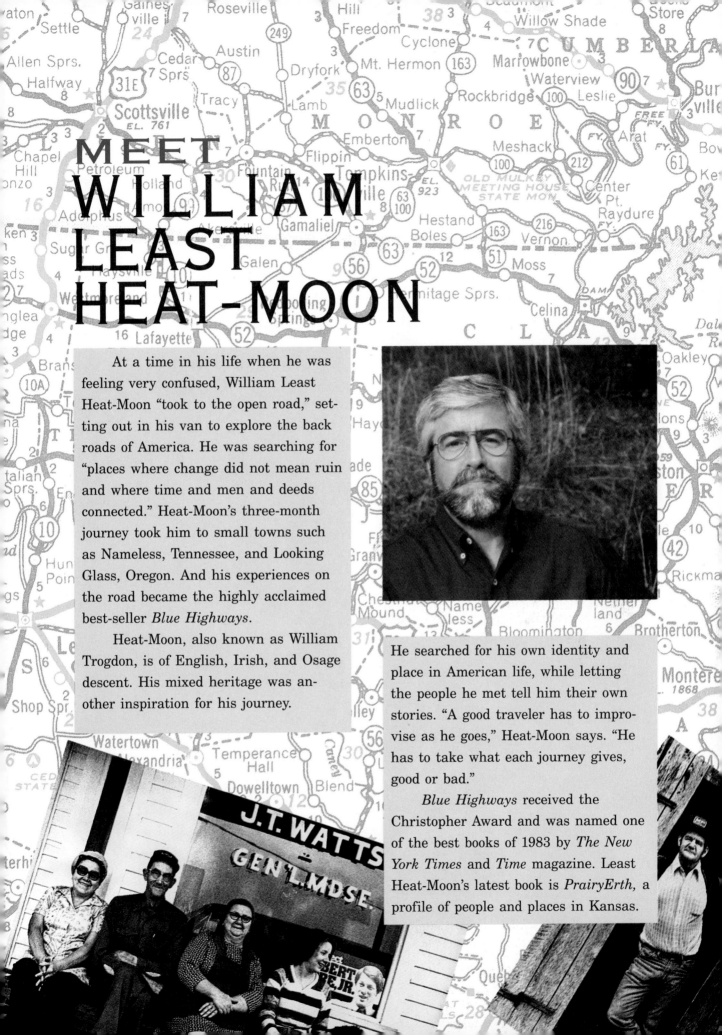

BACKROADS

Some days it doesn't rhyme,
doesn't even scan,
and the verse is much worse than free,
dumber than a hundred bars
of statuary—

Straight on, like driving
from Elko to Green River
one salt-flat night
a hundred years ago
when the river darkened to my right
and blinding walls of rock
slammed the other side
of a black-and-white highway.

On that all-night-long drive home
I thought we'd never see the light again.

And then
the highway ended
in a line across the land
and the sky descended
stony
on a Wyoming morning
as the river
churned green
and we kept on driving
into the nacreous
day
through a barren, unfenced, windmill
dawn.

by Kenneth Lincoln
with Al Logan Slagle

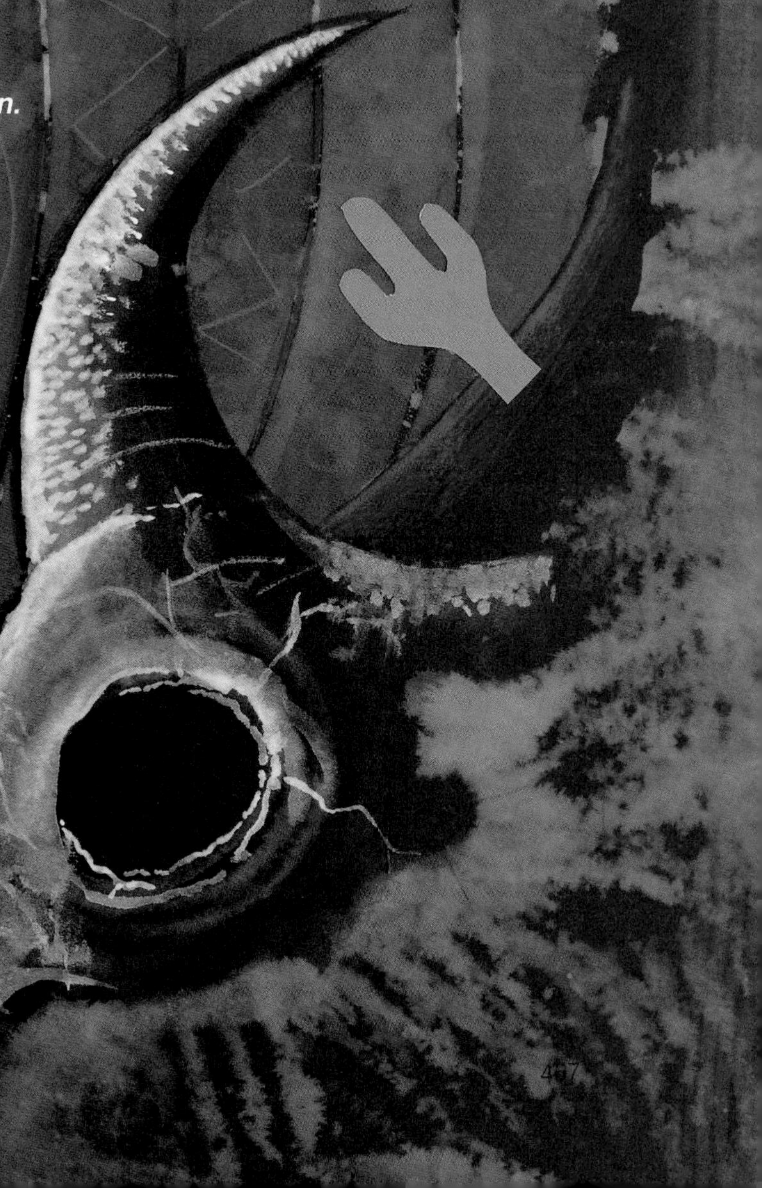

**The Children's Homer**

by Padraic Colum

Collier, 1982

**The Dark Is Rising**

by Susan Cooper

Collier, 1986

# CLASSIC QUESTS

# DRAGONSONG

ILLUSTRATED BY CATHERINE HUERTA

# I

n a distant galaxy, the planet Pern orbits the golden star Rukbar. Threatened by Threadfall, a periodic occurrence in which destructive thread-like spores fall from a neighboring planet and devour anything organic in their way, the colonists of this cool and beautiful world live in fortified caves called Holds. During Threadfall, trained riders sweep the sky atop dragons whose fiery breath destroys the threads before they can reach the ground. Smaller dragonlike creatures called fire lizards also inhabit the planet.

Menolly and Sella are daughters of the Sea Holder of Half Circle Sea Hold. Menolly longs to be a Harper. But Harpers, whose songs teach, entertain, and also perpetuate the history of the people, are traditionally men. Menolly, therefore, is forbidden by her father to spend much time on her music. When she accidentally cuts her hand, making it very difficult to play musical instruments, she believes that she will probably have to give up music entirely. Unhappy about her fate, she takes long walks along the seashore. On one of these walks, she encounters a flock of the shy fire lizards.

## BY ANNE MC CAFFREY

# DRAGONSONG

When spring was fully warming the air and making the marshes brilliant with green and blossom color, spiderclaws began to walk in from the sea to lay their eggs in the shallower cove waters. As these plump shellfish were a delicacy in themselves, besides adding flavor to every dish when dried or smoked, the young people of the Hold—Menolly with them—were sent off with traps, spades and nets. Within four days the nearby coves were picked clear of spider-claws and the young harvesters had to go farther along the coast to find more. With Thread due to fall anytime, it was unwise to stray too far from the Hold, so they were told to be very careful.

There was another danger that concerned the Sea Holder considerably: tides had been running unusually high and full this Turn. Much higher water in the harbor and they'd not get the two big sloops in or out of the Cavern unless they unstepped the masts. Due notice was taken of the high-tide lines, and there was much shaking of heads when it was observed that the line was two full hands higher than ever before recorded.

The lower caverns of the Hold were checked against possible seepage. Bags of sand were filled and placed along the lower portions of the seawalls around the harbor.

A good storm and the causeways would be awash. Yanus was concerned enough to have a long chat with Old Uncle to see if he

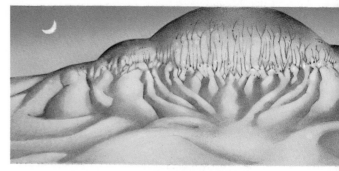

remembered anything from his earlier and clearer days of Sea Holding. Old Uncle was delighted to talk and ranted on about the influence of the stars, but when Yanus, Elgion and two of the other older shipmasters had sifted through what he'd said, it was not to any great increase in knowledge. Everyone knew that the two moons affected the tides, not the three bright stars in the sky.

They did, however, send a message about these curious tides to

# DRAGONSONG

Igen Hold to be forwarded with all possible speed to the main Seacraft Hold at Fort. Yanus didn't want to have his biggest boats caught out in the open, so he kept careful check on the tides, determined to leave them within the Dock Cavern if the tide rose another hand higher.

When the youngsters went out to gather spiderclaws, they were told to keep their eyes open and report back anything unusual, espe-

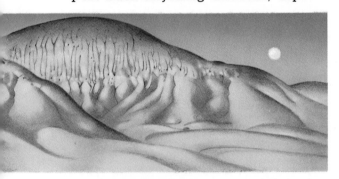

cially new high-water marks on the coves. Only Thread deterred the more adventurous lads from using this as an excuse for ranging far down the coast. Menolly, who preferred to explore the more distant places alone, mentioned Thread to them as often as possible.

Then, after the next Threadfall, when everyone was sent out for spiderclaws, Menolly made certain that she got a headstart on the boys, making good use of her long legs.

It was fine to run like this, Menolly thought, putting yet another rise between her and her nearest pursuers. She altered her stride for uneven ground. It wouldn't do to break an ankle now. Running was something even a girl with a crippled hand could do well.

Menolly closed her mind to that thought. She'd learned the trick of not thinking about anything: she counted. Right now she counted her strides. She ran on, her eyes sweeping ahead of her to save her feet. The boys would never catch her now, but she was running for the sheer joy of the physical effort, chanting a number to each stride. She ran until she got a stitch in her side and her thighs felt the strain.

She slowed, turning her face into the cool breeze blowing offshore, inhaling deeply of its freshness and sea odors. She was somewhat surprised to see how far she had come down the coast. The Dragon Stones were visible in the clear air, and it was only then that she recalled the little queen. Unfortunately, she also remembered the tune she'd made up that day: the last day, Menolly now realized, of her trusting childhood.

# DRAGONSONG

She walked on, following the line of the bluffs, peering down to see if she could spot new high-water marks on the stone escarpments. Tide was halfway in now, Menolly decided. And yes, she could see the lines of sea debris from the last tide, in some places right up against the cliff face. And this had been a cove with a deep beach.

A movement above, a sudden blotting of the sun, made her gaze upwards. A sweep rider. Knowing perfectly well that he couldn't see her, she waved vigorously any-how, watching the graceful glide as the pair dwindled into the distance.

Sella had told her one evening when they were preparing for bed that Elgion had flown on dragons several times. Sella had given a quiver of de-lighted terror, vowing that she wouldn't have the courage to ride a dragon.

Privately Menolly thought that Sella wouldn't likely have the op-portunity. Most of Sella's comments, and probably thoughts, were cen-tered on the new Harper. Sella was not the only one, Menolly knew. If Menolly could think how silly all the Hold girls were being about Harper Elgion, it didn't hurt so much to think about harpers in general.

#  D R A G O N S O N G

Again she heard the fire lizards before she saw them. Their excited chirpings and squeals indicated something was upsetting them. She dropped to a crouch and crept to the edge of the bluff, overlooking the little beach. Only there wasn't much beach left, and the fire lizards were hovering over a spot on the small margin of sand, almost directly below her.

She inched up to the edge, peering down. She could see the queen darting at the incoming waves as if she could stop them with her violently beating wings. Then she'd streak back, out of Menolly's line of sight, while the rest of the creatures kept milling and swooping, rather like frightened herdbeasts running about aimlessly when wild wherries circled their herd. The queen was shrieking at the top of her shrill little voice, obviously trying to get them to do something. Unable to imagine what the emergency could be, Menolly leaned just a little further over the edge. The whole lip of the cliff gave way.

Clutching wildly at sea grasses, Menolly tried to prevent her fall. But the sea grass slipped cuttingly through her hand and she slid over the edge and down.

She hit the beach with a force that sent a shock through her body. But the wet sand absorbed a good deal of the impact. She lay where she'd fallen for a few minutes, trying to get her breath into her lungs and out again. Then she scrambled to her feet and crawled away from an incoming wave.

She looked up the side of the bluff, rather daunted by the fact that she'd fallen a dragon length or more. And how was she going to climb back up? But, as she examined the cliff face, she could see that it was not so unscalable as she'd first thought. Almost straight up, yes, but pocked by ledges and holds, some fairly large. If she could find enough foot and hand holds, she'd be able to make it. She dusted the sand from her hands and started to walk towards one end of the little cove, to begin a systematic search for the easiest way up.

She'd gone only a few paces when something dove at her, screeching in fury. Her hands went up to protect her face as the little queen came diving down at her. Now Menolly recalled the curious behavior of the fire lizards. The little queen acted as if she were protecting something from Menolly

as well as the encroaching sea, and she looked about her. She was within handspans of stepping into a fire lizard clutch.

"Oh, I'm sorry. I'm sorry. I wasn't looking! Don't be mad at me," Menolly cried as the little fire lizard came at her again. "Please! Stop! I won't hurt them!"

To prove her sincerity, Menolly backtracked to the far end of the beach. There she had to duck under a small overhang. When she looked around, there wasn't a sign of the little queen. Menolly's relief was short-lived, for how was she to find a way up the cliff if the little fire lizard kept attacking her every time she approached the eggs. Menolly hunched down, trying to get comfortable in her cramped refuge.

Maybe if she kept away from the eggs? Menolly peered up the cliff directly above her. There were some likely looking holds. She eased herself out the far side, keeping one eye on the clutch, basking in the hot sun, and reached for the first ledge.

Immediately the fire lizard came at her.

"Oh, leave me alone! Ow! Go away. I'm trying to."

The fire lizard's talons had raked her cheek.

# DRAGONSONG

"Please! I won't hurt your eggs!"

The little queen's next pass just missed Menolly, who ducked back under the ledge.

Blood oozed from the long scratch, and Menolly dabbed at it with the edge of her tunic.

"Haven't you got any sense?" Menolly demanded of her now invisible attacker. "What would I want with your silly eggs? Keep 'em. I just want to get home. Can't you understand? I just want to go home."

Maybe if I sit very still, she'll forget about me, Menolly thought and pulled her knees up under the chin, but her toes and elbows protruded from under the overhang.

Suddenly a bronze fire lizard materialized above the clutch, squeaking worriedly. Menolly saw the queen swooping to join him, so the queen must have been on the top of the ledge, waiting, just waiting for Menolly to break cover.

And to think I made up a pretty tune about you, Menolly thought as she watched the two lizards hovering over the eggs. The last tune I ever made up. You're ungrateful, that's what you are!

Despite her discomfort, Menolly had to laugh. What an impossible situation! Held under a cramped ledge by a creature no bigger than her forearm.

At the sound of her laughter, the two fire lizards disappeared.

Frightened, were they? Of laughter?

"A smile wins more than a frown," Mavi was fond of saying.

Maybe if I keep laughing, they'll know I'm friendly? Or get scared away long enough for me to climb up? Saved by a laugh?

Menolly began to chuckle in earnest, for she had also seen that the tide was coming in rather quickly. She eased out of her shelter, flung the carry-sack over her shoulder, and started to climb. But it proved impossible to chuckle and climb. She needed breath for both.

Abruptly both the little queen and the bronze were back to harry her, flying at her head and face. The fragile looking wings were dangerous when used as a weapon.

No longer laughing, Menolly ducked back under her ledge, wondering what to do next.

If laughter had startled them, what about a song? Maybe if she gave that pair a chorus of her tune, they'd let her go. It was the first time she'd sung since she'd seen the lizards, so her voice sounded

477

rough and uncertain. Well, the lizards would *know* what she meant, she hoped, so she sang the saucy little song. To no one.

"Well, so much for that notion," Menolly muttered under her breath. "Which makes the lack of interest in your singing absolutely unanimous."

No audience? Not a fire lizard's whisker in sight?

As fast as she could, Menolly slipped from her shelter and came face to face, for a split second, with two fire lizard faces. She ducked down, and they evidently disappeared because when she cautiously peered again, the ledge where they'd been perched was empty.

She had the distinct impression that their expressions had registered curiosity and interest.

"Look, if wherever you are, you can hear me . . . will you stay there and let me go? Once I'm on the top of the cliff, I'll serenade you til the sun goes down. Just let me get up there!"

She started to sing a dutiful dragon song as she once again emerged from her refuge. She was about five steps upward when the queen fire lizard emerged, with help. With squeaks and squeals she was driven back down. She could

even hear claws scraping on the rock above her. She must have quite an audience by now. When she didn't need one!

Cautiously she looked up, met the fascinated whirling of ten pairs of eyes.

"Look, a bargain! One long song and then let me up the cliff? Is that agreed?"

Fire lizard eyes whirled.

Menolly took it that the bargain was made and sang. Her voice started a flutter of surprised and excited chirpings, and she wondered if by any possible freak they actually understood that she was singing about grateful holds honoring dragonriders. By the last verse she eased out into the open, awed by the sight of a queen fire lizard and nine bronzes entranced by her performance.

"Can I go now?" she asked and put one hand on the ledge.

The queen dived for her hand, and Menolly snatched it back.

"I thought we'd struck a bargain."

The queen chirped piteously, and Menolly realized that there had been no menace in the queen's action. She simply wasn't allowed to climb.

"You don't want me to go?" Menolly asked.

The queen's eyes seemed to glow more brightly.

"But I have to go. If I stay, the water will come up and drown me." And Menolly accompanied her words with explanatory gestures.

Suddenly the queen let out a shrill cry, seemed to hold herself midair for a moment and then, her bronzes in close pursuit, she glided down the sandy beach to her clutch. She hovered over the eggs, making the most urgent and excited sounds.

If the tide was coming in fast enough to endanger Menolly, it was also frighteningly close to swamping the nest. The little bronzes began to take up the queen's plaint and several, greatly daring, flew about Menolly's head and then circled back to the clutch.

"I can come there now? You won't attack me?" Menolly took a few steps forward.

The tone of the cries changed, and Menolly quickened her step. As she reached the nest, the little queen secured one egg from the clutch. With a great laboring of her wings, she bore it upward. That the effort was great was obvious. The

bronzes hovered anxiously, squeaking their concern but, being much smaller, they were unable to assist the queen.

Now Menolly saw that the base of the cliff at this point was littered with broken shells and the pitiful bodies of tiny fire lizards, their wings half-extended and glistening with egg fluid. The little queen now had raised the egg to a ledge, which Menolly had not previously noticed, about a half-dragon length up the cliff face. Menolly could see the little queen deposit the egg on the ledge and roll it with her forelegs towards what must be a hole in the cliff. It was a long moment before the queen reappeared again. Then she dove towards the sea, hovering over the foamy crest of a wave that rolled in precariously close to the endangered clutch. With a blurred movement, the queen was hovering in front of Menolly and scolding like an old aunt.

Although Menolly couldn't help grinning at the thought, she was filled with a sense of pity and admiration for the courage of the little queen, single-handedly trying to rescue her clutch. If the dead fire lizards were that fully formed, the

clutch was near to hatching. No wonder the queen could barely move the eggs.

"You want me to help you move the eggs, right? Well, we'll see what I can do!"

Ready to jump back if she had mistaken the little queen's imperious command, Menolly very carefully picked up an egg. It was warm to the touch and hard. Dragon eggs, she knew, were soft when first laid but hardened slowly on the hot sands of the Hatching Grounds in the Weyrs. These definitely must be close to hatching.

Closing the fingers of her damaged hand carefully around the egg, Menolly searched for and found foot and hand holds, and reached the queen's ledge. She carefully deposited the egg. The little queen

appeared, one front talon resting proprietarily on the egg, and then she leaned forward, towards Menolly's face, so close that the fantastic motion of the many-faceted eyes were clearly visible. The queen gave a sort of sweet chirp and then, in a very businesslike manner, began to scold Menolly as she rolled her egg to safety.

Menolly managed three eggs in her hand the next time. But it was obvious that between the onrushing tide and the startling number of eggs in the clutch, there'd be quite a race.

"If the hole were bigger," she told the little queen as she deposited three eggs, "some of the bronzes could help you roll."

The queen paid her no attention, busy pushing the three eggs,

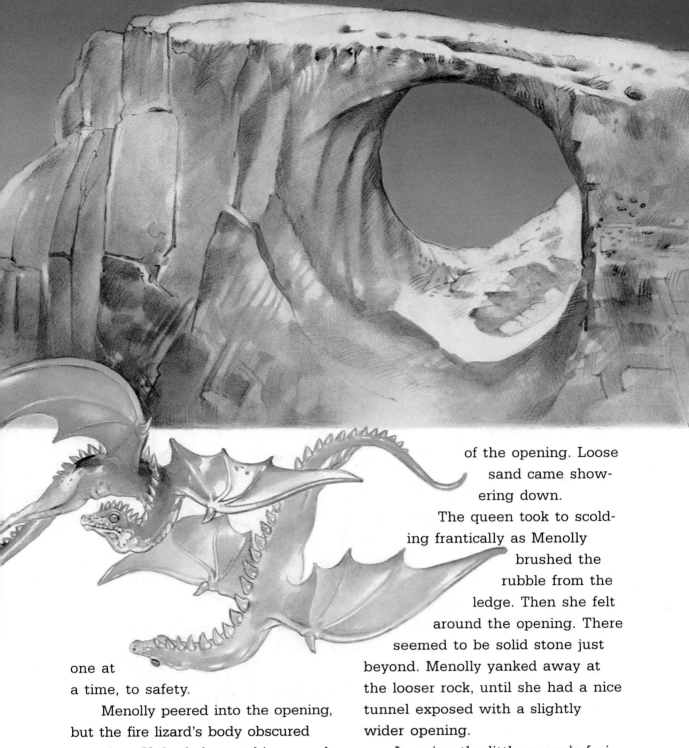

of the opening. Loose sand came showering down.

The queen took to scolding frantically as Menolly brushed the rubble from the ledge. Then she felt around the opening. There seemed to be solid stone just beyond. Menolly yanked away at the looser rock, until she had a nice tunnel exposed with a slightly wider opening.

Ignoring the little queen's furious complaints, Menolly climbed down, unslinging her sack when she reached the ground. When the little queen saw Menolly putting the eggs in the sack, she began to have hysterics, beating at Menolly's head and hands.

one at a time, to safety.

Menolly peered into the opening, but the fire lizard's body obscured any view. If the hole was bigger and the ledge consequently broader, Menolly could bring the rest of the eggs up in her carry-sack.

Hoping that she wouldn't pull down the cliffside and bury the queen, clutch and all, Menolly prodded cautiously at the mouth

481

"Now, look here," Menolly said sternly, "I am not stealing your eggs. I am trying to get them all to safety in jig time. I can do it with the sack but not by the handful."

Menolly waited a moment, glaring at the little queen who hovered at eye level.

"Did you understand me?" Menolly pointed to the waves, more vigorously dashing up the small beach. "The tide is coming in. Dragons couldn't stop it now." Menolly put another egg carefully in the sack. As it was she'd have to make two, maybe three trips or risk breaking the eggs. "I take this," and she gestured up the ledge, "up there. Do you understand, you silly beast?"

Evidently, the little creature did because, crooning anxiously, she took her position on the ledge, her wings half-extended and twitching as she watched Menolly's progress up to her.

Menolly could climb faster with two hands. And she could, carefully, roll the eggs from the mouth of the sack well down the tunnelway.

"You'd better get the bronzes to help you now, or we'll have the ledge stacked too high."

It took Menolly three trips in all, and as she made the last climb,

the water was a foot's width from the clutch. The little queen had organized her bronzes to help, and Menolly could hear her scolding tones echoing in what must be a fair-sized cave beyond the tunnel. Not surprising since these bluffs were supposed to be riddled with caverns and passages.

Menolly gave a last look at the beach, water at least ankle deep on both ends of the little cove. She glanced upward, past the ledge. She was a good halfway up the cliff now, and she thought she could see enough hand and foot holds ahead.

"Good-bye!" She was answered by a trill of chirps, and she chuckled as she imagined the scene: the queen marshalling her bronzes to position her eggs just right.

Menolly did not make the cliff top without a few anxious moments. She was exhausted when she finally flopped on the sea grasses at the summit, and her left hand ached from unaccustomed gripping and effort. She lay there for some time, until her heart stopped thudding in her ribs and her breath came more easily. An inshore breeze dried her face, cooling her; but that reminded her of the emptiness of her stomach. Her exertions had reduced the rolls in

her pouch to crumby fragments, which she gobbled as fast as she could find them.

All at once the enormity of her adventure struck her, and she was torn between laughter and awe. To prove to herself that she'd actually done what she remembered, she crept cautiously to the bluff edge. The beach was completely underwater. The sandy wallow where the fire lizard eggs had baked was being tideswept smooth. The rubble that had gone over the edge with her had been absorbed or washed away. When the tide retreated, all evidence

of her energies to save herself and the clutch would be obliterated. She could see the protuberance of rock down which the queen had rolled her eggs but not a sign of a fire lizard. The waves crashed with firm intent against the Dragon Stones when she gazed out to sea, but no bright motes of color flitted against the somber crags.

Menolly felt her cheek. The fire lizard's scratch was crusted with dried blood and sand.

"So it did happen!"

However did the little queen know I could help her? No one had ever suggested that fire lizards were stupid. Certainly they'd been smart enough for endless Turns to evade every trap and snare laid to catch them. The creatures were so clever, indeed, that there was a good deal of doubt about their existence, except as figures of overactive imaginations. However, enough trustworthy men had actually seen the creatures, at a distance, like her brother Alemi when he'd spotted some about the Dragon Stones, that most people did accept their existence as fact.

Menolly could have sworn that the little queen had understood her. How else could Menolly have helped her? That proved how smart the little beast was. Smart enough certainly to avoid the boys who tried to capture them . . . Menolly was appalled. Capture a fire lizard? Pen it up? Not, Menolly supposed with relief, that the creature would stay caught long. It only had to pop *between*.

Now why hadn't the little queen just gone *between* with her eggs, instead of arduously transporting them one by one? Oh, yes, *between* was the coldest place known. And cold would do the eggs harm. At least it did dragon eggs harm. Would the clutch be all right now in the cold cavern? Hmmm. Menolly peered below. Well, if the queen had as much sense as she'd already shown, she'd get all her followers to come lie on the eggs and keep them warm until they did hatch.

Menolly turned her pouch inside out, hoping for some crumbs. She was still hungry. She'd find enough early fruits and some of the succulent reeds to eat, but she was curiously loath to leave the bluff. Though, it was unlikely that the queen, now her need was past, would reappear.

Menolly rose finally and found herself stiff from the unaccustomed exercise. Her hand ached in a dull way, and the long scar was red and slightly swollen. But, as Menolly flexed her fingers, it seemed that the hand opened more easily. Yes, it did. She could almost extend the fingers completely. It hurt, but it was a stretchy-hurt. Could she open her hand enough to play again? She folded her fingers as if to chord. That hurt, but again, it was a stretchy-hurt. Maybe if she worked her hand a lot more . . . She had been favoring it until today when she hadn't given it a thought. She'd used it to climb and carry and everything.

"Well, you did me a favor, too, little queen," Menolly called, speaking into the breeze and waving her hands high. "See? My hand is better."

There was no answering chirp or sound, but the soft whistle of the seaborne breeze and the lapping of the waves against the bluff. Yet Menolly liked to think that her words had been heard. She turned inland, feeling considerably relieved and rather pleased with the morning's work.

She'd have to scoot now and gather what she could of greens and early berries. No point in trying for spiderclaws with the tide so high.

# Meet

## ANNE McCAFFREY

"Dragons have always had a bad press," according to the award-winning science fiction writer Anne McCaffrey. To help improve their image, she created the fantasy world of Pern, where mind-reading dragons help humans find their way through the perils of life. The dragons are major forces in the three McCaffrey novels known as the Harper Hall trilogy: *Dragonsong*, *Dragonsinger*, and *Dragondrums*.

McCaffrey is very much at home with all kinds of animals—both real and imaginary. Her farm in Ireland, where she lives in a house named Dragonhold, is populated by cats, dogs, and horses. Although she admits to having "quite a goodly crowd of human friends," including her three children, she says, "I continue to think that I understand animals better than humans."

In response to questions about why she writes science fiction, McCaffrey has answered, "It's one of the few fields of fiction that gives you hope."

# WORLDS

## The Fantastic Worlds of Science Fiction

STAR WARS

PLANET OF THE APES

**Science fiction has been irresistible to filmmakers from the very beginning. In fact, one of the first movies of all time was science fiction. Made in France in 1902, the movie was called *A Trip to the Moon.* Of the many science fiction films made since then, here's a sampling of three of the most famous. You'll notice that each of them, like Anne McCaffrey's *Dragonsong,* describes a wondrous world.**

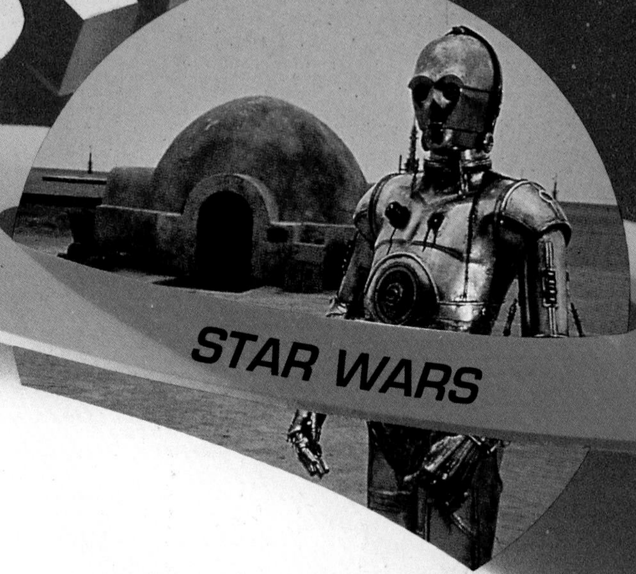

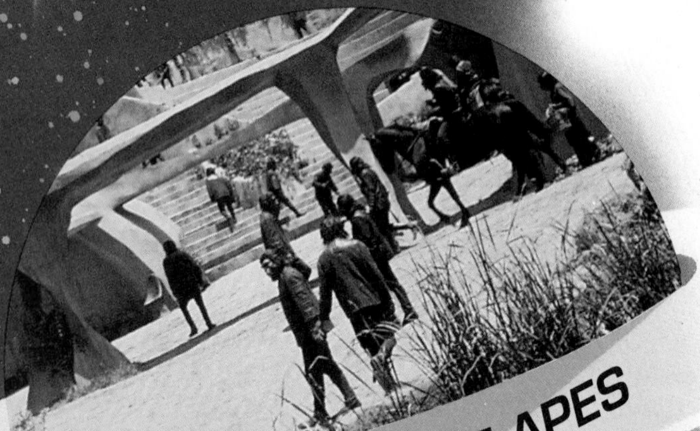

# APART

## Planet of the Apes

In *Planet of the Apes*, a spaceship travels through a time warp thousands of years in the future and crash lands on a strange planet. The astronauts discover that the planet on which they've landed is actually ruled by apes; they are soon captured and taken in chains to the ape city. In the film's incredible final scene, an astronaut who has escaped from the ape city encounters a half-buried Statue of Liberty and suddenly realizes—to his horror—that this supposedly alien world, in which humanity has been enslaved by apes, is actually the future Earth!

## Star Wars

*Star Wars* is probably the most famous science fiction film of all. Set "a long, long time ago in a galaxy far, far away," the film follows young Luke Skywalker as he journeys from his home planet of Tattooine—accompanied by his copilot Han Solo and two friendly robots—into outer space to rescue Princess Leia from the clutches of the evil Darth Vader. To create Tatooine, the filmmakers traveled to the Sahara in North Africa, where they built a futuristic landscape with an incredible collection of modern junk, like sections of jet engines and drainage pipes.

## Fantastic Voyage

A very different kind of world—and a very different kind of journey—is featured in the film *Fantastic Voyage*. A group of doctors is *miniaturized* and injected into the bloodstream of a patient in order to perform a complicated brain operation that cannot be accomplished by normal procedures. On the way to the brain, their submarine winds its way past massive replicas of the complex mechanisms that exist within the human body. (The heart built for the film, for instance, was the largest working model of a heart ever made—forty feet (12 m) wide and thirty feet (9 m) high.) But perhaps the most ingenious thing about this film is its subtle message: The most "fantastic" world of all exists not in space but inside each of us.

FANTASTIC VOYAGE

by Nikki Giovanni

It's a journey . . . that I propose . . . I am not the guide . . . nor technical assistant . . . I will be your fellow passenger . . .

Though the rail has been ridden . . . winter clouds cover . . . autumn's exuberant quilt . . . we must provide our own guide-posts . . .

I have heard . . . from previous visitors . . . the road washes out sometimes . . . and passengers are compelled . . . to continue groping . . . or turn back . . . I am not afraid . . .

I am not afraid . . . of rough spots . . . or lonely times . . . I don't fear . . . the success of this endeavor . . . I am Ra . . . in a space . . . not to be discovered . . . but invented . . .

I promise you nothing . . . I accept your promise . . . of the same we are simply riding . . . a wave . . . that may carry . . . or

BY NATHANIEL HAWTHORNE

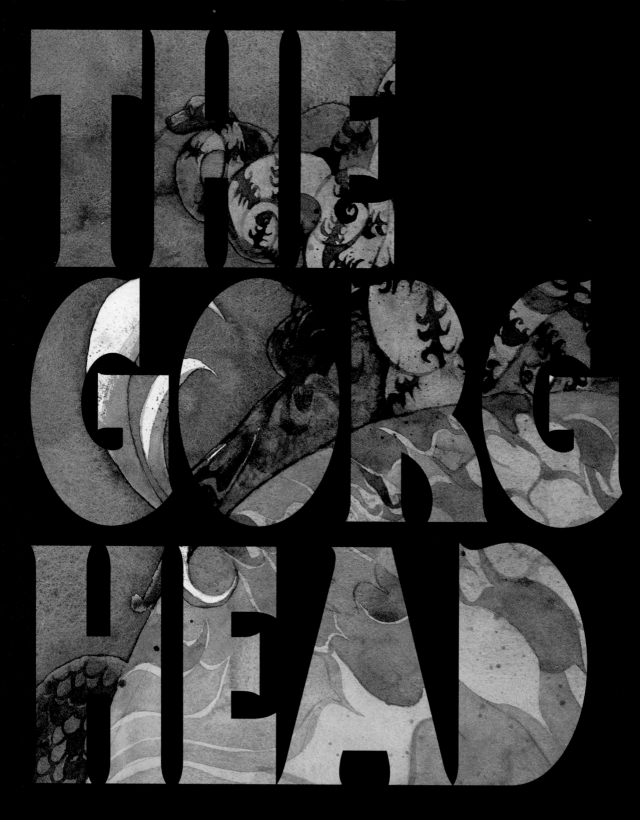

THE GORGON HEAD

ILLUSTRATED BY ROBERT ROTH

Perseus was the son of Danaë, who was the daughter of a king. And when Perseus was a very little boy, some wicked people put his mother and himself into a chest, and set them afloat upon the sea. The wind blew freshly, and drove the chest away from the shore, and the uneasy billows tossed it up and down; while Danaë clasped her child closely to her bosom, and dreaded that some big wave would dash its foamy crest over them both. The chest sailed on, however, and neither sank nor was upset; until, when night was coming, it floated so near an island that it got entangled in a fisherman's nets, and was drawn out high and dry upon the sand. The island was called Seriphus, and it was reigned over by King Polydectes, who happened to be the fisherman's brother.

This fisherman, I am glad to tell you, was an exceedingly humane and upright man. He showed great kindness to Danaë and her little boy, and continued to befriend them, until Perseus had grown to be a handsome youth, very strong and active, and skilful in the use of arms. Long before this time, King Polydectes had seen the two strangers—the mother and her child—who had come to his dominions in a floating chest. As he was not good and kind, like his brother the fisherman, but extremely wicked, he resolved to send Perseus on a dangerous enterprise, in which he would probably be killed, and then to do some great mischief to Danaë herself. So this bad-hearted king spent a long while in considering what was the most dangerous thing that a young man could possibly undertake to perform. At last, having hit upon an enterprise that promised to turn out as fatally as he desired, he sent for the youthful Perseus.

The young man came to the palace, and found the king sitting upon his throne.

"Perseus," said King Polydectes, smiling craftily upon him, "you are grown up a fine young man. You and your good mother have received a great deal of kindness from myself, as well as from my worthy brother, the fisherman, and I suppose you would not be sorry to repay some of it!"

"Please your majesty," answered Perseus, "I would willingly risk my life to do so."

"Well, then," continued the king, still with a cunning smile on his lips, "I have a little adventure to propose to you; and, as you are a brave and enterprising youth, you will doubtless look upon it as a great piece of good luck to have so rare an opportunity of distinguishing yourself. You must know, my good Perseus, I think of getting married to the beautiful Princess Hippodamia; and it is customary, on these occasions, to make the bride a present of some far-fetched and elegant curiosity. I have been a little perplexed, I must honestly confess, where to obtain anything likely to please a princess of her exquisite taste. But, this morning, I flatter myself, I have thought of precisely the article."

"And can I assist your majesty in obtaining it?" cried Perseus eagerly.

"You can, if you are as brave a youth as I believe you to be," replied King Polydectes, with the utmost graciousness of manner. "The bridal gift, which I have set my heart on presenting to the beautiful Hippodamia, is the head of the Gorgon Medusa, with the snaky locks; and I depend on you, my dear Perseus, to bring it to me. So, as I am anxious to settle affairs with the princess, the sooner you go in quest of the Gorgon, the better I shall be pleased."

"I will set out tomorrow morning," answered Perseus.

"Pray do so, my gallant youth!" rejoined the king. "And, Perseus, in cutting off the Gorgon's head, be careful to make a clean stroke, so as not to injure its appearance. You must bring it home in the very best condition, in order to suit the exquisite taste of the beautiful Princess Hippodamia."

Perseus left the palace, but was scarcely out of hearing before Polydectes burst into a laugh; being greatly amused, wicked king that he was, to find how readily the young man fell into the snare. The news quickly spread abroad, that Perseus had undertaken to cut off the head of Medusa with the snaky locks. Everybody was rejoiced; for most of the inhabitants of the island were as wicked as the king himself, and would have liked nothing better than to see some enormous mischief happen to Danaë and her son. The only good man, in this unfortunate island of Seriphus, appears to have been the fisherman. As Perseus walked along, therefore, the people pointed after him, and made mouths, and winked to one another, and ridiculed him as loudly as they dared.

"Ho, ho!" cried they. "Medusa's snakes will sting him soundly!"

Now, there were three Gorgons alive, at that period; and they were the most strange and terrible monsters that had ever been seen, since the world was made, or that have been seen in after days, or that are likely to be seen, in all time to come. I hardly know what sort of creature or hobgoblin to call them. They were three sisters, and seem to have borne some distant resemblance to women, but were really a very frightful and mischievous species of dragon. It is indeed difficult to imagine what hideous beings these three sisters were. Why, instead of locks of hair, if you can believe me, they had each of them a hundred enormous snakes growing on their heads, all alive, twisting, wriggling, curling, and thrusting out their venomous tongues, with forked stings at

the end! The teeth of the Gorgons were terribly long tusks; their hands were made of brass; and their bodies were all over scales, which, if not iron, were something as hard and impenetrable. They had wings, too, and exceedingly splendid ones, I can assure you; for every feather in them was pure, bright, glittering, burnished gold, and they looked very dazzlingly, no doubt, when the Gorgons were flying about in the sunshine.

But, when people happened to catch a glimpse of their glittering brightness, aloft in the air, they seldom stopt to gaze, but ran and hid themselves as speedily as they could. You will think, perhaps, that they were afraid of being stung by the serpents that served the Gorgons instead of hair—or of having their heads bitten off by their ugly tusks—or of being torn all to pieces by their brazen claws. Well, to be sure, these were some of the dangers, but by no means the greatest, nor the most difficult to avoid. For the worst thing about these abominable Gorgons was, that, if once a poor mortal fixed his eyes full upon one of their faces, he was certain, that very instant, to be changed from warm flesh and blood into cold and lifeless stone!

Thus, as you will easily perceive, it was a very dangerous adventure that the wicked King Polydectes had contrived for this innocent young man. Perseus himself, when he had thought over the matter, could not help seeing that he had very little chance of coming safely through it, and that he was far more likely to become a stone image, than to bring back the head of Medusa with the snaky locks. For, not to speak of other difficulties, there was one which it would have puzzled an older man than Perseus to get over. Not only must he fight with and slay this golden-winged, iron-scaled, long tusked, brazen-clawed, snaky-haired monster, but he must do it with his eyes shut, or, at least, without so much as a glance at the enemy with whom he was contending. Else, while his arm was lifted to strike, he would stiffen into stone, and stand with that uplifted arm for centuries, until time, and the wind and weather, should crumble him quite away. This would be a very sad thing to befal a young man, who wanted to perform a great many brave deeds, and to enjoy a great deal of happiness, in this bright and beautiful world.

So disconsolate did these thoughts make him, that Perseus could not bear to tell his mother what he had undertaken to do. He therefore took his shield, girded on his sword, and crossed over from the island to the mainland, where he sat down in a solitary place, and hardly refrained from shedding tears.

But while he was in this sorrowful mood, he heard a voice close beside him.

"Perseus," said the voice, "why are you sad?"

He lifted his head from his hands, in which he had hidden it; and, behold! all alone as Perseus had supposed himself to be, there was a stranger in the solitary place. It was a brisk, intelligent, and remarkably shrewd-looking young man, with a cloak over his shoulders, an odd sort of cap on his head, a strangely twisted staff in his hand, and a short and very crooked sword hanging by his side. He was exceedingly light and active in his figure, like a person much accustomed to gymnastic exercises, and well able to leap or run. Above all, the stranger had such a cheerful, knowing, and helpful aspect, (though it was certainly a little mischievous, into the bargain,) that Perseus could not help feeling his spirits grow livelier, as he gazed at him. Besides, being really a courageous youth, he felt greatly ashamed that anybody should have found him with tears in his eyes, like a timid little schoolboy, when, after all, there might be no occasion for despair. So Perseus wiped his eyes, and answered the stranger pretty briskly, putting on as brave a look as he could.

"I am not so very sad," said he—"only thoughtful about an adventure that I have undertaken."

"Oho!" answered the stranger. "Well; tell me all about it, and possibly I may be of service to you. I have helped a good many young men through adventures that looked difficult enough beforehand. Perhaps you may have heard of me. I have more names than one; but the name of Quicksilver suits me as well as any other. Tell me what your trouble is; and we will talk the matter over, and see what can be done."

The stranger's words and manner put Perseus into quite a different mood from his former one. He resolved to tell Quicksilver all his difficulties; since he could not easily be worse off than he already was, and, very possibly, his new friend might give him some advice that would turn out well in the end. So he let the stranger know, in few words, precisely what the case was;—how that King Polydectes wanted the head of Medusa with the snaky locks, as a bridal gift for the beautiful Princess Hippodamia, and how that he had undertaken to get it for him, but was afraid of being turned into stone.

"And that would be a great pity," said Quicksilver, with his mischievous smile. "You would make a very handsome marble statue, it is true; and it would be a considerable number of centuries before you crumbled away. But, on the whole, one would rather be a young man for a few years, than a stone image for a great many."

"Oh, far rather!" exclaimed Perseus, with the tears again standing in his eyes. "And, besides, what would my dear mother do, if her beloved son were turned into stone!"

"Well, well, let us hope that the affair will not turn out so very badly," replied Quicksilver, in an encouraging tone. "I am the very person to help you, if anybody can. My sister and myself will do our utmost to bring you safe through the adventure, ugly as it now looks."

"Your sister?" repeated Perseus.

"Yes; my sister," said the stranger. "She is very wise, I promise you; and as for myself, I generally have all my wits about me, such as they are. If you show yourself bold and cautious, and follow our advice, you need not fear being a stone image yet awhile. But, first of all, you must polish your shield till you can see your face in it as distinctly as in a mirror."

This seemed to Perseus rather an odd beginning of the adventure; for he thought it of far more consequence that the shield should be strong enough to defend him from the

Gorgon's brazen claws, than that it should be bright enough to show him the reflection of his face. However, concluding that Quicksilver knew better than himself, he immediately set to work, and scrubbed the shield with so much diligence and good-will, that it very quickly shone like the moon at harvest-time. Quicksilver looked at it with a smile, and nodded his approbation. Then, taking off his own short and crooked sword, he girded it about Perseus, instead of the one which he had before worn.

"No sword but mine will answer your purpose," observed he. "The blade has a most excellent temper, and will cut through iron and brass as easily as through the slenderest twig. And now we will set out. The next thing is to find the Three Gray Women, who will tell us where to find the Nymphs."

"The Three Gray Women!" cried Perseus, to whom this seemed only a new difficulty in the path of his adventure. "Pray, who may the Three Gray Women be? I never heard of them before."

"They are three very strange old ladies," said Quicksilver, laughing. "They have but one eye among them, and only one tooth! Moreover, you must find them out by starlight, or in the dusk of the evening; for they never show themselves by the light either of the sun or moon."

"But," said Perseus, "why should I waste my time with these Three Gray Women? Would it not be better to set out at once in search of the terrible Gorgons?"

"No, no," answered his friend. "There are other things to be done, before you can find your way to the Gorgons. There is nothing for it, but to hunt up these old ladies; and when we meet with them, you may be sure that the Gorgons are not a great way off. Come; let us be stirring!"

Perseus, by this time, felt so much confidence in his companion's sagacity, that he made no more objections, and professed himself ready to begin the adventure immediately. They accordingly set out, and walked at a pretty brisk pace; so brisk, indeed, that Perseus found it rather difficult to keep up with his nimble friend Quicksilver. To say the truth, he had a singular idea that Quicksilver was furnished with a pair of winged shoes, which, of course, helped him along marvellously. And then, too, when Perseus looked sideways at him, out of the corner of his eye, he seemed to see wings on the side of his head; although, if he turned a full gaze, there were no such things to be perceived, but only an odd kind of cap. But, at all events, the twisted staff was evidently a great convenience to Quicksilver, and enabled him to proceed so fast, that Perseus, though a remarkably active young man, began to be out of breath.

"Here!" cried Quicksilver, at last—for he knew well enough, rogue that he was, how hard Perseus found it to keep pace with him—"Take you the staff, for you need it a great deal more than I. Are there no better walkers than yourself, in the island of Seriphus?"

"I could walk pretty well," said Perseus, glancing slily at his companion's feet, "if I had only a pair of winged shoes."

"We must see about getting you a pair," answered Quicksilver.

But the staff helped Perseus along so bravely, that he no longer felt the slightest weariness. In fact, the stick seemed to be alive in his hand, and to lend some of its life to Perseus. He and Quicksilver now walked onward, at their ease, talking very sociably together; and Quicksilver told so many pleasant stories about his former adventures, and how well his wits had served him on various occasions, that Perseus began to think him a very wonderful person. He evidently knew the world; and nobody is so charming to a young man, as a friend who has that kind of knowledge. Perseus listened the more eagerly, in the hope of brightening his own wits by what he heard.

At last, he happened to recollect that Quicksilver had spoken of a sister, who was to lend her assistance in the adventure which they were now bound upon.

"Where is she?" he inquired. "Shall we not meet her soon?"

"All at the proper time," said his companion. "But this sister of mine, you must understand, is quite a different sort of character from myself. She is very grave and prudent, seldom smiles, never laughs, and makes it a rule not to utter a word, unless she has something particularly profound to say. Neither will she listen to any but the wisest conversation."

"Dear me!" ejaculated Perseus. "I shall be afraid to say a syllable."

"She is a very accomplished person, I assure you," continued Quicksilver, "and has all the arts and sciences at her fingers' ends. In short, she is so immoderately wise, that many people call her Wisdom personified. But, to tell you the truth, she has hardly vivacity enough for my taste; and I think you would scarcely find her so pleasant a travelling companion as myself. She has her good points, nevertheless, and you will find the benefit of them in your encounter with the Gorgons."

By this time, it had grown quite dusk. They were now come to a very wild and desert place, overgrown with shaggy bushes, and so silent and solitary that nobody seemed ever to have dwelt or journeyed there. All was waste and desolate, in the gray twilight, which grew every moment more obscure. Perseus looked about him, rather disconsolately, and asked Quicksilver whether they had a great deal farther to go.

"Hist! Hist!" whispered his companion. "Make no noise! This is just the time and place to meet the Three Gray Women. Be careful that they do not see you before you see them; for though they have but a single eye among the three, it is as sharp-sighted as half-a-dozen common eyes."

"But what must I do," asked Perseus, "when we meet them?"

Quicksilver explained to Perseus how the Three Gray Women managed with their one eye. They were in the habit, it seems, of changing it from one to another, as if it had been a pair of spectacles, or—which would have suited them better—a quizzing-glass. When one of the three had kept the eye a certain time, she took it out of the socket and passed it to one of her sisters, whose turn it might happen to be, and who immediately clapt it into her own head, and enjoyed a peep at the visible world. Thus it will easily be understood, that only one of the Three Gray Women could see, while the other two were in utter darkness; and, moreover, at the instant when the eye was passing from hand to hand, neither of the poor old ladies was able to see a wink. I have heard of a great many strange things, in my day, and have witnessed not a few, but none, it seems to me, that can compare with the oddity of these Three Gray Women, all peeping through a single eye.

So thought Perseus, likewise, and was so astonished that he almost fancied his companion was joking with him, and that there were no such old women in the world.

"You will soon find whether I tell the truth or no," observed Quicksilver. "Hark! Hush! Hist! Hist! There they come, now!"

Perseus looked earnestly through the dusk of the evening, and there, sure enough, at no great distance off, he descried the Three Gray Women. The light being so faint, he could not well make out what sort of figures they were; only he discerned that they had long gray hair; and, as they came nearer, he saw that two of them had but the empty socket of an eye, in the middle of their foreheads. But, in the middle of the third sister's forehead, there was a very large, bright and piercing eye, which sparkled like a great diamond in a ring; and so penetrating did it seem to be, that Perseus could not help thinking it must possess the gift of seeing in the darkest midnight, just as perfectly as at noon-day. The sight of three persons' eyes was melted and collected into that single one.

Thus the three old dames got along about as comfortably, upon the whole, as if they could all see at once. She, who chanced to have the eye in her forehead, led the other two by the hands, peeping sharply about her, all the while; insomuch that Perseus dreaded lest she should see right through the thick clump of bushes, behind which he and Quicksilver had hidden themselves. My stars! It was positively terrible to be within reach of so very sharp an eye!

But, before they reached the clump of bushes, one of the Three Gray Women spoke.

"Sister! Sister Scarecrow!" cried she. "You have had the eye long enough. It is my turn now!"

"Let me keep it a moment longer, Sister Nightmare," answered Scarecrow. "I thought I had a glimpse of something behind that thick bush."

"Well; and what of that?" retorted Nightmare, peevishly. "Can't I see into a thick bush as easily as yourself? The eye is mine as well as yours; and I know the use of it as well as you, or may be a little better. I insist upon taking a peep immediately!"

But here the third sister, whose name was Shake-joint, began to complain, and said that it was her turn to have the eye, and that Scarecrow and Nightmare wanted to keep it all to themselves. To end the dispute, old Dame Scarecrow took the eye out of her forehead, and held it forth in her hand.

"Take it, one of you," cried she, "and quit this foolish quarrelling. For my part, I shall be glad of a little thick darkness. Take it quickly, however; or I must clap it into my own head again!"

Accordingly, both Nightmare and Shake-joint stretched out their hands, groping eagerly to snatch the eye out of the hand of Scarecrow. But, being both alike blind, they could not easily find where Scarecrow's hand was; and Scarecrow, being now just as much in the dark as Shake-joint and Nightmare, could not at once meet either of their hands, in order to put the eye into it. Thus, (as you will see with half an eye, my wise little auditors,) these good old dames had fallen into a strange perplexity. For, though the eye shone and glistened like a star, as Scarecrow held it out, yet the Gray Women caught not the least glimpse of its light, and were all three in utter darkness, from too impatient a desire to see.

Quicksilver was so much tickled at beholding Shake-joint and Nightmare both groping for the eye, and each finding fault with Scarecrow and one another, that he could scarcely help laughing aloud.

"Now is your time!" he whispered to Perseus. "Quick, quick; before they can clap the eye into either of their heads! Rush out upon the old ladies, and snatch it from Scarecrow's hand!"

In an instant, while the Three Gray Women were still scolding each other, Perseus leaped from behind the clump of bushes, and made himself master of the prize. The marvelous eye, as he held it in his hand, shone very brightly, and seemed to look up into his face with a knowing air, and an expression as if it would have winked, had it been provided with a pair of eyelids for that purpose. But the Gray Women knew nothing of what had happened, and, each supposing that one of her sisters was in possession of the eye, they began their quarrel anew. At last, as Perseus did not wish to put these respectable dames to greater inconvenience than was really necessary, he thought it right to explain the matter.

"My good ladies," said he, "pray do not be angry with one another! If anybody is in fault, it is myself; for I have the honor to hold your very brilliant and excellent eye in my own hand!"

"You! You have our eye! And who are you?" screamed the Three Gray Women, all in a breath; for they were terribly frightened, of course, at hearing a strange voice, and discovering that their eyesight had got into the hands of they could not guess whom. "Oh, what shall we do, sisters, what shall we do! We are all in the dark! Give us our eye! Give us our one, precious, solitary eye! You have two of your own! Give us our eye!"

"Tell them," whispered Quicksilver to Perseus, "that they shall have back the eye, as soon as they direct you where to find the Nymphs, who have the flying slippers, the magic wallet, and the helmet of darkness."

"My dear, good, admirable old ladies," said Perseus, addressing the Gray Women, "there is no occasion for putting yourselves into such a fright. I am by no means a bad young man. You shall have back your eye, safe and sound, and as bright as ever, the moment you tell me where to find the Nymphs!"

"The Nymphs! Goodness me, sisters, what Nymphs does he mean?" screamed Scarecrow. "There are a great many Nymphs, people say:—some that go a-hunting in the woods, and some that live inside of trees, and some that have a comfortable home in fountains of water. We know nothing at all about them. We are three unfortunate old souls that go wandering about in the dusk, and never had but one eye amongst us, and that one you have stolen away. Oh, give it back, good stranger!—whoever you are—give it back!"

All this while, the Three Gray Women were groping with their outstretched hands, and trying their utmost to get hold of Perseus. But he took good care to keep out of their reach.

"My respectable dames," said he—for his mother had taught him always to use the greatest civility—"I hold your eye fast in my hand, and shall keep it safely for you, until you please to tell me where to find these Nymphs. The Nymphs, I mean, who keep the enchanted wallet, the flying slippers, and the—what is it?—the helmet of invisibility!"

"Mercy on us, sisters, what is the young man talking about?" exclaimed Scarecrow, Nightmare, and Shake-joint, one to another, with great appearance of astonishment. "A pair of flying slippers, quoth he! His heels would quickly fly higher than his head, if he were silly enough to put them on! And a helmet of invisibility! How could a helmet make him invisible, unless it were big enough for him to hide under it? And an enchanted wallet! What sort of a contrivance may that be, I wonder? No, no, good stranger! We can tell you nothing of these marvellous things. You have two eyes of your own, and we but a single one amongst us three. You can find out such wonders better than three blind old creatures, like us!"

Perseus, hearing them talk in this way, began really to think that the Gray Women knew nothing of the matter; and, as it grieved him to have put them to so much trouble, he was just on the point of restoring their eye, and asking pardon for his rudeness in snatching it away. But Quicksilver caught his hand.

"Don't let them make a fool of you!" said he. "These

Three Gray Women are the only persons in the world, that can tell you where to find the Nymphs; and, unless you get that information, you will never succeed in cutting off the head of Medusa with the snaky locks. Keep fast hold of the eye, and all will go well!"

As it turned out, Quicksilver was in the right. There are but few things that people prize so much as they do their eyesight; and the Gray Women valued their single eye as highly as if it had been half-a-dozen, which was the number they ought to have had. Finding that there was no other way of recovering it, they at last told Perseus what he wanted to know. No sooner had they done so, than he immediately, and with the utmost respect, clapt the eye into the vacant socket in one of their foreheads, thanked them for their kindness, and bade them farewell. Before the young man was out of hearing, however, they had got into a new dispute; because he happened to have given the eye to Scarecrow, who had already taken her turn of it, when their trouble with Perseus commenced.

It is greatly to be feared, that the Three Gray Women were very much in the habit of disturbing their mutual harmony by bickerings of this sort; which was the more pity, as they could not conveniently do without one another, and were evidently intended to be inseparable companions. As a general rule, I would advise all people, whether sisters or brothers, old or young, who chance to have but one eye amongst them, to cultivate forbearance, and not all insist upon peeping through it at once.

Quicksilver and Perseus, in the mean time, were making the best of their way in quest of the Nymphs. The old dames had given them such particular directions, that they were not long in finding them out. They proved to be very different persons from Nightmare, Shake-joint and Scarecrow; for instead of being old, they were young and beautiful; and instead of one eye amongst the sisterhood, each Nymph had two exceedingly bright eyes of her own, with which she looked very kindly at Perseus. They seemed to be acquainted with Quicksilver; and when he told them the adventure which Perseus had undertaken, they made no difficulty about giving him the valuable articles that were in their custody. In the first place, they brought out what appeared to be a small purse, made of deer-skin, and curiously embroidered, and bade him be sure and keep it safe. This was the magic wallet. The Nymphs next produced a pair of shoes, or slippers, or sandals, with a nice little pair of wings at the heel of each.

"Put them on, Perseus," said Quicksilver. "You will find yourself as light-heeled as you can desire, for the remainder of our journey."

So Perseus proceeded to put one of the slippers on, while he laid the other on the ground by his side. Unexpectedly, however, this other slipper spread its wings, fluttered up off the ground, and would probably have flown away, if Quicksilver had not made a leap, and luckily caught it in the air.

"Be more careful," said he, as he gave it back to Perseus. "It would frighten the birds, up aloft, if they should see a flying slipper amongst them!"

When Perseus had got on both of these wonderful slippers, he was altogether too buoyant to tread on earth. Making a step or two, lo and behold! upward he popt into the air, high above the heads of Quicksilver and the Nymphs, and found it very difficult to clamber down again. Winged slippers, and all such high-flying contrivances, are seldom quite easy to manage, until one grows a little accustomed to them. Quicksilver laughed at his companion's involuntary activity, and told him that he must not be in so desperate a hurry, but must wait for the invisible helmet.

The good-natured Nymphs had the helmet, with its dark tuft of waving plumes, all in readiness to put upon his head. And now there happened about as wonderful an incident as anything that I have yet told you. The instant before the helmet was put on, there stood Perseus, a beautiful young man, with golden ringlets and rosy cheeks, the crooked sword by his side, and the brightly polished shield upon his arm; a figure that seemed all made up of courage, sprightliness, and glorious light. But, when the helmet had descended over his white brow, there was no longer any Perseus to be seen! Nothing but empty air! Even the helmet, that covered him with its invisibility, had vanished!

"Where are you, Perseus?" asked Quicksilver.

"Why, here, to be sure!" answered Perseus, very quietly, although his voice seemed to come out of the transparent atmosphere. "Just where I was a moment ago. Don't you see me?"

"No indeed!" answered his friend. "You are hidden under the helmet. But if I cannot see you, neither can the Gorgons. Follow me, therefore, and we will try your dexterity in using the winged slippers."

With these words, Quicksilver's cap spread its wings, as if his head were about to fly away from his shoulders; but his whole figure rose lightly into the air, and Perseus followed. By the time they had ascended a few hundred feet, the young man began to feel what a delightful thing it was to leave the dull earth so far beneath him, and to be able to flit about like a bird.

It was now deep night. Perseus looked upward, and saw the round, bright, silvery moon, and thought that he should desire nothing better than to soar up thither, and spend his life there. Then he looked downward again, and saw the earth, with its seas, and lakes, and the silver courses of its rivers, and its snowy mountain-peaks, and the breadth of its fields, and the dark cluster of its woods, and its cities of white marble; and, with the moonshine sleeping over the whole scene, it was as beautiful as the moon or any star could be. And, among other objects, he saw the island of Seriphus, where his dear mother was. Sometimes, he and Quicksilver approached a cloud, that, at a distance, looked as if it were made of fleecy silver; although, when they plunged into it, they found themselves chilled and moistened with gray mist. So swift was their flight, however, that, in an instant, they emerged from the cloud into the moonlight again. Once, a high-soaring eagle flew right against the invisible Perseus. The bravest sights were the meteors, that

gleamed suddenly out, as if a bonfire had been kindled in the sky, and made the moonshine pale for as much as a hundred miles around them.

As the two companions flew onward, Perseus fancied that he could hear the rustle of a garment close by his side; and it was on the side opposite to the one where he beheld Quicksilver. Yet only Quicksilver was visible.

"Whose garment is this," inquired Perseus, "that keeps rustling close beside me, in the breeze?"

"Oh, it is my sister's!" answered Quicksilver. "She is coming along with us, as I told you she would. We could do nothing without the help of my sister. You have no idea how wise she is. She has such eyes, too! Why, she can see you at this moment, just as distinctly as if you were not invisible; and I'll venture to say, she will be the first to discover the Gorgons."

By this time, in their swift voyage through the air, they had come within sight of the great ocean, and were soon flying over it. Far beneath them, the waves tossed themselves tumultuously, in mid-sea, or rolled a white surf-line upon the long beaches, or foamed against the rocky cliffs, with a roar that was thunderous, in the lower world; although it became a gentle murmur, like the voice of a baby half-asleep, before it reached the ears of Perseus. Just then, a voice spoke in the air, close by him. It seemed to be a woman's voice, and was melodious, though not exactly what might be called sweet, but grave and mild.

"Perseus," said the voice, "there are the Gorgons."

"Where?" exclaimed Perseus. "I cannot see them!"

"On the shore of that island, beneath you," replied the voice. "A pebble, dropt from your hand, would strike in the midst of them."

"I told you she would be the first to discover them," said Quicksilver to Perseus. "And there they are!"

Straight downward, two or three thousand feet below him, Perseus perceived a small island, with the sea breaking into white foam all round its rocky shore, except on one side, where there was a beach of snowy sand. He descended towards it, and looking earnestly at a cluster or heap of brightness, at the foot of a precipice of black rocks, behold! there were the terrible Gorgons. They lay fast asleep, soothed by the thunder of the sea; for it required a tumult that would have deafened everybody else, to lull such fierce creatures into slumber. The moonlight glistened on their steely scales, and on their golden wings, which drooped idly over the sand. Their brazen claws, horrible to look at, were thrust out, and clutched the wave-beaten fragments of rock, while the sleeping Gorgons dreamed of tearing some poor mortal all to pieces. The snakes, that served them instead of hair, seemed likewise to be asleep; although, now and then, one would writhe, and lift its head, and thrust out its forked tongue, emitting a drowsy hiss, and then let itself subside among its sister snakes.

The Gorgons were more like an awful, gigantic kind of insect—immense, golden-winged beetles, or dragon-flies, or things of that sort—at once ugly and beautiful—than like anything else; only that they were a thousand and a million times as big. And with all this, there was something partly human about them, too. Luckily for Perseus, their faces were completely hidden from him by the posture in which they lay; for, had he but looked one instant at them, he would have fallen heavily out of the air, an image of senseless stone.

"Now," whispered Quicksilver, as he hovered by the side of Perseus, "now is your time to do the deed! Be quick; for if one of the Gorgons should awake, you are too late!"

"Which shall I strike at?" asked Perseus, drawing his sword and descending a little lower. "They all three look alike! All three have snaky locks! Which of the three is Medusa?"

It must be understood, that Medusa was the only one of these dragon-monsters, whose head Perseus could possibly cut off. As for the other two, let him have the sharpest sword that ever was forged, and he might have hacked away by the hour together, without doing them the least harm.

"Be cautious!" said the calm voice which had before spoken to him. "One of the Gorgons is stirring in her sleep, and is just about to turn over. That is Medusa. Do not look at her! The sight would turn you to stone! Look at the reflection of her face and figure, in the bright mirror of your shield."

Perseus now understood Quicksilver's motive for so earnestly exhorting him to polish his shield. In its surface, he could safely look at the reflection of the Gorgon's face. And there it was—that terrible countenance—mirrored in the brightness of the shield, with the moonlight falling over it, and displaying all its horror. The snakes, whose venomous natures could not altogether sleep, kept twisting themselves over the forehead. It was the fiercest and most horrible face that ever was seen or imagined, and yet with a strange, fearful, and savage kind of beauty in it. The eyes were closed, and the Gorgon was still in a deep slumber; but there was an unquiet expression disturbing her features, as if the monster were troubled with an ugly dream. She gnashed her white tusks, and dug into the sand with her brazen claws.

The snakes, too, seemed to feel Medusa's dream, and to be made more restless by it. They twined themselves into tumultuous knots, writhed fiercely, and uplifted a hundred hissing heads, without opening their eyes.

"Now, now!" whispered Quicksilver, who was growing impatient. "Make a dash at the monster!"

"But be calm!" said the grave, melodious voice, at the young man's side. "Look in your shield, as you fly downward, and take care that you do not miss your first stroke!"

Perseus flew cautiously downward, still keeping his eyes on Medusa's face, as reflected in his shield. The nearer he came, the more terrible did the snaky visage and metallic body of the monster grow. At last, when he found himself hovering over her within arm's length, Perseus uplifted his sword; while, at the same instant, each separate snake upon the Gorgon's head stretched threateningly upward, and Medusa unclosed her eyes. But she awoke too late. The sword was sharp; the stroke fell like a lightning-flash; and the head of the wicked Medusa tumbled from her body!

"Admirably done!" cried Quicksilver. "Make haste, and clap the head into your magic wallet!"

To the astonishment of Perseus, the small, embroidered wallet, which he had hung about his neck, and which had hitherto been no bigger than a purse, grew all at once large enough to contain Medusa's head. As quick as thought, he snatched it up, with the snakes still writhing upon it, and thrust it in.

"Your task is done," said the calm voice. "Now, fly; for the other Gorgons will do their utmost to take vengeance for Medusa's death."

It was indeed necessary to take flight; for Perseus had not done the deed so quietly, but that the clash of his sword, and the hissing of the snakes, and the thump of Medusa's head as it tumbled upon the sea-beaten sand, awoke the other two monsters. There they sat, for an instant, sleepily rubbing their eyes with their brazen-fingers, while all the snakes on their heads reared themselves on end with surprise, and with venomous malice against they knew not what. But when the Gorgons saw the scaly carcass of Medusa, headless, and her golden wings all ruffled, and half spread out on the sand, it was really awful to hear what yells and screeches they set up. And then the snakes! They sent forth a hundred-fold hiss, with one consent, and Medusa's snakes answered them, out of the magic wallet.

No sooner were the Gorgons broad awake, than they hurtled upward into the air, brandishing their brass talons, gnashing their horrible tusks, and flapping their huge wings so wildly that some of the golden feathers were shaken out, and floated down upon the shore. And there, perhaps, those very feathers lie scattered, till this day. Uprose the Gorgons, as I tell you, staring horribly about, in hopes of turning somebody to stone. Had Perseus looked them in the face, or had he fallen into their clutches, his poor mother would never have kissed her boy again! But he took good care to turn his eyes another way; and, as he wore the helmet of invisibility, the Gorgons knew not in what direction to follow him; nor did he fail to make the best use of the winged slippers, by soaring upward a perpendicular mile or so. At that height, when the screams of those abominable creatures sounded faintly beneath him, he made a straight course for the island of Seriphus, in order to carry Medusa's head to King Polydectes.

I have no time to tell you of several marvellous things that befel Perseus, on his way homeward; such as his killing a hideous sea-monster, just as it was on the point of devouring a beautiful maiden; nor how he changed an enormous giant into a mountain of stone, merely by showing him the head of the Gorgon. If you doubt this latter story, you may make a voyage to Africa, some day or other, and see the very mountain, which is still known by the ancient giant's name.

Finally, our brave Perseus arrived at the island, where he expected to see his dear mother. But, during his absence, the wicked king had treated Danaë so very ill, that she was compelled to make her escape, and had taken refuge in a temple, where some good old priests were extremely kind to her. These praiseworthy priests—and the kind-hearted fisherman, who had first shown hospitality to Danaë and little Perseus, when he found them afloat in the chest—seem to have been the only persons in the island who cared about doing right. All the rest of the people, as well as King Polydectes himself, were remarkably ill-behaved, and deserved no better destiny than that which was now to happen.

Not finding his mother at home, Perseus went straight to the palace, and was immediately ushered into the presence of the king. Polydectes was by no means rejoiced to see him; for he had felt almost certain, in his own evil mind, that the Gorgons would have torn the poor young man to pieces, and have eaten him up, out of the way. However, seeing him safely returned, he put the best face he could upon the matter, and asked Perseus how he had succeeded.

"Have you performed your promise?" inquired he. "Have you brought me the head of Medusa with the snaky locks? If not, young man, it will cost you dear; for I must have a bridal present for the beautiful Princess Hippodamia, and there is nothing else that she would admire so much!"

"Yes; please your majesty," answered Perseus, in a quiet way, as if it were no very wonderful deed for such a young man as he to perform. "I have brought you the Gorgon's head, snaky locks and all!"

"Indeed! Pray let me see it!" quoth King Polydectes. "It must be a very curious spectacle, if all that travellers tell about it be true!"

"Your majesty is in the right," replied Perseus. "It is really an object that will be pretty certain to fix the regards of all who look at it. And, if your majesty think fit, I would suggest that a holiday be proclaimed, and that all your majesty's subjects be summoned to behold this wonderful curiosity. Few of them, I imagine, have seen a Gorgon's head before, and perhaps never may again!"

The king well knew that his subjects were an idle set of reprobates, and very fond of sight-seeing, as idle persons usually are. So he took the young man's advice, and sent out heralds and messengers, in all directions, to blow the trumpet at the street-corners, and in the market-places, and wherever two roads met, and summon everybody to court. Thither, accordingly, came a great multitude of good-for-nothing vagabonds, all of whom, out of pure love of mischief, would have been glad if Perseus had met with some ill-hap, in his encounter with the Gorgons. If there were any better people in the island, (as I really hope there may have been, although the story tells nothing about any such,) they staid quietly at home, minding their own business, and taking care of their little children. Most of the inhabitants, at all events, ran as fast as they could to the palace, and shoved, and pushed, and elbowed one another, in their eagerness to get near a balcony, on which Perseus showed himself, holding the embroidered wallet in his hand.

On a platform, within full view of the balcony, sat the mighty King Polydectes, amid his evil-counsellors, and with his flattering courtiers in a semi-circle round about him. Monarch, counsellors, courtiers, and subjects, all gazed eagerly towards Perseus.

"Show us the head! Show us the head!" shouted the people; and there was a fierceness in their cry, as if they would tear Perseus to pieces, unless he should satisfy them with what he had to show. "Show us the head of Medusa with the snaky locks!"

A feeling of sorrow and pity came over the youthful Perseus.

"Oh, King Polydectes," cried he, "and ye many people, I am very loth to show you the Gorgon's head!"

"Ah, the villain and coward!" yelled the people, more fiercely than before. "He is making game of us! He has no Gorgon's head! Show us the head, if you have it, or we will take your own head for a foot-ball!"

The evil-counsellors whispered bad advice in the king's ear; the courtiers murmured, with one consent, that Perseus had shown disrespect to their royal lord and master; and the great King Polydectes himself waved his hand, and ordered him, with the stern, deep voice of authority, on his peril to produce the head.

"Show me the Gorgon's head; or I will cut off your own!"
And Perseus sighed.

"This instant," repeated Polydectes; "or you die!"

"Behold it, then!" cried Perseus, in a voice like the blast of a trumpet.

And suddenly holding up the head, not an eyelid had time to wink before the wicked King Polydectes, his evil-counsellors, and all his fierce subjects, were no longer anything but the mere images of a monarch and his people. They were all fixed, forever, in the look and attitude of that moment. At the first glimpse of the terrible head of Medusa, they whitened into marble! And Perseus thrust the head back into his wallet, and went to tell his dear mother that she need no longer be afraid of the wicked King Polydectes.

As a college student, Nathaniel Hawthorne jokingly asked his mother, "What do you think of my becoming an author, and relying for support upon my pen? I think the illegibility of my handwriting is very author-like."

After he graduated in 1825, Hawthorne began writing in earnest while living at home in Salem,

# MEET NATHANIEL HAWTHORNE

Massachusetts. There, living a lonely life in his "chamber," he created a great volume of novels, short stories, and tales, among them *The House of the Seven Gables*, *Twice-Told Tales*, and *A Wonder-Book and Tanglewood Tales*, in which "The Gorgon's Head" appears.

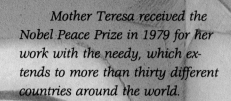

*Mother Teresa received the Nobel Peace Prize in 1979 for her work with the needy, which extends to more than thirty different countries around the world.*

*Arthur A. Schomburg devoted his life to researching and collecting materials on African-American history, which are now part of the Schomburg Center for Research in Black Culture in New York City.*

# THE IMPOSSIBLE *Dream*

**Lyric by JOE DARION**

To dream the impossible dream, to fight the unbeatable foe,
To bear with unbearable sorrow, to run where the brave dare not go.
To right the unrightable wrong, to love pure and chaste from afar,
To try when your arms are too weary, to reach the unreachable star!
This is my quest, to follow that star,
No matter how hopeless, no matter how far;
To fight for the right without question or pause,
To be willing to march into hell for a heavenly cause!
And I know, if I'll only be true
To this glorious quest,
That my heart will lie peaceful and calm,
When I'm laid to my rest,
And the world will be better for this;
That one man, scorned and covered with scars,
Still strove with his last ounce of courage,
To reach the unreachable stars.

*Mohandas K. Gandhi, one of India's most celebrated political and spiritual leaders, helped his people gain independence in 1947 through nonviolent resistance.*

*Corazon Aquino became the first woman president of the Philippines in 1986.*

YOUR GUIDE TO

A WORLD OF

INFORMATION—

# INFORMATION ILLUSTRATED

WITH

EXAMPLES

RELATED TO

THE THEMES

YOU ARE

EXPLORING!

# CONTENTS

# *A*DVERTISEMENTS

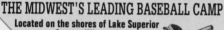

# ALMANAC

## Grammy Awards

Source: National Academy of Recording Arts & Sciences

**1958**
**Record:** Domenico Modugno, Nel Blu Dipinto Di Blu (Volare).
**Album:** Henry Mancini, The Music from Peter Gunn.
**1959**
**Record:** Bobby Darin, Mack the Knife.
**Album:** Frank Sinatra, Come Dance with Me.
**1960**
**Record:** Percy Faith, Theme From a Summer Place.
**Album:** Bob Newhart, Button Down Mind.
**1961**
**Record:** Henry Mancini, Moon River.
**Album:** Judy Garland, Judy At Carnegie Hall.
**1962**
**Record:** Tony Bennett, I Left My Heart in San Francisco.
**Album:** Vaughn Meader, The First Family.
**1963**
**Record:** Henry Mancini, The Days of Wine and Roses.
**Album:** The Barbara Streisand Album.
**1964**
**Record:** Stan Getz and Astrud Gilberto, The Girl From Ipanema.
**Album:** Getz/Gilberto.
**1965**
**Record:** Herb Alpert, A Taste Of Honey.
**Album:** Frank Sinatra, September of My Years.
**1966**
**Record:** Frank Sinatra, Strangers in the Night.
**Album:** Frank Sinatra, A Man and His Music.
**1967**
**Record:** 5th Dimension, Up, Up and Away.
**Album:** The Beatles, Sgt. Pepper's Lonely Hearts Club Band.
**1968**
**Record:** Simon & Garfunkel, Mrs. Robinson.
**Album:** Glen Campbell, By the Time I Get to Phoenix.
**1969**
**Record:** 5th Dimension, Aquarius/Let the Sunshine In.
**Album:** Blood, Sweat and Tears.
**1970**
**Record:** Simon & Garfunkel, Bridge Over Troubled Water.
**Album:** Bridge Over Troubled Water.
**1971**
**Record:** Carole King, It's Too Late.
**Album:** Carole King, Tapestry.
**1972**
**Record:** Roberta Flack, The First Time Ever I Saw Your Face.
**Album:** The Concert For Bangla Desh.
**1973**
**Record:** Roberta Flack, Killing Me Softly with His Song.
**Album:** Stevie Wonder, Innervisions.
**1974**
**Record:** Olivia Newton-John, I Honestly Love You.
**Album:** Stevie Wonder, Fulfillingness' First Finale.
**1975**
**Record:** Captain & Tennille, Love Will Keep Us Together.
**Album:** Paul Simon, Still Crazy After All These Years.
**1976**
**Record:** George Benson, This Masquerade.
**Album:** Stevie Wonder, Songs in the Key of Life.
**1977**
**Record:** Eagles, Hotel California.
**Album:** Fleetwood Mac, Rumours.
**1978**
**Record:** Billy Joel, Just the Way You Are.
**Album:** Bee Gees, Saturday Night Fever.
**1979**
**Record:** The Doobie Brothers, What a Fool Believes.
**Album:** Billy Joel, 52nd Street.
**1980**
**Record:** Christopher Cross, Sailing.
**Album:** Christopher Cross, Christopher Cross.
**1981**
**Record:** Kim Carnes, Bette Davis Eyes.
**Album:** John Lennon, Yoko Ono, Double Fantasy.
**1982**
**Record:** Toto, Rosanna.
**Album:** Toto, Toto IV.

**1983**
**Record:** Michael Jackson, Beat It.
**Album:** Michael Jackson, Thriller.
**1984**
**Record:** Tina Turner, What's Love Got to Do With It.
**Album:** Lionel Richie, Can't Slow Down.
**1985**
**Record:** USA for Africa, We Are the World.
**Album:** Phil Collins, No Jacket Required.
**1986**
**Record:** Steve Winwood, Higher Love.
**Album:** Paul Simon, Graceland.
**1987**
**Record:** Paul Simon, Graceland.
**Album:** U2, The Joshua Tree.
**1988**
**Record:** Bobby McFerrin, Don't Worry, Be Happy.
**Album:** George Michael, Faith.
**1989**
**Record:** Bette Midler, Wind Beneath My Wings.
**Album:** Bonnie Raitt, Nick of Time.
**Male Pop Vocal:** Michael Bolton, How Am I Supposed to Live Without You?
**Female Pop Vocal:** Bonnie Raitt, Nick of Time.
**Duo or Group Pop Vocal:** Linda Ronstadt and Aaron Neville, Don't Know Much.
**Pop Instrumental:** Neville Brothers, Healing Chant.
**New Artist:** Milli Vanilli.
**Male Rock Vocal:** Don Henley, The End of the Innocence.
**Female Rock Vocal:** Bonnie Raitt, Nick of Time.
**Duo or Group Rock Vocal:** The Traveling Wilburys, The Traveling Wilburys, Vol. 1.
**Rock Instrumental:** Jeff Beck's Guitar Shop with Terry Bozzio and Tony Humas.
**Rap:** Young MC, Bust a Move.
**Male Country Vocal:** Lyle Lovett, Lyle Lovett and His Large Band.
**Female Country Vocal:** k.d. lang, Absolute Torch and Twang.
**Duo or Group Country Vocal:** Nitty Gritty Dirt Band, Will the Circle be Unbroken? Vol. 2.
**Country Vocal Collaboration:** Hank Williams Jr. and Hank Williams Sr., There's a Tear in My Beer.
**Country Instrumental:** Randy Scruggs, Amazing Grace.
**Bluegrass:** Bruce Hornsby and the Nitty Gritty Dirt Band, The Valley Road.
**Male R&B Vocal:** Bobby Brown, Every Little Step.
**Female R&B Vocal:** Anita Baker, Giving You the Best That I Got.
**Duo or Group R&B:** Soul II Soul, Back to Life.
**R&B Instrumental:** Soul II Soul, African Dance.
**Male Jazz Vocal:** Harry Connick Jr., When Harry Met Sally...
**Female Jazz Vocal:** Ruth Brown, Blues on Broadway.
**Duo or Group Jazz Vocal:** Dr. John and Rickie Lee Jones, Makin' Whoopee.
**Solo Jazz Instrumental:** Miles Davis, Aura.
**Group Jazz Instrumental:** Miles Davis, Aura.
**Big Band Jazz Instrumental:** Chick Corea, Chick Corea Acoustic Band.
**New Age:** Peter Gabriel, Passion–Music for the Last Temptation of Christ.
**Classical Album:** Emerson String Quartet, Bartok: 6 String Quartets.
**Orchestral Recording:** Leonard Bernstein, New York Philharmonic, Mahler: Symphony No. 3 in D Minor.
**Chamber Music:** Emerson String Quartet, Bartok: 6 String Quartets.
**Solo Classical Vocalist:** Dawn Upshaw, Summer of 1915.
**Opera:** James Levine, Metropolitan Opera Orchestra, Wagner: Die Walküre.
**Musical Original Cast Album:** Jerome Robbins' Broadway.
**Comedy:** Prof. Peter Schickele, The Greater Hoople Area Off-Season Philharmonic, P.D.Q. Bach: 1712 Overture and Other Musical Assaults.
**Non-Musical Spoken Word:** Gilda Radner, It's Always Something.
**Children:** Tanya Goodman, The Rock-a-Bye Collection, Vol. 1.

# Atlas

**INDIAN EMPIRES IN AMERICA**

- Mayan
- Aztec
- Incan

N

0 500 1,000 Miles
0 500 1,000 1,500 Kilometers

NORTH AMERICA
Gulf of Mexico
ATLANTIC OCEAN
Tenochtitlán
Chichén Itzá
Copán
Caribbean Sea
PACIFIC OCEAN
SOUTH AMERICA
ANDES MOUNTAINS
Machu Picchu
Cuzco

**LATIN AMERICA**
**Political**

⊛ National capital · Other city

0 400 800 Miles
0 400 800 1,200 Kilometers

UNITED STATES
Monterrey
MEXICO
Guadalajara
Mexico City
Gulf of Mexico
Havana
CUBA
BAHAMAS
DOMINICAN REPUBLIC
HAITI
PUERTO RICO (U.S.)
San Juan
JAMAICA
Kingston
Port-au-Prince
Santo Domingo
VIRGIN ISLANDS (U.K.)
VIRGIN ISLANDS (U.S.)
ST. KITTS-NEVIS
ANTIGUA AND BARBUDA
BELIZE
Belmopan
GUATEMALA
HONDURAS
Guatemala City
Tegucigalpa
San Salvador
EL SALVADOR
NICARAGUA
Managua
GUADELOUPE (FR.)
DOMINICA
MARTINIQUE (FR.)
ST. LUCIA
BARBADOS
ST. VINCENT AND THE GRENADINES
GRENADA
TRINIDAD AND TOBAGO
COSTA RICA
San José
Panama
PANAMA
NETHERLANDS ANTILLES (NETH.)
ARUBA (NETH.)
Barranquilla
Maracaibo
Valencia
Caracas
VENEZUELA
Medellín
Cali
Bogotá
COLOMBIA
GALAPAGOS ISLANDS (ECUADOR)
ECUADOR
Quito
Guayaquil
Georgetown
Paramaribo
Cayenne
GUYANA
SURINAME
FRENCH GUIANA (FR.)
PACIFIC OCEAN
Iquitos
Manaus
Amazon River
PERU
Trujillo
Belem
Callao
Lima
Cuzco
BRAZIL
São Francisco
Arequipa
La Paz
Brasília
BOLIVIA
Sucre
Belo Horizonte
PARAGUAY
Antofagasta
Tucumán
Asunción
São Paulo
Rio de J
CHILE
Córdoba
Rosario
URUGUAY
Pôrto Alegre
Valparaíso
Santiago
Buenos Aires
Montevideo
Río de la Plata
Concepción
ARGENTINA
Punta Arenas
Strait of Magellan
FALKLAND ISLANDS (U.K.)

ATLANTIC OCEAN
Tropic of
PACIFIC OCEAN

---

# GAZETTEER

This Gazetteer is a geographical dictionary that will help you to pronounce and locate places discussed in this book. Latitude and longitude are given for cities and some other places. The page number tells you where each place appears on a map.

### PRONUNCIATION KEY

| | | | |
|---|---|---|---|
| a | cap | êr | clear |
| ā | cake | hw | where |
| ä | father | ī | bib |
| är | car | ī | kite |
| âr | dare | ng | song |
| ch | chain | o | top |
| e | hen | ō | rope |
| ē | me | ô | saw |

| | |
|---|---|
| oi | coin |
| ôr | fork |
| ou | cow |
| sh | show |
| th | thin |
| th | those |
| th | sun |
| ù | book |

ü moon
ū cute
ûr term
ə about, taken, pencil, apron, helpful
ər letter, dollar, doctor

**Beijing**

**Beijing** (bā jing´) [Peking] The capital of China. Beijing became China's capital in the thirteenth century; 40°N, 116°E. (p. 459)

**Beringia** (ber´ an gē ə) The land bridge connecting Asia and North America during the Ice Age. (p. 567)

**Bering Strait** (bâr´ ing strāt) Narrow waterway connecting the Bering Sea with the Arctic Ocean. The Bering Strait separates the Soviet Union and the state of Alaska. (p. 282)

**Berlin** (bər lin´) The capital of Germany. Following World War II, Berlin was divided into East Berlin and West Berlin. The city was reunited in 1989; 52°N, 13°E. (p. 313)

**Bethlehem** (beth´ lə hem) A town in Israel where Jesus was born; 31°N, 35°E. (p. 183)

**Black Sea** (blak sē) An inland sea between Europe and Asia. (p. 196)

**Bombay** (bom bā´) The largest city and chief port on India's western coast; 19°N, 73°E. (p. 449)

**British Isles** (brit´ ish ī əlz) A group of

in southern China. (p. 459)

**Florence**

**Chichén Itzá** (chē chen´ ēt zä´) A village in Mexico. It was one of the principal centers of the Mayas; 21°N, 87°W. (p. 570)

**Constantinople** (kon stan tə nō´ pəl) A former Greek colony that was made a capital of the Roman Empire by the Emperor Constantine. It is now called Istanbul; 41°N, 29°E. (p. 357)

**Copán** (kō pan´) Ancient city that was a center of Mayan civilization; 15°N, 89°W. (p. 570)

**Corsica** (kôr´ si kə) A French island in the Mediterranean Sea, southeast of France. (p. 196)

**Crete** (krēt) A Greek island in the eastern Mediterranean Sea, southeast of mainland Greece. Crete is the largest of the Aegean Islands. (p. 130)

**Cuzco** (küs´ kō) A city in southern Peru, in the Andes Mountains. It was the capital of the Ancient Incan empire; 14°S, 72°W. (p. 570)

528

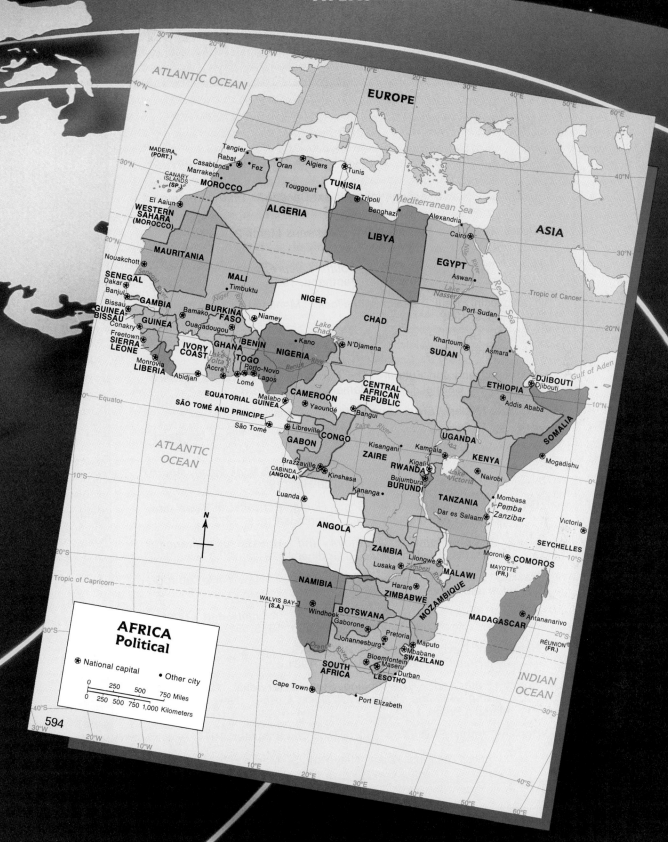

**AFRICA**
Political

⊛ National capital    • Other city

0    250    500    750 Miles

0  250  500  750  1,000 Kilometers

# *B*IBLIOGRAPHY

## FOR FURTHER READING

Barth, J. and M. Wilkins. "Roadside Rock." *Rolling Stone* July 16, 1987: 104+.

Cocks, J. "New Directions for the Next Decade." *Time* September 4, 1989: 63.

Doyle, Kevin. "Rock Goes Gold." *Macleans* March 2, 1987: 2, 30–37.

Frith, Simon. *Sound Effects: Youth, Leisure, and the Politics of Rock 'n' Roll.* New York: Pantheon, 1981.

Gambaccini, Paul. *Masters of Rock.* Menasha, Wis.: Omnibus Press, 1982.

Garland, Phyl. *The Sound of Soul.* Washington, D.C.: Henry Regnery, 1969.

Gill, Chris and Jon Futtrell. *The Illustrated Encyclopedia of Black Music.* Carmel, Calif.: Salamander Books, 1982.

Goldman, Albert. *Elvis.* New York: McGraw-Hill, 1981.

Goldensohn, M. "Midlife Music." *The New York Times Magazine* June 21, 1987: 48+.

Goldstein, Richard. *Goldstein's Greatest Hits: A Book Mostly About Rock 'n' Roll.* New York: Prentice-Hall, 1970.

Guralnick, Peter. *Feel Like Going Home: Portraits in Blues and Rock 'n' Roll.* Menasha, Wis.: Omnibus Press, 1978.

———. *Lost Highway: Journeys and Arrivals of American Musicians.* Boston: David R. Godine, 1979.

Haskins, James. *The Story of Stevie Wonder.* New York: Lothrop, Lee and Shepherd, 1976.

Hemphill, Paul. *The Nashville Sound: Bright Lights and Country Music.* New York: Simon and Schuster, 1970.

Henderson, Davis. *'Scuze Me While I Kiss The Sky: The Life of Jimi Hendrix.* New York: Bantam, 1981.

Herbst, Peter, ed. *The Rolling Stone Interviews, 1967–1980: Talking With the Legends of Rock & Roll.* New York: St. Martin's Press, 1981.

Hopkins, Jerry. *Elvis.* New York: Simon and Schuster, 1971.

———. *Elvis: The Final Years.* New York: St. Martin's Press, 1980.

# CARD CATALOG
## AND LIBRARY CLASSIFICATION SYSTEMS

| | |
|---|---|
| 000-099 | Generalities |
| 100-199 | Philosophy |
| 200-299 | Religion |
| 300-399 | Social Sciences |
| 400-499 | Language |
| 500-599 | Pure Sciences |
| 600-699 | Technology (Applied Sciences) |
| 700-799 | The Arts |
| 800-899 | Literature and Rhetoric |
| 900-999 | General Geography, History, and Related Disciplines |

**DEWEY DECIMAL CLASSIFICATION SYSTEM (DDC)**

**LIBRARY OF CONGRESS CLASSIFICATION SYSTEM (LC)**

| | |
|---|---|
| A | General Works |
| B | Philosophy – Religion |
| C | History – Auxiliary Sciences |
| D | History and Topography (except America) |
| E-F | American History |
| G | Geography, Anthropology, Folklore, Manners and Customs, Recreation |
| H | Social Sciences |
| J | Political Sciences |
| K | Law of the United States |
| L | Education |
| M | Music and Books on Music |
| N | Fine Arts |
| P | Language and Literature |
| Q | Science |
| R | Medicine |
| S | Agriculture – Plant and Animal Industry |
| T | Technology |
| U | Military Science |
| V | Naval Science |
| W | Bibliography and Library Science |

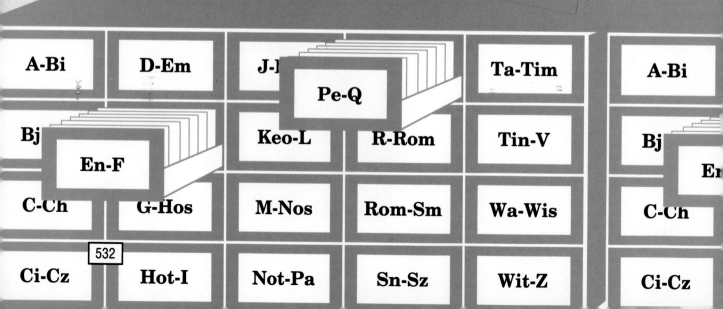

**AUTHOR CARD**

398.2
C

**Courlander, Harold.**
The fourth world of the Hopis, Crown [c1971].
239 p.
A collection of twenty legends of the Hopi people, originating in the different tribes and relating tales of journeys, wars, heroic deeds, and tribal heroes.

1. Indians of North America — Legends.   2. Hopi Indians — Legends.   I. Title.

X23681
LJ Cards, c1971

398.2                   Selection
Young Adult Literary Guild

**TITLE CARD**

**The fourth world of the Hopis**

398.2
C

**Courlander, Harold.**
The fourth world of the Hopis, Crown [c1971].
239 p.
A collection of twenty legends of the Hopi people, originating in the different tribes and relating tales of journeys, wars, heroic deeds, and tribal heroes.

1. Indians of North America — Legends.   2. Hopi Indians — Legends.   I. Title.

X23681
LJ Cards, c1971

398.2                   Selection
Young Adult Literary Guild

| A-Bi | D-Em | J-? | | Ta-Tim | A-Bi |
| | | | Pe-Q | | |
| Bj | | Keo-L | R-Rom | Tin-V | Bj |
| | En-F | | | | |
| C-Ch | G-Hos | M-Nos | Rom-Sm | Wa-Wis | C-Ch |
| Ci-Cz | Hot-I | Not-Pa | Sn-Sz | Wit-Z | Ci-Cz |

532

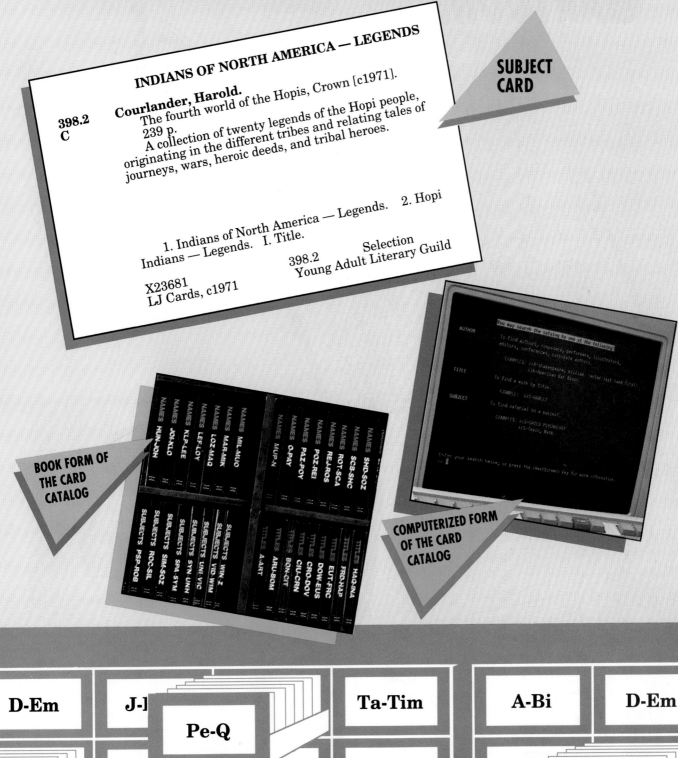

**INDIANS OF NORTH AMERICA — LEGENDS**

**398.2**
**C**

**Courlander, Harold.**
The fourth world of the Hopis, Crown [c1971].
239 p.
A collection of twenty legends of the Hopi people,
originating in the different tribes and relating tales of
journeys, wars, heroic deeds, and tribal heroes.

1. Indians of North America — Legends.    2. Hopi
Indians — Legends.   I. Title.

398.2              Selection
Young Adult Literary Guild

X23681
LJ Cards, c1971

**SUBJECT CARD**

**BOOK FORM OF THE CARD CATALOG**

**COMPUTERIZED FORM OF THE CARD CATALOG**

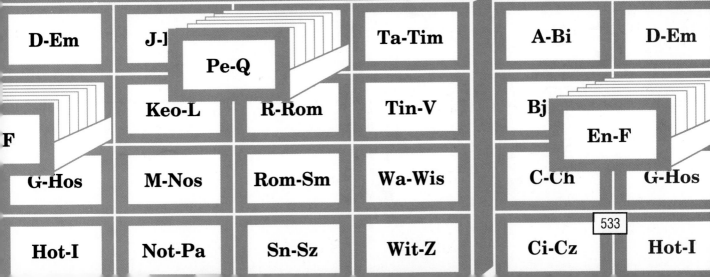

# CARTOONS

"Maybe they'd like us to say 'good night' already."

# CHARTS AND TABLES

## LANGUAGE — SIGNS AND SYMBOLS

| Roman letter or English sound equivalent | Russian alphabet (Cyrillic letters) | Sign language | Braille (raised dots) | Roman letter or English sound equivalent | Russian alphabet (Cyrillic letters) | Sign language | Braille (raised dots) |
|---|---|---|---|---|---|---|---|
| A, a | А а | | | R, r | Р р | | |
| B, b | Б б | | | S, s | С с | | |
| C, c | | | | T, t | Т т | | |
| D, d | Д д | | | U, u | У у | | |
| E, e | Э э | | | V, v | В в | | |
| F, f | Ф ф | | | W, w | | | |
| G, g | Г г | | | X, x | | | |
| H, h | | | | Y, y | Ы ы | | |
| I, i | И и | | | Z, z | З з | | |
| J, j | | | | ch | Ч ч | | |
| K, k | К к | | | kh | Х х | | |
| L, l | Л л | | | oi | Й й | | |
| M, m | М м | | | sh | Ш ш | | |
| N, n | Н н | | | shch | Ш ш | | |
| O, o | О о | | | ts | Ц ц | | |
| P, p | П п | | | ya | Я я | | |
| Q, q | | | | ye | Е е | | |
| | | | | yo | Ё ё | | |
| | | | | yu | Ю ю | | |
| | | | | zh | Ж ж | | |
| | | | | syllable break | a y sound before following vowel  Ъ ъ | | |
| | | | | softens consonant preceding y sound | Ь ь | | |

# MEDIA SPENDING BY SOME LEADING ADVERTISERS: 1988

| ADVERTISER | MEASURED | | | | ESTIMATED UNMEASURED |
|---|---|---|---|---|---|
| | PRINT | TV | RADIO | OUTDOOR | |
| Procter & Gamble | $102,640,000 | $684,158,000 | $41,311,000 | $ 682,000 | $678,100,000 |
| General Motors | 293,515,000 | 573,943,000 | 78,440,000 | 2,997,000 | 345,105,000 |
| Eastman Kodak | 42,615,000 | 194,323,000 | 6,551,000 | 557,000 | 491,900,000 |
| McDonald's | 6,899,000 | 387,798,000 | 5,158,000 | 6,306,000 | 322,159,000 |
| PepsiCo | 9,425,000 | 414,802,000 | 32,140,000 | 3,080,000 | 252,900,000 |
| Kellogg | 23,335,000 | 378,411,000 | 73,000 | 70,000 | 281,200,000 |
| Ford Motor | 155,574,000 | 255,383,000 | 23,870,000 | 2,157,000 | 132,800,000 |
| American Telephone and Telegraph | 104,021,000 | 224,627,000 | 18,494,000 | 361,000 | 200,000,000 |
| General Mills | 43,623,000 | 309,120,000 | 7,020,000 | 295,000 | 110,000,000 |
| Johnson & Johnson | 38,393,000 | 195,263,000 | 1,402,000 | 77,000 | 233,700,000 |
| J.C. Penney | 87,587,000 | 54,442,000 | 11,503,000 | 49,000 | 273,000,000 |
| Coca-Cola | 13,993,000 | 198,758,000 | 15,696,000 | 2,538,000 | 154,100,000 |
| Mars | 15,731,000 | 163,430,000 | 8,673,000 | 23,000 | 151,800,000 |
| Sara Lee | 49,038,000 | 105,756,000 | 1,586,000 | 64,000 | 170,500,000 |
| Macy | 184,463,000 | 15,651,000 | 289,000 | 376,000 | 108,100,000 |
| Walt Disney | 44,865,000 | 103,050,000 | 7,823,000 | 543,000 | 144,300,000 |
| Hershey Foods | 19,362,000 | 69,137,000 | 10,001,000 | 32,000 | 200,100,000 |

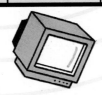

# DIAGRAMS

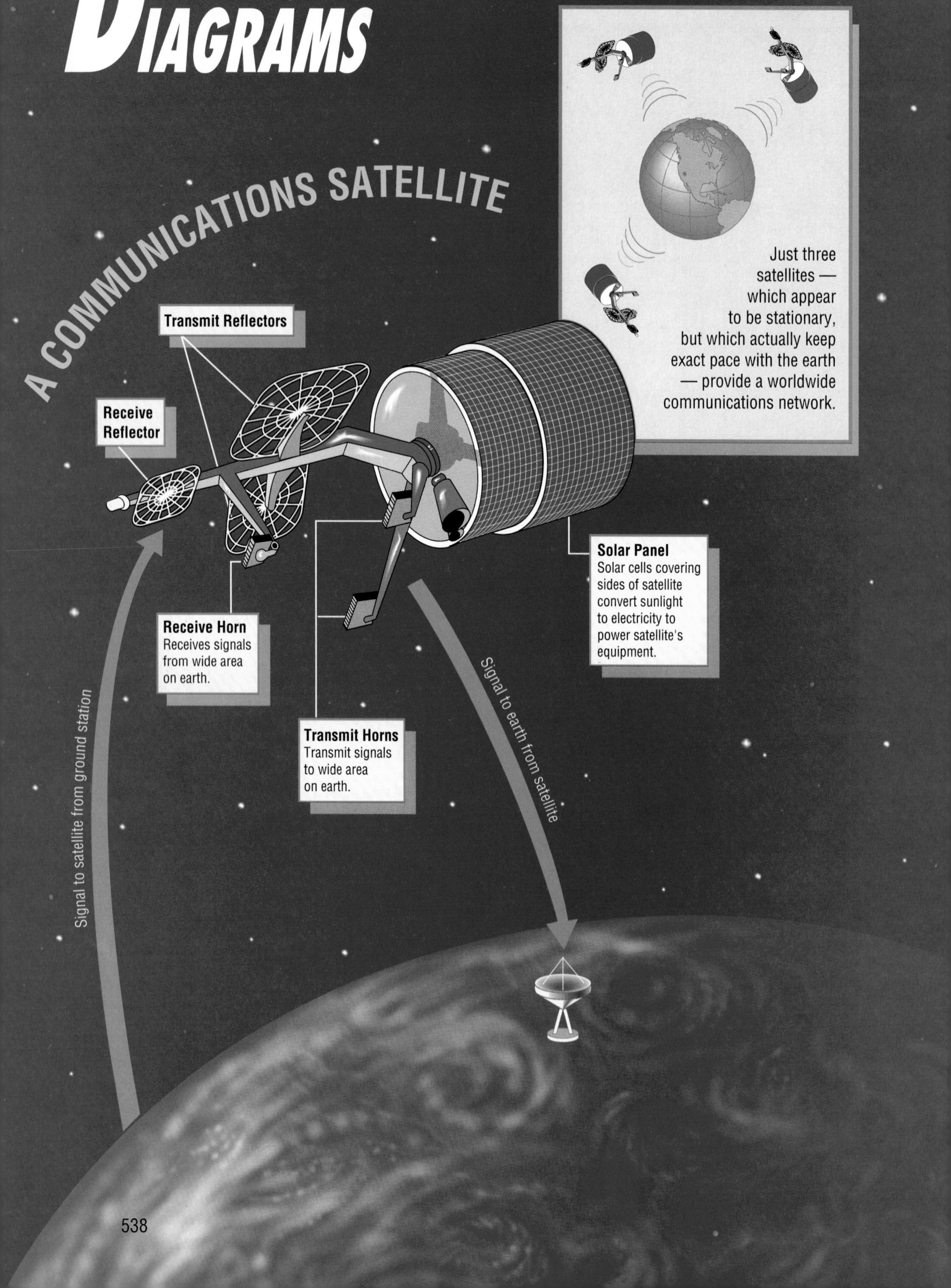

## A COMMUNICATIONS SATELLITE

Just three satellites — which appear to be stationary, but which actually keep exact pace with the earth — provide a worldwide communications network.

**Transmit Reflectors**

**Receive Reflector**

**Receive Horn**
Receives signals from wide area on earth.

**Transmit Horns**
Transmit signals to wide area on earth.

**Solar Panel**
Solar cells covering sides of satellite convert sunlight to electricity to power satellite's equipment.

Signal to satellite from ground station

Signal to earth from satellite

# HARDBACK BOOK

**(also called a hardcover book or a casebound book)**

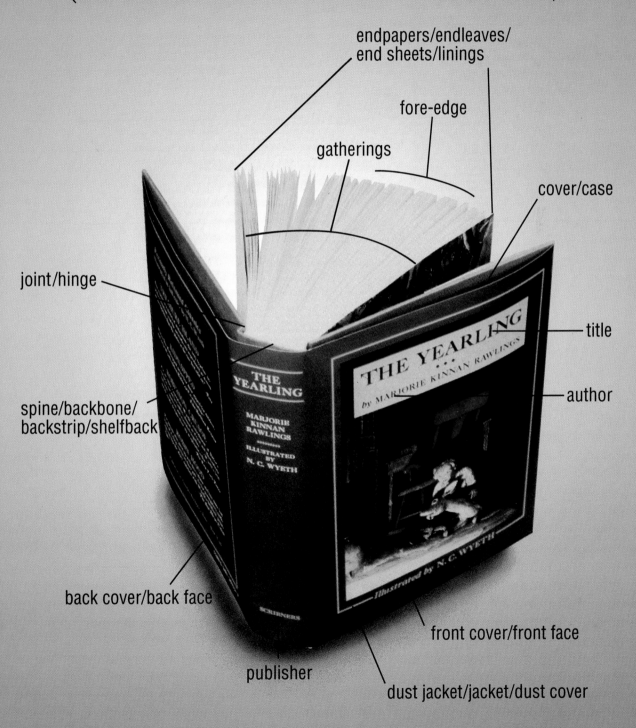

endpapers/endleaves/
end sheets/linings

fore-edge

gatherings

cover/case

joint/hinge

title

author

spine/backbone/
backstrip/shelfback

back cover/back face

front cover/front face

publisher

dust jacket/jacket/dust cover

THE
YEARLING

MARJORIE
KINNAN
RAWLINGS

ILLUSTRATED
BY
N. C. WYETH

THE YEARLING
by MARJORIE KINNAN RAWLINGS

Illustrated by N. C. WYETH

SCRIBNERS

# **D**ICTIONARY

guide words

main entry

syllable division

part of speech

pronunciation

definition

subject label

subentry

etymology

homographs

inflected forms

usage label

illustrative sentence

illustrative phrase

compound

run-on entry

illustration

pronunciation key

---

**mur·rain / musk·rat**

make a faint sound of discontent or protest. —*v.t.* to say in a soft, low voice: *to murmur an apology.* —**mur′mur·er,** *n.*
**mur·rain** (mûr′in) *n.* any of several infectious, usually fatal diseases of cattle and other animals.
**mus·cle** (mus′əl) *n.* **1.** a body tissue made up of fibers that are capable of contracting to produce motion or apply force. **2.** one of the organs of the body composed of these tissues, especially one that is attached by tendons to bones and that functions to move part of the body. **3.** strength or force, especially bodily strength: *No one has the muscle to lift that heavy barrel.*
**mus·cle-bound** (mus′əl-bound′) *adj.* having tight or overdeveloped muscles, as from too much exercise.
**Mus·co·vite** (mus′kə vīt′) *n.* a person who was born or is living in Moscow or, formerly, in Russia.
**mus·cu·lar** (mus′kyə lar) *adj.* **1.** of, relating to, or involving muscles: *muscular coordination.* **2.** having well-developed muscles; strong: *a muscular athlete.* **3.** composed or consisting of muscle: —**mus·cu·lar·i·ty** (mus′kyə lar′i tē), *n.*
**muscular dys·tro·phy** (dis′trə fē) a hereditary disease that is characterized by a gradual weakening and wasting away of the muscles. It commonly begins in early childhood.
**muscular system,** the system of muscles that move the parts of the body of an animal. Some parts of the muscular system, such as the heart, work automatically. Others, such as the skeletal muscles, are mostly under voluntary control.
**mus·cu·la·ture** (mus′kyə lə chər) *n.* the arrangement of the muscles in the body or in a particular part of the body.
**muse** (mūz) *v.i.,* **mused, mus·ing.** to think, reflect, or meditate: *to muse on the events of the day.*
**Muse** (mūz) *n.* **1.** *Greek Mythology.* any of the nine goddesses of the arts and sciences. **2. muse.** a spirit or other source of genius or inspiration.
**mu·se·um** (mū zē′əm) *n.* a building or place where objects of value or interest, as in the fields of art, science, history, or natural history, are preserved and displayed. [From the Latin word *museum* meaning "a building set apart for study," from the Greek word *mouseion* "a philosophical school and library," earlier "a shrine for the Muses," from the word *Mousa* "Muse."]
**mush¹** (mush) *n., pl.* **mush·es. 1.** a thick porridge made by boiling cornmeal. **2.** any soft, thick mass. **3.** *Informal.* anything overly sentimental or romantic. [Probably a form of *mash.*]
**mush²** (mush) *interj.* go or go faster. said as an order to a team of dogs pulling a sled. —*v.i.* to travel by dogsled. [From the Canadian French cry *mouche!* meaning "run!"] —**mush′er,** *n.*
**mush·room** (mush′rūm′, mush′rūm′) *n.* any of various fungi usually shaped like an umbrella. Some mushrooms can be eaten; others are poisonous. —*v.i.* **1.** to spring up or grow suddenly and rapidly: *Buildings mushroomed all over the area.* **2.** to spread out into the shape of a mushroom: *The cloud of smoke from the explosion mushroomed in the sky.*
**mush·y** (mush′ē) *adj.,* **mush·i·er, mush·i·est. 1.** like mush in consistency; soft and thick. **2.** *Informal.* overly sentimental or romantic. —**mush′i·ness,** *n.*

626

**mu·sic** (mū′zik) *n.* **1.** a pleasing or harmonious combination of sounds. **2.** the art of producing and arranging pleasing and expressive combinations of sounds, usually according to principles of rhythm, melody, harmony, and the like. **3.** a musical composition: *Does the pianist know the music to that song?* **4.** the written or printed score of a musical composition: *I can read music.* **5.** any pleasant sound or series of sounds: *Your words of welcome were music to our ears.*
**mu·si·cal** (mū′zi kəl) *adj.* **1.** of, relating to, or producing music: *a musical instrument.* **2.** set to or accompanied by music: *a musical show.* **3.** pleasant to hear: *the musical sounds of children's laughter.* **4.** fond of or skilled in the performance of music. —*n.* a musical comedy or other musical play. —**mu′si·cal·ly,** *adv.*
**musical comedy,** a show or play made up of songs, dances, and spoken dialogue.
**mu·si·cale** (mū′zi kal′) *n.* a party or other social gathering featuring musical entertainment.
**music box,** a box or case containing a device that produces a tune mechanically.
**music hall,** an auditorium or hall for musical performances.
**mu·si·cian** (mū zish′ən) *n.* a person skilled in or professionally engaged in the performance or composition of music. —**mu·si′cian·ship′,** *n.*
**mu·si·col·o·gy** (mū′zi kol′ə jē) *n.* the study of the history, theory, and forms of music. —**mu·si·col′o·gist,** *n.*
**musk** (musk) *n.* **1.** an oily, strong-smelling substance obtained from a gland of the male musk deer. Musk is used in making perfumes, medicine, and soaps. **2.** any similar substance made by humans or obtained from certain other animals, such as the muskrat or civet cat. **3.** the odor of musk.
**musk deer,** a small hornless deer of central and eastern Asia, the male of which has a gland that secretes musk.
**mus·kel·lunge** (mus′kə lunj′) *n., pl.* **mus·kel·lunge.** a large, greenish brown freshwater game fish related to the pike, found especially in the Great Lakes.
**mus·ket** (mus′kit) *n.* a long-barreled gun fired from the shoulder, used before rifles were invented.
**mus·ket·eer** (mus′ki tîr′) *n.* **1.** a soldier armed with a musket. **2.** a member of the royal guard in seventeenth-century France.
**mus·ket·ry** (mus′ki trē) *n.* the art or skill of firing muskets or rifles.
**musk·mel·on** (musk′mel′ən) *n.* **1.** any of several melons that have a netted rind, sweet, juicy orange or green flesh, and small, flat seeds in the center. **2.** any trailing or climbing vine bearing such a fruit.
**musk ox,** an animal somewhat like a buffalo, native to northern Canada and Greenland, and having a shaggy dark brown or black coat. It gives off a musky odor during the mating season.
**musk·rat** (musk′rat′) *n., pl.* **musk·rat** or **musk·rats. 1.** a North American rodent that has webbed hind feet, a flat

**musk ox**

at; āpe; fär; câre; end; mē; it; īce; pîerce; hot; ōld; sông, fôrk; oil; out; up; ūse; rûle; pull; tûrn; chin; sing; shop; thin; this; hw in white; zh in treasure. The symbol ə stands for the unstressed vowel sound heard in about, taken, pencil, lemon, and circus.

---

## Dictionary of the English Language

540

# DICTIONARY

**Prète, Georges** (*b* Waziers, 14 Aug. 1924). French conductor. Studied Douai, Paris Conservatoire, and with Cluytens. Début Marseille, 1946, *Samson et Dalila*. Marseilles 1946–8; Lille 1948–50; Toulouse 1951–4; Lyons 1955; Paris, O.C., 1956 *Mignon, Capriccio*. Premières of *Voix humaine* there, 1959; Paris, O., since 1959. Chicago 1959; San Francisco 1963–4; N.Y. Met., 1964–7; London, C.G., 1965, 1976; Milan, Sc., since 1965. (R)

**Previtali, Fernando** (*b* Adria, 16 Feb. 1907). Italian conductor. Studied Turin. Assisted Gui in organizing the Florence Orchestra and Festival 1928–35. Genoa, C.F., 1935–6, incl. *Elisir* with Schipa. Director Radio Italiana Orchestra 1936–53, and responsible for many fine radio opera performances, including the Verdi cycle of 1951. Rome, Buenos Aires, Milan, Sc., 1942, 1947–8. Naples 1957 Conducted the premières of many modern works, including Ghedini's *Re Hassan* (Venice 1939) and the same composer's *Le Baccanti* (Sc. 1948), Dallapiccola's *Volo di notte* (Florence 1949) as well as revivals of Busoni's *Turandot* and *Doktor Faust*. (R)

voice, a fine technique, and engaging stage personality. (R)

**Preziosilla.** The gipsy girl (mezzo) in Verdi's *La forza del destino*.

**Price, Leontyne** (*b* Laurel, Mississippi, 10 Feb. 1927). American soprano. Studied Juilliard School where she sang Mistress Ford in student performance of *Falstaff*. Chosen by Virgil Thomson to sing in a revival of *Four Saints in Three Acts* in N.Y. and Paris; and then from 1952 to 1954 sang Bess in *Porgy and Bess*. San Francisco 1957 (Madame Lidoine in American première of *Carmélites)*, 1958–9; Chicago 1959, Thaïs and Liù; Vienna since 1958, Pamina and Aida; London, C.G., 1958–9, Aida; Salzburg 1960, Donna Anna and subsequently; N.Y., Met., since 1960; Milan, Sc., since 1962. Created Cleopatra in Barber's *Antony and Cleopatra* at opening of new Met., 1966. Especially admired in Verdi. (R)

**Price, Margaret** (Berenice) (*b* Tredegar, 13 Apr. 1941). Welsh soprano. Studied London, T.C.

## Dictionary of Opera

---

**Eten** \'ā-,ten\. Seaport, Lambayeque dept., NW Peru, ab. 12 m. S of Chiclayo; open roadstead.

**Eter·ni·ty, Cape** \-i-'tər-nət-ē\. Promontory, Quebec, Canada, on S shore of Saguenay river 39 m. from its mouth; 1400 ft. high; forms E portal of inlet of Eternity Bay. See TRINITY, CAPE.

**Ethi·o·pia** \ē-thē-'ō-pē-ə\ *also* **Ab·ys·sin·ia** \,ab-ə-'sin-ēa-'sin-yə\. Independent state, E Africa, bounded on N by the Red Sea, on E by Afars and Issas and Somalia, on S by Somalia and Kenya, and on W and NW by Sudan; 471,775 sq. m.; pop. (1984c) 42,169,203; ✱ Addis Ababa. *Physical features*: Mountainous in N, cen., and S parts with many peaks 7,000 to 13,000 ft., highest point Ras Dashan in N 15,158 ft,; lowlands on E border include Danakil Desert in NE and the Haud in SE extending into coastal Somalia. *Rivers:* Main streams in N and NW the Tekeze and the Abay (Blue Nile), the outlet of Lake Tana, both tributaries of the Nile; in SW the Omo flowing S to Lake Rudolf on Kenya border; in E the Awash, rising in cen. part SE of Addis Ababa and losing itself in Danakil Desert; in SE many streams flowing SE forming headstreams of the Juba and Shebelle rivers in Somalia. *Chief products:* Coffee, barley, corn, sorghum, sugarcane, hides, skins; potash, gold and platinum deposits; manufactured goods include footwear and textiles; ab. 90 percent of labor force is engaged in agriculture. *Chief towns:* Addis Ababa, Atmara, Dire Dawa, Harer, Dese, Gonder, Jima, Debre Markos. Divided into the following 14 provinces (for pronunciation of their names, see their individual entries)

| NAME | AREA (sq. m.) | POP. (1982e) | CAPITAL |
|---|---|---|---|
| Arusi | 9,073 | 1,212,700 | Asela |
| Bale | 48,109 | 927,500 | Goba |
| Eritrea | 45,405 | 2,559,700 | Asmara |
| Gemu Gefa | 15,251 | 1,058,600 | Arba Minch |
| Gojam | 23,784 | 2,150,100 | Debre Markos |
| Gonder | 28,649 | 2,166,400 | Gonder |
| Harer | 100,270 | 3,297,200 | Harer |
| Ilubabor | 18,301 | 855,400 | Metu |
| Kefa | 21,081 | 1,704,300 | Jima |
| Shewa | 32,973 | 6,712,300 | Addis Ababa |
| Sidamo | 45,289 | 2,962,900 | Awasa |
| Tigre | 25,444 | 2,281,100 | Mekele |
| Welega | 27,490 | 2,130,400 | Nekemte |
| Welo | 30,656 | 3,756,400 | Dese |

*History:* Ancient country W of Red Sea, NE Africa, bet. ab. lat. 24° and 10°N; included S Egypt, E Rep. of the Sudan, and N (modern) Ethiopia; sometimes name referred just to the Nile valley above Syene (Aswān), but in classical writings it referred to that part of Africa S from Egypt as far as Zanzibar; dominated by Egypt from XIth dynasty; became independent of Egypt during XXIIId dynasty, the Biblical land of Cush; part of Sabaean kingdom of Aksum ruled by dynasty descended from Menelik, traditionally son of Hebrew King Solomon and Queen of Saba (Sheba) under Jewish influence until converted to Christianity by bishop Frumentius 4th cent. A.D.; became Monophysis Christian 7th cent.; from 675 cut off from rest of Christian world by Muslim conquest of Egypt and Nubia; 1490 resumed contact when visited by Covilhão who was believed to have found kingdom of Prester John; aided by Portuguese in expelling Muslim sultan of the Somali 1541; center of missionary activity of Jesuits until their expulsion 1633; explored 1768–73 by James Bruce who reported decayed empire restricted to region N of Blue Nile. Modern Ethiopia began with reign of Theodore II, established by conquest of other chiefs 1855–56 and terminated by Napier's expedition 1868; cut off from Red Sea by Egypt 1875–79; Aseb (*q.v.*) make Italian 1882; claimed as an Italian protectorate (through Treaty of Uccialli 1889); coastal region made separate Italian colony 1890 (see ERITREA); under Menelik, defeated Italians at Aduwa (see Adwa) 1896; territorial integrity recognized by Great Britain, France, and Italy 1906; admitted to League of Nations 1923; promulgated first constitution 1931; after failure of League to settle an Italo-Ethiopian clash at Walwal 1934, invaded by Italy 1935; formally annexed to Italy and organized with Eritrea and Italian Somaliland as Italian East Africa (1936–41); regained independence after being liberated by British 1941; became federated with Eritrea 1952; adopted revised constitution 1955; Eritrea made a province 1962; founding member of Organization of African Unity 1963; border conflict with Somalia 1964; Emperor Haile Selassie deposed and provisional military government set up Sept. 1974; crown abolished Mar. 21, 1975.

**Et·ive, Loch** \läk-'et-iv, läk-\. Inlet of Atlantic Ocean extending from Firth of Lorn inland E (8 1/2 m.) and NE (10

## Geographical Dictionary

## How To Conduct An
# OPINION POLL

An opinion poll is a system for determining attitudes or opinions of groups of people on particular questions or issues.

**1** Decide what you want to find out by formulating a question or questions. It's a good idea to word the question or questions so that they can be answered "yes" or "no."

**EXAMPLE:** *You want to find out how students in your school feel about having an arts club. Your question is: If an arts club were started, would you join?*

**2** Decide on whom you will question—that is, select a **sample.** You may decide on a **random sample** (the persons to be questioned are selected by chance) or on a **quota sample** (the persons to be questioned belong to a particular group).

**EXAMPLE:** *You decide on a **quota sample**. You will question one fourth of the students in each of the grades (sixth, seventh, eighth) in your school.*

**3** Question your sample, either in person or by telephone. Record the number of "yes" and "no" answers to your question(s). Also keep track of the number of people you question. The number of "yeses" and the number of "noes" should equal the number of people questioned.

**EXAMPLE:** *You question your sample directly, keeping a record of the number of people sampled as well as a record of the number of "yes" and "no" responses. You interview 100 students.*

**4** Tabulate the answers to your question(s) and express the results as percentages. Write a short sentence expressing the results of your poll.

**EXAMPLE:** *You tabulate the number of "yes" and "no" responses. You find that 30 students responded "yes" and 70 students responded "no." You convert these numbers to percents by dividing each by 100 (the total number of interviews). You find that 30% of the sample responded "yes" to the question, and 70% responded "no." You summarize the results of your poll in this sentence: A survey of 100 students in our school showed that only 30% would join an arts club if one were started.*

verbena (*Verbena hybrida*), a grayish trailing plant whose thick stem reaches a length of about a foot. The flowers are usually pink, red, white, blue, or purple, but they may also be striped. A common weedy species is the European vervain (*V. officinalis*), which is native to Europe but also grows wild in North America. It grows from 1 foot to 3 feet (30–90 cm) tall and has spikes of white or purple flowers.

The lemon verbena (*Aloysia triphylla*) is not a true verbena but a related shrub with foliage that smells somewhat like lemons. It grows from 6 to 10 feet (1.8–3 meters) tall and bears clusters of white flowers.

Verbenas are classified as the genus *Verbena* of the family Verbenaceae (vervain). Annual and perennial.
*\*Reed C. Rollins*

**Verdi, Giuseppe** (vär′di, jü zep′pä), *Italian composer. Born Roncole, Italy, Oct. 10, 1813. Died Milan, Italy, Jan. 27, 1901.*

Verdi is generally considered the greatest Italian operatic composer. His works are remarkable for their beautiful melodies and dramatic power. Among his most popular works are *Rigoletto, Il Trovatore, La Traviata,* and *Aïda.* In these, as well as in most of his other operas, Verdi displayed a deep understanding of the expressive power of the human voice and a genius for creating poignant and believable dramatic characters. Perhaps his greatest characterizations and his finest music are contained in his last two operas, *Otello* and *Falstaff,* composed when he was more than 70 years old. Verdi also wrote nonoperatic works. The best known of his nonoperatic compositions is *Requiem Mass.*

Early in his career Verdi followed the established tradition of Italian opera, which subordinated the orchestra to the singers and strongly emphasized set numbers, such as arias, trios, and choruses. Toward the middle of his career, in works such as *Un Ballo in Maschera* (A Masked Ball) and *La Forza del Destino,* he began to assign a more important role to the orchestra, emphasizing a longer, sustained melodic line with fewer breaks between sung parts. Verdi's art reached its culmination in *Otello* and *Falstaff,* in which the music leads into the vocal parts to form a superb artistic and dramatic whole.

**Life.** After studying with local musicians at Roncole and in the nearby town of Busseto, Verdi applied for admission to the Milan Conservatory in 1832. He was rejected, however, and consequently studied privately with the musician Vincenzo Lavigna. In 1836 he married Margherita Barezzi, the daughter of Antonio Barezzi, a merchant who had helped the young composer in pursuing his musical education. Verdi's first opera *Oberto,* was produced at the La Scala opera house in Milan in 1839. In the next year, Verdi's wife died and he temporarily stopped composing.

In 1842, Verdi achieved a great success with *Nabucco,* a stirring Biblical opera about the Jews' captivity in Babylon. This work aroused the patriotic enthusiasm of the Italian people, some of whom were under Austrian rule at the time. Verdi quickly became identified with the struggle for Italian independence, a cause that he supported fervently.

From 1842 to 1850, Verdi composed several operas, of which *Ernani, Luisa Miller,* and *Macbeth* are best known. During this period, Verdi enjoyed the friendship and encouragement of Giuseppina Strepponi, who

later became his wife. In quick succession from 1851 to 1853, Verdi completed *Rigoletto, Il Trovatore,* and *La Traviata,* the three popular masterpieces with which he achieved international fame. Each of these showed a new and different aspect of the composer's genius. These operas were followed by *Simon Boccanegra, Don Carlo,* and the spectacular and successful *Aïda.*

After his great triumph with *Aïda* in 1871, Verdi did not compose any operas for more than a decade. He ended his self-imposed silence with *Otello* and *Falstaff,* both of which were written to the superb librettos of the poet and composer Arrigo Boito. *Otello,* based on Shakespeare's tragedy *Othello,* was produced in 1887. The comic opera *Falstaff,* based on Shakespeare's comedy *The Merry Wives of Windsor,* was produced in 1893. It was Verdi's last major work and his crowning achievement. Helpful studies are *Complete Operas of Verdi* by Charles Osborne (Knopf, 1970) and *Giuseppe Verdi: His Life and Works* by Francis Toye (Vienna House, 1971 reprint of 1946 ed.) *See also* AïDA; DON CARLO; ERNANI; FALSTAFF; MACBETH; MASKED BALL, A; OTELLO; RIGOLETTO; TRAVIATA, LA; TROVATORE, IL.
*\*Boris Goldovsky*

**verdigris** (vèr′də grēs), the common name for basic copper acetate, a blue or green poisonous compound formed when copper reacts with acetic acid. It is sometimes used as a green pigment in paints and as an ingredient in insecticides and fungicides.
*\*Alfred B. Garret*

**Verdun** (vèr dun′), *a city in southern Quebec, Canada; on Montreal Island; on the St. Lawrence River. Pop. (1986) 60,246.*

Verdun is primarily a residential suburb of adjoining Montreal. In addition, some manufacturing is carried on in Verdun. A fort was constructed on the site in 1662. The community that grew up around the fort was originally known as Saverdun. Verdun was incorporated as a city in 1912.
*\*C. Cecil Lingard*

**Verdun, Battle of.** *See under* WORLD WAR I.

**Verdun, Treaty of,** signed in 843 A.D., marking the division of Charlemagne's empire by three of his grandsons. *See also* FRANCE, HISTORY OF: *Beginning of Modern France* (Division of the Empire).

**Verga, Giovanni** (ver′gä, jō vän′nē), *Italian novelist. Born Catania, Sicily, Aug. 31, 1840. Died Catania, Jan. 27, 1922.*

Verga helped develop a style of literary Realism that became known as *verismo.* In such novels as *The House by the Medlar Tree* (I Malavoglia, 1881) and *Mastro-don Gesualdo* (1889) he realistically described the hardships of peasants and fishermen on the island of Sicily. He also wrote outstanding short stories, notably *The Wolf Hunt* (La Lupa), which was made into a play, and *Rustic Chivalry* (Cavalleria rusticana), which was adapted as an opera by Pietro Mascagni.
*\*Thomas G. Bergin*

**Vergennes, Comte de** (ver zhen, kônt də), *French statesman. Born Charles Gravier, at Dijon, France, Dec. 20, 1717. Died Versailles, France, Feb. 13, 1787.*

Vergennes was foreign minister to Louis XVI from 1774 to 1786. Because his foreign policy was directed

# FORMS AND APPLICATIONS

UNITED STATES DEPARTMENT OF STATE

APPLICATION FOR ☒ PASSPORT ☐ REGISTRATION

SEE INSTRUCTIONS—TYPE OR PRINT IN INK IN WHITE AREAS

MIDDLE NAME Barstow

1. NAME FIRST NAME Karen

LAST NAME Redlin

2. MAILING ADDRESS

STREET 348 Lincoln Drive

CITY, STATE, ZIP CODE Fleming, Oregon 00000

IN CARE OF Mr. Walter Redlin

COUNTRY U.S.A.

☐ 5 Yr. ☐ 10 Yr. Issue Date

☐ R ☐ D ☐ DP  Exp.

End. #

3. SEX ☒ Male ☐ Female

4. PLACE OF BIRTH City, State or Province, Country Chicago, Illinois, U.S.A.

5. DATE OF BIRTH 5 / 18 / 80 Mo. Day Year

6. SEE FEDERAL TAX LAW NOTICE ON REVERSE SIDE

SOCIAL SECURITY NUMBER 0 0 0 0 0 0 0 9 0

9. COLOR OF EYES brown

10. (Area Code) HOME PHONE 0 0 0 555 73 8 0

11. (Area Code) BUSINESS PHONE

7. HEIGHT 4 9 Feet Inches

8. COLOR OF HAIR brown

13. OCCUPATION student

16. TRAVEL PLANS (Not Mandatory) COUNTRIES

DEPARTURE DATE

LENGTH OF STAY

12. PERMANENT ADDRESS (Street, City, State, ZIP Code) 348 Lincoln Drive, Fleming, Oregon 00000

☐ Submitted

14. FATHER'S NAME Walter Redlin

BIRTHPLACE Portland, Oregon

BIRTH DATE 6/3/50

U.S. CITIZEN ☒ YES ☐ NO

15. MOTHER'S MAIDEN NAME Barbara Barstow

BIRTHPLACE New Orleans, La.

BIRTH DATE 5/22/55

U.S. CITIZEN ☒ YES ☐ NO

17. HAVE YOU EVER BEEN ISSUED A U.S. PASSPORT? YES ☐ NO ☒

IF YES, SUBMIT PASSPORT IF AVAILABLE. DISPOSITION

IF UNABLE TO SUBMIT MOST RECENT PASSPORT, STATE ITS DISPOSITION: COMPLETE NEXT LINE

NAME IN WHICH ISSUED   MOST RECENT PASSPORT NUMBER   ISSUE DATE (Mo., Day, Yr.)

DATE OF MOST RECENT MARRIAGE Mo. Day Year

18. HAVE YOU EVER BEEN MARRIED? ☐ YES ☒ NO   IF YES, GIVE DATE Mo. Day Year

WIDOWED/DIVORCED? ☐ YES ☐ NO

SPOUSE'S BIRTHPLACE   RELATIONSHIP

SPOUSE'S FULL BIRTH NAME

SUBMIT TWO RECENT IDENTICAL PHOTOS

19. IN CASE OF EMERGENCY, NOTIFY (Person Not Traveling With You) (Not Mandatory)

FULL NAME Mr. and Mrs. Richard Barstow

(Area Code) PHONE NUMBER 0 0 555 4 8 2 8

ADDRESS 7525 Arco, La Vela, Fla. 00000

20. TO BE COMPLETED BY AN APPLICANT WHO BECAME A CITIZEN THROUGH NATURALIZATION

I IMMIGRATED TO THE U.S. (Month, Year)   I RESIDED CONTINUOUSLY IN THE U.S. From (Mo., Yr.) To (Mo., Yr.)   DATE NATURALIZED (Mo., Day, Yr.)   PLACE

21. DO NOT SIGN APPLICATION UNTIL REQUESTED TO DO SO BY PERSON ADMINISTERING OATH

I have not, since acquiring United States citizenship, performed any of the acts listed under "Acts or Conditions" on the reverse of this application (unless explanatory statement is attached). I solemnly swear (or affirm) that the statements made on this application are true and the photograph attached is a true likeness of me.

(SEAL)   X

(Sign in presence of person authorized to accept application)

Subscribed and sworn to (affirmed) before me

Month Day Year

(Signature of person authorized to accept application)

☐ Clerk of Court or PASSPORT Agent
☐ Postal Employee
☐ (Vice) Consul USA At _____

☐ PASSPORT ☐ DRIVER'S LICENSE ☐ OTHER (Specify)

No.

ISSUED IN THE NAME OF

22. APPLICANT'S IDENTIFYING DOCUMENTS

PLACE OF ISSUE

ISSUE DATE Month Day Year   EXPIRATION DATE Month Day Year

APPLICATION APPROVAL

Examiner Name

Office, Date

23. FOR ISSUING OFFICE USE ONLY (Applicant's evidence of citizenship)

☐ Birth Cert.  SR  CR  City  Filed/Issued:
☐ Passport  Bearer's Name:
☐ Report of Birth
☐ Naturalization/Citizenship Cert.  No.:
☐ Other:
☐ Seen & Returned
☐ Attached

24.   FEE   EXEC.   POST

Form Approved OMB No. 1405-0004 (Exp. 8/1/89)

(SEE INSTRUCTIONS ON REVERSE)

FORM DSP-11 (12-87)

# GRAPHS

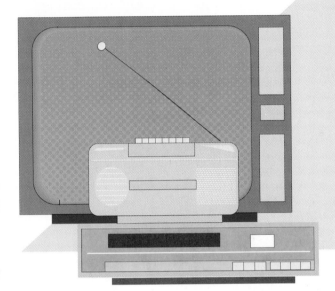

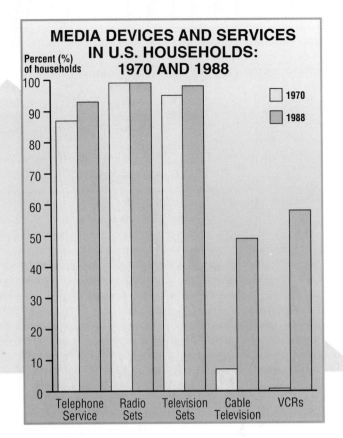

**MEDIA DEVICES AND SERVICES IN U.S. HOUSEHOLDS: 1970 AND 1988**

Percent (%) of households

☐ 1970
▨ 1988

| | Telephone Service | Radio Sets | Television Sets | Cable Television | VCRs |

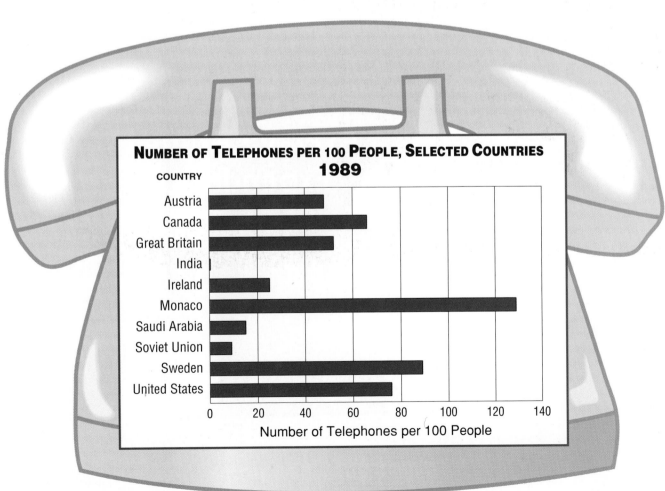

**NUMBER OF TELEPHONES PER 100 PEOPLE, SELECTED COUNTRIES 1989**

COUNTRY

- Austria
- Canada
- Great Britain
- India
- Ireland
- Monaco
- Saudi Arabia
- Soviet Union
- Sweden
- United States

Number of Telephones per 100 People

**BAR GRAPHS**

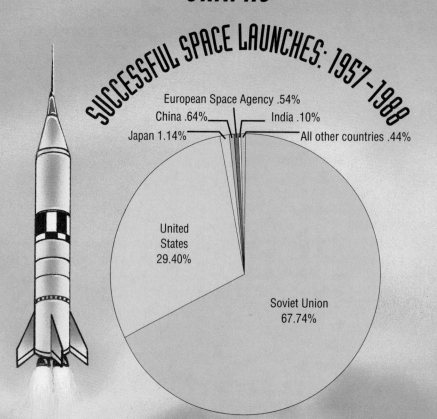

### SUCCESSFUL SPACE LAUNCHES: 1957-1988

European Space Agency .54%

China .64%

India .10%

Japan 1.14%

All other countries .44%

United States 29.40%

Soviet Union 67.74%

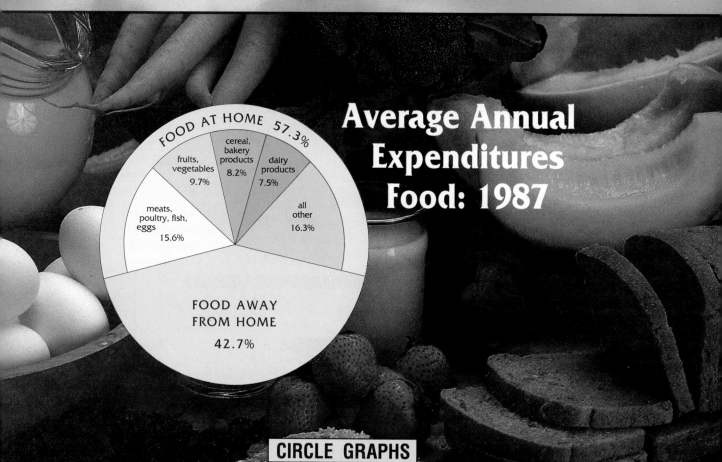

## Average Annual Expenditures Food: 1987

FOOD AT HOME 57.3%

fruits, vegetables 9.7%

cereal, bakery products 8.2%

dairy products 7.5%

meats, poultry, fish, eggs 15.6%

all other 16.3%

FOOD AWAY FROM HOME 42.7%

### CIRCLE GRAPHS

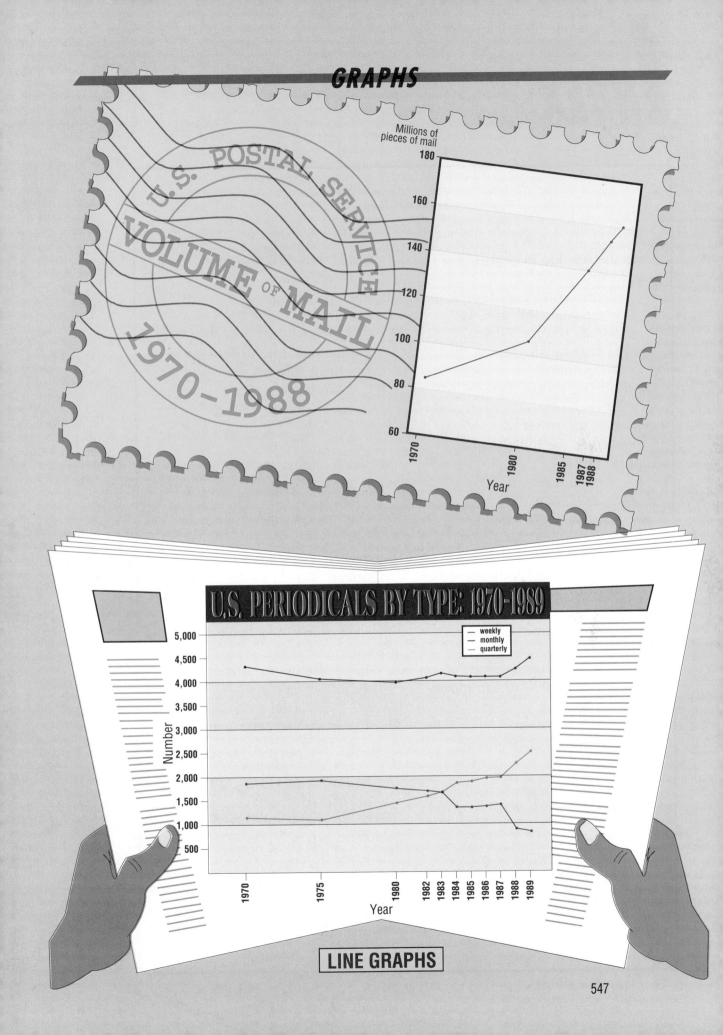

U.S. POSTAL SERVICE VOLUME OF MAIL 1970–1988

Millions of pieces of mail

Year

U.S. PERIODICALS BY TYPE: 1970–1989

- weekly
- monthly
- quarterly

Number

Year

**LINE GRAPHS**

## Index 423

# MAPS

# TECTONIC PLATES

Plate movement is indicated by the direction of the arrows.

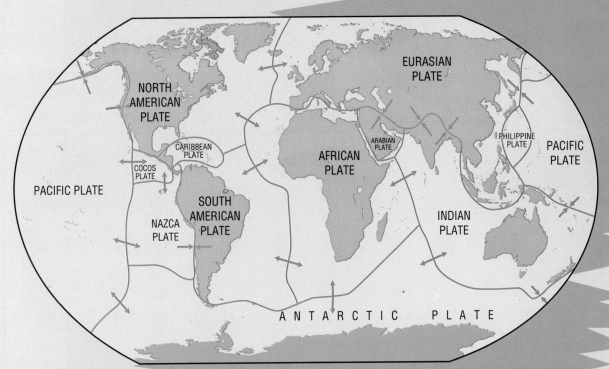

NORTH AMERICAN PLATE

CARIBBEAN PLATE

COCOS PLATE

PACIFIC PLATE

NAZCA PLATE

SOUTH AMERICAN PLATE

EURASIAN PLATE

ARABIAN PLATE

AFRICAN PLATE

PHILIPPINE PLATE

PACIFIC PLATE

INDIAN PLATE

ANTARCTIC PLATE

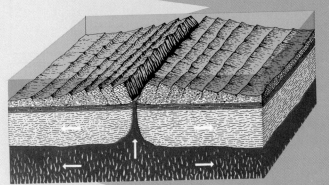

**Lava from the molten interior of the earth** wells up along an oceanic ridge. As the lava cools and hardens, it moves away from both sides of the ridge as great plates (left). The crust of the earth is made up of many such plates, such as A, B, C, and D (below). A plate consists of an upper rocky section, the lithosphere, and a lower, partially molten layer, the asthenosphere. Where two plates collide, one may be pushed beneath the other, forming deep ocean trenches.

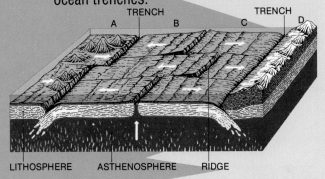

TRENCH

TRENCH

A        B           C        D

LITHOSPHERE        ASTHENOSPHERE        RIDGE

549

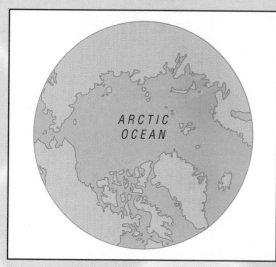

ARCTIC
OCEAN

# Oceans
# of the
# World

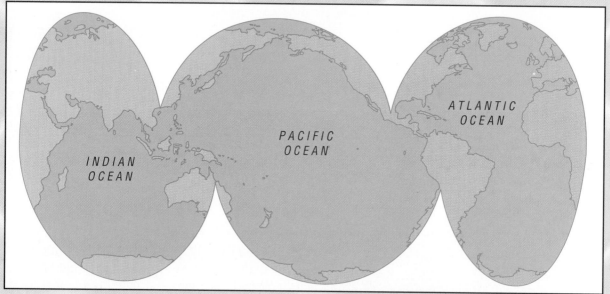

INDIAN
OCEAN

PACIFIC
OCEAN

ATLANTIC
OCEAN

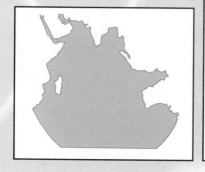

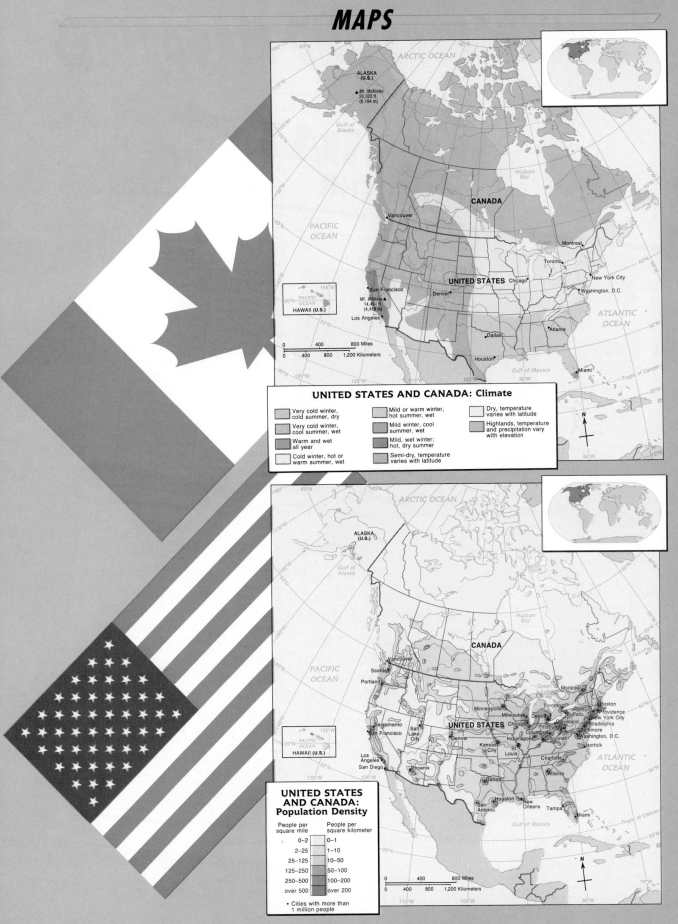

## UNITED STATES AND CANADA: Climate

- Very cold winter, cold summer, dry
- Very cold winter, cool summer, wet
- Warm and wet all year
- Cold winter, hot or warm summer, wet
- Mild or warm winter, hot summer, wet
- Mild winter, cool summer, wet
- Mild, wet winter; hot, dry summer
- Semi-dry, temperature varies with latitude
- Dry, temperature varies with latitude
- Highlands, temperature and precipitation vary with elevation

## UNITED STATES AND CANADA: Population Density

| People per square mile | People per square kilometer |
|---|---|
| 0–2 | 0–1 |
| 2–25 | 1–10 |
| 25–125 | 10–50 |
| 125–250 | 50–100 |
| 250–500 | 100–200 |
| over 500 | over 200 |

- Cities with more than 1 million people

# CLARKSDALE
## COURIER

MONDAY, SEPTEMBER 20, 1993  50¢

CLARKSDALE, IOWA

VOL. 192, No. 263

## State House Crisis Averted As Governor Admits Error

*by Ron Bellum*
Chief Political
Correspondent

Governor Barbara Holden said at a press conference today that state labor negotiators and public employee union officials will sit down tomorrow for a new round of talks on next year's contracts.

The agreement to resume negotiations came after a tense week-long standoff between the Governor and the unions. The crisis came about last Sunday when the wording of an announce-

*Governor Holden blames misunderstanding for crisis and promises new round of talks on labor contracts.*

statement concerned the possibility of layoffs of her executive staff, not of workers who are members of public employee unions.

Political commentators say that the Governor has a strategy behind her public statements. They believe she is sending a message to the union officials that if pushed, she will play "hardball."

A source in the Governor's office told the *Courier* that new wage demands may be placed on the table at tomorrow's meeting.

## NEWS IN BRIEF

*New Downtown Library*

The old Higgins Department store building, vacant since 1977, opened its doors yesterday as the city's newest branch library.

The building, a local landmark in danger of demolition for many years, is the new home of the library's main research division.

The opening was the culmination of years of effort on the part of librarians, historic

for the museum to complete a documentary film about arsenal wildlife and prepare wildlife information packets for teachers who take students on field trips to the arsenal.

problems abound.

The report notes that 60 percent of the mathematics teachers and 40 percent of science teachers do not have college degrees in the subjects they teach.

causing embarrassing problems with some of the elaborate satellites, among them the mirror flaw that blurs the vision of the Hubble Space Telescope.
*please see NASA, on 4A*

more taxpayers could be eligible to claim the earned income credit for 1991. But as things stand now, they will have to deal with a two-page four-part form.
*please see TAXES, on 7A*

expanded the basic benefit and added two supplementary credits. One of them was for families with infants less than a year old; the other was to help families pay health-insurance premiums.

The catch is that families filing for the young-child supplement can't also claim the separate income-tax credit for child-care expenses. And families claiming the health-insurance bonus can't deduct insurance expenses from their income. The paperwork needed to figure all that out has gummed up the form.

The problem is not likely to be fixed before tax time. The reason: Committee leaders fear a free-for-all if they rush a tax bill to the floor.

## Weather Corner

**TODAY:**
Sunny and hazy. High: 67–72; low: 47–53.

**TOMORROW:**
High: 75; low: 48.

**YESTERDAY:**
High: 65; low: 59.

*Complete weather report, 8B*

### Index

## FCC considers cable fee regulation

WASHINGTON (AP)–More than half of the nation's cable-television systems could be subject to local price regulation under rules being considered by the Federal Communications Commission.

The commission scheduled a vote today to revise rules that currently exempt about 97 percent of the nation's 9,600 cable systems from regulation.

The FCC is considering an administration-backed proposal

that would allow only systems facing competition from at least six over-the-air broadcast stations to avoid regulation.

Such a proposal, if adopted, would give local governments control over the prices charged by about 60 percent of cable systems.

The five commissioners still appeared to be deliberating the matter Friday, said an industry source who asked not to be further identified. However, the source

said, it appeared that they were leaning toward the six-signal standard.

Under the 1984 Cable Act, cable systems were exempt from local price regulation beginning in 1987 if they were found to have "effective competition," as determined by the commission.

The FCC defined effective competition as three broadcast stations in a cable system's market, which freed all but a small portion of cable

systems from rate regulation.

But consumer groups and city officials complaining about rapidly increasing cable fees have lobbied Congress to return to cities the right to regulate cable rates.

A month ago, the Senate Commerce Committee approved, 16-3, a re-regulation bill. Senate debate on the measure has been delayed while lawmakers see what the commission will do.

## Cats and Clout

Any cat owner knows how it happens. You see this tabby all wet and shivering in an alleyway and you can't stand the sight of so much misery so you bring him indoors. Next a neighbor arrives and says, "Esmeralda sneaked out before I had a chance to get her spayed and now she's got the cutest kittens and won't you please, please take one." Then your child comes in with the calico she saved from drowning and asks, "Can you imagine anyone being horrible enough to get rid of this cat!" Finally the ginger tom who was the tabby's best friend takes to mewing piteously at your back door and . . . There! You have just exceeded the maximum number of cats or dogs that the Syracuse, N.Y., City Planning Commission would allow.

Dog owners have not complained about the proposed rule, probably because few people would choose to keep more than

three dogs, what with all the care they demand. But since cats ask only for a clean box, a sunny spot and a small bowl of chow it's easy to acquire a houseful. One day you look around and there they are: cats on the windowsill, cats on the bed, cats by the radiator—all of them asleep.

The owners of those sleeping beauties have set up a howl in Syracuse. Punish those who abandon their pets, they say. Arrange for free neutering and spaying. Establish shelters. But don't tell us how many cats we can feed and care for and love.

Love: that's the heart of the matter. Cats don't ask for love, but they get it anyway—simply by being their sinuous, stubborn, stuck-up, snoozing selves. City officials, who've tabled the 3-pet limit, say they misjudged the strength of the cat lobby. That wasn't their only error. Above all, they misjudged the strength of the cat.

**Editorial**

## Dead Sea Scrolls-
## 40-year embargo finally ends

*By Ron Grossman*
*Chicago Tribune*

A long-running, bitter dispute among biblical scholars over access to the Dead Sea Scrolls is about to become moot:

A California museum has decided to release a complete set of photocopies of the priceless Hebrew manuscripts that date to the age of Jesus.

The Huntington Library, a research center and art museum in San Marino, Calif., will make available immediately on microfilm its complete set of 3,000 photographs of the scrolls through the interlibrary loan system that links the nation's universities.

With that stroke, the Dead Sea Scrolls, the greatest archeological find of the 20th century, will become as easy for scholars to view as ordinary books that university libraries routinely exchange on behalf of their researchers.

Until now, some of the world's foremost biblical scholars have been unable to examine large sections of the scrolls, which have been guarded jealously by a tightly knit group of researchers since their discovery more than 40

The few libraries with photocopies of the scrolls have been under strict orders to withhold them from all other scholars.

The Huntington's decision to release the photos to the public, to be announced officially today by its director, William Moffett, comes three weeks after an equally striking circumvention of the embargo on the scrolls.

In early September, two U.S. researchers disclosed that use of a desktop computer had enabled them to reconstruct parts of the Dead Sea Scrolls no outside scholars had been allowed to see.

After being denied access to the scrolls, Ben Zion Wacholder, a professor at Hebrew Union College in Cincinnati, authorized Martin Abegg, a graduate student turned computer hacker, to produce a bootleg version. Abegg programmed his Macintosh to stitch together pieces of the texts from a five-volume concordance.

Wacholder, a widely respected biblical scholar, said he was publishing his computer-generated texts to draw public attention to the embargo on the scrolls. He argued that, as a crucial part of the religious heritage of Christians and Jews,

**Feature Story**

**In Print**

## Newest Stacy Brown Thriller Will Not Disappoint Fans

*Reviewed by*
*Marcia Harmon*

Fiction lovers eagerly await the appearance of each new Stacy Brown mystery novel. Her latest, *The Messenger*, will not disappoint her fans.

In *The Messenger*, we again meet the heroine, Trish Stalling, and many other of Ms. Brown's regular cast of characters. Stalling is still feisty, still independent, still traveling the galaxy.

As her followers know, Stalling makes a living as a kind of 21st-century junk dealer, but she travels the planets in search

of adventure—not in search of good deals on old spaceships.

Ms. Brown's books are popular because they are magnificent, rousing adventure tales. Her books, however, succeed on other levels as well.

In *The Messenger*, Ms. Brown zeros in on language and explores the different ways people communicate.

After landing on the planet Kallos 4, Stalling finds herself smack in the middle of a conflict between the two groups of people who share the planet. Stalling is mystified because for

years Kallos 4 has been a model of peace for the entire galaxy. Her mystification is complete because she can't understand the way the two warring groups—the Margos and the Wysops—communicate.

Communication between the Margos and the Wysops is by the spoken work, but their vocabulary is built on the myths, literature, and proverbs of the past. In order to understand—and possibly help these two groups find peace—Stalling must learn a quite complex language in a very short time.

**Book Review**

# CLASSIFIED ADS

### WANTED

**7000** Stereo, Sound Systems

**AMPEX 800** — solid state reel-to-reel, $150 or best offer. 555-4199

**CD PLAYER RCA $75.**
Call 555-0051

**Entertainment Center,** oak surround., beautiful condition. TV/VCR/DB tape, AM/FM stereo and CD player. Paid $3500, asking $800. 555-0653.

**NEW** Pioneer CD player, home unit, still in box. $175 or best offer. 555-3617

**MacIntosh–Marantz** old-time stereo and speaker. 555-7453

**7220** Video Equipment

**FISHER** Video Camcorder FVC720, brand new, still has warranty. $700 or best offer. Must sell. 555-8582

**7300** Televisions

**COLOR TV 27"**
Sylvania, floor model, $200.
555-4638.

12" Portable Color TV Excellent picture & color. Must sacrifice. $100/offer.

**Classified Ads**

# EYE ON SCIENCE

Vol. 38 • No. 8

August 1993

$2.00

Cover Story

## DOLPHINS

**Magazine — Cover Page**

August 1993

Vol. 38    No. 8

# CONTENTS

## EYE ON SCIENCE

EDITOR-IN-CHIEF
Max Donaldson

DIRECTOR OF DESIGN
Meredith Lowell

EXECUTIVE EDITOR
Esteban Morilla

COPY EDITOR
Barry Fonda

SPECIAL FEATURES
Jennifer Mackay

PHOTOGRAPHS
Douglas Gramzow

REGULAR FEATURES
Ellen Goldman

ART DIRECTOR
Russell Anthony

ASSISTANT TO THE EDITOR
Katherine Neitzel

EDITORIAL/PRODUCTION ASSISTANT
Jesse Lee

PRODUCTION MANAGER
Louise McDowell

MANAGER OF ADVERTISING SERVICES
Laura Delito

NATIONAL SALES MANAGER
Frank Price

NATIONAL MARKETING MANAGER
Darlene Halligan

ASSISTANT TO NATIONAL
SALES MANAGER
Curtis Van Loenen

CIRCULATION DIRECTOR
Arlene Murano

PRESIDENT
Brenda Carmichael

NATIONAL DIRECTOR OF
ADMINISTRATION
Jeremy Little

NATIONAL ADVISORY COMMITTEE
Robert Talley
Francis Tellesen
Dennis Pittman
Juanita Martinez

## STORIES AND ARTICLES

## FEATURES

EYE ON SCIENCE (ISSN 0000-0000) is published monthly by the Educational Guild Council, 1335 W. Acoma, P.O. Box 345, Parrington, WI 00000-0000. $2.00 a copy, $20.00 a year. Outside the United States add $7.50 per year for postage. © 1993 by Educational Guild Council. All rights reserved. Nothing appearing in EYE ON SCIENCE may be reprinted whether wholly or in part without written permission. Postmaster: Send address changes to EYE ON SCIENCE, 446 Sycamore Lane, P.O. Box 334, Landaville, Florida 00000.

**Magazine — Contents Page**

**MYERS, THERESE E.**
*about*
Desqview's different drummer. E. S. Ely. por *Personal Computing* 13:76 Jl '89
Little Quarterdeck throws its weight around. P. Cole. il por *Business Week* p76 Je 19 '89

**MYERSON, BESS**
*about*
Bess Myerson: how I survived. C. Adams. il por *Ladies' Home Journal* 106:106-7+ Jl '89
Bess Myerson: the inside story. J. L. Block. il pors *Good Housekeeping* 208:70+ Ap '89
How Bess got out of the mess. J. Kasindorf. il pors *New York* 22:38-48 Ja 16 '89
Miss America wins again. il por *Time* 133:80 Ja 2 '89
Scraping by on $376,000 a year. L. Touby. il pors *Working Woman* 14:99 My '89

**MYERSON, RALPH M.**
Frederick Albert Cook, M.D. [with editorial comment by Gilbert L. Voss] il por map *Sea Frontiers* 35:3, 8-13 Ja/F '89

**MYLAN LABORATORIES INC.**
Drug abuse [Mylan Laboratories' suspicions of FDA corruption bear fruit] J. Novack. il *Forbes* 143:42-3 Je 26 '89
Mylan is glad it opened this can of worms. M. Schroeder. il *Business Week* p30-1 S 18 '89

**MYLROIE, LAURIE**
Iraq's changing role in the Persian Gulf. bibl f *Current History* 88:89-2+ F '89

**MYOBLASTS**
5-bromo-2'-deoxyuridine blocks myogenesis by extinguishing expression of MyoD1. S. J. Tapscott and others. bibl f il *Science* 245:532-6 Ag 4 '89
Transfer of a protein encoded by a single nucleus to nearby nuclei in multinucleated myotubes. E. Ralston and Z. W. Hall. bibl f il *Science* 244:1066-9 Je 2 '89

**MYOCARDIUM** *See* Heart—Muscle
**MYOFACIAL PAIN DYSFUNCTION SYNDROME** *See* TMJ syndrome

**MYOGLOBIN**
*Spectra and spectroscopy*
Effects of buried ionizable amino acids on the reduction potential of recombinant myoglobin. R. Varadarajan and others. bibl f il *Science* 243:69-72 Ja 6 '89

**MYOPIA**
*Anecdotes, facetiae, satire, etc.*
A pretty girl is like a malady [boy attributes myopia to hours spent reading about sex] P. Freundlich. il *Esquire* 111:122-6 F '89

**MYOSIN**
Assembly of the native heterodimer of Rana esculenta tropomyosin by chain exchange. S. S. Lehrer and others. bibl f il *Science* 246:926-8 N 17 '89
Expression and characterization of a functional myosin head fragment in Dictyostelium discoideum. D. J. Manstein and others. bibl f il *Science* 246:656-8 N 3 '89

**MYRINGOTOMY** *See* Ear—Surgery
**MYRISTIC ACID**
Activation of the cellular proto-oncogene product p21Ras by addition of a myristylation signal. J. E. Buss and others. bibl f il *Science* 243:1600-3 Mr 24 '89
Myristoylated and nonmyristoylated forms of a protein are phosphorylated by protein kinase C. J. M. Graff and others. bibl f il *Science* 246:503-6 O 27 '89

**MYRRH**
Gifts of the Magi: precious resins. D. Dare. *Earth Science* 41:14 Wint '88

**MYRTLE BEACH (S.C.)**
*Description*
Back to the beach. C. F. Wall. il *Southern Living* 24:116+ My '89

**MYSAK, JOE**
The beauty of municipal bonds. il *The American Spectator* 22:18-20 Je '89

**MYSTERY**
A mother's manner of looking to the sky [instilling awareness of mystery of life] J. M. Wall. *The Christian Century* 106:99-100 F 1-8 '89

**MYSTERY OF THE ROSE BOUQUET** [drama] See Puig, Manuel
**MYSTERY STORIES** *See* Detective and mystery stories
**MYSTERY TRAIN** [film] See Motion picture reviews—Single works

**MYSTIC (CONN.)**
*Restaurants, nightclubs, bars, etc.*
A hot movie means a bigger piece of the American pie for a Greek immigrant who owns the real Mystic Pizza [S. Zelepos] D. Chun. il pors *People Weekly* 31:98+ Ja 9 '89

**MYSTIC FIRE VIDEO, INC.**
Making book on video. J. Zinsser. il *Publishers Weekly* 235:32 Ap 14 '89
Video publishers reel in profits with avant-garde offerings. L. Arden. il por *Home Office Computing* 7:45 My '89

**MYSTIC PIZZA (MYSTIC, CONN.: RESTAURANT)** *See* Mystic (Conn.)—Restaurants, nightclubs, bars, etc.

**MYSTIC SEAPORT MUSEUM**
Mystic by the sea. R. S. Peffer. il *Travel Holiday* 172:100-2 Jl '89

**MYSTICISM**
*See also*
Yoga
The owl in the daylight. L. O. Sanneh. il *The Christian Century* 106:1115 N 29 '89
*Catholic Church*
*See also*
Creation spirituality
*Judaism*
*See also*
Cabala

**MYTHICAL ANIMALS** *See* Animals, Mythical
**MYTHOLOGY**
*See also*
Gods and goddesses
Weather in mythology
Women in mythology
Bill Moyers angrily defends Joseph Campbell against charges that his wisdom was only a myth. A. Chambers. il pors *People Weekly* 32:64+ N 27 '89
The faces of Joseph Campbell. B. Gill. il *The New York Review of Books* 36:16+ S 28 '89
Joseph Campbell: an exchange [discussion of September 28, 1989 article, The faces of Joseph Campbell] B. Gill. il *The New York Review of Books* 36:57-61 N 9 '89
Mythics: don't take them too literally [excerpt from Imaginary landscape] W. I. Thompson. *Utne Reader* p103 N/D '89
The power of myth: lessons from Joseph Campbell. B. C. Lane. il *The Christian Century* 106:652-4 Jl 5-12 '89
The stories we live by [personal myths; cover story] S. Keen. il *Psychology Today* 22:42-7 D '88
*Bibliography*
Taking another look at myth. K. Thompson. il *Utne Reader* p102-5+ N/D '89

**MYTHOLOGY, GREEK**
*See also*
Argonauts (Greek mythology)
Jason (Greek mythology)
Palamedes (Greek mythology)
The powers of the primeval goddesses. M. R. Lefkowitz. *The American Scholar* 58:586-91 Aut '89

**MYTHOLOGY, INDIAN (AMERICAN)** *See* Indians of North America—Religion and mythology
**MYTHOLOGY, ROMAN**
*See also*
Hercules (Roman mythology)

**MYTHOLOGY IN POETRY**
Hopkins the mythmaker. J. F. Cotter. *America* 161:106-8 Ag 26-S 2 '89
Poet to poet. D. Dumars. il *The Writer* 102:23-6 Mr '89

**MYTHS** *See* Mythology

## N

**N.S. BIENSTOCK INC.**
When Leibner calls, the networks listen [agent for newscasters] B. Yagoda. il pors *The New York Times Magazine* p36-8+ Je 18 '89

**N.W.A. (MUSICAL GROUP)**
N.W.A. cops an attitude. S. Hochman. il *Rolling Stone* p24 Je 29 '89

**NAACP** *See* National Association for the Advancement of Colored People
**NAACP LEGAL DEFENSE AND EDUCATIONAL FUND** *See* Legal Defense and Educational Fund
**NAAMAN, THE SYRIAN**
*about*
Grateful outcasts. P. J. Ryan. il *America* 161:223 O 7 '89

**NÄBAUER, MICHAEL, AND OTHERS**
Does voltage affect excitation-contraction coupling in the heart? [discussion of May 19, 1989 article, Regulation of calcium release is gated by calcium current, not gating charge, in cardiac myocytes] bibl f *Science* 246:1640 D 22 '89
Regulation of calcium release is gated by calcium current, not gating charge, in cardiac myocytes. bibl f il *Science* 244:800-3 My 19 '89

**NABEL, ELIZABETH G., AND OTHERS**
Recombinant gene expression in vivo within endothelial cells of the arterial wall. bibl f il *Science* 244:1342-4 Je 16 '89

**NABET** *See* National Association of Broadcast Employees and Technicians
**NABOKOV, VLADIMIR VLADIMIROVICH, 1899-1977**
Nabokov's letters: 'Let me explain a few things' [excerpt from Vladimir Nabokov: selected letters, 1940-1977] il por *The New York Times Book Review* 94:1+ S 17 '89
**NABSE** *See* National Alliance of Black School Educators
**NABUCCO** [opera] See Verdi, Giuseppe, 1813-1901

# SCHEDULES

## Symbols and Reference Marks

A — Time symbol for A.M.
CT — Central Time
MT — Mountain Time
N — Time Symbol for Noon
P — Time Symbol for P.M.
PT — Pacific Time
⊞ — Checked Baggage
● — Tickets cannot be purchased at this location. You may purchase your tickets on the train (without penalty) or from any Amtrak appointed travel agency. Please call 1-800-USA-RAIL to make special arrangements when boarding/detraining assistance is required.
○ — Ticket office not open at all train departure times. When ticket office is closed, fare may be paid on train without penalty. Bus drivers cannot accept fares.
✸ — Stops only on signal to receive or discharge passengers; where possible please give sufficient advance notice to agent or conductor.
🦽 — The station and/or platform area is accessible to disabled and elderly passengers. Please call 1-800-USA-RAIL to make special arrangements when boarding/detraining assistance is required.
DP — Departure time
Ar — Arrival time
↓ — Read down
↑ — Read up

## Amtrak
# California Zephyr
### Chicago...Omaha...Denver...
### Salt Lake City...Reno...Oakland

| 5 | Mile | ▼ | ◄Train Number► | Symbol | ▲ | 6 |
|---|---|---|---|---|---|---|
| Daily | | | ◄Days of Operation Daily► | | | Daily |
| Read Down | | | | | | Read Up |
| | | | *(Burlington Northern)* | | | |
| 2:55P | 0 | Dp | Chicago, IL – Union Sta. (CT) | ⊞ 🦽 | Ar | 4:25P |
| 3:31P | 28 | | Naperville, IL | ⊞ 🦽 | ▲ | 3:09P |
| 4:41P | 104 | | Princeton, IL | 🦽 | | 1:59P |
| 5:40P | 162 | | Galesburg, IL | ● | | 1:07P |
| 6:30P | 205 | | Burlington, IA | 🦽 | | 12:14P |
| 7:05P | 233 | | Mt. Pleasant, IA | ⊞ 🦽 | | 11:40A |
| 7:50P | 280 | | Ottumwa, IA | ● | | 10:56A |
| 9:05P | 360 | | Osceola, IA | ⊞ 🦽 | | 9:35A |
| 9:37P | 393 | | Creston, IA | ● | | 8:59A |
| 11:29P 11:44P | 501 | Ar Dp | Omaha, NE | ● 🦽 | Dp Ar | 7:04A 6:39A |
| 12:49A 1:04A | 555 | Ar Dp | Lincoln, NE | ⊞ 🦽 | Dp Ar | 5:39A 5:29A |
| 2:34A | 652 | | Hastings, NE (Grand Island) | ⊞ 🦽 | ▲ | 3:58A |
| 3:23A | 706 | | Holdrege, NE | ⊞ | | 3:06A |
| 4:39A | 784 | | McCook, NE (CT) | ● | | 1:57A |
| 6:04A | 960 | | Fort Morgan, CO (MT) | ● | | 10:29P |
| | | | *(Denver & Rio Grande Western)* | | | |
| 7:50A 9:00A | 1037 | Ar Dp | Denver, CO | ⊞ 🦽 | Dp Ar | 9:10P 8:05P |
| 10:55A | 1100 | | Winter Park, CO | ● 🦽 | ▲ | 4:55P |
| 11:20A | 1113 | | Granby, CO | ● 🦽 | | 4:25P |
| 2:20P | 1222 | | Glenwood Springs, CO | ⊞ 🦽 | | 1:30P |
| 4:25P | 1312 | | Grand Junction, CO | ⊞ 🦽 | | 11:40A |
| ✸5:40P | 1390 | | Thompson, UT | ● 🦽 | ✸9:50A | |
| 7:30P | 1489 | | Helper, UT | ● 🦽 | | 8:20A |
| 9:30P | 1564 | | Provo, UT | ● 🦽 | | 6:25A |
| | | | *(Union Pacific)* | | | |
| 11:20P 12:20A | 1609 | Ar Dp | Salt Lake City, UT (MT) | ⊞ 🦽 | Dp Ar | 5:35A 4:15A |
| 3:33A | 1871 | | Elko, NV (PT) | ● 🦽 | ▲ | 10:38P |
| | | | *(Southern Pacific Lines)* | | | |
| 5:58A | 2005 | | Winnemucca, NV | ● 🦽 | | 8:40P |
| 8:56A 9:11A | 2176 | Ar Dp | Sparks, NV | ● | Dp Ar | 5:45P 5:30P |
| 9:22A | 2179 | | Reno, NV | ⊞ 🦽 | ▲ | 5:00P |
| 10:15A | 2214 | | Truckee, CA (Lake Tahoe) | ● 🦽 | | 4:08P |
| 12:23P | 2278 | | Colfax, CA | ● | | 1:59P |
| 1:29P | 2313 | | Roseville, CA | ● 🦽 | | 1:09P |
| 2:19P | 2331 | | Sacramento, CA | ⊞ 🦽 | | 12:42P |
| 2:39P | 2344 | | Davis, CA | ⊞ 🦽 | | 12:10P |
| 3:03P | 2371 | | Suisun-Fairfield, CA | ● | | 11:43A |
| 3:25P | 2387 | | Martinez, CA | ⊞ 🦽 | | 11:23A |
| 3:54P | 2407 | | Richmond, CA | Φ 🦽 | | 10:53A |
| 5:00P | 2416 | Ar | Oakland, CA (PT) | ⊞ 🦽 | Dp | 10:40A |

### Services On Board the California Zephyr

**Sleeping Car—Reservations required.** Deluxe, special, family and economy bedrooms. First Class Service includes complimentary meals, wine, trak pack, bedtime sweet, morning wake-up service with a newspaper, and coffee, tea and orange juice served between 6:30 a.m. and 9:30 a.m.
**Coaches—Reservations required.**
**Dining Car—**Complete meals.
**Sightseer Lounge Car—**Sandwiches, snacks and beverages.
**Entertainment—**Feature movies, games, railroad history guide (Sacramento to Reno), and hospitality hour.
**Amtrak Thruway Bus Connection—**See inside back cover for details.

# TELEPHONE DIRECTORY

## Emergency Numbers

**Fire**
(Incendio)
**911**

**Police**
(Policía)
**911**

**Ambulance**
(Ambulancia)
**911**

Doctor      Office      Home

### Other Emergency Numbers

Child Abuse & Maltreatment
Reporting Center
(toll-free) **1 800 555-3720**

Coast Guard **1 000 555-7936**

Crime Victims Hotline **1 000 555-7777**

Deaf Emergency TTY
(toll free) **1 800 555-4357**

FBI **555-3140**

Gas Leaks **555-4050**

Poison Control Center **1 000 555-7667**

Sex Crimes Report Line **1 000 555-7273**

U.S.Secret Service **1 000 555-4400**

### Or dial "O" (Operator)

Stay on the line. If you cannot stay on the line, give the Operator the street address and community where help is needed.

### Annoyance calls

If you receive a malicious or annoying phone call, hang up immediately. If the calls persist, please contact our Annoyance Call Bureau on (toll-free) 1 800 555-1122. Calls are answered from 9 a.m. to 4 p.m. weekdays, except holidays.

It is a crime under both Federal and State law to make a telephone call for annoying or harassing purposes or, in the case of the Federal law to knowingly permit a telephone under one's control to be used for such purposes. This includes calls in which the caller remains silent, as well as those in which the offender is threatening or obscene. The penalty under the state law can be imprisonment for one year and a $1,000 fine and under the Federal law, imprisonment for six months and a $500 fine.

### Warning

**Yielding a party line in an emergency**

State law requires you to yield a party line immediately when told the line is needed for an emergency. Emergency calls are those which must be made to get help when human life or property is in jeopardy. The penalty for not relinquishing a party line in an emergency is a fine of $500 and/or imprisonment of up to three months.

EMERGENCY NUMBERS

## WHITE PAGES

**47**

### VOELLER W–WHITMORE          CRESTVIEW

Voeller Wayne 404 Parkway.......555-5645

**W**

Wagner Ed 442 S Adams ............555-2322
Wagner Thomas 628 Jackson.....555-2860
**WAGNER TIRE COMPANY**          **555-4545**
  201 N Washington ....................555-3043
Walker Lucille 114 Emerson..........555-2630
Walker Natalie 615 Emerson........555-2767
Wall Gloria 200 N Ash ................555-2154
Wall John 200 N Ash ..................555-3012
Wall Susan 502 Scott..................555-2598
Walter Matthew 623 Quincy.........555-2598
**WALTER NADINE MD**          **555-3275**
  520 Main...............................555-2734
  Residence 310 College..............555-3160
Walz Mildred 613 Denison ...........555-6___
Warner_____ 1__ Scott ...

**WEBER FURNITURE** 403 E 1......**555-3154**
Weber Geraldine 2121 Webster.......555-2549
Weber Marlene .........................555-2215
  2131 N Lake Shore Dr................555-2581
Weeden Julie 575 Quincy .............555-2224
Weeks Dora 221 Scott.................555-2025
Weeks Ernest 2415 Birch..............
**WEEKS' APOTHECARY**          **555-1235**
  1054 W Washington ..................555-3173
Weems Alvin 103 Emerson ............555-2805
Weinstein Diana 73 Parkway Dr ......555-2362
Weir Josephine 312 E 3................555-2917
Weis Barbara 118 Scott...............555-2215
Weiss B J 508 Quincy..................555-3094
Welch Lila 529 Spencer................
**WESTERN INSURANCE**          **555-6070**
  1650 S Lake Shore Dr................555-2147
Westmore Don 505 Loraine ...........555-____

---

## YELLOW PAGES

### MUSIC

**122**

▶ **Music Boxes**

**MUSIC IN THE AIR** ...............555-4755
  5816 Atlantic ...............

▶ **Music Dealers**
  See "Music Publisher"

▶ **Music Instruction**

American Theater School
**AMERICAN THEATER SCHOOL**
DRAMA - MUSIC - DANCE
Group and Private Instruction
100 years of experience

1275 Pacific
(between 12 & 13 St.) ..............**555-5600**

**BARSTOW MUSIC STUDIOS**
**See Our Display Ad This Page**.....555-8789
  72 Ashland Ct
Carlyle Conservatory .................555-3169
  5209 Ridgewood Rd

Deerfield School of Music and Dance
**Piano - Guitar - Drums**
**Tap - Ballet - Jazz**
Children - Teens - Adults
Weekdays, Saturdays
Daytime and Evenings
1550 Monaco ........................**555-6755**

**STORRS MUSIC**
  Most Instruments – Jazz,
  Classical – Voice
662 Holly...............................**555-4646**

Tempo Teachers' League
**Private Instruction in Our Studio**
**or in Your Home**
SPECIALIZING IN KEYBOARD AND VOICE
5220 King St ...........................**555-3838**

**Time and Time Again** ...........**555-6374**
  789 King St

559

# THESAURUS

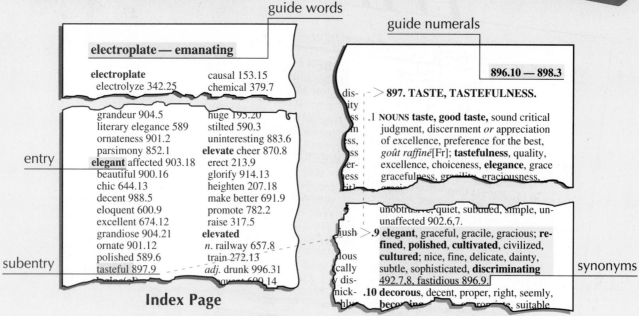

guide words

guide numerals

**electroplate — emanating**

**electroplate**
electrolyze 342.25

causal 153.15
chemical 379.7

grandeur 904.5
literary elegance 589
ornateness 901.2
parsimony 852.1
**elegant** affected 903.18
beautiful 900.16
chic 644.13
decent 988.5
eloquent 600.9
excellent 674.12
grandiose 904.21
ornate 901.12
polished 589.6
tasteful 897.9

huge 195.20
stilted 590.3
uninteresting 883.6
**elevate** cheer 870.8
erect 213.9
glorify 914.13
heighten 207.18
make better 691.9
promote 782.2
raise 317.5
**elevated**
*n.* railway 657.8
train 272.13
*adj.* drunk 996.31

entry

subentry

**Index Page**

**896.10 — 898.3**

**897. TASTE, TASTEFULNESS.**

.1 **NOUNS taste, good taste,** sound critical judgment, discernment *or* appreciation of excellence, preference for the best, *goût raffiné*[Fr]; **tastefulness,** quality, excellence, choiceness, **elegance,** grace gracefulness, gracility, graciousness,

unobtrusive, quiet, subdued, simple, unaffected 902.6,7.

.9 **elegant,** graceful, gracile, gracious; **refined, polished, cultivated,** civilized, **cultured**; nice, fine, delicate, dainty, subtle, sophisticated, **discriminating** 492.7,8, fastidious 896.9.

.10 **decorous,** decent, proper, right, seemly, **becoming,** appropriate, suitable

synonyms

**Numbered Category Page**

# INDEX/NUMBERED CATEGORY STYLE

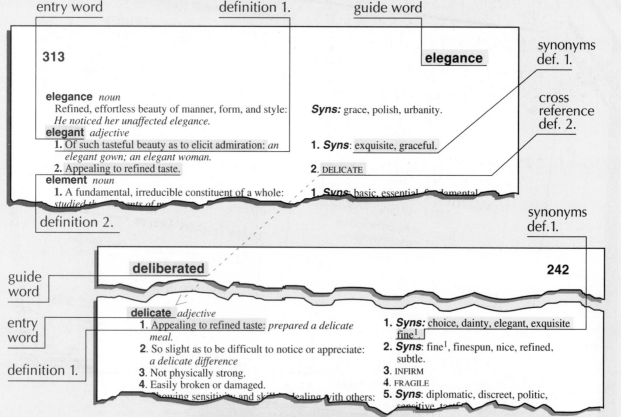

entry word

definition 1.

guide word

synonyms def. 1.

cross reference def. 2.

**313**

**elegance** *noun*
Refined, effortless beauty of manner, form, and style: *He noticed her unaffected elegance.*
**elegant** *adjective*
**1.** Of such tasteful beauty as to elicit admiration: *an elegant gown; an elegant woman.*
**2.** Appealing to refined taste.
**element** *noun*
**1.** A fundamental, irreducible constituent of a whole: *studied the elements of m*

**elegance**

*Syns:* grace, polish, urbanity.

**1.** *Syns*: exquisite, graceful.

**2.** DELICATE

**1.** *Syns*: basic, essential, fundamental,

definition 2.

guide word

entry word

definition 1.

synonyms def.1.

**deliberated**

**242**

**delicate** *adjective*
**1.** Appealing to refined taste: *prepared a delicate meal.*
**2.** So slight as to be difficult to notice or appreciate: *a delicate difference*
**3.** Not physically strong.
**4.** Easily broken or damaged.
**5.** showing sensitivity and skill in dealing with others:

**1.** *Syns:* choice, dainty, elegant, exquisite fine[1].
**2.** *Syns*: fine[1], finespun, nice, refined, subtle.
**3.** INFIRM
**4.** FRAGILE
**5.** *Syns*: diplomatic, discreet, politic, sensitive, tactful

# DICTIONARY STYLE

# TIME LINES

**1939** — World War II begins as Germany invades Poland. Britain and France declare war on Germany.

**1940** — Germany conquers Norway, Denmark, the Netherlands, Belgium, and France. Italy joins Germany, declaring war on Britain and France. Japan takes over European colonies in Southeast Asia.

**1941** — Germany invades Soviet Union. Japan attacks American naval base at Pearl Harbor. United States declares war on Japan, Britain does same. Germany and Italy join Japan in declaring war on U.S.

**1942** — U.S. victory at the Battle of Midway marks turning point against Japan in the Pacific. American offensive against Japan begins.

**1943** — Allies drive Axis troops from North Africa. Soviet Union defeats Germany at Battle of Stalingrad.

**1944** — On June 6—known as D-Day—the Allies land on the beaches of Normandy, France, to begin the liberation of Europe.

**1945** — Germany surrenders to the Allies on May 7—known as V-E Day. The U.S. drops two atomic bombs on Japan. Japan surrenders to the Allies on August 14—known as V-J Day. World War II officially ends on September 2.

# IMPORTANT EVENTS OF WORLD WAR II

# Glossary

This glossary can help you to pronounce and find out the meanings of words in this book that you may not know.

The words are listed in alphabetical order. Guide words tell you the first and last words on the page.

Each word is divided into syllables. The way to pronounce each word is given next. You can understand the pronunciation respelling by using the key to the right. A shorter key appears at the bottom of every other page.

When a word has more than one syllable, a dark accent mark (´) shows which syllable is stressed. In some words, a light accent mark (´) shows which syllable has a less heavy stress.

Information about the history, or etymology, of selected words is presented in brackets following the definition.

The following abbreviations are used in this glossary: *n.* noun, *v.* verb, *v.t.* transitive verb, *v.i.* intransitive verb, *adj.* adjective, *adv.* adverb, *prep.* preposition, *pl.* plural, *interj.* interjection.

The entries in the glossary are based on entries in *The Macmillan/McGraw-Hill School Dictionary 2*.

| | | | |
|---|---|---|---|
| **a** | at, bad | **d** | dear, soda, bad |
| **ā** | ape, pain, day, break | **f** | five, defend, leaf, off, cough, |
| **ä** | father, car, heart | | elephant |
| **âr** | care, pair, bear, their, where | **g** | game, ago, fog, egg |
| **e** | end, pet, said, heaven, friend | **h** | hat, ahead |
| **ē** | equal, me, feet, team, piece, key | **hw** | white, whether, which |
| **i** | it, big, English, hymn | **j** | joke, enjoy, gem, page, edge |
| **ī** | ice, fine, lie, my | **k** | kite, bakery, seek, tack, cat |
| **îr** | ear, deer, here, pierce | **l** | lid, sailor, feel, ball, allow |
| **o** | odd, hot, watch | **m** | man, family, dream |
| **ō** | old, oat, toe, low | **n** | not, final, pan, knife |
| **ô** | coffee, all, taught, law, fought | **ng** | long, singer, pink |
| **ôr** | order, fork, horse, story, pour | **p** | pail, repair, soap, happy |
| **oi** | oil, toy | **r** | ride, parent, wear, more, marry |
| **ou** | out, now | **s** | sit, aside, pets, cent, pass |
| **u** | up, mud, love, double | **sh** | shoe, washer, fish, mission, nation |
| **ū** | use, mule, cue, feud, few | **t** | tag, pretend, fat, button, dressed |
| **ü** | rule, true, food | **th** | thin, panther, both |
| ** u̇** | put, wood, should | **t͟h** | this, mother, smooth |
| **ûr** | burn, hurry, term, bird, word, | **v** | very, favor, wave |
| | courage | **w** | wet, weather, reward |
| **ə** | about, taken, pencil, lemon, circus | **y** | yes, onion |
| **b** | bat, above, job | **z** | zoo, lazy, jazz, rose, dogs, houses |
| **ch** | chin, such, match | **zh** | vision, treasure, seizure |

**a•bash** (ə bash´) *v.t.* to make embarrassed or ashamed; disconcert.

**a•bom•i•na•tion** (ə bom´ə nā´shən) *n.* something disgusting, hateful, or loathsome.

**ab•stract** (ab´strakt, ab strakt´) *adj.* not concerned with real or practical examples or instances; dealing with general ideas. [From the Latin word *abstractus,* past participle of *abstrahere,* meaning "to draw away," from the prefix *ab-,* "from, away" + *trahere,* "to draw, pull."]

*abstract*

**a•cous•tics** (ə küs´tiks) *n.* the qualities of a room, theater, auditorium, or the like that determine how well sound is carried and heard in it. ▲ used with a plural verb.

**ac•qui•esce** (ak´wē es´) *v.i.* to consent or agree by remaining silent or by not raising objections; submit quietly.

**ac•quit** (ə kwit´) *v.t.* **1.** to free or clear from an accusation or charge of crime; declare not guilty. **2.** to conduct (oneself); behave.

**ad-lib** (ad´lib´) *adj.* made up on the spur of the moment; improvised; done or said without previous preparation. [Short for the Latin phrase *ad libitum,* meaning "at one's pleasure."]

**ad•mo•ni•tion** (ad´mə nish´ən) *n.* **1.** a warning. **2.** a mild reprimand.

**A•ï•da** (ī ē´də)

**al•ien** (āl´yən, ā´lē ən) *adj.* **1.** not familiar or natural; strange; unfamiliar. **2.** of or belonging to another country or people; foreign. —*n.* **1.** a person who is not a citizen of the country in which he or she is living. **2.** a supposed being from outer space.

**al•le•vi•ate** (ə lē´vē āt´) *v.t.* to make easier to bear; relieve; lessen.

**A•ma•de•us** (ä´mə dā´əs)

**am•bro•sia** (am brō´zhə) *n.* **1.** something particularly delicious or delightful to the taste or smell. **2.** *Greek and Roman Mythology.* the food of the gods, capable of making anyone who ate it immortal.

**Am•ish** (ä´mish, am´ish) *adj.* of, belonging to, or relating to a Protestant religious denomination, closely related to the Mennonites. It was founded in Switzerland in the seventeenth century. Most members now live in the United States.

*Athens*

**Am•ner•is** (äm ner´is)

**A•mo•nas•ro** (ä´mō näz´rō)

**ap•pall** (ə pôl´) *also,* **ap•pal.** *v.t.* to fill with horror or dismay; terrify or shock.

**ap•peal** (ə pēl´) *v.i.* **1.** *Law.* to bring a case, or request that a case be brought, before a higher court to be heard again. **2.** to make an earnest request. **3.** to be attractive, charming, or interesting.

**ap•pro•ba•tion** (ap´rə bā´shən) *n.* approval, acceptance, or praise; expression of a favorable opinion.

**ar•dent** (är´dənt) *n.* eager; enthusiastic; passionate; having strength of feeling.

**ar•du•ous•ly** (är´jü əs lē) *adv.* in a way requiring great effort, energy, or difficulty.

**ar•son•ist** (är´sə nist) *n.* a person who deliberately sets fire to a dwelling or other property.

**ar•tic•u•late** (är tik´yə lāt´) *v.t.* **1.** to put into words; express effectively. **2.** to pronounce clearly.—*v.i.* **1.** to pronounce syllables and words clearly. **2.** to form a joint or connection.

**Ath•ens** (ath´ənz) the capital of Greece, in the eastern part of the country. It was once the most important and powerful of the ancient Greek city-states.

**au•thor•ize** (ô´thə rīz´) *v.t.* **1.** to approve officially. **2.** to give authority to.

**au•to•mat** (ô´tə mat´) *n.* a cafeteria in which food is obtained from small compartments whose doors open when the proper coins are put into the slots.

**a•venge** (ə venj´) *v.t.* to get revenge for.

**a•vert** (ə vûrt´) *v.t.* **1.** to keep from happening; prevent. **2.** to turn away or aside.

**av•id** (av´id) *adj.* **1.** very eager or enthusiastic. **2.** having a great desire; greedy.

**AZT,** a drug used to suppress the activity of the virus that scientists believe causes AIDS.

at; āpe; fär; câre; end; mē; it; īce; pîerce; hot; ōld; sông; fôrk; oil; out; up; ūse; rüle; půll; tûrn; chin; sing; shop; thin; <u>th</u>is; hw in white; zh in treasure. The symbol ə stands for the unstressed vowel sound in about, taken, pencil, lemon, and circus.

# B

**Ban•gla•desh** (bang´glə desh´, bäng´glə desh´) *also,* **Ban•gla Desh.** a country located at the northern end of the Bay of Bengal and largely surrounded by India. It was formerly the province of **East Pakistan.**

**bar•bar•i•an** (bär bâr´ē ən, bär bar´ē-ən) *n.* **1.** a member of a people whose way of life is considered uncivilized or savage. **2.** a crude, coarse, or brutal person.

**bar•ri•o** (bär´ē ō, bar´ē ō) *n.* in the United States, a neighborhood or section of a city inhabited mainly by Spanish-speaking people. [From the Spanish word *barrio,* "quarter or district of a city," from the Arabic word *barri,* meaning "of the open country."]

**Bar•row, Point** (bar´ō, point) a small Alaskan peninsula, the northernmost point of the United States.

**Beau•fort Sea** (bō´fərt sē) an arm of the Arctic Ocean, bordering northern Alaska and northwestern Canada.

*Point Barrow / Beaufort Sea*

**bed•rock** (bed´rok´) *n.* **1.** the solid rock that lies under the soil and other loose materials on the earth's surface. **2.** a foundation; basis. **3.** the lowest point or level; bottom.

**ben•e•fac•tor** (ben´ə fak´tər) *n.* a person who gives help or financial aid; patron.

**bent•slick** (bent´slik´) *adj.* having the qualities of being either corrupt or chronically intoxicated while also having a stylish appearance and a clever manner.

**Ber•ing Sea** (bîr´ing sē, ber´ing) the northernmost arm of the Pacific Ocean, between Siberia and Alaska.

**bi•fo•cals** (bī fō´kəlz, bī´fō´kəlz) *pl. n.* a pair of eyeglasses having lenses with two parts, one for seeing close objects and one for seeing distant objects.

**big•ot** (big´ət) *n.* a person who is excessively intolerant, as of any race, religion, belief, or opinion differing from his or her own.

**bi•ra•cial** (bī rā´shəl) *adj.* of, relating to, or characteristic of two races.

**bland** (bland) *adj.* **1.** lacking excitement, interest, or distinction; dull. **2.** not irritating; soothing; mild. **3.** smoothly agreeable or pleasant.

**blight** (blīt) *v.t.* **1.** to damage, ruin, or destroy. **2.** to cause to wither or decay. —*n.* **1.** any of several diseases that wither or kill plants. **2.** the organism that causes such a disease. **3.** something that damages, ruins, or destroys.

**blithe** (blī<u>th</u>, blīth) *adj.* **1.** full of joy or gaiety; cheerful; lighthearted. **2.** showing no concern, interest, or responsibility; thoughtless.

**bluff** (bluf) *n.* a high, broad bank or cliff. [Possibly from the Middle Dutch word *blaf,* meaning "broad, flat."]

**bor•ough** (bûr′ō, bur′ō) *n.* **1.** one of the five administrative divisions of New York City. **2.** in some states of the United States, a community having local self-government that is smaller than a city.

**bra•ce•ro** (brä sā′rō) Spanish for "manual laborer," especially a migrant laborer.

**bra•zen** (brā′zən) *adj.* **1.** without shame; bold and impudent. **2.** loud; harsh.

**bron•chi•tis** (brong kī′tis) *n.* an inflammation of the bronchial tubes, the passages through which air flows to and from the lungs.

**brooch** (brōch, brüch) *n.* an ornamental pin fastened by a clasp, often worn at the neck.

**Brook•lyn** (brůk′lin) a borough of New York City.

**buoy•ant** (boi′ənt) *adj.* **1.** able to float or rise in water. **2.** able to keep something afloat. **3.** resilient in spirit; cheerful.

**bur•nished** (bûr′nisht) *adj.* made smooth and shiny; polished.

**bush** (bůsh) *adj. Slang.* unsuitable for eating.

# C

**ca•ca•o** (kə ka′ō, kə kā′ō) *n.* **1.** the seed of a tropical American evergreen tree, valued as the source of cocoa, chocolate, and cocoa butter. **2.** the tree that bears this seed.

**cache** (kash) *n.* **1.** something hidden or stored in a hiding place. **2.** a hiding place, especially for provisions or treasure.

**cam•ass** (cam′əs) *also,* **cam•as.** *n.* **1.** a lily native to the northwestern region of the United States. **2.** the edible bulb of this lily.

cameos

**cam•e•o** (kam′ē ō′) *n.* a piece of jewelry made from a precious or semi-precious stone or a shell, having a carved, raised design on it.

**cam•ou•flage** (kam′ə fläzh′) *v.t.* to disguise or conceal by means of changing the appearance, especially so as to blend into the surroundings.

**Cape Cod•der** (kāp kod′ər) *n.* a kind of house initially found in the Cape Cod region of eastern Massachusetts.

at; āpe; fär; câre; end; mē; it; īce; pîerce; hot; ōld; sông; fôrk; oil; out; up; ūse; rüle; půll; tûrn; chin; sing; shop; thin; this; hw in white; zh in treasure. The symbol ə stands for the unstressed vowel sound in about, taken, pencil, lemon, and circus.

**car•di•o•vas•cu•lar** (kär´dē ō vas´-kyə lər) *adj.* of or relating to the heart and the blood vessels.

**car•ne con chi•le** (kar´nā kōn chē´lā) Spanish for "meat with chili (red peppers)." Also, **chile con carne.**

**cause•way** (kôz´wā´) *n.* a raised road or path, as across a body of water.

**Chad** (chad) a country in north-central Africa.

**Chap•lin, Charles Spenser** (chap´lin) 1899–1977, British film actor and director; known as *Charlie Chaplin.*

**chaste** (chāst) *adj.* **1.** pure in thought and action; moral, virtuous, or decent. **2.** simple in style; not ornate or extreme.

**chat•tel** (chat´əl) *n.* any article of personal property that can be moved, such as furniture, clothing, livestock, or an automobile.

**che•mo•ther•a•py** (kē´mō ther´ə pē, kem´ō ther´ə pē) *n.* the use of chemical substances to treat diseases.

**ches•ter•field** (ches´tər fēld´) *n.* **1.** a large, upholstered sofa, usually having upright, upholstered arms. **2.** a single-breasted topcoat having concealed buttons and a velvet collar. [From the Earl of *Chesterfield.*]

**chron•ic** (kron´ik) *adj.* **1.** done or doing again and again; habitual; constant. **2.** (of an illness) lasting a long time or coming back again and again. [Going back to the Greek word *chronikos,* meaning "of time," from *chronos,* "time."]

**Chuk•chi Sea** (chŭk´chē sē) the part of the Arctic Ocean north of the Bering Strait, between Asia and North America.

**Cic•e•ro** (sis´ə rō´)

**cite** (sīt) *v.t.* **1.** to mention or refer to as support, proof, or confirmation. **2.** to quote (a passage or author), especially as an authority.

**Clas•sics** (klas´iks) *pl. n.* **the Classics.** the literature of ancient Greece and Rome.

**cli•max** (klī´maks) *v.i.* to reach the highest point, as of development, interest, or excitement.

**clutch**[1] (kluch) *n.* **1.** the number of eggs laid or incubated at one time. **2.** all the chicks hatched or cared for at one time. [Probably from the Middle English word *clekken,* meaning "to give birth to, create," from the Old Norse word *klekja,* "to hatch."]

*chesterfield*

**clutch²** (kluch) *v.t.* to grasp or hold tightly or firmly. —*n.* **1.** a strong hold; grip. **2. clutches.** control; power. **3.** a device in a machine, such as an automobile, that connects or disconnects a motor and a drive shaft. [From the Old English word *clyccan,* meaning "to grasp or grip tightly."]

**CNN,** Cable News Network.

*colonnaded*

**col•on•nad•ed** (kol´ə nā´did) *adj.* built with a series of columns, placed at regular intervals, usually supporting a roof or other structure.

**com•mune** (kom´ūn) *n.* a community in which property is owned in common and work and living quarters are shared. [From the French word *commune,* meaning "township," from the Medieval Latin *communia,* "group sharing a common life," from the Latin word *communis,* "common" or "general."]

**com•pa•tri•ot** (kəm pā´trē ət) *n.* a person from one's own country; fellow citizen.

**con•cen•tra•tion camp** (kon´sən trā´shən kamp) *n.* a camp that is fenced and guarded, used by a government or military ruler to confine prisoners of war or other persons deemed threatening or undesirable.

**con•course** (kon´kôrs, kong´kôrs) *n.* **1.** a large gathering; crowd. **2.** a large, open place where crowds gather, as in a bus or train station.

**con•duit** (kon´dü it, kon´dwit, kon´dit) *n.* **1.** a channel, pipe, or tube used to carry liquids. **2.** a tube or pipe that protects electric wires or cables.

**con•script** (kən skript´) *v.t.* to force (someone) by law to serve in the armed forces; draft.

**con•se•cra•tion** (kon´si krā´shən) *n.* **1.** the act of making or declaring holy. **2.** the dedication or devotion to a particular purpose.

**con•sist•en•cy** (kən sis´tən sē) *n.* **1.** the quality or state of keeping to a particular way of thinking or acting. **2.** the degree of firmness, thickness, or stiffness.

**con•tin•gent** (kən tin´jənt) *n.* a group sent by another, larger group as a share or quota. —*adj.* depending on an uncertain condition or event; conditional.

**con•trive** (kən trīv´) *v.t.* **1.** to plan in a clever or ingenious way; scheme; plot. **2.** to bring about or manage, especially with difficulty. **3.** to create or invent; design.

**con•ven•tion•al** (kən ven´shə nəl) *adj.* **1.** following accepted custom or usage; customary. **2.** following generally used practices or standards. **3.** showing little imagination.

**co•rri•dos** (kō rē´dōs) Spanish for "songs like ballads."

at; āpe; fär; câre; end; mē; it; īce; pîerce; hot; ōld; sông; fôrk; oil; out; up; ūse; rüle; pull; tûrn; chin; sing; shop; thin; **th**is; hw in **wh**ite; **zh** in treasure. The symbol ə stands for the unstressed vowel sound in about, taken, pencil, lemon, and circus.

*curry*

**cos•mos** (koz´məs, koz´mōs) *n.* **1.** any ordered and harmonious system. **2.** the universe considered as an ordered and harmonious system.

**co•val•e•dic•to•ri•an** (kō val´i dik-tôr´ē ən) *n.* one of two or more persons who equally share the highest ranking in the class and who usually deliver the farewell address at a graduation exercise.

**crave** (krāv) *v.t.* to long or yearn for; desire eagerly.

**cringe** (krinj) *v.i.* to shrink, flinch, or crouch, as in fear, pain, or horror.

**cri•te•ri•on** (krī tîr´ē ən) *n., pl.* **cri-te•ri•a** (krī tîr´ē ə) or **cri•te•ri•ons.** a rule, standard, or test by which something or someone can be judged or measured.

**cru•cial** (krü´shəl) *adj.* likely to decide or help decide a contest or conflict or be a turning point; critical.

**cru•sade** (krü sād´) *n.* **1.** any vigorous campaign for the advancement of a cause against something seen as evil. **2.** *also,* **Crusade.** any of the military expeditions undertaken by European Christians between 1096 and 1270 to capture the Holy Land from the Muslims. [From the Middle French word *croisade* and the Spanish word *cruzada,* both of which mean "crusade" and both of which go back to the Latin word *crux,* meaning "cross." The crusaders wore the sign of the cross on their uniforms.]

**cur•few** (kûr´fū) *n.* an order or rule requiring certain persons to be indoors or at home before a fixed time, especially at night. [From the Anglo-Norman word *coeverfu,* meaning "cover fire," from the Old French words *covrir,* "to cover" + *feu,* "fire." In medieval European towns, the sounding of a bell was a signal to the people to put out lights and fires and go to bed.]

**cur•ry** (kûr´ē, kur´ē) *n.* **1.** a powder made from various dried, ground spices. Also, **curry powder. 2.** a spicy sauce made from this powder. **3.** food seasoned with this powder or sauce. [From the word *kari,* meaning "sauce," in Tamil, a language of southern India.]

**Cy•re•ne** (sī rē´nē)

# D

**Dan•ä•e** (dan´ə ē´)

**daunt•ed** (dôn´tid) *adj.* frightened or disheartened.

**de•but** (dā bū´, dā´bū) *also,* **dé•but.** *n.* **1.** a first public appearance, as of a performer on stage. **2.** a formal introduction of a young woman into society.

**des•cry** (di skrī´) *v.t.* to catch sight of; make out from afar.

**des•o•la•tion** (des´ə lā´shən) *n.* **1.** a feeling of loneliness or sadness from or as if from a loss. **2.** destruction; devastation.

**de•ter** (di tûr´) *v.t.* to discourage from acting or going ahead, especially by arousing fear or doubt.

**dev•as•tat•ing** (dev´ə stā´ting) *adj.*
**1.** destroying; ravaging. **2.** overwhelming, as with surprise.

**dex•ter•i•ty** (dek ster´i tē) *n.* skill in using the hands, body, or mind.

**dic•tion** (dik´shən) *n.* **1.** the manner and quality of saying or pronouncing words; enunciation. **2.** the way in which ideas are expressed in words; choice and arrangement of words in speaking or writing.

**di•lem•ma** (di lem´ə) *n.* a situation requiring a difficult choice between two or more things, often between things that are equally unpleasant or unsatisfactory.

**dis•con•so•late** (dis kon´sə lit) *adj.* so sad as to be without cheer, hope, or comfort.

**dis•cre•tion** (di skresh´ən) *n.* **1.** good judgment; caution; prudence. **2.** the freedom or power to act according to one's own judgment.

**dis•crim•i•na•tion** (di skrim´ə nā´-shən) *n.* **1.** unfair difference in treatment; prejudice. **2.** the act of noticing differences or making distinctions, especially small ones. **3.** the ability to make distinctions with accuracy; keen judgment.

**dis•cur•sive** (dis kûr´siv) *adj.* wandering from one subject to another.

**dis•cus** (dis´kəs) *n.* a heavy, circular plate that is thrown for distance in athletic contests to test skill and strength.

**di•shev•el•ment** (di shev´əl mənt) *n.* the act or state of being disorderly, rumpled, or untidy.

**dis•pel** (di spel´) *v.t.* to drive away or cause to disappear; disperse.

**doc•ile** (dos´əl) *adj.* easily managed, trained, or taught.

**doc•trine** (dok´trin) *n.* **1.** a belief or set of beliefs held by a particular group, such as a church or political party. **2.** something that is taught; teachings.

**doc•u•men•ta•ry** (dok´yə men´tə rē) *n.* a motion picture, television program, or radio program that deals with a subject in a factual way.

**do•min•ion** (də min´yən) *n.* a territory or country controlled or governed by a particular ruler or government.

*drone*

**drone** (drōn) *n.* a dull, continuous buzzing or humming sound. [Possibly from *drone* (male bee), from Old English *dran,* with the same meaning, in imitation of the sound made by a bee.]

**du•ra•ble** (dùr´ə bəl, dyùr´ə bəl) *adj.* **1.** able to resist wear or decay. **2.** able to resist change or stress; stable; enduring.

at; āpe; fär; câre; end; mē; it; īce; pîerce; hot; ōld; sông; fôrk; oil; out; up; ūse; rüle; pùll; tûrn; chin; sing; shop; thin; <u>th</u>is; hw in white; zh in treasure. The symbol ə stands for the unstressed vowel sound in about, taken, pencil, lemon, and circus.

**eaves** (ēvz) *pl. n.* the overhanging edge or edges of a sloping roof.

*eaves*

**ed•i•ble** (ed´ə bəl) *adj.* that can be eaten; fit to eat.

**ef•fete** (e fēt´) *adj.* without strength or vigor; worn out; decadent.

**el•o•quent** (el´ə kwənt) *adj.* **1.** having or showing the ability to use language effectively. **2.** having or showing the quality of being expressive and effective in regard to language.

**E•man•ci•pa•tion Proc•la•ma•tion** (i man´si pā´shən prok´lə mā´shən) *n.* a public statement by President Abraham Lincoln on January 1, 1863, that officially freed all slaves in the territory still at war with the Union.

**em•i•grant** (em´i grənt) *n.* a person who leaves one place or country to live in another.

**en•croach•ing** (en krō´ching) *adj.* **1.** going beyond usual or natural limits. **2.** intruding on the property or rights of another; trespassing.

**en•ter•prise** (en´tər prīz´) *n.* **1.** a project or undertaking, especially one that is difficult or important. **2.** readiness to take part in such undertakings; enthusiasm; initiative.

**en•trenched** (en trencht´) *adj.* **1.** established firmly or securely. **2.** placed in a trench; surrounded with trenches. Also, **intrenched.**

**es to•do** (es tō´<u>th</u>ō) Spanish for "that's all" or "that's it."

**es•carp•ment** (e skärp´mənt) *n.* **1.** a steep slope or cliff. **2.** a fortification consisting of a steep slope.

**Es•pa•ñol** (es pä nyōl´) Spanish for "the Spanish language."

**E•thi•o•pi•a** (ē´thē ō´pē ə) a country in eastern Africa.

**eth•nic•i•ty** (eth nis´ə tē) *n.* the quality or state of belonging to a particular ethnic group, a group of people having certain characteristics in common, such as language, religion, culture, history, race, or national origin.

**e•vade** (i vād´) *v.t.* **1.** to avoid as by trickery or cunning; elude. **2.** to escape or avoid the responsibility of. **3.** to avoid answering.

**e•voke** (i vōk´) *v.t.* to call forth or bring out; elicit.

**ex•ec•u•tive** (eg zek´yə tiv) *n.* **1.** a person who directs or manages affairs, as of a company. **2.** the branch of government responsible for enforcing laws and for managing the affairs of a nation.

**ex•qui•site** (ek skwiz′it, ek′skwi zit) *adj.* **1.** of great beauty, charm, or perfection. **2.** of great excellence or high quality.

**ex•u•ber•ant** (eg zü′bər ənt) *adj.* **1.** luxuriant in growth. **2.** overflowing with high spirits, enthusiasm, or vigor; elated. **3.** abundant or lavish.

# F

**fal•low** (fal′ō) *adj.* **1.** (of land) left without being planted, usually after being plowed, for one or more growing seasons. **2.** not in use; inactive; dormant. —*n.* fallow land.

**fem•i•nist** (fem′ə nist) *n.* a person who believes in or supports the principle that women are entitled to the same social, economic, and political rights as men.

*feminist*

**fête** (fāt, fet) *also,* **fete.** *n.* a festival or large celebration.

**fet•ish** (fet′ish, fē′tish) *n.* **1.** anything to which unreasonable devotion, concern, or reverence is given. **2.** an object believed to have magical or supernatural powers.

**fig•ment** (fig′mənt) *n.* something imagined or made up; fiction.

**for•bear•ance** (fôr bâr′əns) *n.* **1.** self-control or patience. **2.** the act of keeping from doing something; holding back.

**forge¹** (fôrj) *v.t.* **1.** to heat (metal) in a furnace or hearth and then hammer (it) into shape. **2.** to make or form; fashion. —*n.* **1.** a furnace or hearth in which metal is heated and softened so that it can be hammered into shape. **2.** a workshop in which metals are heated in such a furnace or hearth and then hammered into shape; smithy. [From the Old French word *forge,* meaning "works where one melts iron," going back to the Latin word *fabrica,* "workshop," from the word *faber,* "worker, artisan."]

**forge²** (fôrj) *v.i.* **1.** to move slowly but steadily. **2.** to move ahead with a sudden burst of speed and power. [Of uncertain origin.]

**frank•in•cense** (frang′kin sens′) *n.* a resin from certain Asian and African trees, burned for its fragrant aroma.

**friv•o•lous** (friv′ə ləs) *adj.* **1.** lacking seriousness or sense; silly. **2.** of little importance; trivial.

at; āpe; fär; câre; end; mē; it; īce; pîerce; hot; ōld; sông; fôrk; oil; out; up; ūse; rüle; pu̇ll; tûrn; chin; sing; shop; thin; this; hw in white; zh in treasure. The symbol ə stands for the unstressed vowel sound in about, taken, pencil, lemon, and circus.

*galley*

# G

**gal•ley** (gal´ē) *n.* **1.** a long, low ship of ancient and medieval times, propelled by sails and by a row of oars on either side or sometimes by several rows, one above the other. **2.** the kitchen of a ship or airplane.

**gal•va•nized** (gal´və nīzd´) *adj.* **1.** (of metal, especially iron or steel) covered with a protective coating of zinc to prevent rusting. **2.** roused suddenly; startled; excited.

**gar•land•ed** (gär´lən did) *adj.* decorated with a wreath of flowers, leaves, vines, or similar materials, usually worn on the head, especially as a token of honor.

**gar•ret** (gar´it) *adj.* the uppermost room or floor of a house; attic.

**gri•mace** (grim´əs, gri mās´) *v.i.* to twist the face in a way that shows pain, disgust, or displeasure.

**grist•mill** (grist´mil´) *n.* a mill for grinding grain.

**Gua•te•ma•la** (gwä´tə mä´lə) the northernmost country of Central America.

# H

**har•ried** (har´ēd) *adj.* troubled constantly; tormented; vexed.

**he•mo•phil•i•ac** (hē´mə fil´ē ak´) *n.* a person who has hemophilia, a hereditary disease in which the blood clots very slowly, so that a small injury may result in excessive bleeding.

**Hip•po•da•mi•a** (hip´ə də mī´ə)

**His•pan•ic** (hi span´ik) *n.* a person of Spanish or Spanish-American descent in the United States. —*adj.* of or relating to Spain or to Spanish America.

**hoax** (hōks) *n.* a trick or deception, meant as a practical joke or to fool others.

**ho•log•ra•phy** (hə log´rə fē) *n.* the process or technology of making holograms, three-dimensional photographs made by exposing film to certain kinds of light, such as laser beams. [From the Greek words *holos,* meaning "whole, complete," and *graphein,* meaning "to write."]

**hu•mane** (hū mān´, ū mān´) *adj.* having or showing sympathy and compassion; kind; merciful.

**im•mu•no•de•fic•ien•cy** (im´yə nō-də fish´ən sē, im ū´nō də fish´ən sē) *n.* a condition in which the immune system of the human body fails to provide normal protection against disease.

**im•pe•ri•ous** (im pîr´ē əs) *adj.* **1.** imperative; urgent. **2.** haughty or arrogant; domineering; overbearing.

**im•pov•er•ished** (im pov´ər isht) *adj.* **1.** very poor. **2.** lacking in strength, richness, or resources.

**im•pro•vise** (im´prə vīz´) *v.t.* **1.** to make up and perform without preparation or previous thought. **2.** to make from whatever materials are on hand.

**in•ad•e•quate** (in ad´i kwit) *adj.* less than required; not enough.

**In•di•an O•cean** (in´dē ən ō´shən) an ocean south of Asia, between Africa and Australia.

*Indian Ocean*

**in•dis•pen•sa•ble** (in´di spen´sə bəl) *adj.* that cannot be done without; necessary or essential.

**in•dul•gent** (in dul´jənt) *adj.* characterized by yielding to the whims or wishes of someone.

**in•ex•plic•a•bly** (in´ek splik´ə blē) *adv.* in a way that cannot be explained.

**in•fal•li•ble** (in fal´ə bəl) *adj.* **1.** reliable; unfailing; sure. **2.** not able to make a mistake.

**in•fin•i•ty** (in fin´i tē) *n.* **1.** the state or quality of being boundless, limitless, or endless. **2.** something that is limitless or endless, such as space or time.

**in•her•ent** (in hîr´ənt, in her´ənt) *adj.* forming a permanent or basic part of a person or thing.

**i•ni•tia•tive** (i nish´ə tiv) *n.* **1.** the first step in doing or beginning something; lead. **2.** the ability to take a first step in beginning or doing something.

**in•junc•tion** (in jungk´shən) *n.* **1.** a court order requiring or forbidding some act. **2.** a command; order.

**in•te•gra•tion** (in´ti grā´shən) *n.* **1.** the elimination of racial segregation, as in schools or housing. **2.** the act of bringing parts together into a whole.

**in•ten•sive care** (in ten´siv kâr) *n.* the area of a hospital or health-care institution that provides closely monitored, thorough, and concentrated care.

---

at; āpe; fär; câre; end; mē; it; īce; pîerce; hot; ōld; sông; fôrk; oil; out; up; ūse; rüle; pull; tûrn; chin; sing; shop; thin; this; hw in white; zh in treasure. The symbol ə stands for the unstressed vowel sound in about, taken, pencil, lemon, and circus.

**in•tu•i•tion** (in´tü ish´ən, in´tü ish´ən) *n.* **1.** a direct or immediate perception or understanding of truth without reasoning. **2.** the knowledge or insight resulting from such perception.

**I•vy League School** (ī´vē lēg skül) *n.* one of a group of long-established eastern U.S. colleges widely regarded as high in scholastic and social prestige.

**I•wo Ji•ma** (ē´wə jē´mə) an island in the northwestern Pacific Ocean, captured from Japan by the United States in 1945 during World War II and returned to Japan in 1968.

# J

**jave•lin** (jav´lin, jav´ə lin) *n.* **1.** a lightweight metal shaft that resembles a spear and is thrown for distance in athletic contests. **2.** a light spear, used chiefly as a weapon.

*javelin*

**jes•sies** (jes´ēz) *pl. n. Slang.* things that are false.

**jibe** (jīb) *also,* **gibe.** *n.* a mocking remark; jeer, taunt.

**jive** (jīv) *n. Slang.* **1.** deceptive, glib, or meaningless talk. **2.** jazz music, especially of the late 1930s and 1940s. **3.** the special terms or way of speaking used by jazz musicians and fans.

# K

**knish** (knish) *n.* a baked or fried dumpling filled with potato, cheese, or meat.

# L

**Lab•ra•dor** (lab´rə dôr´) a region in eastern Canada, on the Atlantic Ocean.

**lau•rel** (lôr´əl) *n.* a medium-sized evergreen tree bearing spicy, lance-shaped leaves and clusters of tiny yellow flowers, or the leaves from such a tree.

**leg•a•cy** (leg´ə sē) *n.* something handed down from previous generations or from the past; heritage.

**len•tisk** (len´tisk) *n.* an evergreen tree native to the Mediterranean region. Also, **mastic** or **pepper tree.**

**leth•ar•gy** (leth´ər jē) *n.* **1.** the state or quality of being without strength, energy, or alertness; sluggishness. **2.** an abnormal condition characterized by excessive drowsiness or by prolonged deep sleep. [From the Late Latin word *lethargia,* meaning "drowsiness," going back to the Greek word *lethargos,* "forgetful, sluggish," from *lēthē,* "forgetful" + *argos,* "lazy."]

**Lin, Maya Ying** (lin, mä´yə ying)

**lis•to** (lēs´tō) Spanish for "ready."

**loath** (lōth, lōth) *also,* **loth.** *adj.* reluctant; unwilling.

*longspur*

**long•spur** (lông´spûr) *n.* a brown-feathered bird having long claws on the hind toes, which is native to regions in the north.

**loth** (lōth, lōth) another spelling of **loath.**

**lynch•ing** (lin´ching) *n.* the act of seizing by mob action and putting to death, usually by hanging, without due process of law.

**lyr•i•cal•ly** (lîr´i kə lē, lîr´i klē) *adv.* **1.** in a manner of singing characterized by a light voice and a melodic style. **2.** in a manner characterized by expressing strong personal emotion, as rapture or enthusiasm.

**mal•ice** (mal´is) *n.* the wish to cause harm, injury, or pain to another; spite.

**man•da•to•ry** (man´də tôr´ē) *adj.* required by a law, rule, order, or the like; officially commanded.

**ma•te•ri•al•is•tic** (mə tîr´ē ə lis´tik) *adj.* of, relating to, or characterized by a tendency to be overly or solely concerned with wealth, possessions, and physical comforts.

**mea•sly** (mēz´lē) *adj. Slang.* scanty or worthless.

**me•di•o•cre** (mē´dē ō´kər) *adj.* not exceptional; ordinary; commonplace. [From the French word *médiocre,* from the Latin word *mediocris,* meaning "moderate, ordinary" or "indifferent."]

**med•i•ta•tion** (med´i tā´shən) *n.* **1.** deep reflection on matters of spiritual importance, often as a regular religious practice. **2.** serious and careful thought.

**Me•du•sa** (mə dü´sə, mə dū´sə)

**mi o•lla** (mē ō´yä) Spanish for "my pot."

at; āpe; fär; câre; end; mē; it; īce; pîerce; hot; ōld; sông; fôrk; oil; out; up; ūse; rüle; pull; tûrn; chin; sing; shop; thin; this; hw in white; zh in treasure. The symbol ə stands for the unstressed vowel sound in about, taken, pencil, lemon, and circus.

**mi•nor•i•ty** (mə nôr´i tē, mə nor´i tē, mī nôr´i tē, mī nor´i tē) *n.* **1.** a racial, religious, political, or other group that is different from the majority of the group of which it is a part. **2.** the smaller part of a group or whole.

**mint¹** (mint) *adj.* unused or seeming as if unused. —*n.* **1.** a place where money is coined by the government. **2.** a very large amount of money. —*v.t.* **1.** to coin (money). **2.** to create or invent (a phrase or a word). [From the Old English word *mynet,* meaning "a coin" or "money," from the Latin word *moneta,* "mint" or "money," from (Juno) *Moneta,* a title for the Roman goddess Juno, in whose temple coins were minted.]

*mint²*

**mint²** (mint) *n.* **1.** any of a group of plants, such as the peppermint or spearmint, used as a flavoring or scent. **2.** a piece of candy flavored with mint. [From the Old English word *minte,* meaning "this plant," from the Latin word *menta,* "mint," from the Greek word *mintē,* "mint."]

**min•us•cule** (min´ə skūl´, mi nus´kūl) *adj.* very small; tiny.

**Mi•yax** (mī´aks)

**mole** (mōl) *n.* the stone wall that encloses a harbor and is used to protect it. [From the Latin *moles,* meaning "pier, dam, massive structure."]

**mo•men•tum** (mō men´təm) *n., pl.* **mo•men•ta** or **mo•men•tums.** the force or speed resulting from motion; impetus.

**mo•not•o•ny** (mə not´ə nē) *n.* **1.** a tiresome sameness; lack of variety. **2.** a lack of change, as in tone, sound, or beat.

**mor•tar** (môr´tər) *n.* **1.** a material made of a mixture of sand, water, and lime that hardens as it dries, used especially for binding bricks or stones together in a wall or other structure. **2.** a thick bowl of marble or other hard material in which substances are crushed to a powder by means of a tool called a pestle. [From the Old French word *mortier,* meaning both "plaster" and "mortar (bowl)," from the Latin word *mortarium,* with both meanings.]

**mote** (mōt) *n.* a particle or speck, as of dust.

**mul•ti•tude** (mul´ti tüd´, mul´ti tūd´) *n.* a great number of people or things.

**myr•i•ad** (mir´ē əd) *n.* a great or countless number. —*adj.* too numerous to count; countless.

**myr•tle** (mûr´təl) *n.* any of a group of fragrant evergreen shrubs and trees bearing shiny leaves and white or pink flowers.

# N

**na•cre•ous** (nā´krē əs) *adj.* having the qualities of mother-of-pearl, a hard, rainbow-colored layer lining the shells of pearl oysters and certain other mollusks.

**Neth•er•lands, the** (neth´ər ləndz) a country in northwestern Europe, on the North Sea.

**Niel•sens** (nēl´sənz) *n.* ratings for television programs by the world's largest market-research company.

**Ni•ge•ri•a** (nī jîr´ē ə) a country in western Africa, on the Gulf of Guinea.

**Ni•ko•me•des** (nik´ə mē´dēz)

**non•de•script** (non´di skript´) *adj.* without interesting or striking characteristics or features; not distinctive.

**nymph** (nimf) *n.* **1.** *Greek and Roman Mythology.* any of various goddesses that were believed to live in forests, hills, or rivers and were usually represented as beautiful maidens. **2.** a beautiful young woman.

# O

**ob•jec•tiv•i•ty** (ob´jek tiv´i tē) *n.* the state or quality of not being affected or influenced by personal feelings or opinions; detachment.

**ob•lit•er•at•ed** (ə blit´ə rā´tid) *adj.* destroyed completely; removed without a trace.

**ob•scure** (əb skyùr´) *adj.* **1.** having little or no light; dark; dim. **2.** not clearly expressed; difficult to understand. —*v.t.* **1.** to hide from view; darken or conceal. **2.** to make difficult to understand.

**ob•ses•sive** (əb ses´iv) *adj.* of, relating to, or caused by an idea or desire that continually occupies and troubles the mind.

**ob•sid•i•an** (əb sid´ē ən) *n.* a hard, glassy rock, usually black, formed when molten lava cools.

**oc•cu•pa•tion** (ok´yə pā´shən) *n.* **1.** the act or process of seizing and maintaining control of enemy territory by a military force. **2.** the work that a person does to earn a living; profession; trade.

**O•lym•pi•a** (ō lim´pē ə) a plain in southwestern Greece, site of the ancient Olympic games.

*nymph*

at; āpe; fär; câre; end; mē; it; īce; pîerce; hot; ōld; sông; fôrk; oil; out; up; ūse; rüle; pùll; tûrn; chin; sing; shop; thin; this; hw in white; zh in treasure. The symbol ə stands for the unstressed vowel sound in about, taken, pencil, lemon, and circus.

**o•paque** (ō pāk´) **1.** not letting light shine through. **2.** not shining or lustrous; dull. **3.** hard to understand; obscure.

**op•press** (ə pres´) *v.t.* **1.** to control or govern by cruel and unjust use of force or authority; tyrannize. **2.** to weigh heavily on so as to depress or trouble.

**orb** (ôrb) *n.* **1.** the eye or eyeball. ▲ used in literature. **2.** something round, such as a sphere or globe. **3.** the sun, moon, or any other heavenly body.

**or•gan•ic** (ôr gan´ik) *adj.* **1.** relating to, deriving from, or including living things.

**or•nate** (ôr nāt´) *adj.* having much ornamentation.

**out•mod•ed** (out´mō´did) *adj.* no longer in style, suitable, or useful.

**o•yez** (ō´yes, ō´yez, ō yā´) *interj.* hear ye! ▲ used to announce that a court of law is in session and to ask for silence.

# P

**pag•eant•ry** (paj´ən trē) *n.* an elaborate or spectacular display.

**pal•at•a•ble** (pal´ə tə bəl) *adj.* **1.** pleasant to the taste; pleasing in flavor. **2.** agreeable to the mind or feelings; acceptable.

**par** (pär) *n.* **1.** an equal level. **2.** an average or normal amount, condition, degree, or quality.

**pas•sive** (pas´iv) *adj.* **1.** acted upon without responding or acting back. **2.** giving in without opposition or resistance; submissive. **3.** not active or participating.

**pa•tron•iz•ing** (pāt´rə nī´zing, pat´rə nī´zing) *adj.* **1.** treating others as inferior. **2.** giving support or assistance; acting as a supporter by the use of money or influence.

**pe•di•a•tri•cian** (pē´dē ə trish´ən) *n.* a doctor who specializes in pediatrics, the branch of medicine concerned with the care and treatment of babies and children.

*pediatrician*

*pentathlon*

**pen•tath•lon** (pen tath´lən, pen tath´-lon) *n.* an athletic contest in which each contestant participates in each of five different events.

**per•pe•tra•tor** (pûr´pi trā´tər) *n.* one who commits or performs (a crime, trick, or the like).

**Per•se•us** (pûr´sē əs)

**per•verse** (pər vûrs´) *adj.* **1.** willfully going against what is right, reasonable, or required; wrongheaded. **2.** determined to do as one pleases; stubborn; obstinate. **3.** morally wrong or corrupt; wicked.

**pes•ti•lence** (pes´tə ləns) *n.* any highly infectious, widespread disease; plague.

**Phtha** (ftä)

**pin•ion** (pin´yən) *n.* a bird's wing, especially the endmost segment. —*v.t.* to prevent (a bird) from flying by clipping or binding the pinions. [From the Old French word *pignon,* meaning "a bird's wing," going back to the Latin word *penna,* "feather."]

**Pi•rae•us** (pī rē´əs, pə rā´əs) the principal seaport of Greece and the port of nearby Athens, in the eastern part of the country.

**piv•ot** (piv´ət) *v.i.* to turn on or as if on a point, shaft, or pin.

**poign•ant** (poin´yənt) *adj.* **1.** bringing out deep emotions, especially sadness; touching. **2.** sharply felt; acute. **3.** (of a smell) sharp; penetrating.

**por•ti•co** (pôr´ti kō´) *n., pl.* **por•ti-coes** or **por•ti•cos.** a roofed structure supported by columns or piers and open on at least one side, forming a covered walk and usually attached to a building.

at; āpe; fär; câre; end; mē; it; īce; pîerce; hot; ōld; sông; fôrk; oil; out; up; ūse; rüle; pùll; tûrn; chin; sing; shop; thin; this; hw in white; zh in treasure. The symbol ə stands for the unstressed vowel sound in about, taken, pencil, lemon, and circus.

**prec•i•pice** (pres´ə pis) *n.* a high, steep, often vertical face of rock.

**pro•gen•i•tor** (prō jen´i tər) *n.* **1.** originator. **2.** an ancestor from whom a descendant is traced; forefather.

**proph•e•sy** (prof´ə sī) *v.t.* to tell beforehand (what is to come); foretell; predict. —*v.i.* **1.** to foretell the future; make predictions. **2.** to speak as a prophet.

**pro•pri•e•tor** (prə prī´i tər) *n.* an owner or operator of a small business establishment.

**pru•dent** (prü´dənt) *adj.* **1.** having or showing good judgment or caution; wise; sensible. **2.** showing careful management; economical; frugal.

**psy•cho•log•i•cal** (sī´kə loj´i kəl) *adj.* **1.** of or relating to the mind or mental processes. **2.** of or relating to psychology, the study of the mind, the emotions, and behavior.

# Q

**quay** (kē) *n.* a landing place for boats and ships, usually made of stone.

**Quet•zal•co•a•tl** (ket säl´kō ä´təl, ket säl´kwät´əl)

**quin•ce** (kēn´sā) Spanish for "fifteen."

**quiz•zing glass** (kwi´zing glas) *n.* an eyeglass for one eye with a handle. Also, **monocle** (mon´ə kəl).

**quoth** (kwōth) *v.i. Archaic.* said or spoke.

# R

**Ra** (rä) a sun god of ancient Egypt, depicted with a hawk's head.

*Ra*

**Ra•da•mes** (rä dä mes´)

**ra•di•ance** (rā´dē əns) *n.* **1.** the quality or state of beaming with joy, contentment, or love. **2.** the quality or state of giving off heat or shining brightly.

**Ram•fis** (ram´fis) .

**rapt** (rapt) *adj.* **1.** deeply absorbed. **2.** carried away with joy or delight; enraptured.

**rat•i•fy** (rat´ə fī´) *v.t.* to consent to officially; approve.

**re•but•tal** (ri but´əl) *n.* **1.** an argument or statement that disproves or refutes. **2.** the act of disproving or refuting.

**re•cruit** (ri krüt´) *v.t.* **1.** to hire or get the services of. **2.** to get (someone) to join the armed forces; enlist (someone) for military service.

**re•frain¹** (ri frān´) *n.* a phrase or verse in a song, poem, or the like that is repeated regularly, especially at the end of each stanza; chorus. [From the Old French word *refrain,* from the word *refraindre,* meaning "to resound," going back to the Latin word *refringere,* "to break off," from the prefix *re-,* "back, again" + *frangere,* "to break."]

**re•frain²** (ri frān´) *v.i.* to hold oneself back; restrain oneself. [From the Old French word *refrener,* meaning "to restrain."]

**re•mis•sion** (ri mish´ən) *n.* a temporary lessening of pain, the symptoms of a disease, or the like.

**rem•nant** (rem´nənt) *n.* a remaining piece or part; remainder.

**re•pel** (ri pel´) *v.t.* **1.** to cause to feel dislike or disgust. **2.** to drive back or away.

**rep•ro•bate** (rep´rə bāt´) *n.* a wicked or immoral person. —*adj.* given to wickedness or immorality; sinful.

**res•i•den•cy** (rez´i dən sē) *n.* the period of time during which a physician receives advanced, specialized training, as at a hospital.

**res•i•den•tial** (rez´i den´shəl) *adj.* **1.** characterized by, restricted to, or suitable for homes or the places where people make their homes. **2.** of or relating to the place where someone lives.

**ri•poste** (ri pōst´) *v.i.* **1.** *Fencing.* to make a quick thrust after successfully parrying an opponent's lunge. **2.** to reply in a quick, witty, or sharp way; retort.

**ros•trum** (ros´trəm) *n., pl.* **ros•trums** or **ros•tra** (ros´trə). a raised area, such as a platform or pulpit, used for public speaking.

**ro•tun•da** (rō tun´də) *n.* a circular building or room, especially one having a dome.

*rotunda*

at; āpe; fär; câre; end; mē; it; īce; pîerce; hot; ōld; sông; fôrk; oil; out; up; ūse; rüle; pu̇ll; tûrn; chin; sing; shop; thin; this; hw in white; zh in treasure. The symbol ə stands for the unstressed vowel sound in about, taken, pencil, lemon, and circus.

**rus•set** (rus´it) *adj.* having a yellow-ish-brown or reddish-brown color.

**ruth•less** (rüth´lis) *adj.* without pity, mercy, or compassion.

# S

**sa•gac•i•ty** (sə gas´i tē) *n.* the quality of being very wise; great wisdom.

**sanc•tu•ar•y** (sangk´chü er´ē) *n.* **1.** a holy or sacred place, such as a church or temple. **2.** the most holy part of a church or temple. **3.** any place of refuge or protection.

**sanc•tum** (sangk´təm) *n., pl.* **sanc-tums** or **sanc•ta** (sangk´tə). **1.** a holy or sacred place. **2.** a private room or other place where a person can be undisturbed.

**sa•vor** (sā´vər) *v.t.* **1.** to take great delight in. **2.** to taste or smell with pleasure. [From the Old French word *savor,* meaning "taste" or "smell," from the Latin word *sapor,* "taste, relish, flavor."]

**scrim•mage** (skrim´ij) *v.i.* to partici-pate in a practice session taking the form of a game, as in football and other sports.

*scullery maid*

**scul•lery** (skul´ə rē) *n.* a place, often a small room adjoining a kitchen, where cooking utensils are cleaned and stored and other kitchen chores are done.

**sea•mount** (sē´mount´) *n.* a mountain beneath the sea. The summit of such a mountain is at least 1,000 feet be-low sea level.

**seg•re•gat•ed** (seg´ri gā´tid) *adj.* **1.** having one racial group separated from another or from the rest of soci-ety, as by making them use different schools and social facilities or live in different areas. **2.** set apart from oth-ers or the rest; isolated. [From the Latin word *segregatus,* past participle of *segregare,* meaning "to separate, exclude," from the prefix *se-,* "apart, aside" + *grex,* "flock."]

*scrimmage*

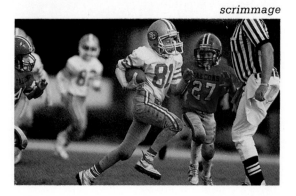

**self•es•teem** (self´e stēm´) *n.* proper regard for or awareness of one's own worth and abilities as a person; self-respect.

**sem•a•phore** (sem´ə fôr´) *n.* **1.** an apparatus for signaling, such as a post with movable arms or an arrangement of lights or flags. **2.** a method of signaling that uses two flags, one held in each hand.

**se•pi•a** (sē´pē ə) *n.* **1.** a dark brown color. **2.** a dark brown pigment made from the inky fluid produced by the cuttlefish. —*adj.* having the color sepia; dark brown.

**ser•en•dip•i•ty** (ser´ən dip´i tē) *n.* the act or ability of making fortunate discoveries by accident.

**shale** (shāl) *n.* a fine-grained rock, formed from hardened clay in very thin layers that separate easily.

**share•crop•per** (shâr´krop´ ər) *n.* a tenant farmer who farms land for the owner in return for a share of the crop that the land yields.

**sick•le** (sik´əl) *n.* a hand tool made up of a sharp, curved blade attached to a short handle, used for cutting grass, grain, or weeds.

**sil•hou•ette** (sil´ü et´) *n.* **1.** a dark outline seen against a lighter background. **2.** the outline of a figure or object filled in with a solid color, usually black. [From the French word *silhouette,* from the French minister of finance Étienne de *Silhouette* (1709–1767), who created amateur portraits of this kind.]

**sin•gu•lar** (sing´gyə lər) *adj.* **1.** strange or peculiar; odd. **2.** out of the ordinary; unusual or remarkable; extraordinary.

**skiff** (skif) *n.* a small, light boat propelled by motor, sail, or oars.

**sloop** (slüp) *n.* a sailboat rigged along its length, with a single mast, a mainsail, and a jib, a smaller, triangular sail in front of the mast.

*sickle*

at; āpe; fär; câre; end; mē; it; īce; pîerce; hot; ōld; sông; fôrk; oil; out; up; ūse; rüle; pùll; tûrn; chin; sing; shop; thin; this; hw in white; zh in treasure. The symbol ə stands for the unstressed vowel sound in about, taken, pencil, lemon, and circus.

**sov•er•eign** (sov´rən, sov´ər ən) *n.* the supreme ruler of a monarchy, such as a king or queen. —*adj.* **1.** having supreme power, rank, or authority. **2.** not controlled by others; independent. [From the Old French word *soverain,* meaning "supreme," going back to the Latin word *super,* "above, on top of."]

**spore** (spôr) *n.* a tiny reproductive body formed by some plants and microscopic animals.

**S.S.,** *Schutzstassel* (shủts´shtä´səl), German for "elite guard," the secret police force of the Nazi government of Germany before and during World War II.

**stat•u•ar•y** (stach´ü er´ē) *n.* **1.** statues as a group. **2.** the art of carving statues.

**stat•ure** (stach´ər) *n.* **1.** level, as of achievement or mental growth; standing. **2.** the height of a person or animal in a normal standing position.

**ster•e•o•type** (ster´ē ə tīp´, stîr´ē ə-tīp´) *v.t.* to develop a fixed, conventional view of. —*n.* an oversimplified or conventional image of a certain person, group, issue, or the like.

**strig•il** (strij´əl) *n.* an instrument used by the ancient Greeks and Romans for scraping moisture off the skin after a bath or exercise.

**sub•cul•ture** (sub´kul´chər) *n.* a smaller division or group, with its own distinctive culture, that exists within a larger society and culture.

**suc•cu•lent** (suk´yə lənt) *adj.* **1.** full of juice; juicy. **2.** having thick, fleshy leaves and stems that can hold large amounts of water. —*n.* a succulent plant.

**suf•fuse** (sə fūz´) *v.t.* to spread through or over, as with a light, color, or emotion.

**su•shi** (sü´shē) *n.* a Japanese dish of cold cooked rice shaped into small cakes and topped or wrapped with garnishes, as of raw fish or seaweed.

*sushi*

# T

**tal•on** (tal´ən) *n.* the claw of a bird or other animal, especially a bird of prey.

**taw•ny** (tô´nē) *adj.* brownish-yellow.

**te•di•ous** (tē´dē əs, tē´jəs) *adj.* causing weariness and boredom because of length, dullness, or the like; boring.

**tem•per** (tem´pər) *n.* **1.** the degree of hardness or strength of a substance, especially a metal, given by mixing it with another substance or by treating it in a particular way. **2.** a tendency to become angry or irritated. **3.** an angry state of mind; rage. **4.** a usual frame of mind; temperament.

**ten•don** (ten´dən) *n.* a strong cord or band of tissue that attaches a muscle to a bone or other part of the body.

**thith•er** (thith´ər) *adv. Archaic.* to or toward that place; in that direction.

**thresh•old** (thresh´ōld) *n.* **1.** a piece of wood, stone, or metal that forms the bottom of a door frame. **2.** a point of entering or beginning.

**Ti•bet•an** (ti bet´ən) *adj.* of or relating to Tibet (a self-governing region in southwestern China, formerly an independent nation), its people, their language, or their culture.

**tie•nen que te•ner cui•da•do** (tyā´-nen kā tā ner´ kwē thä´thō) Spanish for "you (plural) have to be careful."

**tim•bre** (tim´bər, tam´bər) *n.* the special quality of sound, apart from pitch and volume, that distinguishes one voice or musical instrument from another.

**tin•der** (tin´dər) *n.* any substance that burns easily, especially something used to start a fire from a spark, such as dry twigs.

*tinder*

**to•ken** (tō´kən) *adj.* having little or no value, force, or effect. —*n.* **1.** something that serves to indicate or represent some fact, event, object, or feeling; sign; symbol. **2.** something given as an expression of affection or as a memento. **3.** a piece of metal resembling a coin, used as a substitute for money, as in paying for transportation fares.

**to•tal•i•tar•i•an** (tō tal´i târ´ē ən, tō tal´i ter´ē ən) *adj.* of or relating to a system of government in which one leader, group, or political party aims at total control over the lives of people under it. —*n.* a person who favors or supports such a system.

---

at; āpe; fär; câre; end; mē; it; īce; pîerce; hot; ōld; sông; fôrk; oil; out; up; ūse; rüle; pu̇ll; tûrn; chin; sing; shop; thin; this; hw in white; zh in treasure. The symbol ə stands for the unstressed vowel sound in about, taken, pencil, lemon, and circus.

**tran•si•tion** (tran zish´ən) *n.* **1.** a passage from one state, position, condition, or activity to another. **2.** *Music.* **a.** a change of key. **b.** a passage connecting two parts, themes, or the like.

**tri•bu•nal** (trī bū´nəl, tri bū´nəl) *n.* **1.** a court of justice. **2.** any place of judgment.

**tu•mul•tu•ous•ly** (tü mul´chü əs lē, tu mul´chü əs lē) *adv.* **1.** in a stormy way; turbulently. **2.** in a disorderly or excited and noisy way. **3.** in a disturbed or upset manner.

**tur•moil** (tûr´moil) *n.* a state of confused agitation or commotion; turbulence.

*tripod*

**tri•pod** (trī´pod´) *n.* **1.** a pot, stool, table, or similar structure resting on three legs. **2.** a three-legged stand for supporting a camera, surveying instrument, or the like.

**u•nan•i•mous•ly** (ū nan´ə məs lē) *adv.* in a way that is completely agreed upon.

**un•con•sti•tu•tion•al** (un´kon sti tü´shə nəl, un´kon sti tū´shə nəl) *adj.* not in keeping with the constitution of a country, state, or group, especially the Constitution of the United States.

**un•due** (un dü´, un dū´) *adj.* **1.** going beyond what is necessary; excessive. **2.** not just, right, or proper.

**un•du•lat•ing** (un´jə lā´ting) *adj.* **1.** moving in waves or like a wave. **2.** having a wavy outline, form, or appearance.

**un•step** (un step´) *v.t.* to remove (a mast) from a step, a raised frame or platform supporting the lower end of a mast.

**up•pi•ty** (up´i tē) *adj. Informal.* displaying an attitude of exaggerated self-importance; snobbish.

# V

**vá•mo•nos** (bä´mō nōs) Spanish for "let's go."

**var•i•a•tion** (vâr´ē ā´shən) *n.*
**1.** *Music.* the repetition of a theme or tune with changes or additions, as in melody, harmony, rhythm, or key, especially one of a series of such repetitions. **2.** the act, fact, or process of changing. **3.** the extent or amount to which something varies.

**vault¹** (vôlt) *n.* **1.** a burial chamber; tomb. **2.** an arched structure of stone, brick, or concrete serving as a roof or ceiling. **3.** something resembling such a structure. **4.** an underground compartment or room used as a cellar or storeroom. [From the Old French word *volt,* meaning "a vaulted chamber."]

**vault²** (vôlt) *v.t.* to jump over, especially with the aid of the hands or a pole. [From the Old French word *volter,* meaning "to leap, spring."]

*vault²*

**ven•om•ous** (ven´ə məs) *adj.* **1.** able to inflict a poisonous wound, especially by biting or stinging. **2.** containing or full of such poison. **3.** malicious; spiteful.

**ver•sa•tile** (vûr´sə təl, vûr´sə tīl) *adj.*
**1.** having many uses or functions.
**2.** able to do many things well.

**Vic•to•ri•an** (vik tôr´ē ən) *adj.* of or relating to Queen Victoria of England or to the period of her reign (1837–1901).

*Vietnam*

**Vi•et•nam** (vē´et näm´, vē et´näm´) *also,* **Vi•et Nam.** a country in southeastern Asia, divided from 1954 to 1975 into North Vietnam and South Vietnam.

at; āpe; fär; câre; **e**nd; mē; it; īce; pîerce; hot; ōld; sông; fôrk; oil; out; up; ūse; rüle; pull; tûrn; **ch**in; si**ng**; **sh**op; **th**in; **th**is; **hw** in **wh**ite; **zh** in treasure. The symbol ə stands for the unstressed vowel sound in **a**bout, tak**e**n, penc**i**l, lem**o**n, and circ**u**s.

589

**vi•rus** (vī´rəs) *n.* **1.** any of a group of microscopic organisms or complex molecules. Viruses are smaller than any known bacteria and can reproduce and grow only in living cells, where they cause many diseases in humans, animals, and plants. **2.** a disease caused by a virus. [From the Latin word *virus,* meaning "poison" or "slimy liquid."]

**vis•age** (viz´ij) *n.* **1.** the face or facial expression of a person. **2.** the outward aspect or appearance of anything.

**vi•vac•i•ty** (vi vas´i tē, vī vas´i tē) *n.* liveliness or gaiety; animation.

**vo•tive** (vō´tiv) *adj.* given, offered, or performed in fulfillment of a vow.

*wolverine*

**wol•ver•ine** (wŭl´və rēn´) *also,* **wol-ver•ene.** *n.* a meat-eating mammal related to the weasel, native to northern regions, having dark brown fur with pale bands.

# W

**wal•low** (wol´ō) *n.* **1.** a hollow space in the ground formed by or as if by the tossing or rolling about of animals. **2.** the act of tossing or rolling about.

**wan•ton•ness** (won´tən nis) *n.* **1.** extreme thoughtlessness or ill will; complete lack of feeling for others. **2.** immorality; loose morals. **3.** lack of control; unruliness.

# Y

**ya e•so•ra** (yä ā sō´rä) a contraction of *ya es hora* (yä es ō´rä), Spanish for "it's time."

OF CAT CARTOONS, copyright © 1990 by Alfred A. Knopf, Inc. Reprinted by permission of Alfred A. Knopf, Inc. From The New Yorker, Aug. 26, 1991, copyright © 1991 by the New Yorker Magazine, Inc. Reprinted by permission of The New Yorker Magazine, Inc. From MEN, WOMEN AND DOGS, published by Harcourt Brace Jovanovich, Inc., copyright © 1943 by James Thurber. Copyright © renewed 1971 by Helen Thurber and Rosemary A. Thurber. Reprinted by permission of Rosemary A. Thurber. From HERE COMES THE APRIL FOOL! by Charles M. Schulz, Holt, Rinehart and Winston, 1980. Reprinted by permission of United Features Syndicate, Inc.

Dictionary: Excerpt from MACMILLAN DICTIONARY 2, copyright © 1991 by Macmillan/McGraw-Hill School Publishing Company. Reprinted by permission of Macmillan/McGraw-Hill School Publishing Company. Excerpt from THE CONCISE OXFORD DICTIONARY OF OPERA (2nd ed.), edited by Harold Rosenthal and John Warrack. Copyright © 1979 by Oxford University Press, and reprinted with their permission. Excerpt from WEBSTER'S NEW GEOGRAPHICAL DICTIONARY, ©1988 by Merriam-Webster Inc., publisher of the Merriam-Webster R dictionaries. Reprinted by permission of Merriam-Webster Inc.

Encyclopedia: Excerpt from "verbena" by Reed C. Rollins; "Verdi, Giuseppe" by Boris Goldovsky; "verdigris" by Alfred B. Garret; "Verdun" by C. Cecil Lingard; "Verga, Giovanni" by Thomas G. Bergin; and part of "Vergennes, Comte de" by Robert V. Remini, from MERIT STUDENT ENCYCLOPEDIA, vol. 19. Copyright © 1991 by Macmillan Educational Company. Reprinted by permission of the publisher.

Maps: "Tectonic Plates" from WORLD NEIGHBORS, copyright © 1983 by Macmillan Publishing Company. Reprinted by permission of Macmillan Publishing Company. Illustration of geologic plate from "Geology" by Patrick M. Hurley from MERIT STUDENT ENCYCLOPEDIA, vol. 7. Copyright © 1991 by Macmillan Educational Company. Reprinted by permission of the publisher. Maps of oceans from NATIONS OF THE WORLD, copyright © 1982 by Macmillan Publishing Company. Reprinted by permission of Macmillan Publishing Company. "United States and Canada: Climate" and "United States and Canada: Population Density" from WORLD REGIONS, copyright © 1991 by Macmillan/McGraw-Hill School Publishing Company. Reprinted by permission of Macmillan/McGraw-Hill School Publishing Company.

Newspapers and Magazines: "Cats and Clout" from the *New York Times*, July 10, 1991. Copyright © 1991 by The New York Times Company. Reprinted by permission. "Dead Sea Scrolls 40-year embargo finally ends" from *The Denver Post*, Sept. 22, 1991. Reprinted by permission.

Reader's Guide: Excerpt from the READER'S GUIDE TO PERIODICAL LITERATURE, vol. 49, 1989. Copyright © 1989 by The H. W. Wilson Company. Material reprinted with permission of the publisher.

Schedules: Excerpt from AMTRAK National Timetable: California Zephyr, Spring/Summer 1991. Reprinted by permission of AMTRAK/National Railroad Passenger Corp.

Thesaurus: Excerpt from ROGET'S INTERNATIONAL THESAURUS, 4th ed., copyright © 1977 by HarperCollins Publishers. Reprinted by permission of HarperCollins Publishers. ROGET'S II: THE NEW THESAURUS, edited by American Heritage Dictionary. Copyright © 1980 by Houghton Mifflin Company. Reprinted by permission of Houghton Mifflin Company.

**COVER DESIGN:** WYD Design
**COVER ILLUSTRATION:** Wendy Braun, Glen Wexler

**DESIGN CREDITS**
Sheldon Cotler & Associates Editorial Group, *Units 2 & 4*
Designframe Incorporated, 60-61, 154-155, 234-235, 318-319, 394-395, 468-469
Notovitz Design Inc., *Information Illustrated*
Curriculum Concepts, Inc., *Glossary*

**ILLUSTRATION CREDITS**
**Unit 1:** Bert Monroy, 16-19; R. Kenton Nelson, 42-43; Nishi, 70-71; Nancy Stahl, 72-73. **Unit 2:** John Huxtable, 168-169. **Unit 3:** Theo Rudnak, 188-191; Lori Osiecki, 204-205; Zita Asbaghi, 206-207; Joe Fleming, 234-235; Malcolm Farley, 264-265. **Unit 4:** Joyce Patti, 284-287; Dave Maloney, 296-297; Wayne McLoughlin, 338-339; Carlos Ochagavia, 360-361. **Unit 5:** Cary Henrie, 362-365; David Tillinghast, 294-295; Steve Karchin, 412-413; Gil Ashby, 426. **Unit 6:** Ray-Mel Cornelius, 428-431; Teofilo Oliveri, 466-467; Greg Wray, 486-487; Vilma Ortiz, 522-532. **Information Illustrated:** Chris Reed, 537, 557; Randy Chewning, 526; JAK Graphics, 528-529, 538, 549, 550; Alex Bloch, 536, 556; George Ulrich, 542; Graphic Chart & Map Co., 544-545; Bob Pastemak, 546; Brad Hamann, 548, 558-559; Eliot Bergman, 561. **Glossary:** Rodica Prato, 566, 575, 589; Gary Torrisi, 569, 572, 585; James Needham, 571, 577, 590; Alex Bloch, 574; Wendy Smith Griswold, 578; Cary Henrie, 579; Josef Sumichrast, 587.

**PHOTOGRAPHY CREDITS**
All photographs are by the Macmillan/McGraw-Hill School Division (MMSD) except as noted below.

**Unit 1:** 16: t.l. Garry Gay/The Image Bank; t.r. Pete Saloutos/The Stock Market; m.l. George Pickow; b.l. E. Masterson/H. Armstrong Roberts. 16-17: Barry Seidman/The Stock Market. 17; t.r. Jim Zuckerman/H. Armstrong Roberts; 1. Gerard Fritz/FPG; m.r. Martin Cohen/LP Music Group; m. inset D.W. Productions/The Image Bank. 40; Winnie Klotz/The Metropolitan Opera Association. 41: Pat Cummings. 57: t.r., m.r. Sonlight Images for MMSD; b.m. K. Yep/Courtesy of HarperCollins Publishers. 59: The Romare Howard Bearden Foundation/Courtesy of ACA Galleries, New York. 60-61: Geoff Spear. 62-63: Diltz/Gamma-Liaison. 62-69 background: Julian Baum/Science Photo Library/Photo Researchers, Inc. 64: t.l. Jean Claude Dupin/Retna Ltd. 65: m.l., b.l., b.r. Sygma. 67; t.r. Solo/Sipa Press; m.r. T. Orban/Sygma; b.r. Ken Franckling/LGI. 68: t.r. Sygma. 69: b. Neal Preston/*People Weekly* Magazine. 71: t.l., m.l. Dr. Jeremy Burgess/Science Photo Library/Photo Researchers, Inc. 74: b.l. Courtesy of Lerner Publications Co. 75: Courtesy of Macmillan Children's Publicity. 116-117: The Tokyo National Museum Collection. **Unit 2:** 120: L. Scott Halleran/Allsport USA; m. Bob Grant/Comstock; r. Scott Weersing/Allsport USA. 120-121: t. inset Richard Chesnut for MMSD. 121: l.,m. Ken Regan/Camera 5; r. Budd Symes/Allsport USA. 122: b.l. Mary Ann Carter/Sipa Press. 123: Taro Yamasaki/*People Weekly* Magazine. 124: Shelly Henson/Jeanne White. 125: t.r. Taro Yamasaki/*People Weekly* Magazine; b.r. Shelly Henson/Jeanne White. 127 t.r., 128: Mary Ann Carter/Sipa Press. 130: t.m., m.l. Shelly Henson/Jeanne White; b.m. Seth Rossman. 130-131: Taro Yamasaki/*People Weekly* Magazine. 132-133: Shelly Henson/Jeanne White. 134: t. Boys Town Photo. 135, 136 t.l.: Shelly Henson/Jeanne White. 136; t.r. Taro Yamasaki/*People Weekly* Magazine. 137; AP/Wide World Photos. 138: Mary Ann Carter/Sipa. 139: Taro Yamasaki/*People Weekly* Magazine. 140-141: Matt Herron. 143: Herscouici/Art Resource, Inc. 144: t.l. Richard Chesnut for MMSD; m. Jennifer Ashabranner. 146-147: National Park Service. 146 m.l., 147 m.r., 148 l., 149 t.r., b.r.: Jennifer Ashabranner. 150: t. Richard Howard/Black. Star. 150-151: b. Robert Houser/Comstock. 152: t.l. Jennifer Ashabranner. 153: l., b.r. Richard Chesnut for MMSD; m.r. Jennifer Ashabranner. 154-155: Jay Alan Lefcowitz. 156: t.l. Courtesy Francisco Jiménez. 170: m. inset Arnold Zann/Black Star. 170 m.l. inset, 173 t.l., b.l., 174 t.r, 175 t.l. Courtesy of Yuk Ming Liu. 170 b.m. inset, 175 m.r., 176 t.r. Courtesy of Keana Bonds. 170: t.l. inset, 180 b.l., 181 m.l. Courtesy of Angel Stimers. 170-171: Arnold Zann/Black Star. 171: t.m. inset Michael Abramson; b.l. inset Arnold Zann/Black Star. 171 b.r. inset, 177 t.l.,b.l., 178 t.r. Courtesy of Elda Cantu. 171: t.r. inset; 182, 183 b.l., 184 t.r. Courtesy of Esther Barela. 172: Arnold Zann/Black Star. 178: b.r. Michael Abramson. 179: b.l., 180 t.r. Courtesy of Daisy Rosenblum. 185: t.m. Courtesy of Doreen Rappaport; m.l., b.r. Arnold Zann/Black Star. 187: Sef/Art Resource, Inc. **Unit 3:** 203: t.l. Penelope Winslow Brooks/HarperCollins Publishers; b.m. Sonlight Images for MMSD. 205-206: Bud Kemper. 208: t.r. Courtesy of the Philatelic Foundation, NYC; b.l.,b.r. Courtesy of William Swank Family; m.r. Jim Kean/The Marin Independent Journal. 209: t.l.,b. H. Armstrong Roberts; m.l. Courtesy of Time Will Tell Unlimited, NYC. 210-211: t. MMSD. 211: Courtesy of Time Will Tell Unlimited, NYC. 218; m. inset Courtesy of the Philatelic Foundation, NYC. 220: l. Vince Parralla/Stockphotos; r. Francisco Hidalgo/The Image Bank. 224: r. Warren Ogden. 224-225: Scott Harvey for MMSD. 225: l. The Brooklyn Historical Society. 228: t. inset; The Bettmann Archives; b. Scott Harvey for MMSD; b. inset Burt Glinn/Magnum Photos. 263: Courtesy of Penguin USA. 266: t.l. inset Curtis Willocks/Brooklyn Image Group; t.m. inset David Hundley/The Stock Market; t.r. inset John M. Roberts/The Stock Market; m.l. Raga/The Stock Market; b.l. inset Uniphoto; b.m. inset Reginald Wickham; b.r. inset Berenholtz/The Stock Market. 267: t.l. inset Santi Visalli/The Image Bank; t.m. inset Warren Ogden; t.r. inset Joseph Schuyler; b. Tony Stone Worldwide/Chicago; b.l. inset Reginald Wickham; b.m. inset Joseph Schuyler; b.r. inset Angelina Lax/Photo Researchers, Inc., 268; m.l. Jim Brown/The Stock Market. 268-2679: t. Rafael Macia/Photo Researchers, Inc; b. Lawrence Migdale/Photo Researchers, Inc. 270: b.l. John M. Roberts/The Stock Market. 270-271: m. Todd Weinstein/Index Stock Photography, Inc.; b. Michael Quackenbush/The Image Bank. 271: m.r. Joseph Nettis/Photo Researchers, Inc.; b.r. Chris Collins/The Stock Market. 272: l. Warren Ogden; b.l. George E. Jones III/Photo Researchers, Inc. 272-273: t.m. Robert Goldwitz/Photo Researchers, Inc; b.m. George Kleiman/Photo Researchers Inc., 273: r. David Hundley/The Stock Market. 274: m.l. W. Eastep/The Stock Market; m.r. Joseph Schuyler; b.l. Berenholtz/The Stock Market; b.m. Curtis Willocks/Brooklyn Image Group. 278: Steve Elmore/The Stock Market. 278: b.m. inset, 279 m.l.: John Gillmoure/The Stock Market. 279: b., b.r. Sanchez/The Stock Market; b.r. Bruce Wodderi/The Image Bank. 281: Norman Owen Tomalin/Bruce Coleman. **Unit 4:** 295: b.l.,b.m. Richard Chesnut for MMSD. 298: Joan Baron/The Stock Market. 300: t.l. inset Ralph A. Reinhold/Animals Animals/Earth Scenes; m.l. inset Joyce Wilson/Animals Animals/Earth Scenes; b.r. inset Norvia Behling/Animals Animals/Earth Scenes. 300-301: r. Michael Stockey/Comstock. 302: t.l. Richard Gross/The Stock Market. 302-303: J. Barry O'Rourke/The Stock Market. 303: t.m. inset R. Sidney/The Image Works, Inc.; b.m. inset Dana Hyde/Photo Researchers, Inc.; b.r. inset Tibor Bognar/The Stock Market. 304: t.l. inset Tom Nebbia 304-305: J. Pinderhughes/The Stock Market. 306-307: Stephen Green-Armytage/The Stock Market. 308: t.l. inset Julie Habel/Woodfin Camp and Associates, Inc.; b.l. inset Mary Kate Denny/PhotoEdit. 308-309: Andrea Krause/Photo Researchers, Inc. 310; b.l. inset Myrleen Ferguson/PhotoEdit. 310-311: Gabe Palmer/The Stock Market. 311: b.m. inset George W. Gardner/The Image Works, Inc. 312: m.l. inset Michael Newler/The Stock Market: b.m. inset Robbi Newman/The Image Bank. 312-313: Disario/The Stock Market. 314: b.l. inset Tom Nebbia; b.m. inset George Disario/The Stock Market. 314-315: Ulrike Welsch/Photo Researchers, Inc. 316-317: Bill Bachman/Photo Researchers, Inc.; t.r. Comstock. 318-319: John Rizzo. 320: t.m. Ellan Young Photography/HarperCollins Publishers; m.b.,b.r. Richard Chesnut for MMSD. 337: b.l. Robert A Jureit/The Stock Market. 340-359: NASA. 359; m.r. Richard Chesnut for MMSD. **Unit 5:** 377: m.r. Christopher G. Knight; b.m.,b.r. Sonlight Images for MMSD. 380-381: Bonnie Moench/The Image Bank. 382: m.l. Courtesy of Carl DeSantis. 389: t.m. Jill Krementz; b.r. Fritz Menle/Photo Researchers, Inc. 396: m.l. Anne-Marie O'Healy, © Gies-Gold/Courtesy of the Anne Frank Center. 396-397: Anne Frank Fonds, Basel/The Bettmann Archives, Inc. 399: b.r. Gies-Gold. 403: Anne Frank Fonds. Basel/Courtesy of the Anne Frank Center. 404: Jacob de Vries, © Gies-Gold. 405: Anne Frank Fonds, Basel/Culver Pictures, Inc. 407: t.r. © Anne Frank Fonds, Basel. 408: Anne Frank Fonds, Basel/Courtesy of the Anne Frank Center. 409: t.r. AP/Wide World Photos. 411: b.l. Anne Frank Fonds, Basel. 414-415: Schomburg Center for Research in Black Culture, New York Public Library; b. M. Angelo/Westlight. 417: AP/Wide World Photos; r. M. Angelo/Westlight. 419: Culver Pictures, Inc.; r. M. Angelo/Westlight. 421: Elizabeth Hibbs/FPG International Corp.; r. M. Angelo/Westlight. 422: Schomburg Center for Research in Black Culture, New York Public Library. 422 l., 423 r.: M. Angelo/Westlight. 424: b.l. Brad Markel/Gamma-Liaison. 424-425: David W. Hamilton/The Image Bank. **Unit 6:** 449: Scott Harvey for MMSD. 452-465: Map courtesy of the Newberry Library/ © Rand McNally Inc., R. L. 91-s-222. 465: m.r. Courtesy of Houghton Mifflin Company. 468-469: Glen Wexler. 485: b.r. Scott Harvey for MMSD. 486: t.l. © Courtesy of 20th Century Fox Corp. All Rights Reserved. Courtesy of Lucas Film Ltd.; b.l. © Courtesy of 20th Century Fox Corp. All Rights Reserved. Superstock. 487: b.r. © Courtesy of 20th Century Fox Corp. All Rights Reserved. Superstock. 488-489: Index Stock Photography. 521: Courtesy of Essex Institute, Salem, MA. **Glossary:** 562: t.r. The Stock Market; t.l., t.m. Michal Heron for MMSD; b.r. Art Resource. 563: b. Leo de Wys; t.r. Michal Heron for MMSD. 564: Art Resource. 565: The Stock Market. 567: Michal Heron for MMSD. 570: Michal Heron for MMSD. 573: FPG. 576: David Madison. 580; The Stock Market. 581: b.l., t.r., m., b.r., t.l. David Madison. 582: Art Resource. 583: Leo de Wys. 584: b.l. David Madison; t.r. FPG. 586: Michal Heron for MMSD. 588: Michal Heron for MMSD. 589: David Madison. End papers: West Light.